Microsoft®
Outlook® 2000
Bible

Microsoft® Outlook® 2000 Bible

Todd A. Kleinke, CPA, MCSD, MCSE, and Brian Underdahl

IDG Books Worldwide, Inc.
An International Data Group Company

Foster City, CA ✦ Chicago, IL ✦ Indianapolis, IN ✦ New York, NY

Microsoft® Outlook® 2000 Bible

Published by
IDG Books Worldwide, Inc.
An International Data Group Company
919 E. Hillsdale Blvd., Suite 400
Foster City, CA 94404
www.idgbooks.com (IDG Books Worldwide Web site)

ISBN: 0-7645-3365-7

Printed in the United States of America

10 9 8 7 6 5 4 3 2 1

1B/RT/QX/ZZ/FC

Distributed in the United States by IDG Books Worldwide, Inc.

Distributed by CDG Books Canada Inc. for Canada; by Transworld Publishers Limited in the United Kingdom; by IDG Norge Books for Norway; by IDG Sweden Books for Sweden; by IDG Books Australia Publishing Corporation Pty. Ltd. for Australia and New Zealand; by TransQuest Publishers Pte Ltd. for Singapore, Malaysia, Thailand, Indonesia, and Hong Kong; by Gotop Information Inc. for Taiwan; by ICG Muse, Inc. for Japan; by Norma Comunicaciones S.A. for Colombia; by Intersoft for South Africa; by Eyrolles for France; by International Thomson Publishing for Germany, Austria and Switzerland; by Distribuidora Cuspide for Argentina; by Livraria Cultura for Brazil; by Ediciones ZETA S.C.R. Ltda. for Peru; by WS Computer Publishing Corporation, Inc., for the Philippines; by Contemporanea de Ediciones for Venezuela; by Express Computer Distributors for the Caribbean and West Indies; by Micronesia Media Distributor, Inc. for Micronesia; by Grupo Editorial Norma S.A. for Guatemala; by Chips Computadoras S.A. de C.V. for Mexico; by Editorial Norma de Panama S.A. for Panama; by American Bookshops for Finland. Authorized Sales Agent: Anthony Rudkin Associates for the Middle East and North Africa.

For general information on IDG Books Worldwide's books in the U.S., please call our Consumer Customer Service department at 800-762-2974. For reseller information, including discounts and premium sales, please call our Reseller Customer Service department at 800-434-3422.

For information on where to purchase IDG Books Worldwide's books outside the U.S., please contact our International Sales department at 317-596-5530 or fax 317-596-5692.

For consumer information on foreign language translations, please contact our Customer Service department at 800-434-3422, fax 317-596-5692, or e-mail rights@idgbooks.com.

For information on licensing foreign or domestic rights, please phone +1-650-655-3109.

For sales inquiries and special prices for bulk quantities, please contact our Sales department at 650-655-3200 or write to the address above.

For information on using IDG Books Worldwide's books in the classroom or for ordering examination copies, please contact our Educational Sales department at 800-434-2086 or fax 317-596-5499.

For press review copies, author interviews, or other publicity information, please contact our Public Relations department at 650-655-3000 or fax 650-655-3299.

For authorization to photocopy items for corporate, personal, or educational use, please contact Copyright Clearance Center, 222 Rosewood Drive, Danvers, MA 01923, or fax 978-750-4470.

Library of Congress Cataloging-in-Publication Data

Kleinke, Todd A., [DATE]
    Microsoft Outlook 2000 bible / Todd A. Kleinke
    and Brian Underdahl.
        .p. cm.
    ISBN 0-7645-3365-7 (alk. paper)
    1. Microsoft Outlook. 2. Time management--
Computer programs. 3. Personal information
management--Computer programs.
    I. Underdahl, Brian, [DATE]. II. Title.
HD69.T54K582   1999
005.369--dc21   99-15722
                                                           CIP

 is a registered trademark or trademark under exclusive license to IDG Books Worldwide, Inc. from International Data Group, Inc. in the United States and/or other countries.

ABOUT IDG BOOKS WORLDWIDE

Welcome to the world of IDG Books Worldwide.

IDG Books Worldwide, Inc., is a subsidiary of International Data Group, the world's largest publisher of computer-related information and the leading global provider of information services on information technology. IDG was founded more than 30 years ago by Patrick J. McGovern and now employs more than 9,000 people worldwide. IDG publishes more than 290 computer publications in over 75 countries. More than 90 million people read one or more IDG publications each month.

Launched in 1990, IDG Books Worldwide is today the #1 publisher of best-selling computer books in the United States. We are proud to have received eight awards from the Computer Press Association in recognition of editorial excellence and three from Computer Currents' First Annual Readers' Choice Awards. Our best-selling ...For Dummies® series has more than 50 million copies in print with translations in 31 languages. IDG Books Worldwide, through a joint venture with IDG's Hi-Tech Beijing, became the first U.S. publisher to publish a computer book in the People's Republic of China. In record time, IDG Books Worldwide has become the first choice for millions of readers around the world who want to learn how to better manage their businesses.

Our mission is simple: Every one of our books is designed to bring extra value and skill-building instructions to the reader. Our books are written by experts who understand and care about our readers. The knowledge base of our editorial staff comes from years of experience in publishing, education, and journalism — experience we use to produce books to carry us into the new millennium. In short, we care about books, so we attract the best people. We devote special attention to details such as audience, interior design, use of icons, and illustrations. And because we use an efficient process of authoring, editing, and desktop publishing our books electronically, we can spend more time ensuring superior content and less time on the technicalities of making books.

You can count on our commitment to deliver high-quality books at competitive prices on topics you want to read about. At IDG Books Worldwide, we continue in the IDG tradition of delivering quality for more than 30 years. You'll find no better book on a subject than one from IDG Books Worldwide.

John Kilcullen
Chairman and CEO
IDG Books Worldwide, Inc.

Steven Berkowitz
President and Publisher
IDG Books Worldwide, Inc.

Eighth Annual Computer Press Awards ≥1992

Ninth Annual Computer Press Awards ≥1993

Tenth Annual Computer Press Awards ≥1994

Eleventh Annual Computer Press Awards ≥1995

IDG is the world's leading IT media, research and exposition company. Founded in 1964, IDG had 1997 revenues of $2.05 billion and has more than 9,000 employees worldwide. IDG offers the widest range of media options that reach IT buyers in 75 countries representing 95% of worldwide IT spending. IDG's diverse product and services portfolio spans six key areas including print publishing, online publishing, expositions and conferences, market research, education and training, and global marketing services. More than 90 million people read one or more of IDG's 290 magazines and newspapers, including IDG's leading global brands — Computerworld, PC World, Network World, Macworld and the Channel World family of publications. IDG Books Worldwide is one of the fastest-growing computer book publishers in the world, with more than 700 titles in 36 languages. The "...For Dummies®" series alone has more than 50 million copies in print. IDG offers online users the largest network of technology-specific Web sites around the world through IDG.net (http://www.idg.net), which comprises more than 225 targeted Web sites in 55 countries worldwide. International Data Corporation (IDC) is the world's largest provider of information technology data, analysis and consulting, with research centers in over 41 countries and more than 400 research analysts worldwide. IDG World Expo is a leading producer of more than 168 globally branded conferences and expositions in 35 countries including E3 (Electronic Entertainment Expo), Macworld Expo, ComNet, Windows World Expo, ICE (Internet Commerce Expo), Agenda, DEMO, and Spotlight. IDG's training subsidiary, ExecuTrain, is the world's largest computer training company, with more than 230 locations worldwide and 785 training courses. IDG Marketing Services helps industry-leading IT companies build international brand recognition by developing global integrated marketing programs via IDG's print, online and exposition products worldwide. Further information about the company can be found at www.idg.com.   1/24/99

Credits

Acquisitions Editor
David Mayhew

Development Editor
Stefan Grünwedel

Technical Editors
Gayle Ehrenman
Susan Glinert

Copy Editor
Ami Knox

Production
IDG Books Worldwide Production

Proofreading and Indexing
York Production Services

Cover Design
Murder By Design

About the Authors

Todd A. Kleinke, CPA, MCSD, MCSE, is a senior analyst at KSM Consulting, LLC. In his capacity as an accounting and management consultant, he develops custom applications and specializes in the integration and automation of business processes. Currently, Todd designs and develops various intranet applications at Dow AgroSciences, as well as custom sales automation applications that use Outlook and many of the latest Microsoft technologies. Todd presented his Outlook applications at a recent Microsoft Exchange conference.

Brian Underdahl is the best-selling author of over 40 computer books, including several current titles from IDG Books Worldwide: *Small Business Computing For Dummies, Windows 98 One Step at a Time, Internet Bible* (coauthored with Edward Willett), *Teach Yourself Office 97* (coauthored with Keith Underdahl and Faithe Wempen), *Teach Yourself Microsoft Windows 98* (coauthored with Al Stevens), and *Teach Yourself Microsoft Office 2000.* Brian spends most of his time at the keyboard writing about personal computing when he's not attending Mensa meetings or cooking gourmet meals.

This book is dedicated to my beloved wife, Lisa. Without you, everything I do would be meaningless. I'm truly a better person for knowing you, and I love you with all my heart.

—Todd A. Kleinke

To my readers: "Don't stop thinking about tomorrow." (Fleetwood Mac)

—Brian Underdahl

Preface

Welcome to *Microsoft Outlook 2000 Bible* — your complete guide to Outlook 2000! Microsoft Outlook is a great multipurpose program that has many useful features. Despite this fact, Outlook often suffers from an image problem. Most people know that it handles e-mail messages pretty well, but that's about all they use it for. That's really too bad, because Outlook does so much more very well.

By taking an in-depth look at Outlook 2000, this book is intended to open a lot of doors for you. What you'll find may surprise you, because Outlook does so many things so well. Once you learn what you can do with the program, you'll wonder why it took you so long to start doing things the easy and efficient way.

Although the book begins with basic functions and simple tasks, you'll find that the book gradually teaches higher-level tasks at a comfortable pace. Once you reach the later sections of the book, you'll find yourself designing complex workgroup solutions. However, don't feel you have to read this book from cover to cover in order to gain from its content. Perhaps you are only interested in learning certain aspects of Outlook 2000. That's okay; each chapter stands on its own.

In order to drive the point home and help you understand the methodologies behind the tasks, we provide you with in-depth examples of how Outlook 2000 solves problems. The examples demonstrate the same methodologies utilized in the real world and can easily be adapted to suit your specific needs. As a result, you will learn to identify areas in your day-to-day business that Outlook 2000 can help simplify.

Is This Book for You?

Because *Microsoft Outlook 2000 Bible* covers virtually every aspect of Outlook 2000, we have intended this book to help beginning, intermediate, and advanced users. If you're an advanced user interested in developing custom applications using Outlook 2000, you will mostly be interested in the later sections of the book. However, even if you're an experienced Outlook 2000 user, you may want to start at the beginning of the book, because there are many new features in Outlook 2000 that did not exist in prior versions.

So, is this book for you?

Yes, if you don't know how to use e-mail

If your company just implemented an e-mail system or if you want to send e-mail over the Internet from your home computer, this book provides you everything you need to know to get up and running. Once you've mastered the e-mail, you'll be geared up to learn other Outlook 2000 features that will help you work more efficiently.

Yes, if you know how to use Outlook but don't feel you're using it to its full potential

Although it's easy to use once you know what you're doing, Outlook 2000 is a very complex application. Most Outlook users only utilize a small portion of the capabilities this program has to offer. This book provides real-world examples of how Outlook 2000 can be applied to your day-to-day activities to enable you to work more efficiently. Once you understand the intent behind the functionality, you will be able to use Outlook to its fullest potential.

Yes, if you want to develop custom applications using VBScript, Outlook forms, COM add-ins, and Web integration

Custom Outlook forms and VBScript have traditionally been the foundation for custom application development within Microsoft Outlook. However, Outlook 2000 has expanded custom application development to include COM add-ins, Web integration, and collaboration within other Office 2000 applications. The details behind the extended capabilities of Outlook 2000 custom application development are explained in Parts V and VI.

What You'll Find in This Book

The **Quick Start** gives you a quick introduction to a few of the important features of Outlook. You get an idea about some of the things you can do with Outlook along with some pointers if you want to jump right to the section of the book where the topics are covered in more detail.

Part I, Getting Started with Microsoft Outlook 2000, provides you with an in-depth look at the features of Outlook. You learn about each of the major areas of the program, what's new in the latest versions, and how to install and configure Outlook so that it works the best for your needs.

Part II, Mastering E-mail, takes you from the basics of e-mail into both intermediate and advanced topics. You learn how to create, send, and receive e-mail messages — including messages that have attachments. You see how to make your e-mail messages stand out and how to have Outlook automatically process certain messages for you. You learn how to create and use distribution lists so that e-mailing a group is just as easy as e-mailing one person.

Part III, Microsoft Outlook 2000 as a Personal Information Manager, teaches you about Outlook's little-known, but extremely useful, features. You learn how to use contact management, scheduling, to-do lists, document activity tracking, and electronic sticky notes. You also learn how you can use the Outlook Newsreader to access tens of thousands of Internet newsgroups so you can view a vast array of information that you won't find anywhere else.

Part IV, Getting the Most out of Microsoft Outlook 2000, shows you how to customize Outlook so that it works for you the way you want it to. These chapters also show you how to share Outlook information with other people and how to use Outlook with other programs.

Part V, Basics of Microsoft Outlook 2000 Development, is the first of two parts focused on developing custom applications using Outlook 2000 and its related technologies. After getting a general overview of the different types of applications you can create with Outlook, you learn the elements of a simple Outlook form and how to create one. You also learn the specifics behind each of the various form controls and how to use them, and know what custom fields are and when they are appropriate.

Part VI, Advanced Messaging Development, covers advanced application development tasks within Outlook 2000 and its related technologies. These chapters describe how to incorporate Exchange folders into your applications effectively, provide an introduction to collaborative messaging, and introduce the Outlook 2000 Object Model. You also learn how to incorporate COM add-ins into Outlook 2000, what Collaborative Data Objects and Exchange Routing Objects are, and when they are appropriate to use.

Appendix A describes the contents of the CD-ROM and how to use it. **Appendix B** provides reference material for several object models: Outlook 2000, Collaborative Data Objects (CDO), and Collaborative Data Objects for NT Server (CDONTS).

Conventions Used in This Book

We want *Microsoft Outlook 2000 Bible* to be easy to use and informative, so we follow several conventions to help you understand what you're reading. For example, when you need to make a series of selections from a menu, we show the commands like this:

File ➪ Open

This tells you that you need to open the File menu and then choose the Open option from that menu.

When you need to type something exactly as shown in the text, we present the text that you should enter in bold. Here's an example:

Type these exact words

We also use several icons in the margins to alert you to special information. These icons include the following:

This shows you a special tip or trick that can help you do things like a real expert.

Notes are important information that amplifies a subject. They provide a bit more special information that you won't want to miss.

If there's a danger that you need to know about, we display a caution to alert you so that you don't accidentally do something that causes a problem.

The entire *Microsoft Outlook 2000 Bible* team hopes you enjoy this book. We feel it's your best source of up-to-date information about Microsoft Outlook.

Acknowledgments

A project as large as *Microsoft Outlook 2000 Bible* is the result of much hard work by many different people. We'd like to thank everyone personally, but that's just not possible because so many people contributed in one way or another. Here are some of the people who helped make this book possible:

Stefan Grünwedel, our development editor, was instrumental in helping us produce a quality piece of work we can all be proud of. His industry expertise helped kick it up a notch and add those finishing touches that made all the difference. In addition, he did it all while exercising patience and understanding in regard to our busy schedules. Excellent work!

Without Gayle Ehrenman's and Susan Glinert's technical expertise, readers would not be able to obtain the superior level of understanding they can expect. Both have a real talent for seeing things from multiple points of view. Great job!

We also want to thank Ami Knox, our copy editor, whose efforts helped improve our writing and contributed to the overall quality of the book.

Finally, without the coordination and logistical efforts of Andy Cummings, our acquisitions editor, we would have been lost. Andy was also great source for good advice. Thanks a lot!

Additional thanks go to Brad Hehe for his efforts.

Contents at a Glance

• •

Contents

• •

Part II: Mastering E-mail   129

Chapter 6: E-mail Basics 131

Chapter 7: Intermediate E-mail Concepts 151

Part III: Microsoft Outlook 2000 as a Personal Information Manager   203

Part IV: Getting the Most out of Microsoft Outlook 2000   339

Quick Start

Outlook is a multipurpose program. Most people immediately think of e-mail messages when they think of Outlook, but there's really a whole lot more that Outlook can do for you. Outlook can help you keep track of your schedule and make certain that your address book is always up to date. It can help you track the time you spend working on documents, allow you to create electronic "sticky notes," and even make certain that you get around to doing those things that are on your to-do list.

To help you get an idea how Outlook works, this chapter guides you through creating an e-mail message, setting up an appointment, putting a note on your screen, and creating a record of one of your contacts.

Starting Outlook

Depending on your installation of Outlook, the program may automatically open whenever you start your computer, or you may have to launch the program manually. If Outlook starts automatically, consider yourself lucky — you don't have to do anything special to be ready to use the program. If Outlook doesn't automatically run when you start your computer, follow these steps to start Outlook yourself:

1. Click the Start button.

2. Select Programs ⇨ Microsoft Outlook. If you don't see Outlook on the Programs menu, look for it in a folder named Microsoft Office, Office 2000, or something similar.

Outlook opens to display the Outlook Today folder, as shown in Figure QS-1. You can read more about the Outlook Today folder in Chapter 2.

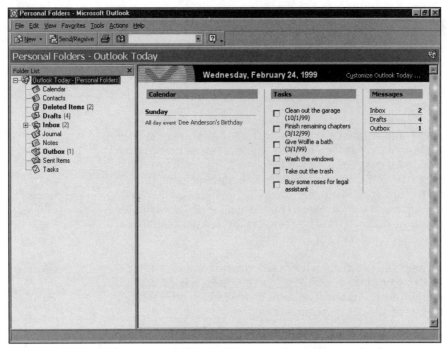

Figure QS-1: Outlook opens and shows you an overview of your active items.

Tip   If you want Outlook to always be available for e-mail messages, faxing, scheduling, and so on, add a shortcut to Outlook to the \Windows\Start Menu\Programs\ StartUp folder. This will cause Outlook to open whenever you start your computer.

Creating a Message

Although Outlook can do many different things, the one thing that almost everyone who uses Outlook does is send and receive e-mail messages. E-mail has certainly changed the way that people communicate. Time and distance are no longer factors in communicating, so if you want to send a message half way around the world, it's just as easy as sending a message down the block. It's also just as inexpensive!

Note   You'll probably send most of your e-mail messages across the Internet, although if you're connected to a private mail system on a network, you can use Outlook to send messages there, too. We aren't going to attempt to tell you how to set up a mail account on the Internet or on your local network. If you don't already have a mail account set up, you'll need to do so before you can send or receive e-mail messages in Outlook.

Creating and sending an e-mail message is very easy. If you have ever typed a letter to someone, you are already familiar with much of the process. The primary difference between a printed letter and an e-mail message is the way you address an e-mail message. A printed letter that you send through the mail requires a valid street address or post office box number. An e-mail message requires a valid electronic address. E-mail addresses aren't very complicated, but because computers aren't very forgiving, you must be very careful to get the address absolutely correct.

Tip　It's generally safe to assume that e-mail addresses are not case sensitive, which means you can use either uppercase or lowercase letters and have everything come out fine. In the past, many mail systems did require you to discriminate between upper- and lowercase letters, but this is generally "not the case" anymore.

If you've never seen one before, an e-mail address may look a little strange. Even so, e-mail addresses are really pretty easy to understand. A typical e-mail address might look like this:

```
someone@someplace.com
```

Someone is the *user name* of the person that you want to send a message to. Usually this isn't quite their real name, but it's probably close. For example, Bob Jones might have a user name like bjones. Following the user name is the *at* sign (@). (You'll generally find this above the 2 key at the top of your keyboard.) Every e-mail address has an *at* sign immediately following the user name. *Someplace.com* is the name of the *mail server*—a computer—where the person receives mail. Compare this example to your own e-mail address, and you'll see just how simple e-mail addresses really are.

To create and send an e-mail message, follow these steps:

1. Click the New button. You may want to hold your mouse pointer over the New button for a few seconds to make certain that the label "New Mail Message" appears. If "New Mail Message" does not appear, click the down arrow at the right edge of the button to display the list of options. As Figure QS-2 shows, the New button can be used to create more than just messages: You can use it to create appointments, tasks, new contacts, and other kinds of Outlook items you'll learn about later. The default new item—the one that appears when you click the button itself, as opposed to the arrow—changes depending upon where you are in Outlook. For example, if you were in the Contacts part of the program, a new Contact form would open when you clicked New.

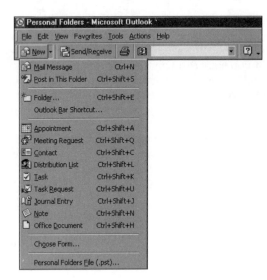

2. In the text box to the right of the To button, enter the e-mail address for the intended message recipient. If you don't know anyone's e-mail address, enter your own e-mail address and send yourself a message. If you already have e-mail addresses in your Address Book, you can also click the To button to select addresses from it.

3. Skip down to the Subject text box and enter a brief description of your message. The subject line is generally the first thing that people see when they receive an e-mail message, so you want this to explain the message in a few words.

4. Click in the large white box below the Subject text box and then enter your message as shown in Figure QS-3. Don't worry about getting fancy at this point, you learn more about making your e-mail messages look a bit more interesting in Chapter 7.

5. Click the Send button to close the message form and place your new message in the Outlook Outbox folder.

6. When you return to Outlook, click the Outbox folder in the folder list or the Outbox icon in the Outlook bar. The message you just wrote should appear in the list on the right. (The Outbox holds messages that are waiting to be sent.)

Place your subject here   Enter your message text here

Figure QS-3: Your message has an address, subject, and body, so it's ready to send.

7. Click the Send/Receive button to send the message. You may have to confirm that you want to connect to the Internet — some computers are set up to connect automatically, whereas others require confirmation.

Once you send an e-mail message, there's really no way to determine how long it will be before the recipient will receive the message. Some people are always connected directly to the Internet, so they may receive a message almost instantly. But if the recipient only occasionally connects to their mail server to check for new messages, your message will have to sit and wait until the next time they log on and check their mail.

Tip

Outlook can automatically check for new e-mail messages on your mail server at intervals that you specify. See Chapter 5 for more information on setting up Outlook to automatically check your mail server.

Setting Up an Appointment

How would you like to have your computer remind you of important events like a meeting with your boss or your sister's birthday? The Outlook Calendar is just the thing to give you those reminders, because it never forgets. Once you've placed a significant occasion on your Outlook Calendar, you can be ensured of being reminded and looking like a hero.

Note Outlook can only give you reminders if Outlook is running. That's one more reason why you may want to load Outlook automatically whenever you start your computer.

Unlike the paper calendar that you may have on your desk or on your wall, your Outlook Calendar never goes out of date. If you need to set up something like next year's vacation, the Outlook Calendar is ready to go. You don't need to buy refills, either!

The Outlook Calendar is also very flexible. If you want to view your workweek schedule, that view is just a click away. In fact, there are probably dozens of different ways to view the Outlook Calendar. To learn more about the possibilities, see Chapter 10.

To add an appointment to your Calendar, follow these steps:

1. Click the Calendar folder in the folder list or the Calendar icon in the Outlook bar to display the Outlook Calendar, shown in Figure QS-4.

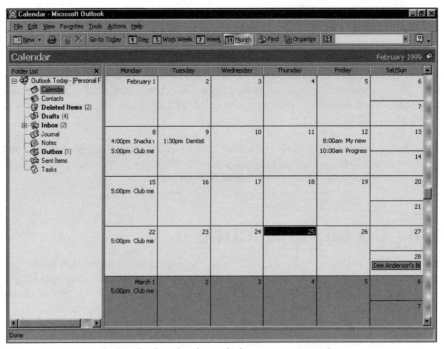

Figure QS-4: Use the Outlook Calendar to help manage your time.

2. Click the Day, Work Week, Week, or Month button on the Outlook toolbar to choose the Calendar display that you prefer. You'll want to choose a view that enables you to find the date of the appointment easily.

3. Scroll the Calendar display until you can see the date of the appointment. If you have selected the Month view, use the scrollbar along the right edge of the Calendar to scroll. In any of the other views, use the small arrows that appear above the month displays to scroll the dates.

4. Double-click the date of the appointment to display the Event form.

5. Enter a brief description of the appointment in the Subject text box. You will only see the first few words of this description in your Calendar, so try to be concise.

6. If this appointment has a specific starting time, remove the check from the *All day event* checkbox. This will display the start and end time list boxes.

7. Click the down arrow at the right edge of the Start time list box and select the time that the appointment begins.

8. Do the same to set the ending time using the End time list box.

9. Click the down arrow next to the Reminder list box and choose how far in advance you would like Outlook to remind you of the event, as shown in Figure QS-5.

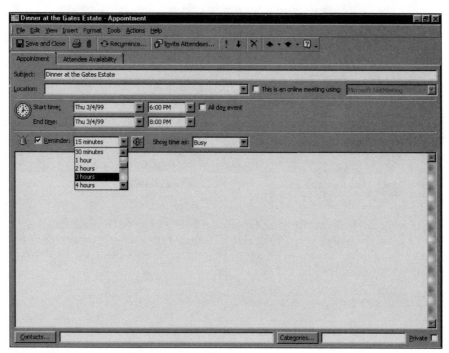

Figure QS-5: Choose when you would like to be reminded of this appointment.

Tip The Reminder list box only displays reminder times up to two days before the appointment, but you can actually specify any amount of time you want. Just go ahead and enter the number of days in the list box. Be sure to specify days, and Outlook will remind you as far in advance as you like.

10. Enter any additional notes about the event in the large text box below the Reminder list box.

11. Click the Save and Close button to close the Event form and save the appointment in your Calendar. Figure QS-6 shows how this new event appears in the Outlook Calendar in Day view.

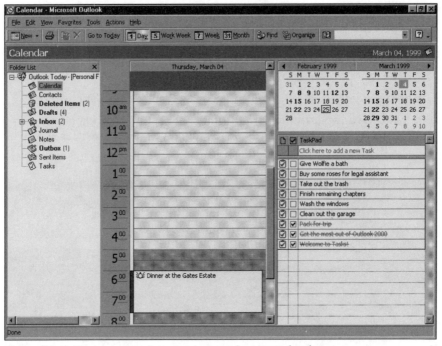

Figure QS-6: The new appointment appears in your Calendar.

You can schedule many different types of events using the Outlook Calendar. Outlook can even help you arrange a meeting at a time when everyone has free time in their schedule. To learn more about scheduling events using the Outlook Calendar, see Chapter 11.

Creating a Note

Are your desk and your monitor covered with a bunch of those little paper sticky notes? If so, you'll probably appreciate another one of Outlook's handy features — electronic sticky notes for your screen. Unlike the paper sticky notes, Outlook's notes won't fall off and get buried under a mound of paper.

Sticky notes are a great idea. You can jot down a quick reminder of a phone number that you need to call, an idea that just popped into your head while you were talking to someone on the phone, or even just a note to remind you to call someone back as soon as you're free. You can do all of these things with paper sticky notes, of course, but those little pads with the blank notes always seem to get lost somewhere on your desk. Even when you do find them, the paper sticky notes are too large or too small for the job. Outlook's notes are always easy to find and just the right size.

To create your own Outlook notes, follow these steps:

1. Click the Notes folder in the folder list or the Notes icon in the Outlook bar to display the Notes folder.

2. Click the New Note button to display a new blank note as shown in Figure QS-7. Remember to hold the mouse pointer over the New button for a few seconds if you aren't certain of the button's current function.

Figure QS-7: Enter your reminder onto the note.

3. Type whatever text you wish onto the note. If you need more or less space, drag the borders of the note to the desired size.

4. Click the Close button in the upper-right corner to close the note and place it in the Notes folder. Alternatively, you can leave a note open when you switch to another program. Figure QS-8 shows how an open note appears on the Windows desktop when Outlook is minimized.

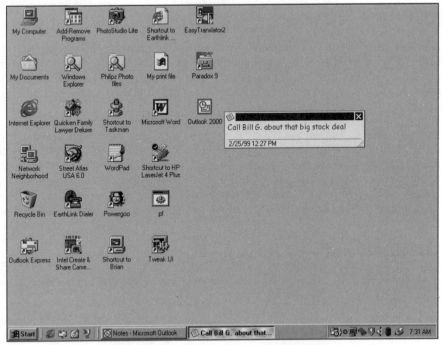

Figure QS-8: You can leave your notes open on your desktop.

 Note   Notes are only visible while Outlook is running. You can minimize Outlook and still have your notes open on your desktop. If another program is covering a note, bring the note to the front by clicking the note's icon on the Windows taskbar.

You can organize your notes by assigning them categories or colors. To learn more about Outlook's notes, see Chapter 14.

Creating a Contact

Most people have some sort of address book that they use to keep track of friends, relatives, or business associates. Often that address book is the well-known "little black book." Address books are handy, but they do have several limitations. When people move, you have to cross out the old information and try to find room for the new. If you're from Minnesota, like one of the authors of this book, there's never quite enough room for all of the Johnsons and Olsons, either!

Outlook refers to all of those people in your address book as *contacts*. The Outlook Contacts folder serves as an extremely versatile electronic address book that always has room—no matter how many entries you have under the letter *J*. But the Outlook Contacts list goes far beyond a simple address book. You can use your Contact records to automatically enter the correct addresses on letters, the correct e-mail addresses on e-mail messages, and even dial the correct phone number when you want to call someone. See Chapter 9 for some more ideas about how you can use the Outlook Contacts list.

To add a new contact, follow these steps:

1. Click the Contacts folder in the folder list or the Contacts icon in the Outlook bar to display the Contacts folder, shown in Figure QS-9.

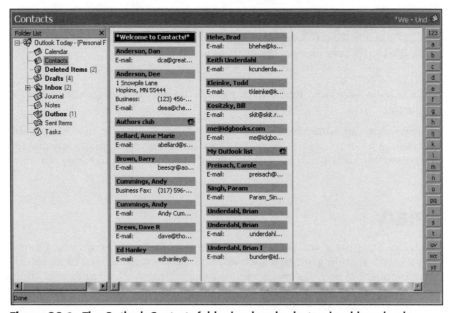

Figure QS-9: The Outlook Contacts folder is a handy electronic address book.

2. Click the New Contact button to display a new blank Contact form.

3. Enter the person's name in the text box to the right of the Full Name button.

4. If you like, enter a job title and company name.

5. Choose the way you would like to file this person's record using the choices in the File as list box. Be sure you enter the name and company before making this selection.

6. Enter any additional information that you need in the remaining text boxes. You can always come back later and add additional items as they become available. Figure QS-10 shows a Contact form that has several of the fields filled in.

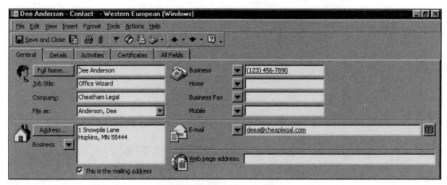

Figure QS-10: Fill in as many of the items as you like.

  7. Click the Save and Close button to save the information and close the Contact form.

You can reopen a Contact form by double-clicking the entry in the Contacts folder. Always remember to use the Save and Close button if you've made any changes — otherwise Outlook will display a message asking if you want to save your changes.

Summary

This Quick Start has given you some ideas about what you can do with Outlook. You've seen a sampling of tasks such as creating a new e-mail message, setting up an appointment in your Calendar, creating an electronic sticky note, and adding a new Contact record to your Outlook address book. Now it's time to start using Microsoft Outlook 2000 to its fullest!

Chapter 1, which follows, provides some basics about how you can use Outlook to get more done with less work.

✦   ✦   ✦

Getting Started with Microsoft Outlook 2000

Part I shows you the basics of Microsoft Outlook 2000. First you see what you can do with Outlook 2000, and then we take you on a guided tour of the program. Next you learn about what is new in this version, compared to earlier releases of Outlook. Finally, you see how to decide which installation and configuration options will work best for you.

What's Outlook 2000 All About?

Have you ever opened a package and been pleasantly surprised when you discovered that it contained a whole lot more than you expected? If so, you'll probably feel the same way with Outlook 2000 — it has many more features and uses than may be apparent at first glance. In this chapter, you have the opportunity to see a sampling of the many features of Outlook 2000 so you can get a feel for just how much is contained in the package.

If you were to ask a cross-section of Outlook users how they use the program, it would be a pretty safe bet that most of them would immediately mention e-mail. Some users would probably also talk about using Outlook to keep track of their calendar and maybe their contacts, but that would likely be about all most people would think about. Very few people actually use Outlook as effectively as they could — in part because they don't know how much Outlook can do for them.

You don't have to use all the features of Outlook any more than you have to eat every type of food you might find at a buffet dinner. On the other hand, you'll probably find that knowing all the different things that are available may stimulate your appetite so you'll want to try some new things. So maybe that's the way you should approach this chapter — as an "appetizer plate" that whets your imagination about what you can do with Outlook.

Increased Productivity

Everyone has certainly heard the old saying, "Time is money." In today's busy world, that old saying is probably even truer than ever. There just isn't enough time for everything you need to accomplish — unless you can get some good help, that is. Outlook can provide lots of that help so you can be more productive and get more done in the time you have available.

Outlook has many different ways to help you increase your productivity. You aren't likely to use all of them, but even using some of them can be very effective. For example, Figure 1-1 shows several items in the Outlook Today folder. The items shown make use of three different Outlook features including the Calendar, the task list, and the messaging features. Just using these three and ignoring the rest of Outlook could make you more productive—but using additional Outlook capabilities will help you to be even more productive.

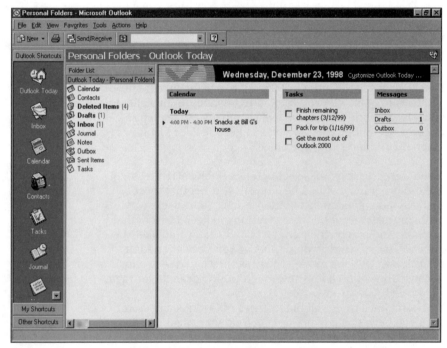

Figure 1-1: Use Outlook's feature to help organize your life so you can be more productive.

Sharing information

Virtually no one works in actual isolation. Even if you were to go off to the top of a mountain to sit in a cave for the rest of your life, you'd still need to communicate with others once in a while—even if that meant creating a fire and sending out smoke signals. Fortunately for those of us with far more normal lives, Outlook is designed to make sharing information pretty simple and straightforward. Outlook isn't likely to make your eyes water as much as smoke signals would, either!

Outlook offers several ways for you to share information. Here are a few possibilities for sharing information through Outlook:

✦ You can send information to other people in the form of e-mail messages. This is by far the simplest method and will serve the needs of many users.

✦ You can use Outlook to schedule meetings — either online or face-to-face meetings — as the need arises. Meetings are an obvious method of sharing information, of course, but you may never have thought of using Outlook for this type of scheduling. To be effective, each of the meeting participants must keep their personal schedule in Outlook.

✦ You can publish information in *net folders* — a special type of Outlook folder that automatically shares information across the Internet. Net folders act as online publishers for information from your computer, but unlike a public Web site, net folders only send information to the people you specify. As the owner of a net folder, you also control how much access each subscriber to the folder is granted. Figure 1-2 shows an Outlook folder that has been shared as a net folder.

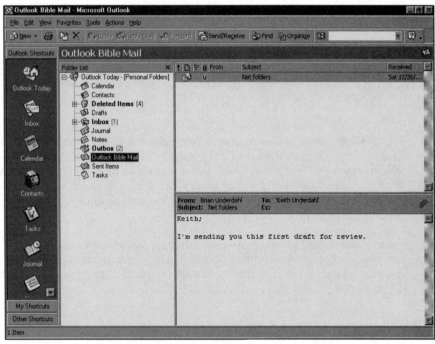

Figure 1-2: Use net folders to publish information to a select group of recipients.

Note With only a few exceptions—e-mail messages being the most notable—you'll have a difficult time sharing most Outlook information with anyone who doesn't also use Outlook. The items on your Calendar, for example, aren't readily usable for scheduling unless everyone in your workgroup is using Outlook. Some types of information, such as your contacts, can be shared indirectly by exporting the information to another format. It is generally not practical to attempt to share such information without user intervention, because you must manually choose the fields that you are importing.

Getting organized

People have different definitions of what it means to be organized. For some people, it's enough that they're able to get up and get to work pretty much on time. Some other people take organization to the extreme and aren't happy unless each pair of socks in their underwear drawer is lined up according to a color chart. Outlook's organization features are intended for people who fit somewhere between these two extremes.

Several of Outlook's capabilities may help you get organized. Depending on your personal definition of what it means to be organized, you many find some or all of these capabilities useful.

Keeping track of your schedule

Figure 1-3 shows the Outlook feature that probably comes to mind first when you're thinking about organization. The Outlook Calendar enables you to plan your schedule, plan for meetings, and even block out time when you don't want to be disturbed.

The Outlook Calendar may look somewhat like the paper calendar that may already sit right there on your desk, but the Outlook Calendar can do things no paper calendar ever could. It's fairly easy to forget to look on your desk calendar to see what might be scheduled for that week when you're planning a vacation, but the Outlook Calendar won't allow you to "accidentally" be gone when you have that dental appointment.

In addition to notifying you about scheduling conflicts, the Outlook Calendar can also provide both visible and audible reminders of important events. With a little planning, you could even have Outlook greet you on your special day by playing *Happy Birthday* when you check your schedule.

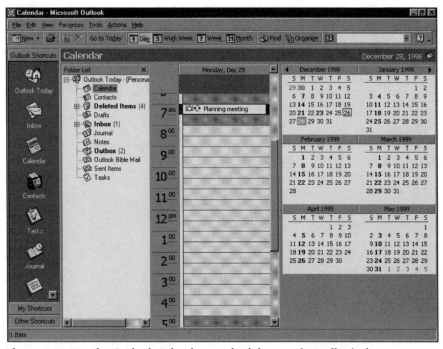

Figure 1-3: Use the Outlook Calendar to schedule your time effectively.

Staying in contact

If you've ever tried to rely on one of those little pocket organizer books to keep track of your address list, you'll quickly come to appreciate the Outlook Contacts list. Gone are the problems of running out of space simply because you know too many people with a last name like Smith or of virtually illegible entries that are the result of making too many corrections.

The Outlook Contacts list can store far more than the obvious e-mail addresses. As Figure 1-4 shows, the Outlook Contacts list has room for additional information such as mailing addresses, phone numbers, business information, and quite a bit more. If you need to keep track of information about someone, the Outlook Contacts list can likely accommodate your needs.

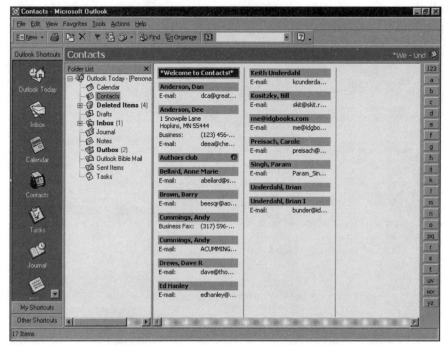

Figure 1-4: Use the Outlook Contacts list to organize your address list.

Tip

If you want to share contact information with people who may not be using Outlook, you may want to send the information as a vCard — an Internet standard for creating and sharing virtual business cards. (More on vCards in Chapter 7.)

Getting even more organized

Outlook doesn't stop at organizing your schedule and your address book. Outlook also keeps track of how you use your computer. You may not realize it, but each time you work on a Microsoft Office document, Outlook can make a note about the document in the Journal. There is an automatic record of not only when you opened each document but also how long you worked on it.

As Figure 1-5 shows, the Outlook Journal automatically tracks information about e-mail messages in addition to Access, Excel, PowerPoint, and Word documents. You can add your own categories such as phone calls to the Journal, too.

Entries in the Outlook Journal are organized by date, so you can scroll to any particular date, click the plus sign (+) in front of the entry type, and see which items are recorded in the Journal for that date. If you want more details about an item, all you need to do is double-click the item to view the Journal entry.

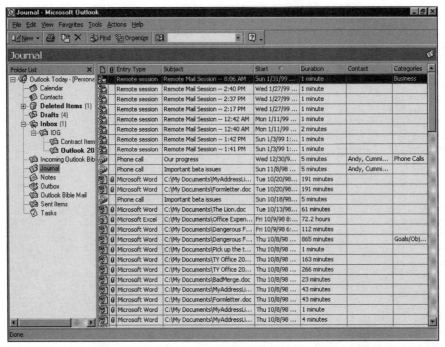

Figure 1-5: The Outlook Journal automatically keeps track of your Office documents.

Tip   The Outlook Journal can be a valuable tool for tracking the time you spent working on a project—especially if you need to bill for projects based on time.

The Tasks list is another important Outlook organizational tool. The Tasks list is
useful for organizing those projects you need to complete but which don't fit neatly
on a calendar. For example, Figure 1-6 shows a Tasks list that includes a number
of items. Some items have a definite due date, whereas others simply need to be
done sometime. What sets all of these items apart from standard Calendar entries is
that tasks are generally somewhat difficult to schedule. It's easy, for example, to
schedule a business trip, because your flight will probably leave at a specified time
whether you're there or not. It's much harder to schedule something like finishing
a manuscript, as it's difficult to foresee any problems that might delay the
completion. In addition, the task of finishing a manuscript is one that you could
finish early—there's no penalty for being ahead of schedule for most task-type
items.

Tip   Be sure to clean out old completed tasks from time to time so that it's easier to
see what's left to be done. Select a completed task and click the Delete button to
remove the task from the list.

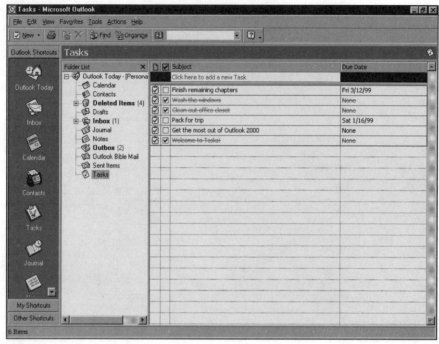

Figure 1-6: Use the Outlook Tasks list to plan items that don't easily fit a calendar-dictated schedule.

Integrating with other applications

Increasing your productivity using Outlook isn't limited to the various tasks you can perform within Outlook itself. A lot of the information that you create or store in Outlook is also quite useful in other applications. You might, for example, want to create a form letter in Word and then use your Outlook Contacts list to address those letters. Sure, you could just create a second address book, but why do all that extra work when Outlook already has just what you need? Besides, do you really want to try to keep two different address lists up-to-date?

One very productive way to integrate Outlook with other applications is a slight variation on the old form letter process. Sure, you've probably used mail merge to create form letters, but did you realize that you could use mail merge to create a series of e-mail messages, too? If you've ever considered changing to a different Internet service provider but decided that notifying all your contacts about your new e-mail address was just too much of a hassle, why not use Outlook and Word together to create an e-mail notification of your new e-mail address? That way each message recipient will receive their personalized copy of your address change and will be far less likely to ignore the message.

Even if you never use mail merge you'll probably find that Outlook has a certain amount of integration with the other Microsoft Office applications. For example, although Outlook has a very rudimentary text editor that you could use to create e-mail messages, it's fairly likely that you'll never actually use this simple editor. It's far more probable that when you click the New Message button that Outlook will start Word than the simple text editor. Word gives you much more control over the format of messages in addition to providing easy access to features like spell checking.

Easy Messaging

You'd be excused if all you thought about doing with Outlook was sending and receiving e-mail messages. Messaging is really at the heart of Outlook, even though only using Outlook for e-mail would be kind of like visiting a family gathering and ignoring all the relatives because you were only interested in seeing your grandma's dog.

What is messaging?

In Outlook, messaging is pretty much synonymous with *e-mail* — electronic mail. E-mail has really changed the way people communicate in a number of pretty fundamental ways. Some of these changes include the following:

✦ Messages can now be delivered virtually instantly nearly anywhere in the world. Although this has been possible for voice messages sent over telephone lines for some time, e-mail encompasses many additional types of messages. (It's also much cheaper than long-distance calls.)

✦ Sending a message is generally much less expensive than in the past. You can, for example, send the entire text of a 500-page book over the Internet without paying a special delivery charge. Compare that to the cost of sending a 500-page printed document via an overnight air express service!

✦ Time zones are far less important when you can send a message, and the recipient can read it at their convenience. As a result, it may be far easier to collaborate on a project with someone half-way around the world than it used to be to collaborate with someone two time zones away.

✦ Because messages can easily include attachments, it's almost as easy to send a photo or a fully formatted document as it is to send a plain text message. This makes it far more likely that the sender and the recipient both understand the message in the same way.

E-mail has truly made the world a bit easier to reach and has brought about many changes in the way people communicate on a daily basis.

Integrating with forms

Outlook *forms* are a method of standardizing the way you send and receive information. You use Outlook forms when you create and store contact information and when you create a new message. Forms make interacting with your computer far easier, as forms are a visual method of presenting information.

You aren't limited to the standard forms Outlook provides for its purposes. As detailed in the last half of this book, you can create your own forms for use with Outlook. You might, for example, create a form that members of your workgroup could use to report on their progress or to report problems with a project.

Outlook forms can effectively connect any other computer in the world into your Outlook information database. If you e-mail someone a message that contains the proper form, the information they enter into the form can be automatically e-mailed back to your computer and used on your system. If you need this type of integration be sure to read all about forms later in this book.

Collaborative Solutions

Many projects can only be successfully completed through the efforts of a number of different people all working together towards a common goal. A book like this one is a good example. It covers a range of topics that is simply too broad for one author to complete in a reasonable amount of time. Only by having a team of authors and editors working in collaboration can a project of this size be completed within a reasonable amount of time.

Collaboration only works if all the members of a team are working together. Those team members may be spread out thousands of miles apart, or they may be office mates, but coordination between team members is usually pretty important. An editor can only begin his or her work once an author has begun submitting pieces of the manuscript. If the authoring team decided to hold all their chapters until the last minute, the editorial team would be hard pressed to complete their work on time. Likewise, if people on a project team all decided to work independently without regard to anyone else's schedule, it would be extremely difficult to finish any project on deadline. Fortunately, Outlook offers some solutions that can help solve these problems.

What is a collaborative solution?

A collaborative solution to a problem is only possible when team members agree to work together. A very simple example of this is seen in a project-planning meeting. It's pretty difficult to hold a successful project-planning meeting unless everyone agrees to attend the meeting at the scheduled time.

Even if you can get everyone to agree that they need to work together, it can still be a lot of work trying to coordinate everyone's schedule. Outlook can make this part of a project somewhat easier by helping you schedule meetings at times when everyone will be available. Figure 1-7 shows how you might use Outlook to begin this process.

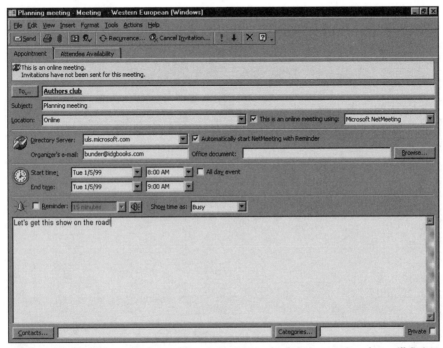

Figure 1-7: Use the Outlook meeting request to schedule a meeting that will fit into the team members' schedules.

As the figure shows, you begin the process by setting up a meeting request. You can include as many details as necessary and determine where you'll hold your meeting. Online meetings require a bit of extra coordination to make certain that everyone uses the correct software and server location, which Outlook enables you to specify (see the example in Figure 1-7).

Tip   It's a good idea to plan a dry run before an important online meeting. Inevitably at least one of the attendees will need to install and configure their online meeting software before they can connect, and this can easily disrupt your entire meeting if it has to be done at the last minute.

Once you've used Outlook to request a meeting, it's time to finalize the schedule and attendance list. If all the people you've invited to the meeting are using Outlook, it's much easier to coordinate this because you'll be able to check on their availability and even automatically log their responses to the meeting request. Figure 1-8 shows an example of an in-progress meeting request. One attendee has indicated he'll attend, and another has tentatively accepted.

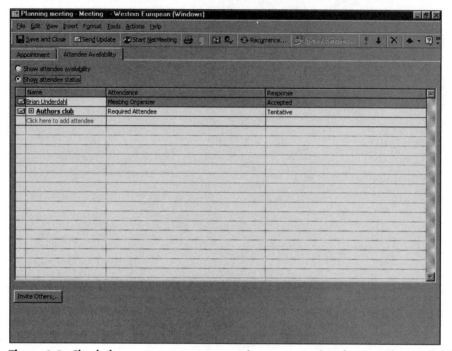

Figure 1-8: Check the responses to your meeting request using the Attendee Availability tab.

Tip   If everyone keeps their schedule in Outlook, you can click the Show attendee availability radio button to help in rescheduling meetings to accommodate the participants.

Business solutions

Business, of course, is about more than just scheduling meetings. There are plenty of business solutions that don't involve meetings but which can use Outlook to help people work together. A common example might be to use net folders to keep everyone informed of important new developments. You might use this method to let everyone know about a workaround for a problem they might encounter.

Another less obvious example would be to use specialized forms to enable people to make standardized requests. Imagine that your company used special letterhead paper but didn't want branch offices to maintain too large a supply because rapid growth was resulting in frequent changes. You might create an Outlook form that enables each branch to easily request letterhead paper on an as-needed basis so that they wouldn't be tempted to hoard too large a supply of possibly outdated materials.

The last half of this book concentrates on many different custom business solutions that use Outlook. You'll find more ideas there about what you can do to make Outlook an important part of your organization's collaborative efforts.

Summary

This chapter has provided a quick sampling of some of the things you can do with Outlook. You probably weren't aware just how versatile and adaptable Outlook could be — especially if you thought Outlook was only another e-mail program. But because this chapter is just a quick sampler, we hope you'll read on and learn much more about this powerful application called Outlook.

The next chapter provides a guided tour of Outlook, where you learn some of the basics of using Outlook for yourself.

✦   ✦   ✦

A Guided Tour of Outlook 2000

Any program that has as many features and capabilities as Outlook can seem pretty confusing at first glance. There are menus, toolbars, icons, status lines, links you can click, and a whole lot of other bits and pieces that may seem designed specifically to make it difficult to know where to begin. Of course, those same screen elements are all really there for another purpose—to help you use Outlook, but that doesn't make it any easier when you're trying to get started. This chapter is intended to help remove some of the confusion you may be feeling if you don't feel quite at home with Outlook.

Note

Outlook 2000—indeed all of Office 2000—uses a new method to install program features as you need them. You may well discover that as you attempt to access certain Outlook features you are prompted to insert your Outlook Program CD-ROM. If you are asked to insert the CD-ROM, you'll have to wait a few minutes while a new feature is installed. You may find this to be a bit of a nuisance, but remember that once a feature is installed, you won't have to install it again in the future. Waiting to install program features until they are first used is intended to minimize the amount of disk space that is used by Office 2000, but it does add some complication to using the programs. Always be sure to keep your Office 2000 CD-ROMs handy so that you'll be able to install program options as needed.

Understanding the Outlook Window

Figure 2-1 shows how the Outlook window may appear when you first open the program. Your copy of Outlook may not look exactly the same as shown in the figure, but for now you can ignore minor differences. Outlook can take on many different appearances depending on how you have configured the view.

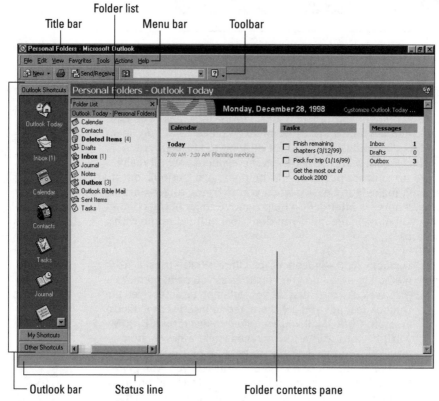

Figure 2-1: The Outlook window has many different elements you can use to get the most out of the program.

To use Outlook effectively you should have an understanding how each of the elements in the Outlook window function. Here's a brief explanation of the major items shown in Figure 2-1:

✦ The *title bar* shows more than just the name of the program. As you open different Outlook folders, the title bar changes to show the name of the open folder. This is especially handy if you hide the folder list, since a quick glance at the title bar can confirm that you have opened the correct folder.

✦ The *menu bar* provides access to all the Outlook commands. The Outlook menu bar is always available because, unlike the toolbars, the menu bar cannot be hidden.

✦ The *toolbars* consist of buttons you can click to perform actions within Outlook — such as the Send/Receive button that sends and receives e-mail. Outlook has several toolbars that you can choose using the View ➪ Toolbars command. As you open different folders, the Outlook toolbars change so that an appropriate set of tools will be displayed. If you like, you can move the toolbars by dragging them to a different location, you can hide the toolbars if you prefer to use menu commands for everything, or you can customize the toolbars to include different sets of tools.

✦ The *Outlook bar* has three different sets of icons that provide one-click access to Outlook folders and to the folders on your computer or network. You can add new shortcut icons to the Outlook bar, remove existing icons, or rename the icons as you please. You can learn more about the Outlook bar in "Using the Outlook bar" later in this chapter.

Tip Numbers in parenthesis next to Outlook bar shortcut icons indicate the number of new items in each folder.

✦ The *folder list* also enables you to access your Outlook folders (as well as the folders on your computer and those available on your network). Because the Outlook bar and the folder list provide virtually the same access to Outlook's features, most people choose to display either the Outlook bar or the folder list by making selections on the View menu. There are, however, a few functions — such as sharing net folders — that can only be done through the folder list and not through the Outlook bar.

Tip Folders whose names appear bold in the folder list contain items awaiting action, such as unread mail.

✦ The *folder contents pane* displays the contents of the currently selected folder. The view of this pane changes considerably as you select different folders, and you also have the option to customize the view of almost any folder.

✦ The *status line* provides a quick summary of the contents of the selected folder (although no summary is shown when the Outlook Today folder is selected). If you select one of the mail folders, the status line tells you both the total number of items and the number of unread items.

Because Outlook is so customizable, there are often several ways to accomplish the same task. You can browse your Outlook folders by clicking either an Outlook bar shortcut icon or by selecting the folder in the folder list, or you can select View ➪ Go To and choose the folder. You can check for new e-mail by clicking the Send/Receive button or by selecting Tools ➪ Send/Receive (and optionally selecting the account you wish to check). In many cases, you'll have access to additional options if you select a menu command rather than simply clicking a button or an icon, but most of the time the default action that is performed when you click the button or icon is really what you want anyway.

You can create more room for the folder contents pane by toggling off either the Outlook bar or the folder list. There's no harm in displaying both of them, but you'll probably find the Outlook window a bit crowded unless you choose one or the other.

Changing the view

It almost seems as though each Outlook user could make their copy of Outlook look completely different from everyone else's copy. There are almost unlimited possible combinations of view settings that enable you to customize the appearance of Outlook. And if that doesn't seem like quite enough for you, remember that each Outlook folder can have its own view settings!

Note

Have you started to hate the way Outlook displays menus yet? If you'd rather see all the commands that are available immediately rather than only the most recently used commands, select Tools ➪ Customize and then click the Options tab in the Customize dialog box that appears. Deselect the *Menus show recently used commands first* checkbox and then click the Close button. You'll now be able to see the complete menus all the time, without delay. (In case you use other Office 2000 applications, you'll notice "smart menus" there, too.)

In addition to choosing to display the Outlook bar, the folder list, or both, you can choose which toolbars you'd like to see. The Outlook toolbars change automatically as you display different types of folders, but you'll probably find that there are times when one or more of the optional toolbars has just what you need. Figure 2-2 shows the four different toolbars that you can display when one of the mail folders — such as Inbox — is selected.

To choose which toolbars are displayed, select View ➪ Toolbars and then the toolbar you wish to display. In Figure 2-2, the toolbars were dragged into four rows to make it a bit easier to differentiate between each of the toolbars. You can also drag the toolbars to other positions if you like. In some cases, more than one toolbar can be fitted into a single row. You can make a toolbar into a floating toolbar rather than one that is docked at the top of the Outlook window by dragging the toolbar down below the toolbar area.

You can drag docked toolbars by moving the mouse pointer over the vertical bar at the left side of the toolbar. When the mouse pointer changes to a four-headed arrow, hold down the left mouse button and drag the toolbar to the new location. Release the left mouse button when the toolbar is in the position where you'd like to drop it. Drag floating toolbars by their title bars.

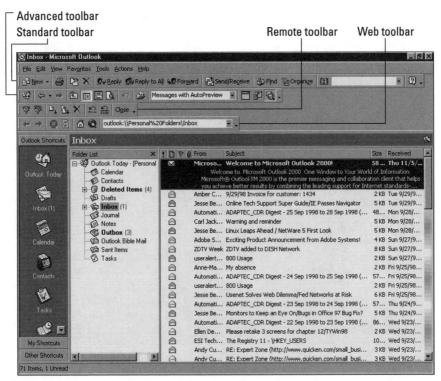

Figure 2-2: Outlook has several different toolbars you can use.

Tip   Choose View ➪ Toolbars ➪ Customize to add or remove buttons from the toolbars. This is often a better choice than displaying several toolbars at the same time, because your customized toolbar can include just the buttons you need without using as much screen space as multiple toolbars would.

In addition to selecting which toolbars are displayed, you can also decide how you'd like the folder contents pane to appear. Each type of Outlook folder has its own unique set of viewing options, and the following sections briefly break down the possibilities by folder type.

Selecting Calendar views

The Outlook Calendar keeps track of your schedule so that you don't miss important meetings or other appointments. You can view the Calendar folder a number of different ways to suit your individual needs. As Figure 2-3 shows, the default view (by selecting View ➪ Current View ➪ Day/Week/Month) looks something like a calendar pad you might have on your desk or hanging on your wall.

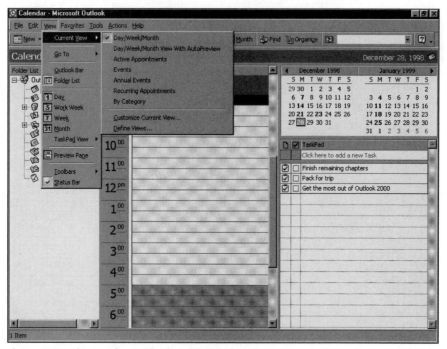

Figure 2-3: Choose the Outlook Calendar view that fits your style of organization.

If you choose either View ➪ Current View ➪ Day/Week/Month or View ➪ Current View ➪ Day/Week/Month With AutoPreview, you can also choose to view a single day, the work week, the entire week, or the entire month at one time. You'll likely find that the number of appointments you track may well dictate which view is most convenient.

Tip   You may find that it is easier to work on your schedule if you temporarily hide both the Outlook bar and the folder list while you are viewing the calendar folder. You can easily move to another folder using the View ➪ Go To command.

Selecting Contacts views

The Outlook Contacts folder helps you keep track of addresses, phone numbers, e-mail addresses, and all sorts of other useful information about the people you deal with. Not surprisingly, you can choose many different ways to view your Contacts list, too. Figure 2-4 shows the Contacts list using the default Address Card view. Notice that the menu changes when you display different types of Outlook folders.

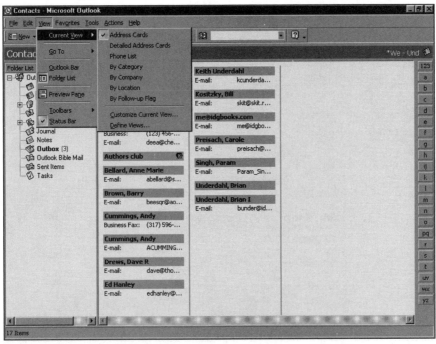

Figure 2-4: Choose the Outlook Contacts list view that works best for you.

Notice in the figure that some entries use the format *last name, first name,* whereas others use the format *first name last name.* Because different entries appear in different formats, the address list may not be sorted quite the way you would expect. Would you look for Keith Underdahl under the letter *K* or the letter *U*? One way to correct this problem would be to use the View ⇨ Current View ⇨ Customize Current View command and then click the Fields button to display the Show Fields dialog box, as shown in Figure 2-5. Select a different field—such as Last Name— rather than the default of File As for the top entry in the *Show these fields in this order* list box to change the sort order. You'll probably want to use First Name as the second entry in the list box and remove File As from the list.

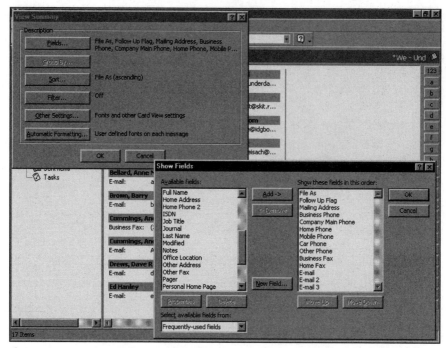

Figure 2-5: Correct sorting problems in the Contacts list by customizing the view.

Selecting mail folder views

Several different Outlook folders fall into the category of mail folders. Typically these include the Deleted Items, Drafts, Inbox, Outbox, and Sent Items folders. If you add additional folders of your own, you may have more mail folders.

Mail folders generally are used to hold e-mail messages and faxes — either incoming or outgoing. Each mail folder can be configured to display its contents differently. You may, for example, want to view your Inbox messages sorted by date received and with a preview of the first few lines of unread messages. You may prefer to sort Sent Items according to the name of the recipient so that you can more easily see who you've sent messages to. Figure 2-6 shows the View ⇨ Current View options you can choose for mail folders.

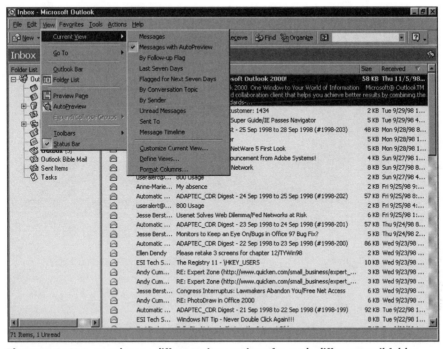

Figure 2-6: You can choose different view options for each different mail folder.

Notice that the mail folder View menu includes a Preview Pane option. If you select this option, the Outlook folder contents pane is split into two panes by a horizontal bar. The upper pane will then show the folder contents, and the lower pane displays the contents of the currently selected message. If you choose this option, you'll probably want to select View ⇨ Current View ⇨ Messages rather than View ⇨ Current View ⇨ Messages with AutoPreview so that you can view more messages in the upper pane.

Selecting Journal views

The Outlook Journal helps you track your time by automatically making a note of when and how long you work on Office documents. You can also add other items to your Journal manually. As Figure 2-7 shows, you have several useful options for viewing the Journal entries.

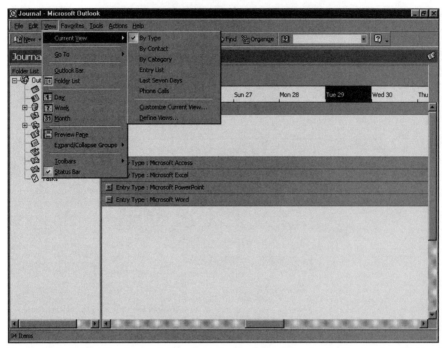

Figure 2-7: Select the Journal view that shows the entries in a style most useful to your way of working.

If you need to track the time you've spent on several different projects, you may find the By Contact view more useful. This view enables you to easily determine how much time you spent working with each client so you can bill for your time.

Selecting Notes views

The Outlook Notes folder holds notes that you create as reminders to yourself. They're essentially the equivalent of those pesky paper sticky notes that people often use to jot down a quick phone number, or remind themselves to take out the garbage or to set up a lunch appointment. Figure 2-8 shows the Notes view options.

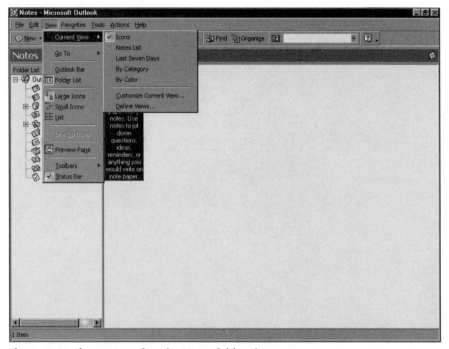

Figure 2-8: Choose your favorite Notes folder view.

Just like paper sticky notes, Outlook notes can be different colors. If you use a lot of notes, you may want to choose the By Color view and then use different colors of notes for different purposes. You could also use the By Category view to sort the notes, but using different colors is probably faster because you can change a note's color with a few quick mouse clicks.

Selecting Task views

The Outlook Tasks folder helps you track things you need to do that you can't easily fit on a calendar schedule. Tasks may or may not have a specified due date. Figure 2-9 shows the Tasks view options.

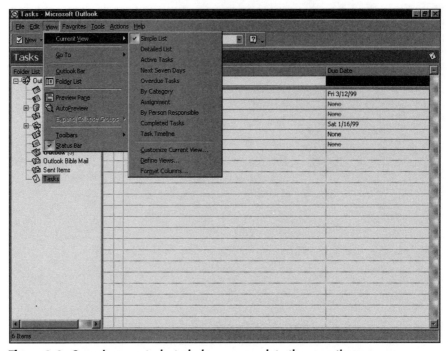

Figure 2-9: Organize your tasks to help you complete them on time.

Even though Outlook allows you to set up tasks without specifying a due date, it's usually best to try and assign due dates. Then you can use a task view that shows when tasks are overdue or are due during the next week. Of course, you may want to assign your own priorities to the tasks and use a view that reflects their importance in your organizational scheme.

Using Outlook Today

Outlook Today is a special folder that summarizes all your active Outlook items so you don't have to hunt around to make certain you keep track of everything yourself. Figure 2-10 shows the Outlook Today folder. It's pretty hard to miss any active item when all of them are listed in one place like this.

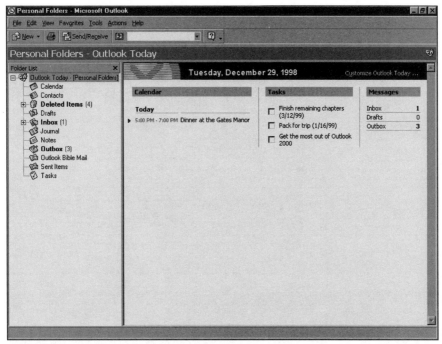

Figure 2-10: The Outlook Today folder organizes all your active items in one place.

The items shown in Outlook Today are linked to their source. This means that you can check off a completed task in Outlook Today, and it will also appear as completed in the Tasks list. Or you can click the Inbox link in Outlook Today to open the Inbox so you can view your new messages.

The Outlook Today calendar section is especially useful because all your upcoming appointments are summarized so you can easily see what's on your schedule. By default, the Outlook Today calendar section shows your appointments for the next five days, but you can easily adjust this to show the number of days your prefer.

It's quite easy to customize Outlook Today. Click the *Customize Outlook Today* button that's usually near the upper-right corner of the Outlook Today folder contents pane to display the customization options as shown in Figure 2-11.

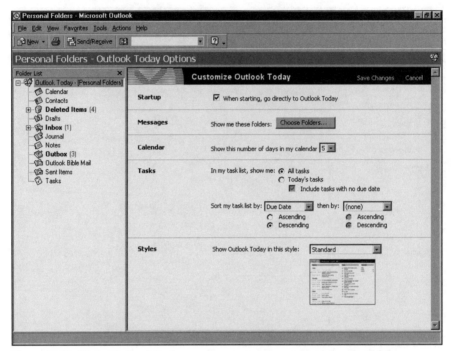

Figure 2-11: Make Outlook Today work your way by customizing the folder.

You have several useful options for customizing the Outlook Today folder:

✦ Remove the check from the checkbox in the Startup section if you would rather have Outlook open the same folder that was open when you last closed Outlook. If you remove this check, you can still open Outlook Today by clicking the Outlook Today folder in the folder list or by clicking the Outlook Today icon in the Outlook Bar.

✦ Use the Choose Folders button to select which folders are included in the Messages section of Outlook Today. The number of unread items in the selected folders will appear in the Messages section.

✦ Use the list box in the Calendar section to select the number of days of appointments you'd like to see in Outlook Today. You can choose between one and seven days of appointments, and you may want to adjust this number according to how full your appointment schedule is normally.

✦ Use the options in the Tasks section to determine which tasks you want to see in Outlook Today and how you'd like them sorted. If you've assigned due dates to each of your tasks, Outlook Today can help you organize your tasks by showing you which ones are due soon and which ones you can delay for a bit longer.

✦ Select a style from the list box in the Styles section to display Outlook Today using a different appearance. Styles are simply a matter of personal preference, but you may find that one of the available styles makes your organization of messages, appointments, and tasks a bit easier.

When you're done customizing the Outlook Today options, click the Save Changes button to apply the changes and view your new version of Outlook Today. You can return to the customization options any time to choose new settings.

Understanding Outlook Folders

The Outlook folder list may give you the impression that Outlook folders are pretty much like any other folders on your computer. While you're working inside Outlook, you can certainly act almost as though this is true. You can easily rename or add new folders, and, within certain limitations, you can move folder contents from one folder to another (the source and destination folders should be the same types of folders).

Outlook folders are unlike ordinary folders in a number of very important ways, however, and you must keep these differences in mind as you use Outlook. First, Outlook folders can only be accessed from within Outlook. You cannot browse your Outlook folders using Windows Explorer. Second, each type of Outlook folder is restricted in the types of items it can hold. You can't, for example, store mail messages in the Calendar folder, nor can you store anything except mail messages in mail folders.

Note   Although you can only store mail messages in mail folders, that doesn't prevent you from storing other types of objects as attachments to mail messages. You can create a new mail message and then add your attachments. If you close the message before it is sent, you can save a copy in the Drafts folder and move the message to any other mail folder later.

Using the Outlook bar

The Outlook bar has several groups of shortcut icons that you can click for quick access to your folders. Just choose the folder you want to view, click the icon, and the folder's contents will be displayed in the folder contents pane.

As you'd probably expect, the Outlook bar is customizable. To change the Outlook bar, right-click any blank space on the Outlook bar, as shown in Figure 2-12. Make certain that the mouse pointer isn't over one of the icons — they appear slightly raised when under the mouse pointer — before you right-click the Outlook bar.

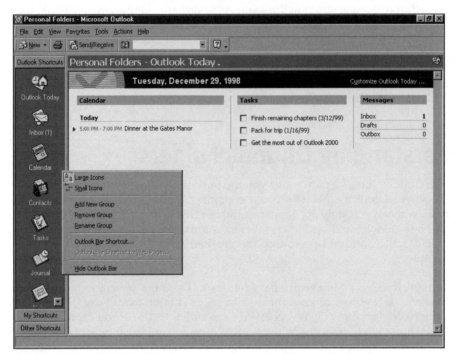

Figure 2-12: Right-click a blank space on the Outlook bar to display the menu so you can customize the Outlook bar.

The first two options on the pop-up menu toggle between large and small icons. Small icons enable you to view more icons at one time, but the icons aren't quite as easy to see or to click — especially if your screen is set to a high-resolution setting — because they present a much smaller target.

The group options enable you to modify the groups of icons shown on the Outlook bar. By default, the Outlook bar includes three groups entitled Outlook Shortcuts, My Shortcuts, and Other Shortcuts. You may want to add a new group that has shortcuts to those folders you use the most.

The third group of options — the Outlook Bar Shortcut options — allow you to add new shortcut icons to your Outlook bar. When you choose one of these options, you'll have the opportunity to browse for the folder you want to add.

The final option—Hide Outlook Bar—simply removes the Outlook bar from the screen. You can display the Outlook bar again by choosing View ➪ Outlook Bar.

You can also right-click any of the shortcut icons on the Outlook bar to view a menu of options for the selected icon. From this menu, you can rename or remove an icon, open the associated folder, search the folder for specified items, or change the folder's properties.

Using the folder list

The folder list serves almost the same purpose as the Outlook bar. You can use the folder list to browse your folders, rename folders, add or delete folders, and move folders within the folder tree. Figure 2-13 shows a typical folder list—albeit with several extra folders added to the folder tree.

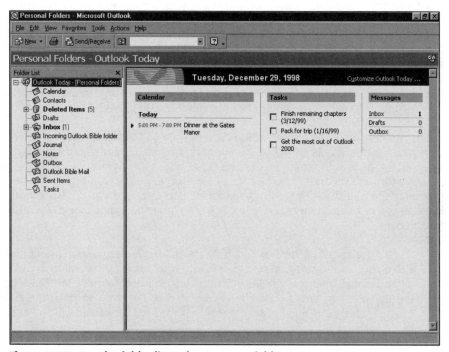

Figure 2-13: Use the folder list to browse your folders.

Tip   Drag the right edge of the folder list to the right or the left to adjust the width of the folder list. If the folder list is too narrow, a scroll bar appears at the bottom of the folder list, and you may need to use the scroll bar to see the entire folder tree.

You can add new folders to the folder list by right-clicking an existing folder and choosing New Folder or by selecting File ➪ New ➪ Folder and then choosing the location for the folder. Folders that contain other folders are indicated by a small box where they connect to the folder tree. If the box contains a minus sign (–), such as the Outlook Today folder in the figure, all the first-level folders contained in the parent folder are shown. If the box contains a plus sign (+), such as the Deleted Items and Inbox folders in the figure, the subfolders are not being shown. Click the minus sign to collapse the tree or the plus sign to expand it.

You probably will want to choose between having the Outlook bar and the folder list displayed. Showing both at the same time wastes considerable space in the Outlook window.

Using the Calendar

The Outlook Calendar is used to keep track of your schedule. If you have appointments, events, or regular meetings that you need to keep track of, the Outlook Calendar is an excellent choice for doing so. This is especially true if you're already using Outlook as your e-mail program, as you'll likely have Outlook running all the time anyway.

Figure 2-14 shows the whole month view of the Calendar. You can use the buttons on the toolbar to select the number of days that are displayed.

When you first open the Calendar, the current date will automatically be selected. Selecting another day is easy, but the method you use depends on the view you've selected. In the month view, you use the scroll bar at the right edge of the Calendar to move through the months. The other Calendar views include small representations of the months with arrows you can click to move forward or backward through the months. In any view, you can click a specific date to view the schedule for the date.

Note   If you'd prefer that all the days (not just weekdays) have equal-sized blocks on the Calendar, select View ➪ Current View ➪ Customize Current View and then click the Other Settings button in the View Summary dialog box. Remove the check from the *Compress weekend days* checkbox and click OK twice to close the dialog boxes. Saturday and Sunday will then be displayed just the same as the other days of the week.

To add an event to your Calendar, double-click the time period where you'd like to add the appointment. Enter the details in the Appointment dialog box and click the Save and Close button to add the item. You may need to adjust the start and end times, especially if you're using the month view, because it may be difficult to double-click the correct time period. You can also drag an appointment to a different time period after it's on your schedule.

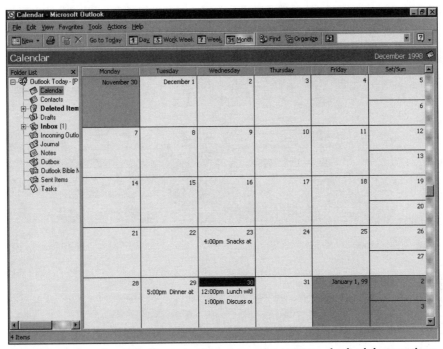

Figure 2-14: Use the Calendar to track your appointments and schedule your time.

Using Contacts

Keeping track of all the information you need to know about people has become pretty complex. Instead of the simple name, address, and phone number that you needed years ago, now you may also need to keep track of someone's e-mail address, fax number, Web site address, and so on. The Outlook Contacts list is just what you need to make certain you never lose that important information again.

Figure 2-15 shows a typical contact card you may create to keep track of all this information. You display this dialog box by double-clicking an existing contact or by clicking the New Contact button. You may only need some of the information that Outlook can track, so it's likely you won't fill in all of the fields.

Notice in the figure that several of the text boxes (such as Business and Home) have a down arrow to the left of the text box. These text boxes work a little differently than the text boxes you've encountered in other applications. When you click the down arrow, you'll see a list of field names, and you can select the field you want from the list. When you do so, the list box name will change to reflect the field you've selected, and you can enter information for that field. Be certain you click Save and Close if you've made any changes.

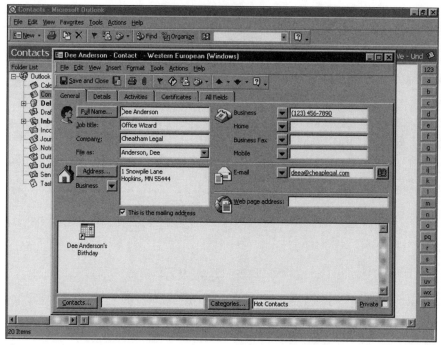

Figure 2-15: Use the Contacts List to track information about people.

Using the Inbox

The Inbox is the place where Outlook stores all your incoming messages. When someone sends you an e-mail message or a fax, the Inbox is the place to look. Figure 2-16 shows a slightly different view of the Inbox than you may have seen before. In the figure, the View ➪ Preview Pane command was used to split the folder contents pane into two windows. When the preview pane is displayed, you can view the contents of the currently selected message in the Inbox in the preview pane below.

Messages that you have not yet read are shown in bold to distinguish them from messages that you have read. Double-click a message to open it so you can read it. If the message includes an attachment — such as a document file — you'll see a paperclip icon just in front of the From column.

Note   Items that appear in your Inbox can stay in the Inbox almost indefinitely unless you do something about them. You have several options for dealing with old messages. In addition to just leaving them where they are, you can move them to another folder, delete them, or export them for use in other programs. In Chapter 17, you'll learn more about managing the items in your Outlook folders.

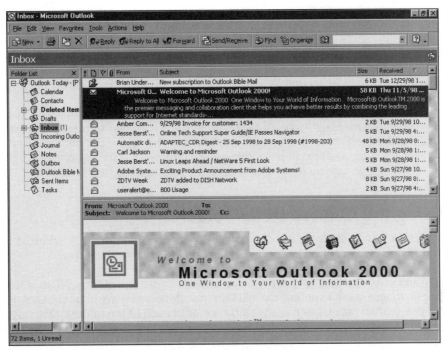

Figure 2-16: The Inbox stores all your incoming messages.

Although Outlook initially places all your incoming messages into the Inbox, you may want certain types of messages placed in other locations. If you're working on an important project, you may want all the messages relating to that project placed in a special folder. Or you may find that someone constantly sends you e-mail that you'd just as soon not bother with and would rather have their messages automatically deleted. Outlook allows you to create rules for handling specified messages.

Cross-Reference

Chapter 8 covers the Rules Wizard that you can use to customize the way Outlook handles incoming messages.

Using the Outbox

The Outbox is the folder where Outlook places all your outgoing messages until they can be sent to the mail server. Depending on just how you have Outlook configured, messages may sit in the Outbox for a few minutes or until you click the Send/Receive button.

E-mail doesn't have an "Unsend" button, but the Outbox is about the closest you'll come to this function. As long as an item remains in the Outbox, you can cancel the message; but once a message has left the Outbox, you should assume that it's on the way to the recipient and can't be stopped (some mail servers may offer the option to cancel a message after you send it, but your timing would have to be absolutely perfect to accomplish this).

Tip   If you forgot to print out a copy of a message before you clicked the Send button, open the message in the Outbox and print it. Click Send to place the message back in the Outbox message queue. Don't use the right-click Print command for items in the Outbox, because this generally prevents Outlook from sending the message unless you remember to open the message and click Send.

Using the Deleted Items folder

Messages you delete from any of the mail folders end up in the Deleted Items folder. This gives you a second chance in case you deleted the item in error.

Like any other Outlook folder, the Deleted Items folder can quickly fill up with items you no longer need. Eventually you'll find that Outlook seems to be running quite a bit slower than normal as it loads all the items in each of the folders. One way to prevent this from becoming a problem is to empty the Deleted Items folder. There are several methods you can use to empty this folder:

✦ Right-click the Deleted Items folder and choose *Empty "Deleted Items" Folder* from the pop-up menu. This method is effective but it is not selective—all items in the folder are deleted.

✦ Open the Deleted Items folder and select the items you want to delete. You can hold down Shift as you click to select a range of items or hold down Ctrl as you click to select noncontiguous items. Once the items are selected, click the Delete button and then confirm the deletion.

✦ Select Tools ➪ Options and click the Other tab. Place a check in the *Empty the Deleted Items folder upon exiting* checkbox and click OK. Your Deleted Items folder will then be emptied automatically whenever you exit from Outlook.

Although it's important to delete items you no longer need and to empty the Deleted Items folder on a regular basis, these steps won't prevent your Outlook Personal Folders file from continuing to grow and eat up your disk space. There's one extra step that's necessary to regain the space that was used by those old items. Select Tools ➪ Services and double-click Personal Folders in the services list. Click the Compact Now button to reclaim the lost space. Close the dialog boxes to return to Outlook.

Using the Drafts folder

The Drafts folder could also be called the "works in progress" folder. If you begin to create a message in Outlook, but then you cancel the message before sending it, Outlook offers to save a copy of the message in the Drafts folder. Messages that you save in the Drafts folder are simply stored in that folder until you decide to delete them, send them, or open them for additional editing.

If you decide that you may need to revise a message before sending it, save that message in the Drafts folder. You won't have to start the message over from the beginning, and you won't have to worry that you've sent off a message that's incomplete or incorrect.

Using the Sent Items folder

The Sent Items folder holds copies of each message that you've sent out. You can check this folder to make certain that you actually did send a message to someone. You can also go to this folder if you need to resend a message that someone had problems receiving. Simply select the message and click the Forward button to open the message editor so you can address the message.

Like any of the other Outlook mail folders, the Sent Items folder can easily become loaded with hundreds of old messages that you've sent out. Unlike some of the other mail folders, however, you may forget to clean out your Sent Items folder on a regular schedule. To avoid the space wasting problems that can result, you can configure the Sent Items folder to automatically empty itself of old items. Right-click the Sent Items folder and choose Properties from the pop-up menu. Click the Auto-Archive tab and select the *Permanently delete old items* radio button. Use the spin control and list box near the top of the tab to select how long items should remain before being deleted. The default setting, 2 months, will probably be adequate in most cases.

Using E-mail

E-mail is usually the first thing that comes to mind when someone talks about Outlook. In fact, many people never even take advantage of all of the power of Outlook and simply use the e-mail features without ever bothering to learn about any of the other things that Outlook can do. That's probably natural, as Outlook started out primarily as an e-mail program, and almost everything else came later.

Creating and sending an e-mail message using Outlook is very easy. Figure 2-17 shows a message that has been created but not yet sent.

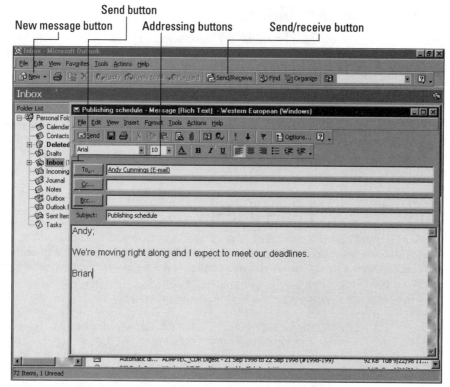

Figure 2-17: You can quickly create and send e-mail using Outlook.

To create and send a simple e-mail message, follow these steps:

1. Select File ➪ New ➪ Mail Message. Click the New message button to open the message editor. (You can also click the New Mail Message button on the toolbar.)

2. Enter the e-mail addresses in the boxes next to the addressing buttons. If the e-mail addresses are in your Contacts list, you can click the addressing buttons and select the addresses from your list.

3. Type a short message description on the subject line.

4. Type your message in the message body area.

5. Click the Send button to place the message in the Outbox.

6. If Outlook is not configured to automatically check for new messages, click the Send/Receive button to send the message to your mail server.

If you want to include an attachment such as a document file or a scanned photo with your message, click the Insert File button on the message editor toolbar before you send the message. The Insert File button is the button that looks like a paper-clip. Choose the file and click Insert to attach it to your message.

Caution   Some people cannot receive e-mail messages that include attachments, and for those who can there is often a limit to the total size of a message. If it's important that the recipient receive your message and the attachment, you may want to send a separate text-only message asking the recipient to confirm that they received the attachment correctly.

Reading your e-mail messages is even easier than creating and sending messages. Open the Inbox folder and double-click the message you want to read. Figure 2-18 shows how Outlook displays a message. You may want to click the maximize button to view more of the message at one time.

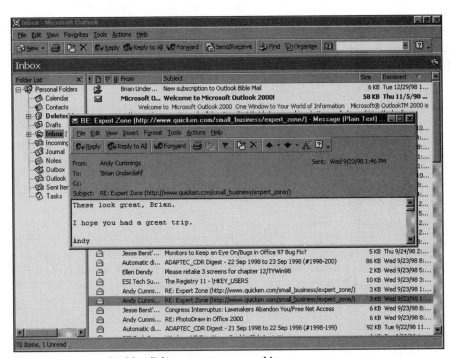

Figure 2-18: Just double-click a message to read it.

Tip   Click the Print button to print a copy of the message. Outlook will include the message date and time on the printout.

Outlook displays your messages in the order they were received, with the newest messages at the top. If you have a lot of messages in your Inbox, you may find it's somewhat difficult to locate a particular message—especially if you don't remember exactly when the message was received. You can quickly sort the messages by clicking any of the column headers. For example, click the column header "From" to sort your messages according to who sent the message. Click the same column header a second time to sort the messages in reverse order.

The chapters in Part II, "Mastering E-mail," show you much more about using e-mail in Outlook.

Creating Tasks

The Outlook Tasks list is a handy way to keep track of those jobs you need to do. There are, of course, many types of tasks and different priority levels for those tasks. Packing for a trip or finishing a book manuscript are examples of tasks that typically have firm due dates. Cleaning up your office is more likely to be a task without a due date—unless you're expecting important clients, of course! Creating and tracking the status of tasks in Outlook is quite simple.

To create a simple task item, follow these steps:

1. Open the Tasks folder.

2. Click the subject line where you see the words "Click here to add a new Task."

3. Type a brief description of the task.

4. Optionally, click the Due Date box and enter a date when the task must be completed.

5. Press Enter to finish.

Figure 2-19 shows a Tasks list that includes several items. Notice that several of the items are checked off to indicate that they have been completed. When you complete a task, click the checkbox to show that it has been completed. You can also click the Delete button to remove a selected task from the list.

To learn more about creating tasks, see Chapter 12.

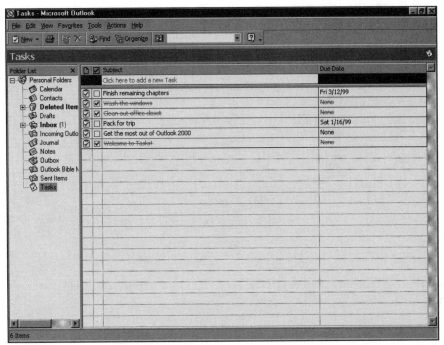

Figure 2-19: Keep track of the tasks you need to complete using the Tasks folder.

Keeping a Journal

If you ever need to track the time you spend on specific projects, you'll probably really appreciate the Outlook Journal. The Journal automatically tracks the time you spend working on Office documents, and you can easily use it to track other activities, too. Figure 2-20 shows an example of how you might use the Journal to log the time spent on phone calls discussing a project.

The Journal uses a scrolling timeline to display the Journal entries. To view the entries in a category, click the plus sign (+) to the left of the entry type and then scroll to the date you'd like to view. Outlook shows the subject in the timeline. To view more details, double-click an item in the timeline. You can also double-click the timeline to create a new entry, as shown in the figure. For manually created entries, you can enter the duration yourself or use the timer by clicking the Start Timer button. When you're done modifying a Journal entry, click the Save and Close button to save your changes.

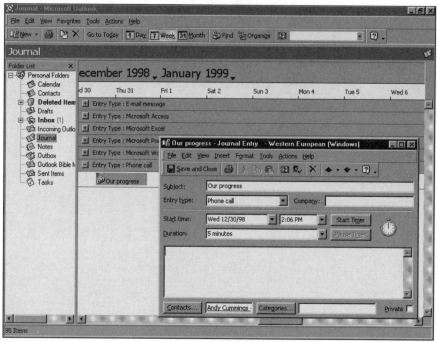

Figure 2-20: Use the Journal to track the time you spend on projects.

Chapter 13 shows you much more about using the Outlook Journal to track the time that you spend on particular tasks.

Taking Notes

Is your monitor covered with a bunch of those sticky notes? Do you jot down reminders and then discover that you've misplaced the one you really need? The Outlook Notes folder can help. Figure 2-21 shows how you can use Outlook's sticky notes to create reminders that won't get lost.

The notes you create in Outlook can't get lost because they're always in one place — the Notes folder. You can use different colors or separate your notes into categories if you need a bit more organization. You can even send notes to someone else.

You can learn much more about notes in Chapter 14.

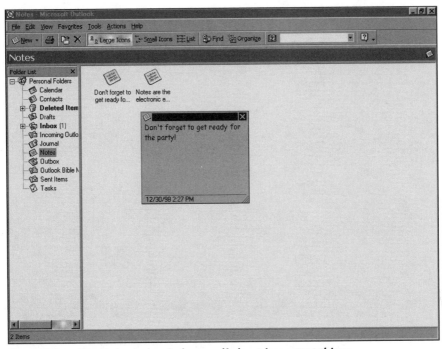

Figure 2-21: Use Notes to remind yourself about important things.

Summary

This chapter provided you a quick guided tour of Outlook 2000. You learned about the various parts of the Outlook screen and how you can modify the appearance of almost anything in Outlook. You also had a look at the different folders and learned how to use them. Finally, you learned about some of the things you can do with Outlook.

The next chapter introduces the newest features of Outlook 2000. If you've used past versions of Outlook, the next chapter will help you learn how much more you can do with this new version. But even if you're new to Outlook, you'll find some exciting new capabilities that you probably didn't know Outlook possessed in the next chapter.

✦   ✦   ✦

What's New in Outlook 2000?

Outlook is a program that has evolved from fairly simple origins into a powerful, multipurpose application. In this chapter, you learn more about that evolution and what you'll find new in the latest versions.

The evolution of Outlook has really been a path of constant change. The original version of Outlook was called Exchange and was one of the accessories that Microsoft included with Windows 95. Eventually, the program was renamed the Windows Messaging System, and later it became Outlook. Currently, there are two versions of Outlook. The full version — the subject of this book — is a part of Microsoft Office, whereas the "lite" version — Outlook Express — is available as a part of Internet Explorer.

Several different "full" versions of Outlook have existed along the way, so in this chapter we're going to try and present as clear a picture as possible of features that have been introduced or enhanced either in Outlook 2000 or a bit earlier in Outlook 98. The decision to include coverage of features added in Outlook 98 was easy — the short time that Outlook 98 was available means that most people who are new to Outlook 2000 probably never used Outlook 98 (or if they did, they likely didn't learn about most of the newest features).

Understanding the E-mail Enhancements

There have been a lot of e-mail enhancements in Outlook. In the early days of e-mail, most people were pleased that they were even able to send a simple text-based message and that it would arrive at its destination in a relatively short time. Those times have certainly changed as people have come to expect more from their e-mail program. The simple text message has in many cases been replaced by complex messages that include fancy formatting, multimedia presentations, and even animation.

Outlook's e-mail enhancements go beyond just making your messages look a bit fancier. Some of the improvements also help to make e-mail easier to use and less prone to confusing problems. The following sections show you the important improvements that have been made to Outlook's e-mail capabilities.

Using the new formatting options

When you send an e-mail message using plain text, only the text of your message and none of the formatting that you've applied is sent. Although that may get your message across, it certainly can't compare with a message that includes bold, italics, underlining, colors, and so on. Formatting adds a lot of visual impact that can really get your message noticed.

Outlook now enables you to send messages with the formatting intact, and makes it easier for you to apply that formatting as well.

Understanding the new formatting options

You can use several different formatting options while you're composing a message. In the past, though, choosing a formatting option wasn't always easy:

+ If you wanted to be sure that anyone could read the message, you could skip all formatting and send your message as plain old text. This wasn't very fancy, but it did guarantee that the recipient wouldn't have any trouble reading your message.

+ If you were absolutely certain that the recipient was using a compatible version of Microsoft Word, you could use Word's native format. All of your formatting would be retained, but the message would be unreadable if the recipient lacked the proper version of Word.

+ You could compromise by using *rich text format*—RTF—a file format that enabled different types of word processors to understand at least some of the formatting that had been applied to a document. Unfortunately, there were several different types of RTF, and this sometimes resulted in unreadable messages.

Outlook 98 introduced a new option—*HTML mail*. HTML—HyperText Markup Language—is the standard programming language used to create pages on the World Wide Web. In effect, HTML mail messages could be considered the equivalent of Web pages. Because HTML is a standard format that almost anyone who uses the Internet is able to read, using HTML to create mail messages means that almost anyone should be able to read your messages, including any fancy formatting that you use in creating the message.

Outlook 98 also introduced another enhancement for messages that you create in HTML. You can now use *stationery*—a background image that looks like fancy paper—when creating your messages. There's no longer any reason to create boring-looking messages!

You can choose your mail format on a message-by-message basis, or you can decide to send all your messages as HTML mail, either with or without stationery. To send a single message as HTML mail without stationery, follow these simple steps:

1. Select Actions ⇨ New Mail Message Using ⇨ HTML (No Stationery), as shown in Figure 3-1.

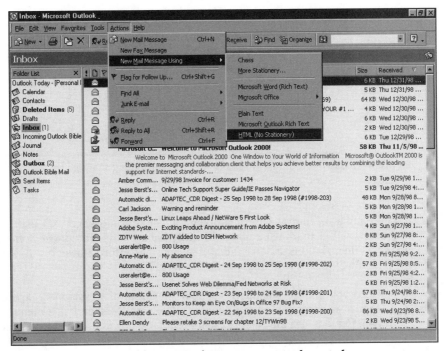

Figure 3-1: Outlook enables you to choose many more formats for your messages.

2. Create your message as you normally would.

3. Use the toolbar buttons to apply formatting either as you type or when you've finished typing your message.

4. Click the Send button to send the message. Figure 3-2 shows just a few of the options you can use in HTML format.

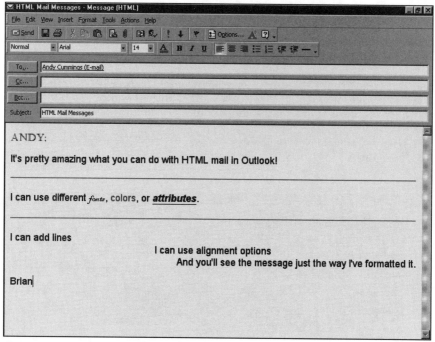

Figure 3-2: Use the toolbar buttons to add text formatting that will be sent with the message.

If you really want to dress up the appearance of your messages, try using some stationery rather than just a plain old white background. To choose some stationery, select Actions ➪ New Mail Message Using ➪ More Stationery to display the Select a Stationery dialog box, as shown in Figure 3-3.

Tip   Once you choose stationery for your messages, that stationery selection will appear as an option on the Actions ➪ New Mail Message Using menu, and you won't have to use the Select a Stationery dialog box to use the same stationery in the future.

Scroll down through the choices to select the stationery you want to use. You'll likely find that some choices cannot be previewed unless you first insert the Outlook CD-ROM so that the stationery can be installed. If you can't find the perfect choice, you can try clicking the Get More Stationery button. This will start Internet Explorer and connect you to the Office Update Web site, where you can find other choices that may be just what you want.

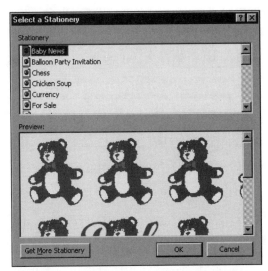

Figure 3-3: Choose some stationery for your messages.

As you scroll through the choices in the Select a Stationery dialog box, notice that some stationery adds a background color or image that covers much or all of the page. Other stationery is a bit subtler and just adds a border along the left edge of the page. Figure 3-4 shows a message created using the Tech Tools stationery — an example of the subtler type of stationery. In most cases, you'll probably find that your message is easier to read if you stick with stationery that only adds a subtle left border.

You can also instruct Outlook to use HTML and, optionally, stationery as the default for all new messages. If you set these options, Outlook will automatically send your messages as HTML when you click the New Message button, and you won't have to wade through the menus to make the selections.

To set HTML as the default mail format, select Tools ➪ Options to display the Options dialog box. Click the Mail Format tab to pick the mail format options. In the *Send in this message format* list box, select HTML, as shown in Figure 3-5.

If you also want to add stationery to your default settings, choose an option in the *Use this stationery by default* list box. If the choice you want to use does not appear in the list box options, click the Stationery Picker button to select your choice. When you've completed your selections, click the OK button to close the dialog box and return to Outlook.

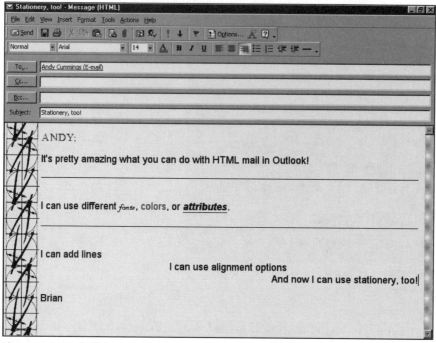

Figure 3-4: Including some stationery adds a fancy touch to your e-mail messages.

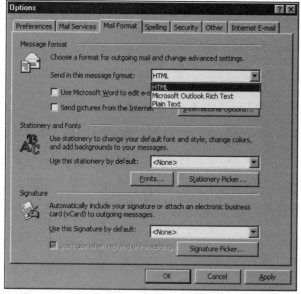

Figure 3-5: Set HTML as the default message format so you don't have to select the format for each new message.

Tip

You can override the default mail format and stationery settings for a single new message by making a selection from the Actions⇨ New Mail Message Using menu.

Using the new formatting tools

Along with providing new formatting options, Outlook also makes those options easier to use. You can now choose any supported mail format regardless of whether you're using the Outlook message editor or Word to create your e-mail messages. Either editor will automatically create messages using the current default settings or using the options you select for an individual message.

To use Word as your e-mail editor, select Tools ⇨ Options and select the *Use Microsoft Word to edit e-mail messages* checkbox. No matter which editor you use to create e-mail messages, you can change the message format of Outlook e-mail messages by selecting an option from the Actions ⇨ New Mail Message Using menu. Using Word as your e-mail editor gives you access to all of Word's proofing tools, such as spell checking, the grammar checker, and the thesaurus.

Using the new usability enhancements

Several of the new items in Outlook fall into the category of e-mail usability enhancements. None of these are really big changes, but they do make Outlook e-mail a bit easier to use. The following sections detail these improvements.

Internet read receipts

You may not realize it, but you can get confirmation that someone has received and read your e-mail messages. There is, in fact, a standard way to generate and send these confirmations that is now supported by Outlook.

To receive a message telling you when someone reads a message you've sent, click the Options button while you are creating the message. This opens the Message Options dialog box, as shown in Figure 3-6. Place a check in the *Request a read receipt for this message* checkbox to receive the confirmation. You can also place a check in the *Request a delivery receipt for this message* checkbox to receive a confirmation that the message has been delivered. Remember that just because a message has been delivered does not mean that the recipient has bothered to actually read the message.

Note

Although you can request both delivery and read confirmation for messages, there's no guarantee that the confirmation messages will actually be sent to you. The recipient may be using a mail system that is behind a *firewall,* which prevents confirmation messages from being sent, or the recipient may manually delete the confirmation messages before they are sent. Even so, this is the best method available to check whether your messages have been delivered.

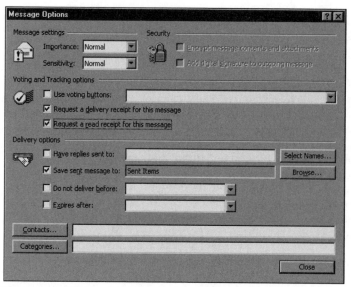

Figure 3-6: Use the Message Options dialog box to request confirmation that your message was delivered and read.

Multiple signatures

You probably end most of your messages with pretty much the same information. Perhaps you include your name, job title, phone numbers, address, e-mail address, and so on. Typing all of that same information each time can quickly become a real drag. One way to make this task a little less boring is to create an e-mail signature that you include at the end of all your messages. Once you create your e-mail signature, Outlook will automatically place that signature at the end of each message.

As handy as e-mail signatures may be, there's just one problem — you may not always want to use the same signature. You may, for example, want to use one standard e-mail signature for all your business-related messages, another for your personal messages, and a third for messages you send as an officer in a social organization. Outlook now makes it easy for you to create multiple e-mail signatures and then pick the one you want when you create a message.

Figure 3-7 shows how you can select from your list of e-mail signatures. Select Tools ⇨ Options and click the Mail Format tab. Choose a signature from the *Use this Signature by default* list box or click the Signature Picker button to select from the Signature Picker dialog box.

Cross-Reference

To learn more about creating signatures, see Chapter 7.

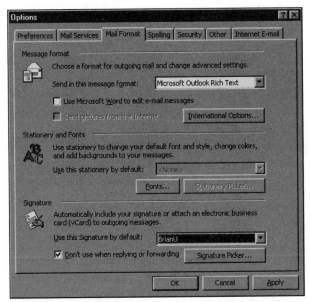

Figure 3-7: Create and select an e-mail signature to always sign your messages with the same information.

Auto format reply

If you send someone a message in a format that their e-mail program doesn't understand, there's a good chance the recipient won't be able to read your message. This is particularly true if your message includes an attachment.

To reduce the likelihood of problems with the message format, Outlook now sends any reply in the same format as the corresponding message was received. This ensures that when you reply to a message you've received, the original sender will be able to read your response.

Note

If you send someone a message with an attachment, but all they receive is a cryptic message with WINMAIL.DAT attached, the problem is the format you used to send the message. Open the recipient's e-mail properties dialog box in your address book and remove the check from the checkbox that refers to sending messages in Microsoft rich text format (the checkbox label will vary according to where you keep your e-mail addresses). This will enable you to successfully send messages to this recipient. One additional clue that incorrect message format is indeed the problem is if the recipient can read replies you send but not new messages.

Getting Organized

Do you need a little help getting organized? If so, Outlook offers some features that can at least make your e-mail messages better organized. If you receive a lot of messages, you can use these features to make really important messages stand out from all the rest and to send some messages right where they belong—in the Deleted Items folder.

Filtering using the Rules Wizard

The Rules Wizard helps you set up *rules* or *filters*—methods for dealing with certain types of messages. You may want to use several types of rules to deal with different types of messages:

✦ You may want to create a "bozo filter" that sends all messages from a particular person directly to the Deleted Items folder without your ever reading them. This could be quite useful if, for example, all a particular person ever sends your way are lame jokes and bogus warning messages that they're forwarding to several dozen people at the same time.

✦ You may want to create a rule that moves all messages relating to a particular project directly into the project's folder. This would help you keep all of the information for the project in one place.

✦ You could create a rule that saves a copy of every message you send to your boss into a special folder so that you could later show that you had indeed warned him about potential problems in a timely manner.

✦ You could create another rule that gave you a special notice when certain very important messages were received. For example, if you have an account with an online brokerage and have set up your account to send you e-mail when a certain stock reaches a set price level, you'd probably want to know about that message immediately.

Figure 3-8 shows an example of how you might create a rule using the Rules Wizard. In this case, the rule specifies that e-mail from a specified group of senders should be moved into a folder that relates to a specific project.

Cross-Reference   Chapter 8 covers the use of the Rules Wizard in much more detail.

Using the Organize tool

The Organize tool also helps you organize your e-mail messages. The Organize tool is quite similar to the Rules Wizard, but is in some ways a bit easier to use because it works by example. In Figure 3-9, the Organize tool is proposing to create a rule that uses the currently selected message as an example of the type of message to move.

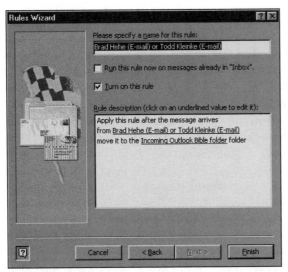

Figure 3-8: Create rules for handling your e-mail using the Rules Wizard.

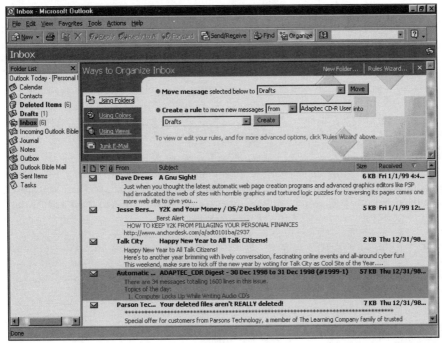

Figure 3-9: Use the Organize tool to create rules by using examples that are already in the Inbox.

The Organize tool includes several different options for organizing your e-mail messages:

✦ **Using Folders** enables you to specify that particular messages should be moved from the Inbox to another folder. You can use this option to move selected messages or to create a rule that affects future messages.

✦ **Using Colors** enables you to make certain messages stand out by displaying them in a different color. You can differentiate between messages sent to several recipients and those that were only sent to you by choosing two different colors.

✦ **Using Views** changes the way your messages are sorted in the Inbox. This can be handy when you want to find specific messages, such as those flagged for follow-up during the next week.

✦ **Junk E-Mail** enables you to set rules for handling both junk e-mail and messages with adult content. These rules work based on keywords that Outlook searches for in incoming messages, and they enable you to flag those messages with a specific color or to move them to a specified folder.

Note The junk and adult content e-mail filters won't catch all messages that you may consider to fit in these two categories. People who send out these types of messages are always looking for ways around such filters. There are several ways you can improve the filtering of messages you find offensive. You can select Help ➪ Office on the Web to visit the Microsoft Office Web site and download any updates to Outlook. Such updates may include improved filters. In addition, you can set specific rules that filter out messages from anyone who has sent you offensive messages in the past.

Managing and Exchanging Information

We live in an age when managing and exchanging information is literally as important as the production of material goods. Many of today's businesses deal exclusively in information rather than in an actual physical product. Your job may not be so completely tied to managing and exchanging information as this, but it's a sure bet that information is important to you.

Outlook has a number of improvements that are directly tied to managing and exchanging information. Between them these enhancements can make it easier for you to accomplish what you need to do. The following sections provide a quick look at the important Outlook improvements in these areas.

Using the improved Scheduler

Planning a meeting can be a real nightmare. You may need to check the schedules for each of the required attendees, make certain the meeting room is available, and determine the availability of additional resources such as video equipment. In a busy organization, it's a wonder that any meeting can ever be scheduled.

Outlook provides a powerful tool for scheduling meetings — the Meeting Request form, shown in Figure 3-10. In this figureaa, a Monday morning meeting has been scheduled. When the electronic invitations aaare sent out, Outlook will show whether the proposed meeting actually fits into each person's schedule.

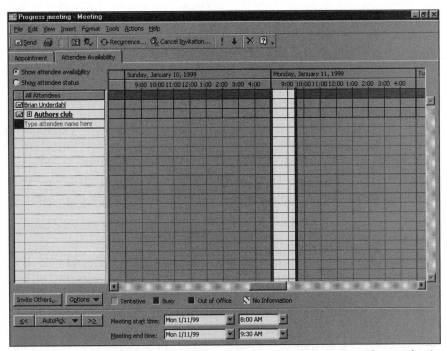

Figure 3-10: Use Outlook to schedule meetings and make certain each attendee is available.

In the figure, the attendee list includes a *distribution list* — a group of people who will all receive the same invitation to the meeting. Distribution lists are a handy way to make certain everyone in a group is sent the same information. But the distribution list you use to disburse information may not be totally appropriate for meeting planning purposes. Consider a situation where several people are part of a project team, and let's say you create a distribution list so that everyone receives all the project information updates. Suppose that one member of the team was working in an office several thousand miles distant from the rest of the team. If you were to plan a meeting, you probably wouldn't require that the distant team member come into the office for the meeting. One of the new features in Outlook 2000 enables you to work around this problem by expanding the distribution list while you're planning the meeting so that you can select individuals from the distribution list. Just click the box with the plus sign (+) in front of the name of the distribution list, and then select the individuals you want.

If all the attendees use Outlook to manage their schedule, your meeting request can determine a more suitable time should the proposed schedule not work out. You can click the AutoPick button to find a time that does fit into everyone's schedule.

Note   If you use Exchange Server in your organization, you can also set up schedules for resources such as meeting rooms. These can be set up to accept and decline meeting invitations automatically, based on their availability.a

Cross-Reference   See Chapter 8 for more information on distribution lists and Chapter 11 for more detailed information on using Outlook for scheduling.

Understanding improved protocol support

Another important part of managing and exchanging information is support for the *protocols* — standards — used on the Internet for messaging, directory access, newsgroups, and security. Outlook 98 added support for a number of new protocols:

✦ *POP3/SMTP* provides Internet mail with multiple-account support.

✦ *IMAP4* is another protocol that provides Internet mail and server-based mail storage with multiple-account support.

✦ *LDAP* provides Internet directory access, including search and name-checking capabilities and multiple-account support. LDAP includes built-in support for the leading public directories on the Internet.

✦ *S/MIME* enables you to send and receive signed and encrypted Internet mail.

✦ *NNTP* enables you to read your newsgroups with the newsreader. The newsreader is shared with Microsoft Internet Explorer.

Note   The newsreader is available when you use Outlook in Internet Only mail configuration or with Microsoft Exchange Server. Chapter 4 provides more information on the differences between the Outlook Internet Only and the Corporate or Workgroup mail configuration options.

Using the improved searching features

All the information in the world would be useless if you couldn't find the information you really need. The right tools can help you search for what you need and ignore all of the extraneous information. Outlook provides the tools to assist you in finding that "needle in a haystack" in your e-mail messages.

One interesting search tool is the Outlook Today folder. You may not immediately think of Outlook Today as a search tool, but when you consider that Outlook Today summarizes your active schedule items, tasks, and mail messages (as shown in Figure 3-11), you can see that Outlook Today really does fit into the category of a search tool.

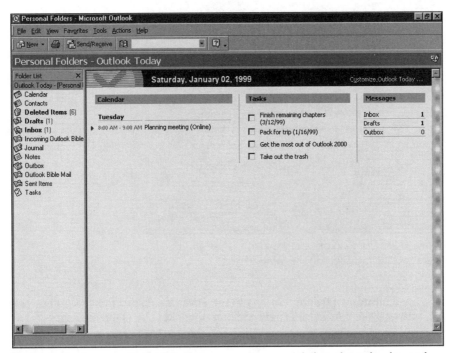

Figure 3-11: Because Outlook Today summarizes your daily tasks, Calendar, and e-mails, use it to find active items without searching throughout Outlook.

Outlook also has some more formal search tools that you can use to find specific pieces of information. If you need to find an e-mail message that discusses a certain project, but you don't remember exactly when you received the message, you could simply open each message from the person who sent the message and look for yourself. But what if the search is complicated by an Inbox that is full of hundreds of messages or worse—you can't remember exactly who sent the message?

If you simply want to search for specified text within your messages, you can use the Find tool that was added in Outlook 98. Click the Find button on the toolbar to display the Find tool. Enter your search phrase in the Look for text box and click the Find Now button.

To create a more sophisticated set of search parameters, select Tools ➪ Advanced Find to display the Advanced Find dialog box, as shown in Figure 3-12. This dialog box enables you to specify an incredibly complex set of conditions that should narrow down your results to exactly the message you're seeking.

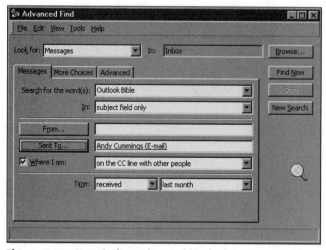

Figure 3-12: Use Find or Advanced Find when you need to locate specific messages in the Inbox.

Try the Find tool before resorting to the Advanced Find command. You can easily create a set of Advanced Find conditions that filter out all the messages.

Also, select File ➪ Save Search to save an advanced find for future use.

Using the Improved Calendar Options

You've already learned in the first two chapters that the Outlook Calendar has improved scheduling capabilities. The Outlook Calendar has some other important improvements as well. The two most important of these are Internet-related, as you'll see in the following sections.

Using iCalendars

iCalendar is the name of an Internet standard used to share calendar information. Normally, when you send a meeting request using Outlook, all the attendees must also be using Outlook in order to use Outlook's scheduling features. This makes it difficult to schedule meetings if some people use another program to handle their schedule. You can work around this problem by sending your meeting request as an iCalendar, as shown in Figure 3-13. To send the meeting request as an iCalendar, select Tools ➪ Send as iCalendar before you click the Send button. This option is a toggle, and a checkmark in front of the menu selection indicates that the option is selected.

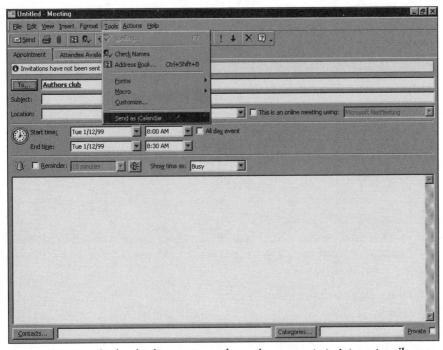

Figure 3-13: Use iCalendar format to send meeting requests to Internet mail users who may not be using Outlook.

Saving your Calendar as a Web page

You can also save your Outlook Calendar as a Web page. Saving a Calendar as a Web page offers several advantages. If you e-mail the page to someone, they won't need Outlook to view the Calendar. In addition, you can easily add the Calendar Web page to your Web site so anyone visiting the Web site can view the Calendar.

To save a Calendar as a Web page, follow these steps:

1. Open the Calendar folder in the view you want to save.

2. Select File ➪ Save as Web Page to open the Save as Web Page dialog box, as shown in Figure 3-14.

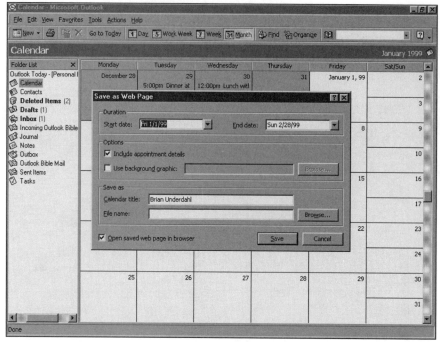

Figure 3-14: Save your Calendar as a Web page for publication on the Internet.

3. Select the options you want for the Calendar.

4. Click Save and then specify the name for the Web page.

You can use the Save as Web Page option for several very useful purposes. For example, if you maintain a Web site for a social organization, you may want to use this option to publish the monthly event schedule. That would enable your members to quickly browse the Web site to determine if there had been any schedule changes since your printed newsletter was mailed.

Managing Your Contacts

If you haven't used Outlook to manage your address books in the past, it may be a good time to start. Outlook now offers a number of new features and enhancements that make this task easier than ever.

Here's a sampling of some of the new contact management features you'll find in Outlook:

✦ **Automatic map of address** can be generated by the Microsoft Expedia Web site, which will plot a map to any address in the United States. When you have a contact open, as shown in Figure 3-15, click the Display Map of Address button to see a map that shows the contact's address.

Display Map of Address button

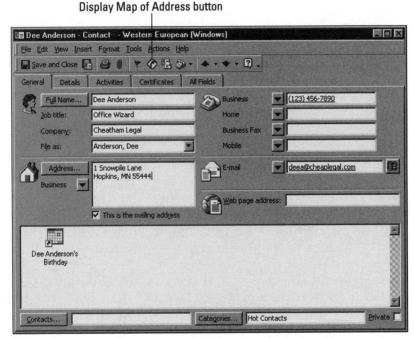

Figure 3-15: Use the Display Map of Address button to see where your contacts are.

✦ **Contact activity tracking** enables you to keep track of all e-mail, tasks, appointments, journal entries, and documents related to a contact. Whenever you create an Outlook item that is tied to one of your contacts, Outlook keeps a list of those items that can be displayed on the Activities tab of the Contact dialog box, as shown in Figure 3-16. This makes it much easier to see everything that you've set up for a particular contact.

✦ **Enhanced mail merge** enables you to create a mailing list that's a subset of your Contacts folder. This means you can filter the Contacts list to select just those contacts you want and then use the filtered list for a mail merge.

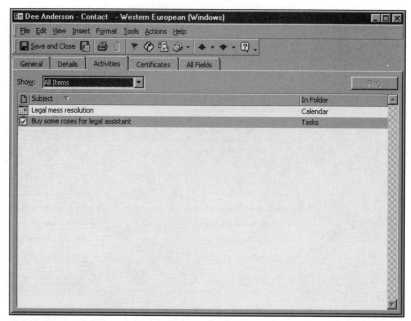

Figure 3-16: Use the Activities tab to view all activities related to the selected contact.

✦ **Flag contacts for follow up** enables you to set a follow-up reminder for a contact so that you can be reminded to call, meet with, or send a message to the person. You can specify a date and time for Outlook to send you a reminder, as shown in Figure 3-17. To flag a contact for a follow up, right-click the contact and select Flag for Follow Up.

✦ **Merge contact information** checks new contacts that you add to make certain they aren't duplicates of existing contacts. If the contact is a duplicate, you have the option to automatically merge the new information with the existing contact entry.

✦ **Personal distribution lists** enable you to make it easier to send messages to a group of people or to set up a meeting with a group. You can use contacts from both your Contacts folder and, if you are using Exchange Server, the global address list.

✦ **vCards** — Internet contacts format — enables you to send contact information over the Internet to anyone using a contact manager that understands the vCard standard. You could create your own electronic business card as a vCard and then send it as an attachment to your e-mail messages.

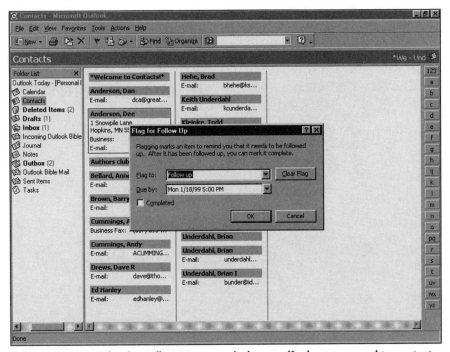

Figure 3-17: Use Flag for Follow Up to remind yourself when you need to contact someone.

Integrating Outlook with Other Applications

Even though you use Outlook to manage your e-mail, your schedule, and your contacts, you'll probably use a number of other applications for many other tasks. But just because you use different applications for different purposes doesn't mean you should have to lose the benefits of Outlook while you're using those other programs. There's no reason, for example, that you shouldn't be able to use the contact information you've stored in Outlook when you're creating a Word document.

Taking advantage of better integration with Office

The integration between Outlook and the other programs in Office 2000 means that your work is much easier, as the features of one program can often enhance another of the programs. If you create a document in any Microsoft Office program—including Word, Excel, Access, or PowerPoint—you can send the document as a message without switching to Outlook. Not only that, but your messages can easily be sent in HTML format so virtually anyone can read them even if they don't have Office 2000 installed on their computer.

Figure 3-18 shows an example of how you can create a letter in Word and then send the letter as an e-mail message. There's no need to open Outlook to send the message. In Word, select File ➪ Send To ➪ Mail Recipient.

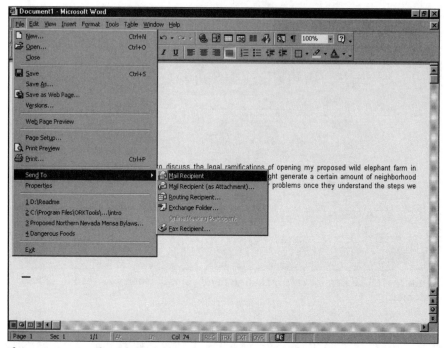

Figure 3-18: Send any Office document as an e-mail message.

Tip   Use the Outlook Actions ➪ New Letter to Contact command to quickly begin a letter to one of your contacts. This will enable you to automatically use the information from your Contacts list to address the letter.

Integrating with Internet-related programs

The Internet has really had a tremendous effect on the way people work. Outlook takes full advantage of the Internet in a number of ways that go well beyond its obvious use of the Internet—for e-mail messages. The following sections show a few of the other ways Outlook works together with some of the Internet-related programs to help you do even more.

Using Outlook with NetMeeting

When you schedule a meeting using the Outlook meeting request, you can set up the meeting to be online via NetMeeting to enable everyone to attend, regardless of their location. Using NetMeeting, you have audio, video, and chat capabilities, all available during your meeting (assuming the participants have the proper equipment). Figure 3-19 shows how you can schedule an online meeting using NetMeeting.

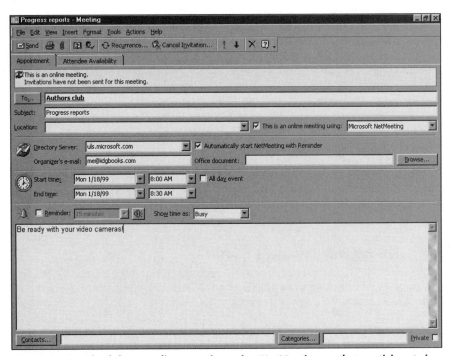

Figure 3-19: Schedule an online meeting using NetMeeting so that participants in many different locations can join in.

NetMeeting provides some very useful and interesting capabilities for online meetings. During your meeting, you can share programs and documents with the other attendees — even if they don't have the programs installed on their computers. In addition, NetMeeting provides a whiteboard that the participants can use as a drawing board during the meeting.

Caution Although NetMeeting can be used for online meetings, performance is generally pretty poor for anyone attending the meeting via dial-up connections. Video and application sharing are especially poor over dial-up connections. If you intend to use NetMeeting as a serious method of holding online meetings, consider investing in higher-speed connections for your attendees. You might, for example, use NetMeeting only for meetings between remote offices that all have high-speed Internet connections.

Using Outlook with NetShow Services

NetShow is a type of *streaming* broadcast service you can use on the Internet. When you schedule an online meeting with Outlook, you can choose to use NetShow Services rather than NetMeeting to provide the content.

Using NetShow would be appropriate for a meeting where one person is giving a presentation—such as if the company president were giving an annual report to the employees. Because NetShow is streaming content, both video and audio can be used even over dial-up connections. The content is broadcast to the recipients, and the viewer *buffers*—stores—the content until enough has been received for playback. As the playback begins, additional content can be downloaded. If the participants have relatively high-speed connections, the playback can be virtually real-time.

Because of the one-way nature of a NetShow broadcast, you may find NetShow quite useful for lectures, training seminars, or any other type of meeting where one person is speaking to a group. The one-way flow of data provides much better performance than you would experience using NetMeeting for these types of presentations.

Using Outlook with Internet Explorer

If you install the latest version of Internet Explorer along with Outlook, you'll find that these two programs work together very well, too. Here are some of the ways Outlook and Internet Explorer work together:

✦ If you open a Web page in Outlook, you can quickly switch between viewing the page in Outlook and Internet Explorer. This may be very useful if you discover that you need to navigate within a Web site that you've opened in Outlook, as Internet Explorer provides much easier Web site navigation.

✦ You can open Outlook from the Internet Explorer Tools menu or use the Internet Explorer File menu to send e-mail messages and create Outlook contacts. This enables you to quickly send e-mail messages while you're browsing the Web.

✦ You can copy images from Web pages directly into HTML-format Outlook e-mail messages. This enables you to more easily share information that you've found on the Internet.

Summary

This chapter has introduced you to the important new features and enhancements in Outlook. These include e-mail enhancements, better organizational capabilities, improved methods of managing and exchanging information, new Calendar options, more capable means of managing your contacts, and better integration with other applications.

The next chapter discusses the Outlook installation options. You'll discover that Outlook can be installed with different sets of capabilities and learn how to choose the options that are right for you.

✦　　✦　　✦

Installing Outlook 2000

Outlook has many different options you can choose while you're installing the program. These options directly affect how well the program will work for you, and they even determine whether you'll be able to access certain of the program's features. This chapter discusses those options and shows you how to take charge of your Outlook installation so that the program does what you need and want it to do.

If you upgrade to a newer version of Outlook, you'll probably find that you aren't given the option to decide just how you want to install Outlook. Upgrades generally use the existing settings — no matter what they may be. But because you probably weren't aware of the options that were available when you first installed Outlook, there's a good chance that you don't have the best choices installed for your uses. As you learn in this chapter, this is not a serious problem, because once you know the options, you can change your settings to fit your needs.

Note   Several Outlook options change depending on the e-mail configuration you select. In this book, we are primarily covering the Corporate or Workgroup e-mail option. If you choose the Internet Only configuration, you may see some differences in a few of Outlook's menus compared to what you see in this book.

What Are the Options?

Outlook has three basic configuration options. The type of e-mail mode that you wish to use determines which of these options you should select. The e-mail mode you choose also affects some of the add-in services that you can use with Outlook. For more information on the Outlook add-in services, see "Adding Outlook Services" later in this chapter.

The following sections discuss the e-mail mode options and how they affect your use of Outlook. Be sure to read through each of these options so that you can select the e-mail mode that best suits your needs.

Understanding the Internet Only option

The Internet Only e-mail option is intended for individual Outlook users who aren't part of a workgroup and don't need to connect to an Exchange Server. One feature of Outlook is only available if you select the Internet Only option: IMAP4 is a new protocol that is sometimes used by newer Internet mail servers. IMAP4 is an alternative to the more common POP3/SMTP mail protocols. It's not too likely that you'll connect to a mail server that requires you to use IMAP4, as most older e-mail programs don't support this option. Still, if your mail server is one of the rare ones that does require IMAP4, you can only use this protocol option if you've selected Internet Only e-mail mode.

One Outlook feature — the NNTP newsreader — is available in both Internet Only and the Corporate or Workgroup e-mail configuration. But unless you are connected to an Exchange Server, you won't be able to use the newsreader except in Internet Only mode. The newsreader enables you to view the messages posted in news-groups using NNTP — Network News Transfer Protocol — the Internet standard for newsgroup messages.

The Outlook installation CD-ROM includes a fax program for use with the Internet Only e-mail configuration. Because the Symantec Fax Starter Edition program is designed to send or receive faxes only with the Internet Only e-mail option, you may be inclined to choose this option simply for the faxing capabilities. But because Symantec Fax Starter Edition is a pretty bare-bones faxing solution, you probably shouldn't base your decision just on its availability. Symantec Fax Starter Edition certainly isn't the equal of Symantec's far more capable WinFax Pro. (And some users have described Symantec Fax Starter Edition in far less complementary terms!)

Fortunately, as you'll learn in "Adding Outlook Services" later in this chapter, it's easy to find another faxing solution that both works with the Corporate or Work-group e-mail configuration and is free. Not only that, it's pretty likely you already have that solution right at your desk and may not even know it!

Microsoft claims that the Internet Only e-mail option offers "significant perfor-mance benefits for dial-up users." You'd probably be wise to take this claim with a grain of salt. This is especially true if you consider how little time you actually spend manually sending and receiving e-mail. If you're like most Outlook users, you probably just let Outlook check your e-mail automatically at regular intervals and aren't really affected by any small differences in performance, regardless of which e-mail mode you choose. It's far better to choose your Outlook installation options based on the features you need than to give much thought to performance differences.

Understanding the Corporate or Workgroup option

The Corporate or Workgroup e-mail option adds support for several types of mail servers. These types of mail servers are typically used to manage the e-mail on a network and include Microsoft Exchange Server, Microsoft Mail 3.x, and Lotus cc:Mail server. If you need to connect to any of these, you must choose the Corporate or Workgroup e-mail option.

Caution   If you use the original version of MSN—the Microsoft Network—that came with Windows 95, you must choose the Corporate or Workgroup option to use Outlook for your e-mail program. Later versions of MSN aren't quite so picky about which Outlook option you select. To determine which version of MSN you are using, click Help ➪ About. If the version is 1.x, you must use the Corporate or Workgroup option unless you first upgrade your MSN version to at least 2.0.

Certain Outlook features are available only when you use Exchange Server as your mail server:

✦ **Delegate access and folder permissions:** This option enables you to give another person delegate access permission to your Outlook folders; to send messages on your behalf; and to read, modify, or create items in your public and private folders on a Microsoft Exchange Server computer. You may want to use this feature to allow an assistant to handle your e-mail messages while you are away from the office on a vacation or a business trip.

✦ **Group scheduling:** When you use Exchange Server, you can also reserve a location and equipment in addition to sending a meeting request to the meeting attendees. Resources such as meeting rooms and video equipment can have their own Outlook Calendar to specify free and busy times.

✦ **Message recall:** This enables you to recall a message from recipients who haven't read it yet, and, if you want, replace the recalled message with a new message. This is essentially an *unsend* option but will only work for messages that have not yet been read.

✦ **Offline folders and offline address book:** This enables you to use Outlook folders and an address book that are on the Exchange Server computer. You can also synchronize your folders and address book with those on the server so that you always have the latest information. This is especially handy if you work in a large company where one person is responsible for maintaining information centrally and sharing that information with those people who work in remote locations.

✦ **Organize Web pages in a public folder:** This feature enables you to collect Web pages for a group to share. You can also keep track of how often the pages are used, when they are updated, and who owns them. You may want to use this feature to ensure that a group of remote users always has access to the latest important company information, such as price lists or inventory levels.

✦ **Out of office assistant:** This feature helps you to manage your e-mail messages while you're out of the office. You can set up an automatic response to incoming messages to let people know that you are away.

If you set up the out of office assistant to respond to messages while you are away, you may want to suspend any subscriptions that you have to Internet mailing lists. Otherwise, the list server may be flooded with useless messages, and the list coordinator may cancel your subscription.

✦ **Public folders:** These enable you to collect, organize, and share files and Outlook items with others on your team or across your organization. You can use this feature to set up public, online discussions with others or to share a contact or Tasks list with a group.

Although you need access to an Exchange Server to use public folders, there's no such requirement for net folders. Net folders and public folders serve essentially the same function, although net folders use the Internet rather than an Exchange Server to publish the folder contents.

✦ **Voting:** This feature enables you to request and tally responses to multiple-choice questions that you send in a message. You can then consolidate the voting results in the original message.

The Corporate or Workgroup option does not include a fax program, but this option is available from your Windows 95, Windows 98, or Windows NT 4 CD-ROM. See "Adding Outlook Services" later in this chapter for more information on adding the fax service to Outlook.

Understanding the No E-mail option

The third choice for installing Outlook is the No E-mail option. You may want to choose this option if you prefer to use another program, such as Netscape Mail, to manage your e-mail messages. If you choose this option, you can still use the non–e-mail-related functions in Outlook. You could, for example, use the Outlook Calendar to maintain your schedule and the Outlook Contacts list to manage your address book even if you don't install the e-mail options.

Changing Your Installation

It probably should come as no surprise that you may not have the optimum Outlook e-mail option installed. If you were even given a choice while installing Outlook — which you probably weren't if you upgraded from an earlier version of Outlook — you likely had no real idea which option you should install.

Before deciding to change to a different e-mail option, it would be pretty handy to know which e-mail option is currently installed. You can easily determine this by selecting Help ⇨ About Microsoft Outlook from the Outlook menu. As Figure 4-1 shows, the About Microsoft Outlook dialog box shows which e-mail option you currently have installed.

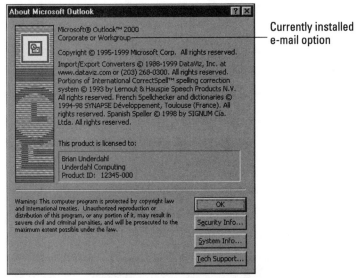

Currently installed e-mail option

Figure 4-1: Use the About Microsoft Outlook dialog box to determine which e-mail option is installed.

If you do decide to change to a different e-mail configuration, follow these steps:

1. Select Tools ⇨ Options. This displays the Options dialog box so that you can select the Outlook options you prefer.

2. Click the Mail Services tab, shown in Figure 4-2, to access the options for your mail services.

3. Click the Reconfigure Mail Support button to continue.

4. Choose the e-mail option you prefer, as shown in Figure 4-3.

Figure 4-2: Switch to the Mail Services tab to configure the mail service options.

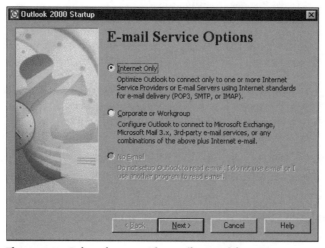

Figure 4-3: Select the type of e-mail you wish to use.

5. Click Next to continue. If you keep the same option you already have, you'll simply return to the Options dialog box without making any changes. If you select a new option, you'll see a warning message similar to the one shown in Figure 4-4.

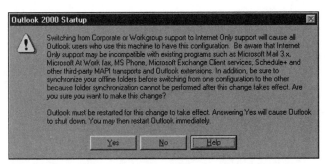

Figure 4-4: Changing your e-mail option may mean that you'll have to make additional changes to your system.

6. Select Yes to confirm that you wish to change your e-mail option. Whenever you change your e-mail option, you must shut down and restart Outlook for the change to take effect. If the proper components aren't already installed, you may be prompted for your Outlook CD-ROM.

Changing your e-mail option will result in several important changes that will require you to perform additional steps to complete the Outlook setup. First, you'll likely have to reinstall your fax program regardless of which new option you select. Second, if you switch from Corporate or Workgroup to Internet Only support, you'll need to manually re-create any addresses or links that refer to Exchange Server folders. Be certain you have all the resources you need available before you change your e-mail option.

Once you've restarted Outlook, use the Help ➪ About Microsoft Outlook command to confirm that the change was successful.

Adding New Outlook Features

When you installed Outlook, you probably didn't install all of Outlook's features. Outlook, like all of the Office 2000 programs, often uses an installation option that is known as *install on first use*. This means that some features Microsoft thought you might not use probably won't be installed until you really need to use them.

As a concept, the idea of installing features the first time they're really needed may not sound too bad. Like many theories, though, this one has some holes in it that could end up causing you considerable grief. Here are some reasons why you may want to be proactive and install the features you need now, rather than waiting until the first time you attempt to use them:

✦ When you need a feature, you may not have the time to locate your Outlook CD-ROM, wait while the feature is installed, and then restart your system to allow the feature to work.

✦ If you like to store your original program CD-ROMs in a safe place after you've installed programs, you may find that installing each individual feature one at a time is becoming a real hassle. In addition, each time you take out the program CD-ROMs, you increase the risk of damaging them.

✦ Probably the worst thing that could happen is that Outlook will attempt to install a new feature when your original program CD-ROMs simply aren't available — perhaps when you're away from your office with your laptop PC and the CD-ROMs are safely back at the office.

If you still aren't convinced that you should take charge of your Outlook installation, you can skip the rest of this section. But don't say that you weren't warned!

To add new Outlook features, follow these steps:

1. If Outlook is running, close the program before continuing. Because you may have to restart your system, it's a good idea to close all programs before continuing.

2. Click the Start button and choose Settings ➪ Control Panel.

3. Double-click the Add/Remove Programs icon (single-click if your system is set up for single-clicking rather than double-clicking) to open the Add/Remove Programs Properties dialog box, as shown in Figure 4-5.

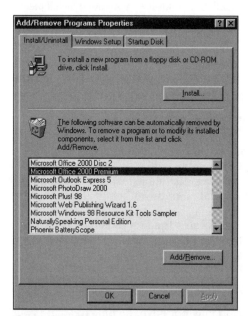

Figure 4-5: Open the Add/Remove Programs Properties dialog box to change the installed Outlook features.

4. Select Outlook 2000 (or Microsoft Office 2000, if you installed Outlook along with Office) and then click the Add/Remove button (the button will be grayed out until you select a program from the list).

5. Click the Add or Remove Features button, shown in Figure 4-6. This will enable you to select which features are installed.

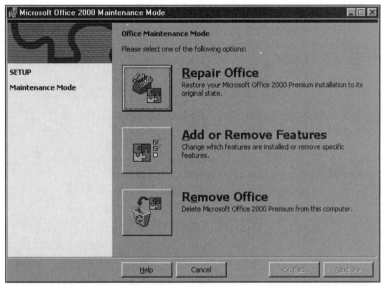

Figure 4-6: Click the Add or Remove Features button to change the currently installed features.

6. Click the box to the left of Microsoft Outlook for Windows to expand the list of features, as shown in Figure 4-7.

7. Click the down arrow by a feature to see which options are available for that feature. Some features include all the options that are shown in Figure 4-8, whereas others may not include all the options.

Be especially wary of any features that have the "1" symbol shown on their icon. This means that the feature will be installed the first time it is used. Features that have a CD-ROM icon are not installed on your hard disk and require the Outlook CD-ROM in order to function.

8. When you have completed your changes, select Update Now to apply your changes. If you've changed any features to *Run from My Computer* status, you'll probably need to insert your Outlook CD-ROM to complete the installation.

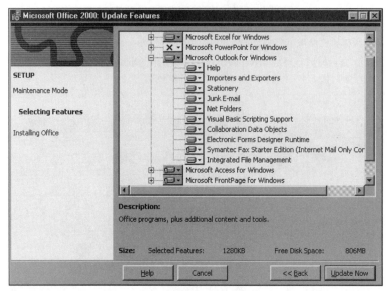

Figure 4-7: Expand the Outlook feature list so you can see the status of each feature.

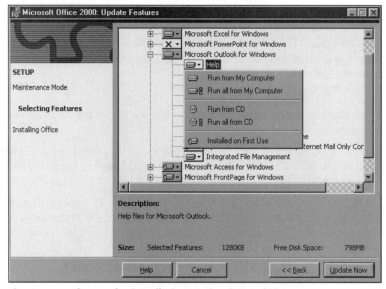

Figure 4-8: Choose the installation option for each feature.

Tip Watch the size number for the selected features near the bottom of the dialog box as you change the feature selections. The dialog box does not specifically inform you how much your changes will affect the use of disk space, so you'll have to make note of the difference as you change the selections.

Adding Outlook Services

Outlook also has a number of options—*services*—that simply aren't installed unless you specifically choose to do so. It doesn't matter whether you need these services or not, Outlook won't offer to automatically install them. You're pretty much on your own when it comes to making certain that all the services you need are installed.

In this section, you'll learn how to install additional Outlook services. You'll also learn how to work around the infamous lack of fax support in Outlook's Corporate or Workgroup mode.

Understanding the available services

Outlook's services enhance the way Outlook functions, but you probably won't be able to use all the available services. Unless you are connected to the proper server, services such as Microsoft Exchange Server and MS Outlook support for Lotus cc:Mail won't do anything for you. In addition, if you are using the Internet Only e-mail configuration, you cannot use the Microsoft Fax service.

Some Outlook services are automatically built into Outlook. The Rules Wizard is one example of a service that was an optional add-in in earlier versions of Outlook but is now an integral part of Outlook. Other Outlook services—such as Internet e-mail—are normally installed automatically but can be removed if you don't use them. Finally, there are services—such as Internet Folders—that you can add if you need to.

To add most services, follow these steps:

1. Select Tools ➪ Services to display the Services dialog box, as shown in Figure 4-9. This dialog box enables you to add, remove, or configure Outlook services.

2. Click the Add button to display the Add Service to Profile dialog box, as shown in Figure 4-10.

3. Choose an information service to add from the *Available information services* list box and click OK to add the service.

4. Once the service has been added, close the dialog boxes and exit from Outlook. The service should be available the next time you start Outlook.

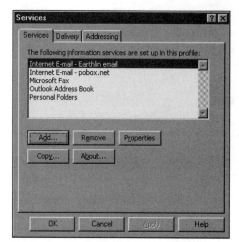

Figure 4-9: Use the Services dialog box to set up Outlook services.

Figure 4-10: Choose the Outlook services you want to add.

Some service providers may add their own Outlook services that don't appear in the Add Service to Profile dialog box. If you want to add one of these types of services, click the Have Disk button in Step 3 and then specify the location of the setup files.

Tip Although Outlook only advises you to close and restart Outlook after adding a new service, it's often advisable to shut down and restart your PC as well. Some services need a system restart in order to properly register their required settings with your computer.

Adding the fax service

For some reason that is known only to Microsoft, Outlook 2000 does not include a fax service for the Corporate or Workgroup e-mail mode. Oh, Microsoft Fax shows up as one of the available information services, all right, but that doesn't mean that Microsoft Fax is really there on the Outlook CD-ROM. Indeed, all that is included with Outlook is the configuration information to allow the use of Microsoft Fax if you already have a copy of Microsoft Fax available from another source.

To make matters worse, Outlook will happily enable you to select and add the Microsoft Fax service without making any protest — until you try to restart Outlook, that is. That's when you'll be greeting by a rather cryptic message informing you that a dll could not be loaded properly.

As if someone were trying to add insult to injury, you may encounter problems adding the fax service even if you do locate a copy of Microsoft Fax and install it on your system. It turns out that you must install Microsoft Fax and add the Microsoft Fax service to Outlook in precisely the correct order for all of this to work. And that's what you learn here.

To successfully add the fax service to your Corporate or Workgroup mode copy of Outlook, you need to do things in the following order:

1. Make certain that Microsoft Fax is not listed as one of the installed services. Use Tools ⇨ Services to view the Services tab of the Services dialog box. If Microsoft Fax is shown, select it and click the Remove button. Confirm the deletion and then close Outlook.

2. Install Microsoft Fax. If you are using Windows 98, double-click the file awfax.exe in the \tools\oldwin95\message\us\ folder of your Windows 98 CD-ROM. Ignore any other files that you see in this folder.

   If you are using Windows 95, add Microsoft Fax (or Microsoft At Work Fax — it's the same thing) by using the Windows Setup tab of the Add/Remove Programs dialog box. This will probably be found in the Accessories group, but the exact location may vary depending on your version of Windows 95.

   If you are using Windows NT, add the Microsoft Personal Fax service. You may have to use the Windows Help system to find the exact sequence necessary in your version.

3. Start Outlook again.

4. Select Tools ⇨ Services to open the Services dialog box.

5. Click the Add button to display the Add Service to Profile dialog box.

6. Select Microsoft Fax from the list of services.

7. Click OK to add the new service. (If you have not yet used your modem, you will also be asked to configure it.)

8. Click OK to close the Services dialog box.

9. Close Outlook and restart your system. The next time you start Outlook, the fax service should be ready to use.

If you are unable to locate the Microsoft Fax files using the procedures detailed in Step 2, you may want to search the Microsoft Web site at www.microsoft.com. Use a search phrase such as "fax AND Outlook" — be sure to capitalize the word *AND* so that the search engine understands that you want to find both words. You may have to hunt around some to locate the files. Another site you may want to try is the Microsoft FTP site at `ftp://ftp.microsoft.com/softlib/MSLFILES/`. The FTP site won't give you much help finding specific files, so you'll need to be a little creative looking at the filenames.

Cross-Reference   You'll need to configure the fax service before you can use it. In particular, the default setting does not receive incoming faxes. See Chapter 5 for more information on configuring the fax service.

Summary

This chapter explained the options that are available when you install Outlook and showed you how to add the options and services you need. You also learned how to make certain that items are installed when it is convenient for you — not necessarily when they would otherwise be installed.

The next chapter shows you how to configure Outlook so that it works the way you want it to. You'll see how to make certain that Outlook helps you accomplish what you want rather than making you do extra work.

✦   ✦   ✦

Configuring Outlook 2000

✦   ✦   ✦   ✦

In This Chapter

Configuring e-mail

Setting your e-mail
options

Configuring Microsoft
Fax

Using profiles

✦   ✦   ✦   ✦

Who should decide how your computer operates? This question is not quite as off the wall as it might sound. If you think that you should have some say in how your computer functions, then you need to consider one thing: Unless you take an active role in configuring your system, someone else has made the decisions about how your computer works.

Outlook has a large number of configuration options that directly affect how the program works for you. The default settings for these options may not be right for you, however. A prime example of this occurs when you install Microsoft Fax for use with the Corporate or Workgroup e-mail configuration. The default settings for the fax service enable you to send faxes but not to receive them! (Then again, if you have a small office with several networked computers, you may only want one modem in the group to receive faxes. In that case, the default would make sense.)

This chapter shows you how to access and set most of Outlook's major configuration settings. Although most of the default settings may be a little less bizarre than the default fax settings, it's still worth a few minutes of your time to see how to make certain that Outlook has the best possible configuration to suit your needs. You're almost certain to discover that Outlook can do a whole lot more than you realized, and all it takes is changing a few configuration options.

Configuring E-mail Services

In spite of all the other powerful features of Outlook, you probably use the e-mail capabilities quite a bit more than anything else in the program. It makes sense, therefore, to begin the configuration journey by looking at all the different e-mail-related configuration options. In the following sections, you learn how to find and properly set these options.

Note Depending on the type of mail server you use, some of the settings shown in the following sections may not apply to your situation. In particular, if you use a LAN-based mail server, you may not need to configure the dial-up options. Likewise, if you only send e-mail within your company network, you may not need to configure such options as the Internet e-mail format. The examples shown will attempt to cover as much ground as possible, so if you feel an option does not apply in your case, you can probably just leave the default settings in place and skip to the next section of the chapter.

There are a lot of different configuration options that can affect your Outlook e-mail messages. In this section, you learn about the basic settings that you must set for the Internet e-mail service. Configuring the Internet e-mail service first makes the most sense because none of the other e-mail configuration options will work until your e-mail service is properly installed and configured.

Note If you don't already have an e-mail service installed, please refer to Chapter 4 for more information on installing Outlook and its optional features and services.

Setting the basic configuration options

To view and modify the configuration for your Internet e-mail service, follow these steps:

1. Select Tools ⇨ Services to display the Services dialog box, shown in Figure 5-1.

Figure 5-1: Open the Services dialog box to select the service you wish to configure.

2. Select the service you wish to configure. If you have more than one Internet e-mail account, as shown in the figure, you need to configure each account separately.

3. Click the Properties button to display the General tab of the properties dialog box for the selected e-mail account, as shown in Figure 5-2. You'll use this tab to enter some basic information about your account.

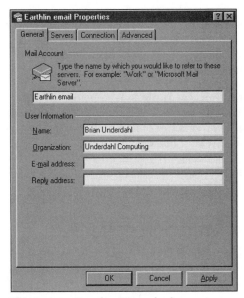

Figure 5-2: Use the General tab to set up your basic user information.

4. Check the name shown in the account name text box. You can enter any name for this account that you prefer, as this name is simply the one that you will use to identify the account.

5. Use the Name text box to enter the name that you want people to see on the From line when they receive one of your messages. Here, too, the choice is totally up to you — but it's a good idea to use a name that people will recognize.

6. The Organization text box entry is completely optional. Most e-mail messages won't even display the information you add to this text box — but on the off chance that this information is displayed, you'll probably want to avoid entering something that might be considered offensive.

7. Enter your actual e-mail address in the E-mail address text box. This must be in the proper format, such as brianu@idgbooks.com. If you aren't sure of your e-mail address, you can ask your Internet service provider (ISP).

Tip   Your e-mail address will probably consist of your account name, an at sign (@), and the name of the mail server.

8. If you want replies sent to a different e-mail address, enter that address in the Reply address text box. You might want to supply this information if you use a Web-based e-mail server such as Hotmail to collect all your incoming e-mail messages for the purposes of accessing those messages from any computer that connects to the Internet.

Tip   Set up a separate Internet e-mail account that uses your company e-mail account to send messages but your home e-mail address as the Reply address. That way you can send a quick personal message from work when necessary but have any replies sent to your home computer.

9. If you've made any changes, click the Apply button before continuing. Although it's not really necessary to apply the changes you've made until you are finished making changes in the entire dialog box, clicking the Apply button does make it much easier if you later make a change on another tab and then decide you'd rather cancel the change. If you've clicked Apply before leaving each tab, you won't have to go back and redo those changes if you later click the Cancel button.

Setting the server configuration options

Once you've set up the basic information on the General tab, it's time to set up the *mail servers* using the Servers tab. Mail servers are the computers that process incoming and outgoing e-mail messages.

To set up the mail server options, follow these steps:

1. If necessary, open the Properties dialog box for the Internet e-mail service you want to configure.

2. Click the Servers tab, as shown in Figure 5-3.

3. Enter the correct address for the incoming mail server in the Incoming mail (POP3) text box. You can generally use the server name as shown in the figure, but in some cases, you may need to use the *IP address* — the Internet address that consists of four numbers separated by periods, as in 123.1.56.256.

4. Enter the address for the outgoing mail server in the Outgoing mail (SMTP) text box. Depending on your ISP, this may be the same as the incoming mail server shown in the figure, or it may be a different address.

5. Enter your account name — generally the name you use to log on to the Internet — in the Account name text box. Your account name and password may be case sensitive, so make certain you enter them correctly, or you may create an almost impossible to find problem that later prevents you from logging onto the mail servers.

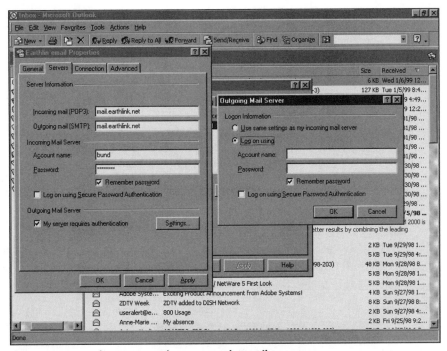

Figure 5-3: Use the Servers tab to set up the mail servers.

6. Enter your password in the Password text box. As you type your password, asterisks (*) will appear in place of each character. It's very easy to make a mistake entering your password, so if you have any doubts that you entered it correctly, double-click the Password text box and very carefully reenter the password.

7. If you want Outlook to be able to automatically log on to send and receive e-mail, make certain the Remember password checkbox is selected. It's true that this allows anyone who uses your computer to send and receive e-mail using your account, but if you don't select this option, you'll have to type your password each time Outlook checks for e-mail.

8. Select the *Log on using Secure Password Authentication* checkbox only if your ISP has informed you that this is required to access the mail servers. Most mail servers do not use this option.

9. Outgoing mail servers generally don't require a separate logon, but if your ISP has informed you that yours does, select the *My server requires authentication* checkbox and then click the Settings button to display the Outgoing Mail Server dialog box, also shown in Figure 5-3.

10. If you need to use a different account name and password for the outgoing mail server, click the *Log on using* radio button. Then enter the correct account and password information for the outgoing mail server. Click the OK button to close the Outgoing Mail Server dialog box and return to the properties dialog box.

11. Click Apply to confirm the changes you've made on this tab of the dialog box.

Setting the connection configuration options

Next, you must choose the method that you use to connect to the Internet. To do so, you use the Connection tab of the Properties dialog box. If you use a modem to connect, you'll also be able to set the modem properties for the connection.

To configure the connection options, follow these steps:

1. If necessary, open the Properties dialog box for the Internet e-mail service you want to configure.

2. Click the Connection tab, shown in Figure 5-4.

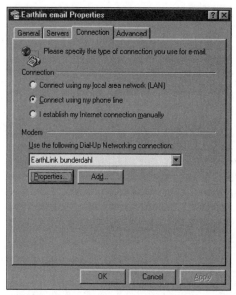

Figure 5-4: Use the Connection tab to specify how you connect to the mail server.

3. Select the proper radio button for your type of connection:

   - Use *Connect using my local area network (LAN)* if you connect to a mail server that is available through another computer on your network. You would probably use this type of connection if your network is connected directly to the Internet or if it is connected through a proxy server.

   - Use *Connect using my phone line* if you want Outlook to automatically establish a dial-up connection using your modem. If you are a stand-alone user, or if your network does not offer another method of connecting directly to the Internet, this is your most likely choice.

   - Use *I establish my Internet connection manually* if you don't want Outlook to attempt to connect to the Internet. You'll need to open the connection to the Internet before you tell Outlook to send or receive e-mail messages.

4. If you have more than one Dial-Up Networking connection set up on your system, choose the correct one from the drop-down list box. You may want to have more than one connection set up if you sometimes use your system while traveling and have multiple accounts.

5. To check the settings for the selected Dial-Up Networking connection, click the Properties button to display the dialog box shown in Figure 5-5.

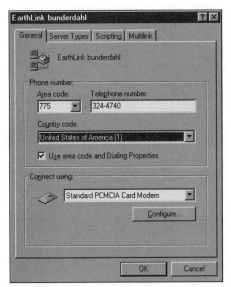

Figure 5-5: Use this dialog box to configure the Dial-Up Networking connection.

6. Verify that the correct area code, phone number, and country code are shown. If the *Use area code and Dialing Properties* checkbox is not selected, only the telephone number will be used; you'll need to make certain the phone number includes any special codes you need to dial for outside lines or long distance.

7. Make certain the correct modem is specified. If you change modems, you'll probably have to reselect your modem in order for the Dial-Up Networking connection to continue working.

8. Click the Configure button if you need to change your modem settings. You may need to do so if you install a new modem or change the modem to a different port.

9. Click the Server Types tab to configure the connection for the correct type of dial-up server, as shown in Figure 5-6.

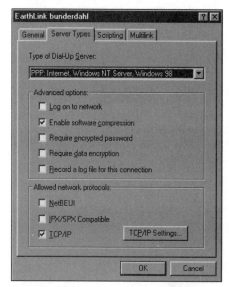

Figure 5-6: Use the Server Types tab to specify the Dial-Up Server settings.

10. In most cases, you'll want to select the PPP option as the type of dial-up server. Your ISP will tell you if you need to use one of the other types.

11. As a general rule, the only advanced option you're likely to select is the *Enable software compression* checkbox. The remaining options in this section should only be selected if you've been advised to do so by your ISP.

12. If you're connecting to the Internet, make certain the only protocol that is selected is TCP/IP. Selecting either of the other two protocols may slow your connection and could result in a security risk.

13. Click the TCP/IP Settings button to display the TCP/IP Settings dialog box, shown in Figure 5-7.

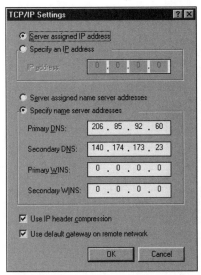

Figure 5-7: Use the TCP/IP Settings dialog box to specify the IP addresses.

14. In most cases, you should select the *Server assigned IP address* radio button. Unless you are running a Web server on your computer, your IP address is generally assigned when you establish your dial-up connection.

15. You may need to select the *Specify name server addresses* radio button and then enter the addresses in the text boxes. The name servers are the computers that enable you to enter a Web site address such as `http://www.idgbooks.com` rather than a numeric IP address.

16. Unless your ISP instructs otherwise, make certain the two checkboxes near the bottom of the dialog box are selected. These two settings generally improve the speed of your Internet connection.

17. Click the OK button to close the TCP/IP Settings dialog box.

18. Click the Scripting tab, shown in Figure 5-8. In most cases, you will not need to use any of the options on this tab. In rare cases, you may need to use a logon script to connect to the Internet, and you would specify the script file in the File name text box.

Note

Logon scripts are text files that are sometimes needed to connect to a remote computer correctly. Although logon scripts are rarely needed today, you can still use one if necessary. To create or edit a logon script, enter the name of the script in the File name text box and then click the Edit button.

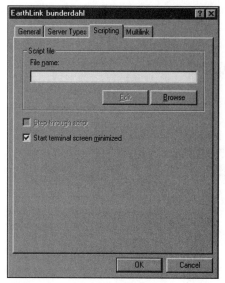

Figure 5-8: Use the Scripting tab if you need to specify a logon script.

19. Click the Multilink tab, shown in Figure 5-9. You'll use this tab if you have more than one modem and will be using both at the same time to create a faster connection to the Internet.

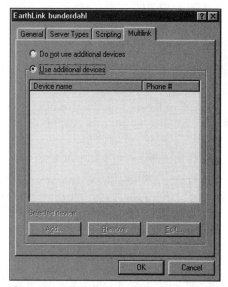

Figure 5-9: Confirm your changes to begin using the new settings.

If you have more than one modem installed, and if your ISP allows multiple connections to the same account, you can click the *Use additional devices* button and then select the additional modems or other types of Internet connections to use. You may need to pay extra fees in order to connect using more than one connection at a time. Check with your ISP to see if this service is available.

20. Click OK to confirm any changes you've made in this dialog box.

21. Click Apply to confirm any changes you've made on the Connection tab.

Setting the advanced configuration options

In most cases, you won't have to adjust any of the options on the Advanced tab. There are instances, however, where you may need to make some adjustments—especially to handle unusual situations.

To configure the advanced options, follow these steps:

1. If necessary, open the Properties dialog box for the Internet e-mail service you want to configure.

2. Click the Advanced tab, shown in Figure 5-10.

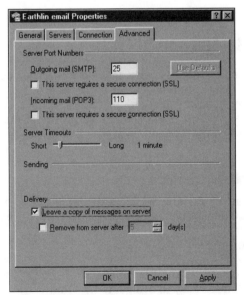

Figure 5-10: Use the Advanced tab to make some special adjustments.

3. Don't change any of the server port number section settings unless directed to do so by your ISP. The default settings enable you to connect to most mail servers — changing those settings could cause connection problems.

4. Drag the Server Timeouts slider to the left or to the right, depending on how quickly your servers respond to your requests. If you are constantly receiving error messages that tell you the server is not responding, you may want to set a slightly longer timeout. Be careful not to set this too high, though, because you'll have to wait for the entire timeout period whenever you attempt to access a server that really isn't responding to requests.

5. Select the *Leave a copy of messages on server* checkbox if you don't want Outlook to automatically delete messages that you've received from the incoming mail server. You might consider using this option if you wanted to check messages using your laptop PC while you were on vacation, but still be able to access those messages on your desktop system when you return home.

6. If you decide to leave messages on the server, you may want to also select the *Remove from server after x day(s)* option. Most mail servers limit the amount of space that you can use. If you don't delete old messages, your mailbox can become full and refuse to accept new messages.

7. Click the OK button to close the properties dialog box, and then click OK to close the Services dialog box.

Setting Your E-mail Options

Once you have the Internet e-mail service properly configured, you can set your e-mail options. There are lots of these options — some more critical than others. In the following sections, you have the opportunity to take a look at these settings so that you can learn how the e-mail options affect you and your use of Outlook. Some of these settings will also be covered in more detail in Part II of this book.

Setting the e-mail preferences

The e-mail preference settings affect the appearance and handling of your e-mail messages — from what happens to messages you send to how replies are handled.

To set your e-mail options, follow these steps:

1. Select Tools ➪ Options to display the Options dialog box, shown in Figure 5-11. Click the Preferences tab if necessary to bring it to the front.

2. Click the E-mail Options button to display the E-mail Options dialog box, shown in Figure 5-12.

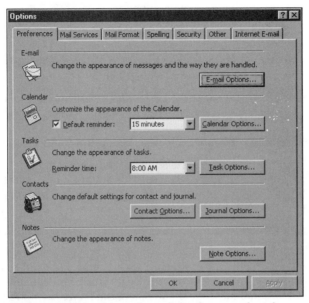

Figure 5-11: Use the Options dialog box to select the e-mail options.

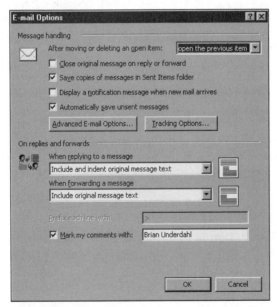

Figure 5-12: Choose the basic e-mail options in this dialog box.

3. Select an action from the *After moving or deleting an open item* drop-down list box. This specifies what you want to do when you close a message.

4. Select the *Close original message on reply or forward* so that you won't return to a message you've replied to or forwarded. If you don't select this checkbox, you'll need to close the original message yourself.

5. Select *Save copies of messages in Sent Items folder* to always save a copy of any messages you send. If you don't select this option, there will be no record that you've sent messages except in the Journal. Be sure to clean out the Sent Items folder occasionally if you've selected this option.

6. Select *Display a notification message when new mail arrives* to have Outlook notify you when you receive new messages. This setting is independent of the New Mail Notification event that you can set in the Sounds applet in the Control Panel. You can have both types of notifications — audio and visual — if you like.

7. Select *Automatically save unsent messages* to place copies of messages you've begun but not yet sent in the Drafts folder.

8. Use the *On replies and forwards* options to specify how you want to handle the original text of a message that you reply to or forward. You can only choose a line prefix for the original message if you select the *Prefix each line with* option. It's become an Internet e-mail custom to prefix the original message lines with a greater-than symbol (>), but you can use the options you prefer.

Some of these e-mail option settings are codependent, whereas others are mutually exclusive. For example, you will not be able to use a character to prefix the lines of the original messages when replying to messages if you also choose to include and indent the original message.

9. Click the Advanced E-mail Options button to display the Advanced E-mail Options dialog box, shown in Figure 5-13.

10. Choose the options you prefer from this dialog box.

Although you can set the importance and sensitivity level for messages, these settings generally accomplish very little in the real world. Mail recipients can choose to observe or ignore both of these settings with impunity — which is one of the reasons that they are seldom used.

11. Click OK to close the Advanced E-mail Options dialog box.

12. Click the Tracking Options button to display the Tracking Options dialog box, shown in Figure 5-14.

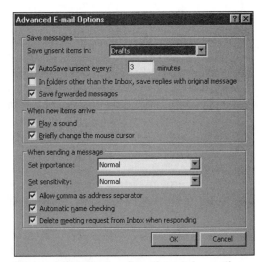

Figure 5-13: Choose the advanced e-mail options in this dialog box.

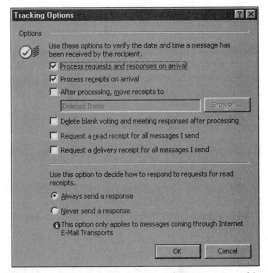

Figure 5-14: Choose the e-mail message tracking options in this dialog box.

13. Choose the tracking options you prefer. Be aware of the differences between the two receipt request options:

- A *read receipt* is a message that tells you the recipient has actually opened your message.

- A *delivery receipt* is a message that simply tells you your message was delivered. The message recipient may choose to ignore all your messages, even if they are delivered, so a delivery receipt won't confirm that your message was actually read.

14. Choose how you want to respond to read receipt requests.

Note

Notice that because you can turn off responses to read receipts, a sender can never be certain that you've actually opened a message. It's relatively difficult to block the sending of delivery receipts, so both types of receipt requests do serve a useful function when it's important to know that your message arrived at its destination.

15. Click OK to close the Tracking Options dialog box.

16. Click OK to close the E-mail Options dialog box.

Setting the mail service options

The mail service options enable you to specify which *profile* — set of user options — and which services are used for your e-mail messages. As you learned in Chapter 4, these options also enable you to reconfigure your e-mail support to change between Internet Only, Corporate or Workgroup, and no e-mail support.

To set your mail service options, follow these steps:

1. If necessary, select Tools ➪ Options to display the Options dialog box. Click the Mail Services tab to bring it to the front, as shown in Figure 5-15.

2. Unless you share your computer with someone else, it's usually best to select the *Always use this profile* radio button. To learn more about profiles, see "Using Profiles" later in this chapter.

3. Select the mail services that you would like Outlook to check for e-mail messages. If Microsoft Fax is selected, as shown in the figure, you'll probably want to deselect it, because checking for new e-mail on Microsoft Fax really doesn't accomplish anything except waste time when Outlook checks for e-mail.

Caution

Unless you intend to change your e-mail mode, as described in Chapter 4, it's best not to click the Reconfigure Mail Support button. Clicking this button can easily lead you into accidentally wiping out your current fax setup if you're not careful.

4. Click Apply to confirm any changes you've made on this tab of the Options dialog box.

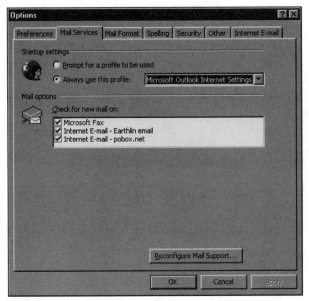

Figure 5-15: Use the Mail Services tab to select profiles and service options.

Setting the mail format options

The mail format options affect the default appearance of outgoing e-mail messages that you create. These options are covered extensively in Chapter 7, but Figure 5-16 shows the Mail Format tab of the Options dialog box so you can get a feel for all the available mail options.

For now, you should simply note that you can only send pictures from the Internet or use stationery if you select HTML as the message format. Remember, though, that you can set the message format for each message as you create it.

Setting the Internet e-mail options

The Internet e-mail options determine the type of encoding that is used for your messages and the procedures that Outlook uses to connect to the mail server. Message encoding is required because the Internet is largely based on the outmoded standards of UNIX operating systems.

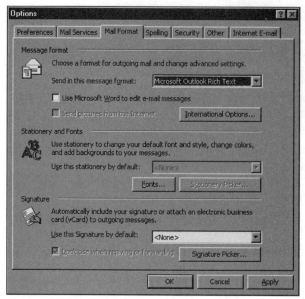

Figure 5-16: Use the Mail Format tab to set the default appearance options for new messages you create.

Note

The Internet standards for message transmission require that messages be broken down into *7-bit* characters so those UNIX-based computers can handle and forward the messages. 7-bit characters were adequate for the transmission of simple plain-text messages but are completely inadequate for sending other things such as program files, graphics images, or foreign language characters.

Encoding schemes such as Multipurpose Internet Mail Extensions (MIME) and UNIX-to-UNIX Encoding (UUEncode) work around this problem by changing messages into 7-bit characters before they are sent and then changing them back into 8-bit (or 16-bit in some cases) characters when they are received. This encoding and decoding process is normally hidden from the user, but it does have one serious drawback—it increases the size of messages considerably during their transmission. That's one reason why messages you send to someone may be rejected as too large for their mailbox, even though the file you are sending is well below the limit. For example, a 1.5MB file attachment can easily exceed 2.2MB as an encoded message and will be rejected if the recipient's mailbox is limited to files no larger than 2MB. Your only options, if this occurs, are to try and reduce the size of the file, break the attachment into several pieces, or hope that the recipient can convince their ISP to remove or adjust the message size limitations.

To set your Internet e-mail options, follow these steps:

1. If necessary, select Tools ➪ Options to display the Options dialog box. Click the Internet E-mail tab to bring it to the front, as shown in Figure 5-17.

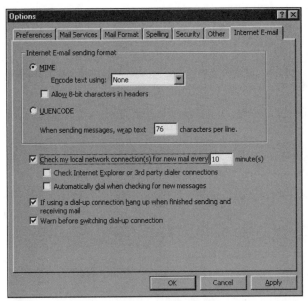

Figure 5-17: Use the Internet E-mail tab to select encoding and connection procedure options.

2. Select the encoding option that you wish to use. Generally it's best to select MIME rather than UUENCODE, because MIME offers much better support for sending file attachments. You may need to choose UUENCODE if you are sending messages to someone who is working on an older UNIX-based computer system.

3. It's generally best to select None in the *Encode text using* drop-down list box. If you use one of the other options, the message recipient may have to use a special program to decode your message.

4. It's also safest to not select the *Allow 8-bit characters in headers* checkbox. Although this option will enable you to use foreign characters in your message headers, some older e-mail programs have trouble reading messages when this option is selected.

5. The *When sending messages, wrap text xx characters per line* option causes Outlook to limit the length of the lines in your messages to the number of characters shown in the text box. This setting makes it easier for people who are using simple text editors to read your messages, because they won't have to scroll right and left to see the whole message.

6. If you want Outlook to automatically check for new messages periodically, select the *Check my local network connection(s) for new mail every xx minute(s)* checkbox. This poorly worded selection really doesn't have anything to do with your network — you need to use this option to make Outlook automatically check for e-mail even if you don't have a network! Specify the time interval that you'd like in the text box.

Caution

If you use a single phone line for your modem and for voice calls, remember that Outlook will automatically dial at the interval you select (if you've selected the correct set of options). If you set too short a time interval, your phone line may be constantly tied up as Outlook dials your ISP, logs in, and checks for new messages. The time interval you specify is between the beginning of each connection attempt — not the free time between those attempts.

7. Select the *Check Internet Explorer or 3rd party dialer connections* checkbox if you want Outlook to first determine if you're already connected to the Internet before attempting to dial. If you choose this option and Outlook can find the mail server on the current connection, Outlook won't try to hang up and redial.

8. Select the *Automatically dial when checking for new messages* checkbox if you want Outlook to automatically connect if you aren't already connected. If both this and the *Check my local network connection(s) for new mail every xx minute(s)* option are selected, Outlook will be able to send and receive e-mail automatically at the intervals you specify.

9. Select the *If using a dial-up connection hang up when finished sending and receiving mail* checkbox to make certain that after Outlook automatically dials in, it disconnects the call when the sending and receiving is complete. If you don't select this option, Outlook will dial in, but will leave you connected. Your ISP will probably object if you leave your system connected, even when you aren't doing anything online.

10. Select the *Warn before switching dial-up connection* checkbox to make certain Outlook doesn't disconnect you if you are online and Outlook wants to check for e-mail. This is generally only a problem if you have more than one Dial-Up Networking connection.

11. Click OK to close the dialog box and confirm your selections.

Configuring Microsoft Fax

Even though e-mail has greatly reduced the use — and indeed the need for — faxing, there still are times when nothing but a fax will do the job. Some documents simply cannot be sent by e-mail, and there still are people who have a fax machine but no computer. Fortunately, all modern modems can also send and receive faxes if the right software is available. With Outlook and Microsoft Fax (or Symantec Fax Starter Edition, if you use the Internet Only e-mail mode) you can easily handle your faxing needs.

In the following sections, you'll learn how to configure Microsoft Fax. Although Symantec Fax Starter Edition is not specifically shown in these examples, you should be able to use the information that is shown to similarly configure that program if you use it in place of Microsoft Fax.

Configuring fax message options

The fax message options determine when faxes are sent, the fax message format, and which cover page — if any — is sent along with your faxes. You access all the Microsoft Fax settings through the Microsoft Fax Properties dialog box. This makes configuring your fax settings a little less confusing that configuring the e-mail message settings.

To set your fax message options, follow these steps:

1. Select Tools ⇨ Services to display the Services dialog box.

2. Select Microsoft Fax and then click the Properties button to display the Message tab of the Microsoft Fax Properties dialog box, shown in Figure 5-18.

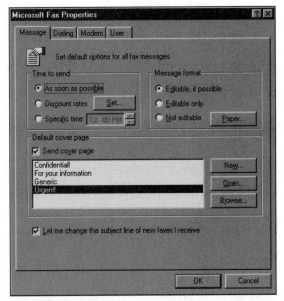

Figure 5-18: Use the Message tab to select the time, format, and cover letter options.

3. Select the time option you prefer. In most cases, you'll want to select *As soon as possible* so that there is no delay in sending out faxes. If you want to delay your faxes to take advantage of lower long-distance rates, either use the *Discount rates* or *Specific time* options. Use the Set button to specify when the discount rate period occurs.

4. Select the message format you prefer:

- *Editable, if possible* sends your fax as a document file if the receiving fax system is a computer and is using fax software that is compatible with Microsoft Fax. Otherwise, the fax is sent as a fax image. This is generally the best choice unless you want to prevent someone from receiving a document file.

- *Editable only* will only send the fax as a document file. If the receiving system cannot receive faxes in this format, your fax will not be sent.

- *Not editable* sends a fax image without even attempting to send a document file.

5. Click the Paper button to choose the paper size, orientation, and image quality. Unless you make prior arrangements to have the receiving fax machine load special-sized paper, it's usually safest to set the size for letter-sized paper and portrait orientation. In almost all cases, you should select the *Best Available* image quality option. Lower-quality image settings may save a few seconds per page, but generally it's not enough to make up for the image quality degradation. Click OK to close the Message Format dialog box.

6. If you'd like to send a cover page, select the *Send cover page* checkbox and choose a page from the list box. To view or edit a cover page, select the page and click Open to open the cover page editor.

7. Select the *Let me change the subject line of new faxes I receive* checkbox so that you can change the Outlook subject line for faxes. Outlook generally lists incoming faxes with a very brief description that doesn't really describe the subject of the fax. Choosing this option allows you to enter a more descriptive subject so you can more easily locate a particular fax in the Inbox later.

Configuring fax dialing options

The fax dialing options enable you to configure the way the fax application dials out and what happens if a successful connection cannot be made on the first attempt. With all of the area code changes that seem to be happening almost on a daily basis, you'll probably need to use these settings more than you can imagine!

To set your fax dialing options, follow these steps:

1. If necessary, display the Microsoft Fax Properties dialog box and then click the Dialing tab, shown in Figure 5-19.

2. Click the Dialing Properties button to set up your area code, to specify which area codes are local calls, and to specify the codes you need to enter to access outside lines, long-distance services, or calling cards, or to disable call waiting.

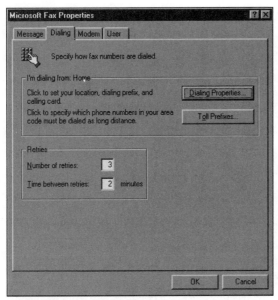

Figure 5-19: Use the Dialing tab to set up phone numbers and retry attempts.

3. Click the Toll Prefixes button to specify which telephone prefixes must be dialed as long distance numbers, even though they are in your area code.

4. Specify the number of times you would like to retry sending a fax and how long to wait between failed attempts. If you attempt to send a fax and there is no answer, a busy signal, or a person answers the line, these settings will determine how persistent the fax program will be in trying again.

Configuring fax modem options

The fax modem properties actually enable your system to use your modem for sending faxes and for sharing your fax modem on your network. Also hidden within these properties is the setting that makes your system capable of receiving faxes. This last setting often causes considerable frustration, because it is buried so deeply.

To set your fax dialing options, follow these steps:

1. If necessary, display the Microsoft Fax Properties dialog box and then click the Modem tab, shown in Figure 5-20.

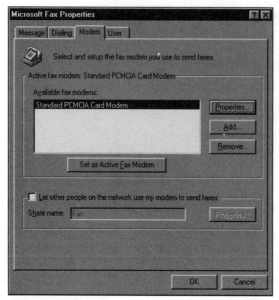

Figure 5-20: Use the Modem tab to set up your fax modem.

2. Select your modem from the Available fax modems list box and click the *Set as Active Fax Modem* button to enable the use of your modem for faxing.

3. If you want other people on your network to be able to send faxes using your modem, select the *Let other people on the network use my modem to send faxes* checkbox. You can also specify a name for the shared fax modem and, by clicking the Properties button, set passwords for its use.

Note   If you share your fax modem, any incoming faxes will appear on your computer. Microsoft Fax does not include the capability to distribute incoming faxes to the intended recipients across the network.

4. Click the Properties button next to the Available fax modems list box to display the Fax Modem Properties dialog box, shown in Figure 5-21.

5. Select the answer mode option you prefer. The default setting, *Don't answer*, prevents you from receiving faxes. If you select *Manual*, a dialog box will appear when the phone rings, and you can then choose to pick up the call as an incoming fax. If you have a dedicated line for your modem, it's usually best to select the *Answer after x rings* option so that faxes can be received automatically.

6. Set the speaker options as you prefer. Remember that these options will have no effect if the modem does not have a speaker.

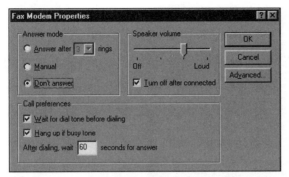

Figure 5-21: Use the Fax Modem Properties dialog box to set your fax modem for receiving faxes.

7. Set the Call preferences options to suit your phone lines. The default settings generally work well for standard phone lines, but you may need to adjust the settings if you call out on a special type of line that does not provide the normal dial tone and busy signals.

8. You can usually ignore the advanced settings that are available through the Advanced button. These settings are most useful for troubleshooting purposes.

9. Click OK to close the Fax Modem Properties dialog box.

Configuring fax user options

The fax user options provide information that is displayed on cover letters and at the top of each page of faxes you send. Much of this information is optional, but certain of the information must be provided to comply with existing laws.

To set your fax user options, follow these steps:

1. If necessary, display the Microsoft Fax Properties dialog box and then click the User tab, shown in Figure 5-22.

2. Enter your name and fax number in the appropriate boxes. This information is required by law and must be accurate.

3. Enter any additional information you might want included on cover pages. This additional information is all optional, but including it here enables the cover letters to automatically include it in the appropriate fields.

4. Click OK to close the dialog box and confirm your changes.

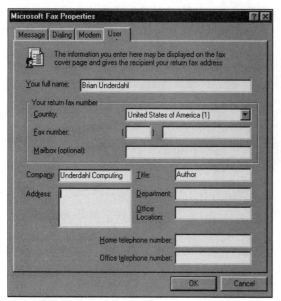

Figure 5-22: Use the User tab to enter your personal information.

Using Profiles

Now that you've learned how to configure Outlook, it's time to take a quick look at an Outlook feature—*profiles*—that can make it possible for you to have more than one set of Outlook configurations available on your computer. You'll find this feature especially useful if you share your PC with other people, because each person could have their own set of configuration options stored in their own profile. No one would have to put up with someone else's quirky way of setting up Outlook, and each user could easily access the settings they prefer simply by loading their own profile when they used the system.

It's also possible for an individual user to have multiple profiles. Although it's not real common, you may want to set up multiple profiles for special purposes. An example of this might be if you wanted to have one profile that you used for business and allowed you to use your company's Exchange server for all e-mail messages. You might then create a second profile for your personal use that specified your private ISP account for e-mail.

Adding a profile

You use the Mail applet in the Windows Control Panel to add a new profile. You cannot add a profile from within Outlook itself. To add a new profile, follow these steps:

1. Click the Start button and then choose Settings ⇨ Control Panel to display the Control Panel.

2. Double-click the Mail icon to display the dialog box shown in Figure 5-23. This dialog box looks very similar to the Services dialog box within Outlook, but it includes an extra option that enables you to work with profiles.

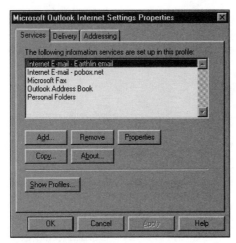

Figure 5-23: Use the Control Panel Mail applet to work with profiles.

3. Click the Show Profiles button to display the Mail dialog box, shown in Figure 5-24. You'll use this dialog box to create, remove, modify, or copy profiles.

4. Click Add to start a new profile from scratch or Copy to make a copy of the currently selected profile. If you are creating a new profile that is quite similar to an existing profile, it's far easier to use a copy of an existing profile and then simply modify those settings you prefer to change.

5. Depending on your selection in Step 4, you may need to follow through the steps of the Inbox Setup Wizard or simply specify a name for your new profile.

It's probably pretty clear from Figure 5-24 that you can delete a profile by selecting it and clicking the Remove button. Likewise, you can configure the settings for a selected profile by clicking the Properties button. You'll probably find that it's a bit easier to set the properties for a profile by first opening it in Outlook and then setting the properties.

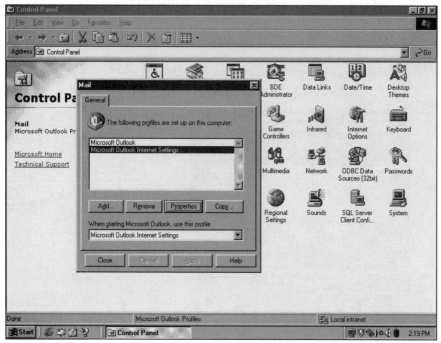

Figure 5-24: Open the Mail dialog box to access your profiles.

Using multiple profiles

You must be able to select the profile to use in order for multiple profiles to be of any value. You can choose the profile to use by default, or you can have Outlook prompt for the profile to use whenever you start the program.

To set the profile selection options, follow these steps:

1. In Outlook, select Tools ➪ Options to display the Options dialog box.

2. Click the Mail Services tab, shown in Figure 5-25.

3. Choose the option you prefer. Select *Prompt for a profile to be used* to be able to choose the profile whenever you start Outlook, as shown in Figure 5-26. This is the best option for people who are sharing a computer and want to use their individual profile settings.

4. Click OK to close the dialog box.

Caution

If you choose a default profile by selecting a choice from the *Always use this profile* list box, Outlook will continue to use the existing profile until the next time you restart Outlook. You must close and restart Outlook before the new profile will become active.

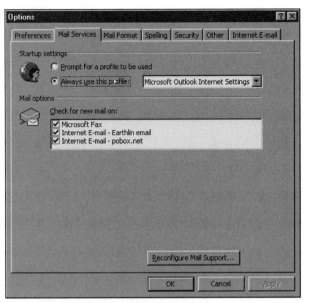

Figure 5-25: Select the profile selection options on the Mail Services tab.

Figure 5-26: Select the profile to use when you open Outlook.

Summary

This chapter showed you how to configure Outlook so that it will work the way you want it to. There are literally dozens of configuration settings and options that you can use to customize Outlook, and this chapter explained not only where to find those settings but also why you may want to make certain choices.

The next chapter covers the basics of e-mail. You'll learn how to use Outlook's e-mail services more effectively to handle your e-mail messaging needs.

✦   ✦   ✦

Mastering
E-mail

P A R T

✦ ✦ ✦ ✦

In This Part

Chapter 6
E-mail Basics

Chapter 7
Intermediate E-mail
Concepts

Chapter 8
Advanced E-mail
Concepts

✦ ✦ ✦ ✦

Part II deals with e-mail—the one thing that almost everyone uses Outlook for. These chapters take you from the basics of e-mail through intermediate and advanced e-mail concepts. If you'd like to make certain your e-mail messages are noticed, you'll want to learn about all the formatting options. If you want to learn how to route certain messages automatically, you'll find the sections on rules quite interesting. Finally, if you need to send messages to groups of people, you'll want to learn about distribution lists.

E-mail Basics

CHAPTER 6

I f Outlook did nothing other than enable you to efficiently send and receive e-mail messages, it would still likely be one of the most often used programs on your PC. For many different reasons, e-mail has become one of the most prevalent forms of communications in the modern world. There is no other method of sending messages that has quite the combination of speed, convenience, and low cost that e-mail offers.

This chapter shows you the basics of using Outlook to send and receive e-mail. Along the way, you learn a number of handy little tricks that will make common e-mail tasks just a bit easier. In no time at all, you'll be completely comfortable with using Outlook's e-mail features to manage all your e-mail messages.

Composing a Message

Composing an e-mail message isn't a whole lot different than writing a letter to someone. Sure, your e-mail message is likely to be delivered a lot faster than a letter that you mail, but you're still using the written word to communicate your thoughts in either case.

If you aren't much of a letter writer, you may discover that composing your first e-mail messages is a bit harder than you thought it might be. This may be especially true if you're the type of person who uses a lot of gestures or vocal inflections to help convey much of the meaning when you're talking to someone. Sometimes it can be really hard to find the right words to explain just how you feel about a subject. If this happens to you, don't worry — using e-mail will become a lot easier as time goes along and you have more experience with this communications medium.

Tip   It's best to keep your e-mail messages short and to the point. No one wants to read *War and Peace* in an e-mail message.

Starting a new message

Outlook offers you a number of ways to begin composing a new e-mail message. Figures 6-1 and 6-2 demonstrate several of these methods. As Figure 6-1 shows, you can select File ➪ New ➪ Mail Message to open the message editor.

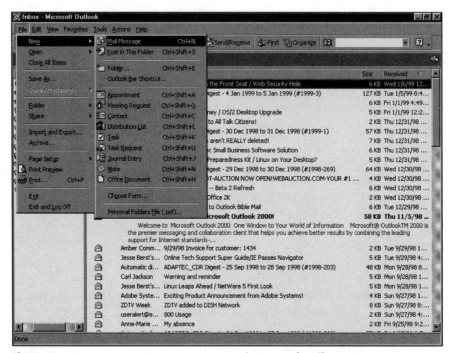

Figure 6-1: One way to start a new message is to use the File menu.

Figure 6-2 shows several additional methods of starting a new message, as listed here:

✦ Select Actions ➪ New Mail Message.

✦ Press Ctrl+N.

✦ Select Actions ➪ New Mail Message Using and then select an option from the list of choices.

✦ Click the New Mail Message button at the left side of the Outlook toolbar when a mail folder is open.

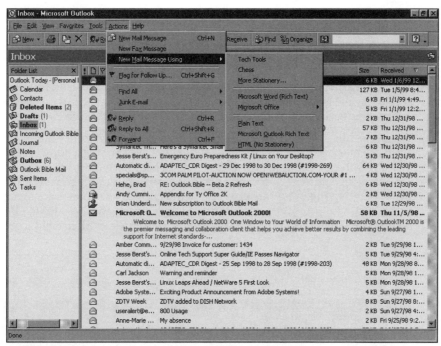

Figure 6-2: Outlook offers several additional ways to start a new message.

Tip

> The New button's default changes function depending on what folder is currently open. Hold the mouse pointer over the button for a few seconds to verify which type of new object will be created.

Unless you choose the Actions ➪ New Mail Message Using command and then select from one of the choices on the menu, Outlook will open the message editor using the default message format that you selected when you configured Outlook. If you'd prefer to set a different default message format, see Chapter 5 for information on configuring Outlook.

Addressing your message

The new message window has several different places for you to enter information, as you can see in Figure 6-3. To begin your message, you'll most often start by adding the addresses that are used to deliver your message. Each of the address text boxes has a labeled button to the left of the text box that identifies the text box. Here's an explanation of those text boxes:

✦ The *From* text box can be used to enter an e-mail address that identifies the sender. This text box is rarely used because Outlook automatically enters your return e-mail address when sending messages. You may want to use this text box if you need to send a message but want replies to be routed to a different e-mail address instead of your own. You can display this text box by selecting View ➪ From Field.

✦ The *To* text box is used to specify the e-mail addresses for the primary message recipients. You must always specify this address.

✦ The *Cc* — carbon copy — text box is used to specify the e-mail addresses for secondary message recipients. Use the Cc text box for people who need to be aware of a message but who aren't expected to respond to the message.

✦ The *Bcc* — blind carbon copy — text box is used to specify the e-mail addresses for message recipients to whom you are sending a copy of the message without informing the primary and secondary message recipients. For example, if you need to send copies of certain messages to your attorney without letting the other message recipients know that copies were being sent to the attorney, you would enter the attorney's e-mail address into the Bcc text box. You can display this text box by selecting View ➪ Bcc Field.

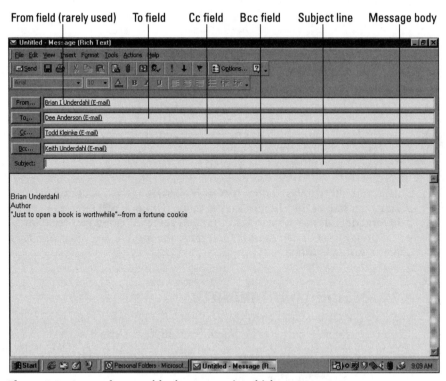

Figure 6-3: Areas of a new, blank message in which to enter text

You need to address e-mail messages properly in order for your messages to be delivered. This is really no different from with any type of message. If you drop a letter that is addressed simply to "John Smith" in the mailbox, it's pretty likely your letter won't be delivered. On the other hand, a letter addressed to "John Smith, 1 Dirt Road, Virginia City, NV 89440" has a pretty good chance of being delivered — assuming, of course, that the address were a real address.

E-mail addresses use a standard format that allows e-mail messages to be routed to the intended recipient. This format is *name@mailserver*. For our friend John Smith, this might be something like johns@vcnv.net, where *johns* is John's e-mail account name and vcnv.net is the name of John's mail server. Here are a few rules about e-mail addresses that you should know:

✦ The account name and the mail server name are always separated by an at sign (@).

✦ Spaces are not allowed in e-mail addresses.

✦ E-mail addresses are not generally case-sensitive. JohnS@VcNv.net and johns@vcnv.net should be equivalent in most cases.

✦ If you have even one character incorrect in an e-mail address, your message will not go to the intended recipient; however, it may end up in someone else's inbox if their e-mail address happens to match the address you entered incorrectly.

Note

If you address an e-mail message incorrectly (and the address you entered did not match someone else's e-mail address), the mail server will usually *bounce* your message back to you. Usually this happens fairly quickly, but some mail servers can take several days to bounce messages. If a message bounces back to you, it will generally be accompanied by an automatic message from the mail system administrator informing you that the message was undeliverable and that no message transport was available for the intended recipient. If this happens, check the e-mail address very carefully, correct any errors, and resend the message. Unfortunately, you'll also see this same automatic message returned on correctly addressed messages if your ISP has incorrectly configured the IP addresses on their mail server. If e-mail addresses that you've used successfully in the past suddenly stop working, you may need to call your ISP for assistance.

You can enter e-mail addresses into the address text boxes several different ways. You can, of course, simply type the address into the appropriate text box. This may be the best choice for an address you won't use again and don't want to add to your address book. If you already have someone's e-mail address in your Contacts list, you can also just type that person's name into the text box. When you send the message, Outlook will verify the e-mail addresses and replace the name with the correct e-mail address. You can request that Outlook immediately check the names by clicking the Check Names button. As Figure 6-4 shows, Outlook will ask you to help verify any entries that it cannot positively identify.

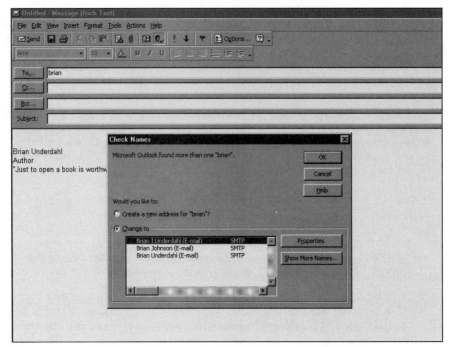

Figure 6-4: Outlook sometimes needs a little help identifying addresses.

If Outlook displays the Check Names dialog box, as shown in Figure 6-4, you have several options:

✦ Select the correct entry from the list and click OK.

✦ Verify that you've selected the correct entry by using the Properties button to view the selected contact record.

✦ Select the *Create a new address for* radio button and click OK to create a new contact record.

✦ Click the Show More Names button to select the correct recipient from your contact list.

If Outlook can identify the message recipient without any extra help, it will replace the name you entered with an underlined link that indicates a correct e-mail address. You can verify that the correct recipient was selected by double-clicking the underlined link to display the contact record, as shown in Figure 6-5.

Double-click the name . . .   . . . to display the contact record.

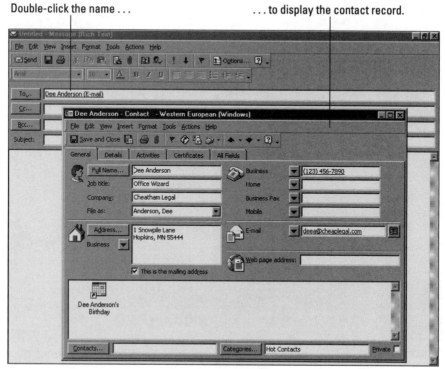

Figure 6-5: Verify that the correct recipient is selected by opening the contact record.

If you prefer clicking to typing, Outlook offers another method of addressing your e-mail messages that is fast, easy, and very unlikely to result in an incorrect e-mail address. In place of typing anything in the address text boxes, click the appropriate button and select the names from a list. In Figure 6-6, for example, clicking the To button displayed the Select Names dialog box. Double-clicking on Dee Anderson added her name to the To box in the dialog box, and clicking OK added her name to the To text box at the top of the message. In the figure, the Select Names dialog box is still shown to illustrate the process better.

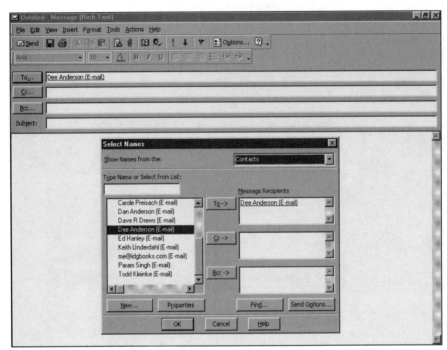

Figure 6-6: Click the appropriate address button to select the recipients from a list.

While the Select Names dialog box is open, you can select additional names and add them to any of the address fields by clicking the appropriate button. If the desired recipient isn't already in the list, click the New button to create a new address entry. Verify that you've selected the correct recipient by clicking the Properties button. If you have more than one address list — such as a list in Contacts and another in a separate Outlook address book, use the drop-down *Show Names from the* list box to select the correct address list.

Tip   You can quickly verify a recipient by right-clicking the recipient's entry and selecting Properties.

Entering a subject

Once you've addressed your e-mail message, you should enter a brief description of the message in the subject text box. Adding a subject is actually optional, but highly recommended. When you look at the messages in your Inbox, it's easy to see why the subject line is so important. The Inbox typically displays several pieces of information about each message, but the two items that really stand out are the name of the sender and the subject. A catchy subject line can be the difference between your message getting immediate attention and one that sits around until the recipient finds some spare time.

There is, of course, more to devising a good subject line than simply coming up with something that catches the eye. Sure, you want the recipient to read your message, but you probably want the recipient to be able to associate messages with the actual message topic, too. Remember that the recipient may well receive hundreds of e-mail messages, and it's important for them to be able to locate specific messages based on the topic. An example of this might be e-mail messages you send to your lawyer. You would probably want to include a reference to a specific case in the subject line. That way the lawyer would be able to quickly see which of your messages concerned your lawsuit against the apple grower who sold you an apple that contained a worm, and which of your messages were related to redoing your will.

Caution   Many people use filters or rules to automatically delete junk or adult-content e-mail messages. You could accidentally cause your messages to be seen as fitting into one of these categories by trying to be too sensational in creating your message subject lines. You may want to refer to Chapter 8 to learn more about the Outlook Rules Wizard so you can see how to avoid this problem when sending your messages.

Entering the message text

Entering the text of your message is your chance to express your thoughts and make your point. Unfortunately, it also can turn into a chance to really embarrass yourself if you're not careful.

Just because e-mail messages are quick and cheap to send doesn't mean that you should throw all of your good sense out the window when you create a new message. If you wouldn't think of allowing misspellings, poor grammar, or foul language to appear in a letter that you were writing to someone, why would you lower your standards and allow them into your e-mail messages? Because e-mail messages are so immediate, people sometimes allow their emotions to rule the day. They may send out an e-mail that is poorly written or contains derogatory statements that they would never use in a face-to-face conversation. The term for this type of boorish message is a *flame*. The result of a flame is seldom the desired one. Frequently flames result in *flame wars* in which both sides trade insults endlessly — certainly not a productive use of anyone's time!

Certain conventions are often used in the text of e-mail messages. One example is the use of several acronyms — such as BTW for "by the way" — that slightly reduce the amount of typing in creating a message. Another common convention is the use of *emoticons* — sets of characters used to express an emotion — such as "<G>" for "big grin." It's generally best to limit the use of acronyms and emoticons in any message — especially in any business-related correspondence, which you hope to be taken seriously.

In reality, creating the text of an e-mail message is no different than writing a letter. In some cases, a casual style makes sense, and in others, it's important to put on a more formal appearance. Only you can decide what is appropriate in your messages.

Figure 6-7 shows a completed e-mail message that is ready to be sent. The recipient's e-mail address has been added, a descriptive subject line was entered, and the text in the body of the message has been completed.

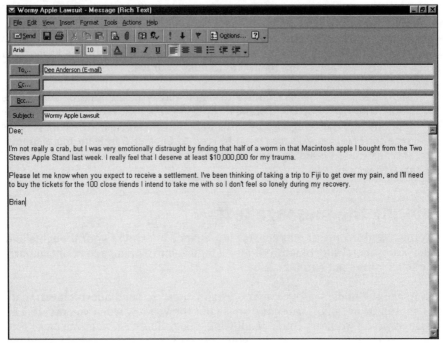

Figure 6-7: The e-mail message has an address, subject, and message body so it is now ready to send.

Sending a Message

Once you've created your message and are ready to send it, you have a couple of questions to consider. Should the message simply go out immediately? Do you want replies sent to someone else? Do you need to know if the message was delivered? In most cases the answer is simple — no special handling is needed. Outlook does give you several options that you can use in those instances where special handling is required. In the following sections, you learn how to use those options — and how to simply ignore them and send the message on its way.

Sending a message immediately

When you finish creating an e-mail message, you'll likely just want to send it immediately. In most cases, all you need to do is just click the Send button to place the message in the Outbox. If you have Outlook configured to automatically check for new e-mail messages at regular intervals, your message will probably sit in the Outbox for a short time until Outlook next logs onto the mail server.

Tip   To send any outgoing messages immediately, click the Send/Receive button. Outlook will immediately log onto the mail server to send the messages from the Outbox and download any new messages into the Inbox.

Remember that you can only cancel or edit messages that you've sent while they're still in the Outbox. Once a message leaves the Outbox, you might as well consider it as delivered. The one exception to this is if you use an Exchange Server. You can cancel a message that has left your Outbox if that message is still sitting at the Exchange Server waiting for the recipient to collect their mail. Still, the best time to cancel any e-mail message is before you send it!

Setting message options

For those times when your messages require special handling, Outlook offers a number of very useful options. For example, you could delay a message telling your boss that you have absconded with the company bank account until the day after you leave on your flight to Fiji. Or you could prepare your new product announcement ahead of time but have Outlook hold the messages until the date of the official announcement.

To set the message options, follow these steps:

   1. Click the Options button (or select View ➪ Options) to display the Message Options dialog box, shown in Figure 6-8.

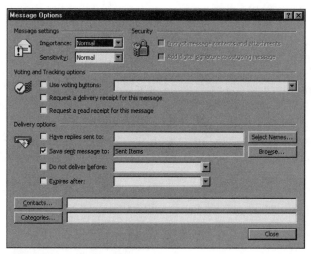

Figure 6-8: Use the Message Options button to control how your message is sent.

2. Select the *Use voting buttons* if you want to attach reply buttons to your message so that the recipients can easily send a reply. This option only applies if you are using an Exchange Server.

3. Select the *Request a delivery receipt for this message* checkbox to automatically receive a message informing you that your message was delivered. Remember, though, that just because a recipient receives your message does not guarantee that they will read the message.

4. Select the *Request a read receipt for this message* checkbox to automatically receive a message informing you that your message was read. Unfortunately, there are several factors that can prevent you from receiving this confirmation message. As you learned in Chapter 5, you can configure Outlook so that it does not send read receipts for messages you receive. In addition, some mail systems automatically reject these requests.

5. Select the *Have replies sent to* checkbox to have any replies sent to someone else. You might use this option, for example, if you are sending out a survey and want your assistant to tally the results. You can use the Select Names button to choose the reply recipient.

6. Select the *Save sent message to* checkbox to keep a copy of the message in the Sent Items folder. You can also click the Browse button to select a different Outlook folder for saving the message copy.

7. Select the *Do not deliver before* checkbox and select a date from the drop-down list box to delay sending the message until a specified date. Outlook will hold the message until the date you select.

8. Select the *Expires after* checkbox and select a date from the drop-down list box to make the message unavailable if it is not delivered by a specific date. This option may not work with all mail servers. You might use this option to send out a message that tells recipients that you'll be on vacation for the next week, but to delete the message if it isn't delivered before you return.

9. Click the Contacts button to link this message to specific contacts. This will add a link in their contact cards so you can easily refer to this message when viewing those cards. This option is handy if you aren't sending the message to the contact but perhaps want to send a message about the contact to someone else. That way you'll easily be able to find all messages relating to the contact.

10. Click the Categories button to link this message to specific categories of messages. This, too, is intended to make it easier for you to find related messages.

11. Click the Close button to close the dialog box. You will still need to send your message after you've set the message options.

The remaining message options are discussed in Chapter 7.

Reading a Message

Almost everyone likes to get mail—at least the kind that doesn't come in those window envelopes! Reading your e-mail messages is usually fun, too, especially since most bills still come as regular mail rather than as e-mail.

By default, Outlook places all new messages into the Inbox folder. As Figure 6-9 shows, messages that you have not yet read are distinguished from the messages you have read by being displayed in bold type. In addition, the default settings display a brief preview of the text of unread messages.

Tip   Select Edit ⇨ Mark as Read or Edit ⇨ Mark as Unread to change the status of messages in your Inbox. Because unread messages are bold, making a message "unread" can help you prioritize your pile of e-mail messages.

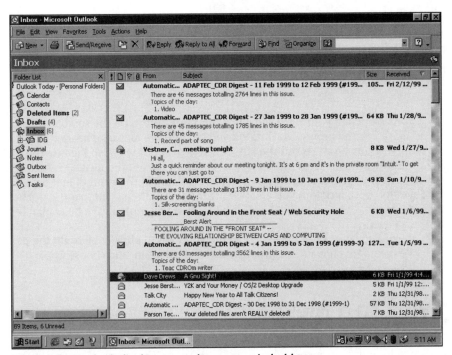

Figure 6-9: Outlook displays unread messages in bold type.

In addition to displaying unread items in bold, Outlook indicates the number of unread items in the folder list, in the Outlook bar, and in the Outlook Today window.

The easiest way to read a message is to double-click the message. This works whether the message has been read or not.

Tip To sort your messages in a different order, click the column header of the column you want to use to control the sort. Click again to sort in reverse order.

Outlook generally opens messages without any fanfare. As Figure 6-10 shows, however, messages sent in certain formats can contain *scripts* — executable code that runs on your computer — that could cause you problems. If you see a message similar to the warning shown in the figure, it's a good idea to select the Disable Script button unless you are absolutely certain that the scripts are safe to run.

Figure 6-10: Outlook warns you if the message you are opening may contain harmful code that could damage your computer.

Once you've opened your message, click the Print button on the toolbar if you would like a printed copy of it. Outlook will include the message header so you can see who sent the message and the subject. The printout will also include the date and time when the message was sent. To print just part of the message, highlight the portion you wish to print and then select File ➪ Print. In the Print dialog box, click the Selection option before you click OK. Outlook will then print just the portion of the message that you've highlighted. (This option may not always be available.)

Tip To copy some or all of a message to the Windows Clipboard, highlight the part of the message you want to copy, right-click the selection, and choose Copy.

Replying to a Message

Replying to an e-mail message that you've received is very simple. You just click a button, add your response, and send off your reply. There are, of course, a few things to consider when sending a reply, and they are discussed in this section.

Choosing the type of reply

You've probably noticed that the Outlook toolbar has three buttons that you can use when replying to a message. Each of these buttons has a slightly different purpose:

✦ The *Reply to Sender* button opens the message editor, adds the sender to the To address box, adds RE: in front of the message subject, and places the insertion point at the beginning of the message so you can type a reply.

✦ The *Reply to All* button functions very much like the *Reply to Sender* button except that all the original message recipients — except you — are added to the To or Cc address boxes.

✦ The *Forward* button opens the message editor, adds Fwd: in front of the message subject, and places the insertion point at the beginning of the message so you can type a message. You must manually select the message recipient.

Regardless of who Outlook adds to the address boxes, you can add additional recipients or delete recipients as you please. You can even add a Bcc recipient if you don't want to advertise the fact that you're sending a copy of the message to someone.

Composing and sending your reply

Composing and sending a reply is a virtually identical process to that of creating a new e-mail message from scratch. As Figure 6-11 shows, a message reply generally does have one important difference from an original message — the original message usually appears in the body of the reply below the reply text that you add. This makes it easier for everyone to keep track of the complete message stream.

Caution

Although there's no rule that says you must include the original message text in your reply, leaving out the original message can lead to confusion. Suppose, for example, that someone sends you five messages during a day, and you reply to each one with a simple yes or no. Unless the original sender knows for certain which message you are replying to, it's very likely that at least one of your responses will be misinterpreted.

As you learned in Chapter 5, you have several options for how the original message text is included in your reply. Many people prefer to use the convention of prefixing each reply line with a greater-than symbol (>). This convention has both good and bad points. On the good side, it's easy to follow the message stream, because each time someone replies to a message another greater-than symbol is added to the beginning of each line. This convention also makes it easier to include responses within the original message text, since new lines won't be prefixed with the greater-than symbol. On the bad side, prefixing the original lines with greater-than symbols often results in hard-to-read text composed of a mixture of long and short lines, which is caused by the line length limit setting that breaks lines over a certain length.

Once you've composed your reply, click the Send button to send the message. Outlook adds a small curved arrow to the Inbox icon for messages after you send a reply or if you forward the message. The direction of the arrow is different for replies and forwards. The reply arrow points left and the forward arrow points right.

New text   Original text

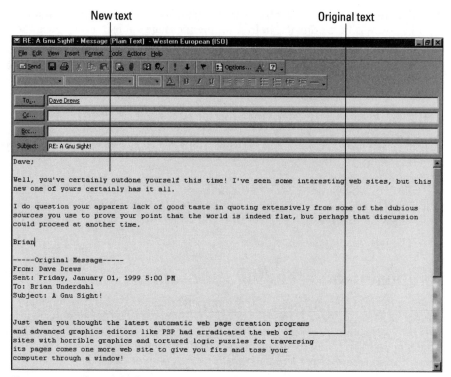

Figure 6-11: The original message is normally included below your reply.

Managing the Mail Folders

The Outlook mail folders handle all your incoming and outgoing messages. Although the mail folders may look a lot like normal folders that appear in Windows Explorer, Outlook's mail folders are quite different from those types of folders. Here are some of the important differences:

✦ Mail folders don't exist as actual separate folders on your hard disk. Rather, they are contained within a special database type file in the Outlook Personal Folders file.

✦ Mail folders can hold messages that include multiple attachments.

✦ The items in your mail folders continue to use disk space even after they've been deleted. You must *compact* the mail folders from time to time to recover this lost space.

✦ You cannot move items directly between Outlook mail folders and Windows Explorer folders. You can import and export certain items, but this generally changes the item's format.

✦ You cannot move folders between Outlook and Windows Explorer.

Outlook periodically *archives* old items that are in your mail folders. This removes those items from the mail folders and stores them in a file that Outlook can open if you need to refer back to an old message. The archive file is normally named Archive.pst and can usually be found in the C:\Windows\Application Data\ Microsoft\Outlook folder.

Outlook automatically creates a standard set of mail folders, but you are not limited to just those folders. As Figure 6-12 shows, you can create new folders as needed to help you better organize your messages. In the figure, the Inbox contains a new folder named "IDG," and that folder contains another folder named "Outlook 2000 Stuff." Creating, renaming, copying, moving, or deleting Outlook folders is just as easy as working with Windows Explorer folders. Right-click the folder to display the pop-up menu, as shown in the figure, and then make your selection.

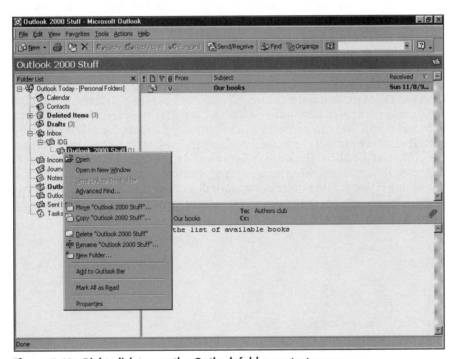

Figure 6-12: Right-click to see the Outlook folder context menu.

Notice that each folder can have its own view settings. In Figure 6-12, for example, the folder has the preview pane active so that you can see the message contents without even opening the message. Use the options on the View menu to set the view for each folder.

When you first start Outlook, five different mail folders are created by default:

✦ The *Inbox* holds all of your incoming messages. Unread messages appear in bold type to alert you to the messages you haven't viewed yet. Double-click a message to open it.

✦ The *Drafts* folder holds copies of messages that you started but have not yet sent. If you begin composing a new message, but click the Close button rather than the Send button, Outlook will ask you if you want to save a copy in the Drafts folder. You can reopen messages that are in the Drafts folder for further editing before you send them.

✦ The *Outbox* folder holds messages that you have sent but which have not yet been delivered to the mail server. Generally speaking, the Outbox provides your last chance to successfully recall a message to prevent its delivery.

✦ The *Sent Items* folder holds copies of messages that you have sent. Items appear in the Sent Items folder after they are removed from the Outbox.

✦ The *Deleted Items* folder holds those items that you have deleted from another folder.

An important part of managing your Outlook folders and the items they contain is getting rid of unnecessary clutter. You may not realize it, but the Deleted Items folder can continue to hold onto old items long after they are of no use. Figure 6-13 shows how you can control this excess more carefully by making certain the Deleted Items folder is emptied periodically. Select Tools ➪ Options to display the Options dialog box. Click the Other tab and then make certain you select the *Empty the Deleted Items folder upon exiting* checkbox. You may not want to select this option if you would rather exert more direct control over the Deleted Items folder — but you'll have to remember to manually empty the Deleted Items folder yourself occasionally.

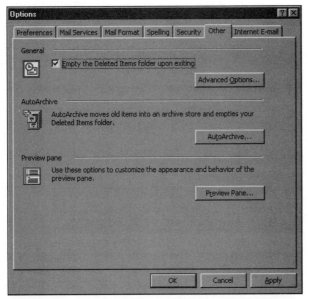

Figure 6-13: Choose this option to empty the Deleted Items folder automatically whenever you close Outlook.

Summary

In this chapter, you learned the basics of using e-mail in Outlook. The chapter didn't assume that you were already a seasoned e-mail user but rather showed you everything that a beginning e-mail user would want to know to get started. You learned how to compose and send messages, how to read your messages, and how to reply to messages. Finally, the chapter covered the subject of managing your mail folders.

The next chapter builds on the topics covered in this chapter. You'll see how you can get a bit more creative and make your messages look a little fancier. You'll also learn how to include files with messages as well as how to use features like an automatic signature. You'll also see a bit more about how you can use mail folders to effectively organize your e-mail messages.

✦   ✦   ✦

Intermediate E-mail Concepts

In the very early days of e-mail messages, people were quite happy with the idea that it was possible to send a simple text message from one computer to another. Everyone understood that an e-mail message was quite different from something like a formal business letter. Fancy formatting and attachments simply weren't a part of the e-mail game — plain old text was all there was.

Today the picture is quite different. E-mail messages are no longer limited to looking plain and boring. If you want to create an e-mail message that really stands out, Outlook gives you plenty of fancy options. If you want to send a file along with your message, that's also quite easy to do. In many ways, e-mail messages have gone well beyond the capabilities of most other types of communications to combine style, immediacy, and utility into a medium that has transformed the way people communicate. In this chapter, you learn how you can use these capabilities in creating your Outlook e-mail messages.

Using Message Format Options

Outlook 2000 supports three major e-mail message formats. Each of these formats varies in the level of message formatting options they allow and also in the ability of message recipients to successfully read the message and view the formatting that you have applied. In the following sections, you learn about the Outlook e-mail message formats.

Sending messages as plain text

The simplest e-mail message format is *plain text*. Messages sent in plain text format do not include any character formatting, background images, or other elements to make the message look fancy. Plain text messages can include *attachments* — files that are transmitted along with the message.

As detailed in Chapter 5, Outlook enables you to set a default message format that will be used whenever you select File ➪ New ➪ Mail Message or Actions ➪ New Mail Message, or when you click the New Mail Message button. As Figure 7-1 shows, you can override the default by selecting Actions ➪ New Mail Message Using ➪ Plain Text to begin creating a new message in the plain text format.

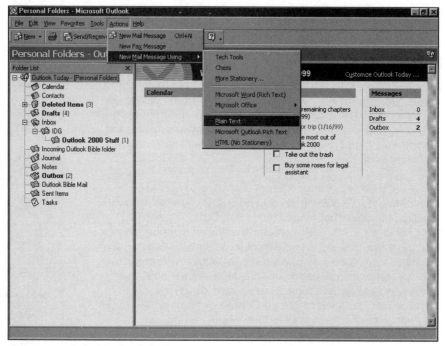

Figure 7-1: Override the default message format by selecting the format for an individual message.

The plain text message format may not be very exciting, but it does offer one major advantage over any other message format — plain text messages can be successfully received and read using any e-mail client software. It doesn't matter if the recipient has the fanciest graphical workstation or the simplest character-based Braille terminal device — plain text messages can always get through.

Caution   Although plain text messages can include file attachments, there's no guarantee that your intended recipients will be able to open and use those attachments. If you must be absolutely certain that your message will be delivered, it's safest to use the plain text format with no attachments.

Figure 7-2 shows a simple e-mail message that is being created in plain text format. Notice that although the Formatting toolbar is displayed, all the toolbar controls are inactive. No character formatting — not even something as simple as making text bold or italic — can be used in plain text format.

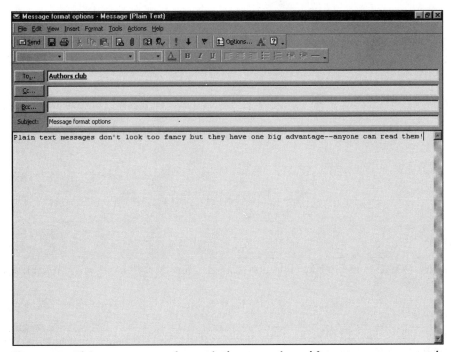

Figure 7-2: Plain text message format is the one universal format anyone can read.

Outlook does provide one character format setting for plain text messages. Because different languages use different sets of characters, you may need to choose a different character set to correctly create messages in foreign languages. Outlook provides quite a few character set options. You can choose an option by selecting Format ⇨ Encoding ⇨ More and then selecting the character set, as shown in Figure 7-3.

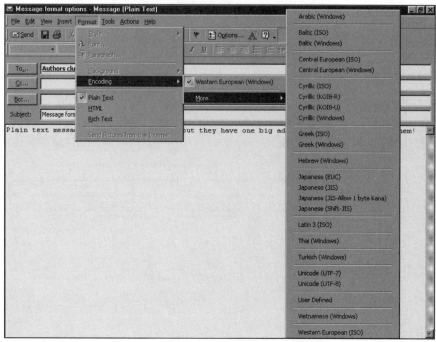

Figure 7-3: You may need to select the correct character set for messages in foreign languages.

Tip

If you receive an e-mail message or need to send an e-mail message in a language that you do not understand, you may be able to use software to translate the message for you. For example, *EasyTranslator* from Transparent Language can automatically translate e-mail messages between English and German, French, Spanish, Italian, and Portuguese. For more information, visit the Transparent Language Web site at www.transparent.com. At the Web site, you'll also learn about additional products, such as *31 Languages of the World,* that can help you learn to read and speak the world's major languages quickly. You can also do limited translations online at http://babelfish.altavista.digital.com.

Sending messages as rich text

Rich text format — also known as RTF — was originally created as a word processing document format. Easy word processing software used quite a few different and incompatible methods of specifying character formatting. If you created a document in a version of WordPerfect, for example, you wouldn't be able to share that document with someone who was using Microsoft Word or WordStar. Nor could those people share their document files with you.

Eventually, document format translators became a standard part of most word processing programs, but these had several problems. First, you had to know the format of a document before you could successfully translate it. Second, the translators typically left quite a bit of room for improvement. Word processor manufacturers simply didn't have much incentive to produce translators that were very good—if translating document formats was too much trouble, maybe users would decide to stick with one brand of word processor.

Rich text format was intended as a type of universal document format. If you created an RTF document in one word processor and then opened the document in a different word processor, the document would look the same—in theory, that is. The reality was usually somewhat less than full fidelity. The reason for this was simple— RTF is one of those "standards" that everyone sees in their own way. Microsoft's definition of RTF might include a few enhancements that are slightly different from WordPerfect's RTF enhancements. The result is that while RTF started out as a good idea, using the RTF message format may not always be a good idea. In particular, if you create a message using rich text as the format and then include an attachment, some recipients will receive a message that includes an unusable attachment named Winmail.dat.

If rich text is so troublesome, you may be wondering why anyone would ever use that format for messages. The simple answer is this—Outlook 2000 is the first version of Outlook that offers another message format option that is intended to eliminate the rich text problems. The longer answer is that rich text message format does offer several features that simply aren't available in any other message format. Here are some character formatting options that you'll find only in rich text message format:

✦ *Font sizes*—A full range of font sizes is available in rich text. Plain text format does not include any font size information, and HTML format offers a limited range of choices.

✦ *Multiple text alignments*—A rich text message can easily include different text alignment for each line of text. HTML messages can use different text alignments but only by breaking the document into separate page elements— not always the easiest thing to accomplish!

✦ *Flush left bullets*—When you create a bulleted list in a rich text message, the bullets can appear flush with the left margin rather than indented. In HTML format, bullets are always indented.

Note If you use Word 97 or Word 2000 as your e-mail editor, your only message format options will be plain text and rich text.

Figure 7-4 shows a message being created in rich text format. Notice that the Formatting toolbar is active and has been used to apply a number of different character formatting options to the message.

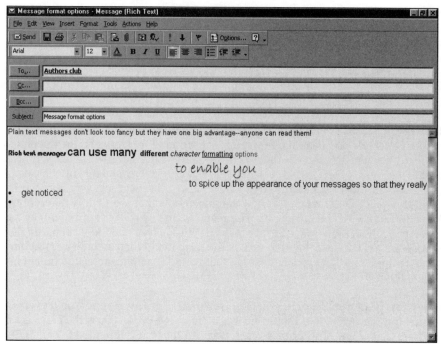

Figure 7-4: Rich text format includes many character formatting options.

Sending messages as HTML

Because the rich text message format can be rather troublesome, Outlook 2000 has added a new message format, HTML—the same document format that is used to create Web pages. HTML-based messages offer one very large advantage over rich text messages—virtually everyone can successfully view HTML documents. If you can view Web pages, you can view HTML messages.

HTML—HyperText Markup Language—was originally designed as a page layout language that was intended to make it easy to link different documents on the World Wide Web. The original language specification has been extended considerably, but HTML-based documents still don't have all the capabilities that you would find in a native word processor format document. For example, if you are creating a document in Word, you have the ability to select virtually any font size for your text. When you're creating an HTML document, Outlook gives you seven different font size choices. Also, if you want to change the text alignment on a line-by-line basis, you'll find that this is very easy in a Word document, but rather difficult in an HTML document.

These minor hassles aside, HTML is a very good choice for the message format of your Outlook e-mail messages. The nearly universal ability for anyone to read HTML messages would by itself be a very good reason to use this message format. Figure 7-5 shows an HTML-based message with examples of some of the elements you can use in this type of message.

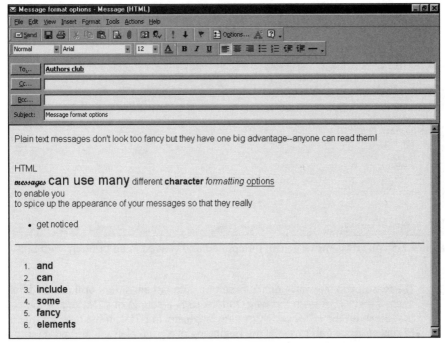

Figure 7-5: HTML format ensures that almost anyone can read the message and see the formatting.

Figure 7-6 demonstrates how easy it is to read HTML messages. In this case, the same message that was shown in Figure 7-5 has been opened in Internet Explorer. If you compare the two figures, you can see that all of the character formatting that was placed in the message when it was created in Outlook is still visible when the message is opened in Internet Explorer.

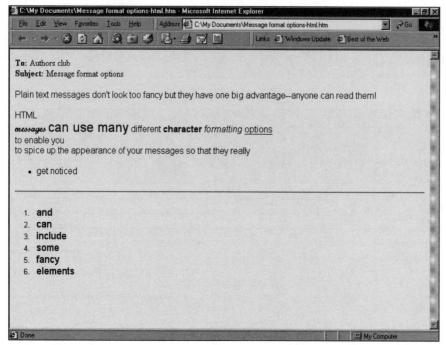

Figure 7-6: An HTML message can be opened and viewed in an ordinary Web browser.

Note

The reason you may have difficulty setting different alignment options for different lines of text stems from the way Outlook uses a couple of HTML *tags* — the codes that make up the HTML programming language. In HTML, most tags are made up of sets of tags — one to signal the beginning of a page element and another to signal the end of that element. The most basic set of tags for creating a paragraph are <P> and </P>. Anything located between these two tags will be considered part of the same paragraph. Another tag, <BR>, is used to indicate a line break. Unlike the paragraph tag, the line break tag is a singular tag. Several line break tags can appear in the same paragraph.

Because Outlook is so sparing in the use of paragraph tags, what may appear as several paragraphs to the human eye can actually be considered part of the same paragraph. In Figure 7-5, everything above the "get noticed" bullet is included in a single paragraph. Because HTML only allows a single alignment option per paragraph, all of the text in that extended paragraph will be aligned the same.

If you really need to use different alignment options, you'll have to split the different areas of text into separate elements. You can do this by adding a horizontal line, bullets, or a numbered list. You can also edit the HTML source code manually using an editor such as Notepad to create separate paragraph elements. This option, however, is really only for those people with far too much time on their hands!

Sending messages as Office documents

Outlook enables you to create and send messages that are really Office documents. This means that the recipient will be able to open and work with the document. In "Attaching Files," later in this chapter, you learn how to use Outlook to send these types of messages. Sometimes, though, you may want to use one of the Office applications to create a message without actually sending a file that the recipient can manipulate. For example, you may want to use Excel to create a budget worksheet to show your managers how the company is doing, but you don't want anyone playing around with the formulas to make their division look better than the rest of the company. Figure 7-7 shows how to begin this process by selecting Actions ➪ New Mail Message Using ➪ Microsoft Office ➪ Microsoft Excel Worksheet.

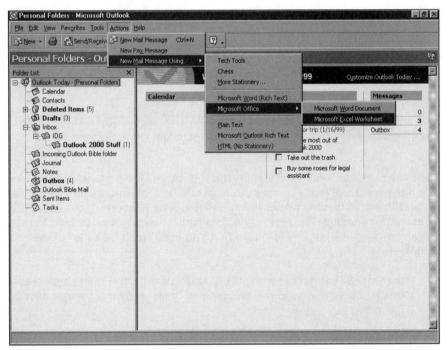

Figure 7-7: You can use different Office applications to create and send mail messages.

The options shown in the Actions ➪ New Mail Message Using ➪ Microsoft Office menu will vary according to which Office applications you have installed on your system. As Figure 7-8 shows, you can create your message as though it were a standard document—an Excel worksheet, in this example. You can use any formulas, text formatting, and so on that you like to create the message.

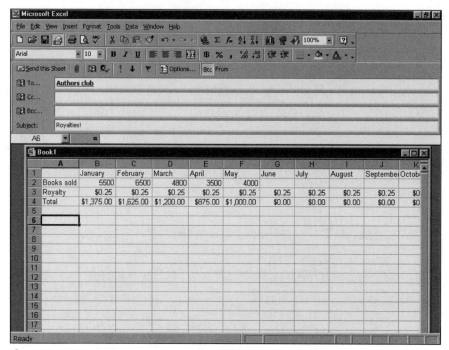

Figure 7-8: Create your message as if it were a standard Office document.

When you click the Send the Sheet button to send the message, something you may not quite expect will happen. Your message will be sent, but it won't be sent as an actual Office document—rather the message will be converted into an HTML document for sending. The recipient will be able to view your message complete with any formatting, but any formulas that you used won't be a part of the document.

Tip   If the recipient will need to manipulate the document rather than simply read your message, be sure to send the document as a file attachment rather than as an HTML message.

Using Advanced Message Options

Outlook offers you several advanced message options that you can use to personalize your messages. In the following sections, you learn how to use these options to make your messages stand out a bit from ordinary e-mail messages.

Flagging a message

Flagging a message means that you're marking the message for special treatment. You might use a flag to indicate that the message recipient is expected to reply to the message no later than a specific date. You might use the *No Response Necessary* flag to inform a message recipient that they don't need to send any reply, or the *Do Not Forward* flag to ask the recipient to refrain from forwarding your message.

You can flag outgoing messages before you send them or incoming messages that you've received. Figure 7-9 shows how you can choose a message flag while you're creating a message. Click the Flag button on the toolbar to display the Flag for Follow Up dialog box, shown in the figure. Choose the type of flag in the drop-down Flag to list box. If you want to add a due date, choose a date using the Due by list box.

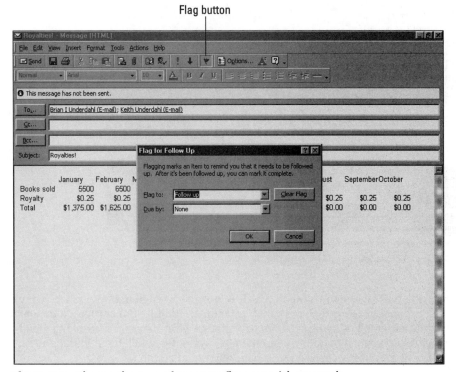

Figure 7-9: Choose the type of message flag you wish to attach.

Caution Recipients can choose to ignore message flags if they want. You shouldn't depend on message flags to make certain a recipient will actually follow up as you'd like. It may be more effective to simply send the recipient a reminder as necessary— especially if you're not certain that the recipient is using Outlook for their e-mail messages.

Setting message importance and sensitivity

In addition to flagging a message for follow up, you can set indicators of the message's importance and sensitivity. Like the follow up flag, these settings are mostly advisory in nature—the recipient can simply ignore these settings if he or she prefers.

To change the importance and sensitivity settings for a message, click the Options button to display the Message Options dialog box, shown in Figure 7-10. You can also use the Importance High and Importance Low buttons to quickly make one of those two importance settings.

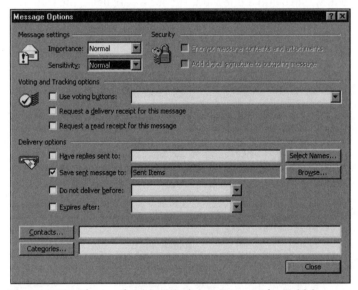

Figure 7-10: Choose the message importance and sensitivity settings in the Message Options dialog box.

Outlook messages can be labeled as low, normal, or high in importance. They can also be labeled as normal, personal, private, or confidential in regards to sensitivity. No matter which of these settings you choose, your messages probably won't receive any special handling from the mail system—you'll have to depend on the recipient to follow your wishes in handling the message.

Creating an auto signature

A *signature* is a tagline that Outlook adds to your outgoing messages. Your signature can include information such as your mailing address, phone number, job title, or any other bits and pieces that you want to include with each message. Once you create and tell Outlook to use a signature, that same information will automatically be included with your messages so that you won't have to type it in every time you create a new message.

Caution   Make certain you only include information in your signature that you want every-one to see. If you don't want every e-mail recipient to know your home address, then don't include that information in your signature (or create a second, optional signature with different information).

To create a signature, follow these steps:

1. Select Tools ➪ Options to display the Options dialog box. Once you have created a signature, you'll use this dialog box to select a default signature to use with each new e-mail message.

2. Click the Mail Format tab, shown in Figure 7-11.

Figure 7-11: Use the Mail Format tab to set up your signature.

3. Click the Signature Picker button to display the Signature Picker dialog box, shown in Figure 7-12. If you have any existing signatures, they will be listed in the Signature list box, and a preview of the selected signature will be shown in the Preview box.

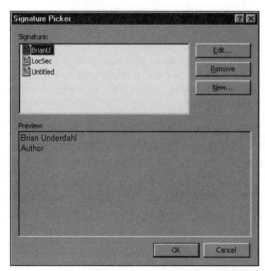

Figure 7-12: Use the Signature Picker dialog box
to preview any existing signatures.

4. Click the New button to begin creating a new signature. This will display the
   Create New Signature dialog box.

5. Type a descriptive name for your signature in the *Enter a name for your new
   signature* text box, shown in Figure 7-13. This name should be descriptive
   enough so that you'll easily be able to identify which signature you are
   selecting when you later choose a default signature. The name you enter
   here won't appear in your e-mail messages — it's simply to help you identify
   a particular signature.

Figure 7-13: Enter a descriptive name so
you'll be able to easily choose a signature later.

6. Choose one of the radio buttons to specify whether you want to begin a totally new signature or if you'd rather base it upon an existing signature or other file. For now choose the *Start with a blank signature* radio button.

7. Click Next to continue.

8. Type the signature text shown in Figure 7-14.

Figure 7-14: Enter the text that you want included with each of your e-mail messages.

9. To change the font options for the signature, click the Font button to display the Font dialog box. Remember, though, that any font selections you choose will have no effect if you create a plain text message or if the message recipient is unable to read the formatting.

10. Click the OK button to close the Font dialog box after you've made any changes to the font settings.

11. Click the Paragraph button to display the Paragraph dialog box. In this dialog box, you can select the alignment options for the signature and you can choose to display the signature as a list of bulleted items.

12. Click the OK button to close the Paragraph dialog box after you've made any changes to the paragraph settings.

13. If you wish to clear out any existing text and start over, click the Clear button.

14. If you want to use Word to create your signature, click the Advanced Edit button. You might want to do this if you wish to use the spell checker to make certain you haven't made any typos.

15. Click the Finish button to return to the Signature Picker dialog box.

16. Click the OK button to return to the Options dialog box. Your new signature will appear in the *Use this signature by default* list box.

17. Click OK to confirm your selection and return to Outlook.

When you have specified a default signature, Outlook automatically appends the signature to new messages that you create. Figure 7-15 shows how Outlook adds the signature automatically when you choose one of the new message options.

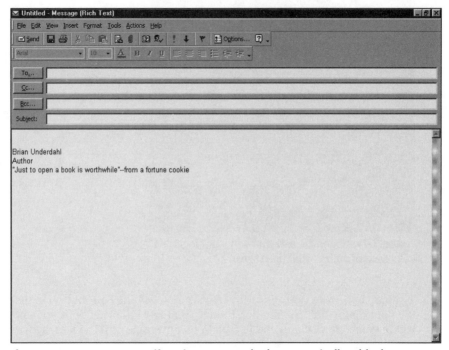

Figure 7-15: Once you specify a signature, Outlook automatically adds that signature to all new messages.

If you like, you can edit the signature that Outlook has added to the new blank message. Creating a signature can save you considerable time when you send e-mail messages, because you don't have to retype the same information for each new message.

Tip   Keep your signature short. It's generally considered poor form to use signature files that are longer than five or six lines.

Using business cards

Outlook enables you to exchange contact information in the form of electronic business cards known as *vCards*. A vCard file is a standard way of exchanging such information over the Internet. Just as a printed business card provides a convenient method of passing along information, vCards make it easy to ensure your message recipients have accurate information about how they may contact you.

Outlook uses records in the Contacts folder to create vCards. If you want to create a vCard file to send along with your messages, you'll have to start by first creating a Contact record for yourself. If you've never created a Contact record, you may wish to refer to Chapter 9 for more information about this process.

To create a vCard file from an existing Contact record, follow these steps:

1. Open the Outlook Contacts folder.

2. Double-click the Contact record you wish to use to open the record.

3. Select File ➪ Export to vCard file.

4. As shown in Figure 7-16, specify a name for the file in the File Name text box. You will normally want to use the same name as the Contact record name, but you can use a more descriptive name if necessary so that you can more easily identify the vCard file.

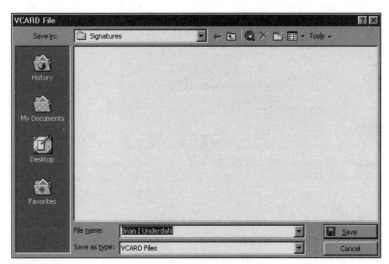

Figure 7-16: Save your vCard file to send it along with messages.

5. Click the Save button to save the file.

6. Click the Close button to close the Contact record.

To attach a vCard file to your messages, you include the vCard as part of your signature. To modify your signature file to include a vCard, follow these steps:

1. Select Tools ➪ Options to open the Options dialog box.

2. Click the Mail Format tab to view the mail format options.

3. Click the Signature Picker button to display the Signature Picker dialog box.

4. Choose the signature file you wish to modify.

5. Click Edit to open the Edit Signature dialog box.

6. Choose the vCard file from the *Attach this business card (vCard) to this signature* drop-down list box, as shown in Figure 7-17.

   If you haven't already created a vCard file, as shown earlier, you can also create a new vCard file by using the *New vCard from Contact* button to create the vCard file now.

Figure 7-17: Select the vCard you wish to include with your signature.

7. Click OK to close the Edit Signature dialog box.

8. Click OK to close the Signature Picker dialog box.

9. Click OK to close the Options dialog box.

Although vCards are a convenient method of distributing your contact information, you probably won't want to automatically include a vCard with each new message. Not only will this increase the size of your messages, but it's also likely to annoy message recipients who receive multiple copies of the same vCard each time they receive one of your messages. It might be better to create a separate signature that includes your vCard file, and then select that signature for use with specific messages rather than as your default signature.

Using stationery

Stationery is a background image that you can use to make your e-mail messages appear as though they were written on a fancy pad of paper. Whether using stationery really adds to the quality of e-mail messages is open to personal interpretation. Some people like the often interesting visual effects, whereas others find that stationery can make messages more difficult to read—especially if the sender isn't careful to select contrasting background and text colors!

Caution
Stationery may look pretty, but it increases the file size of your e-mail messages and takes longer for you to upload them and for recipients to download them.

To create a new message using stationery, follow these steps:

1. Select Actions ⇨ New Mail Message Using ⇨ More Stationery to open the Select a Stationery dialog box, shown in Figure 7-18.

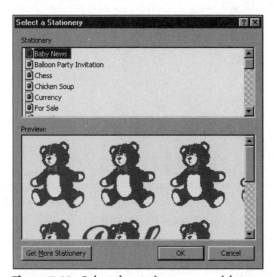

Figure 7-18: Select the stationery you wish to use.

2. Scroll down through the stationery choices until you find the stationery you wish to use.

   You'll likely find several stationery choices that display the message *Stationery not installed yet. It will be installed when you compose mail.* If you wish to choose one of these options, you will need to have your Outlook 2000 CD-ROM available so that your selection can be copied to your hard disk.

3. If the choices shown in the Select a Stationery dialog box don't quite fit your needs, you can click the Get More Stationery button to visit the Office 2000 Web site. There you'll find additional stationery options that you can download.

4. Click the OK button to close the dialog box and begin creating a new message using your selected stationery. Figure 7-19 shows an example of using stationery.

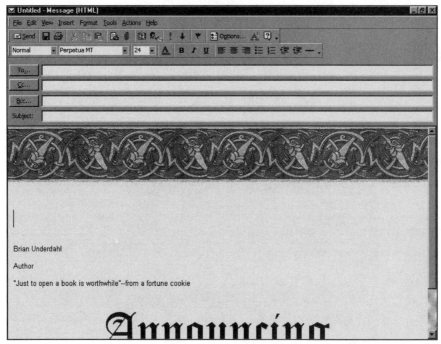

Figure 7-19: The stationery you select will appear as a background image in your message.

Tip   Make certain the text of your message stands out — especially if the stationery you choose uses a dark background. It may be necessary to change the text color and size to make sure your message is readable.

Attaching Files

As fancy as a rich text or HTML message may appear, all the e-mail message enhancements discussed so far in this chapter have really done little other than improve the appearance of the message text. Changing the font or adding a background image doesn't increase the functionality of your messages. For that, you need something that's just a bit more practical.

Attaching a file to a message enables the message to carry a lot more than a simple text note. Rather than trying to describe the view out your office window, you could attach a digital image that shows the view. In place of telling someone where they could find the latest version of a shareware program, you could attach a copy of the program file so that the message recipient would be sure to get the correct program. Instead of sending a complex word processing document through the mail on a disk, you could attach the document file to a message to deliver the file immediately. These are just some of the ways that file attachments can make your e-mail messages more effective.

A few mail systems will not accept e-mail messages that include attachments. But even those that do accept message attachments often limit the overall size of messages. Because of the way messages must be encoded for sending over the Internet, these message size limitations generally prevent you from sending a message that is more than about two-thirds the stated message size limit. Therefore, if someone's mail system rejects messages over 2MB in size, you probably won't be able to successfully send messages that exceed about 1.3MB.

Attaching files while composing a message

When you send a file attachment along with a message, the recipient receives a single e-mail message that consists of both your message text and the file that you attached. Each file attachment is, however, kept separate from the text and from any other attachments. This enables the recipient to open or save the attachment just as he or she would if you handed him or her a disk containing the file.

Although plain text e-mail messages pose no threat to your system, files that are attached to a message could be dangerous. If you aren't completely sure of the source of e-mail file attachments, it's best not to open those attachments. You may also wish to save any attachments in a special folder and then use a virus scanner to check for computer viruses before opening the files.

To include file attachments with an e-mail message, follow these steps:

1. Open a new message by clicking the New Mail Message button (or by using any of the other Outlook new mail message options).

2. Address and compose your message as you would any other message.

3. Select Insert ⇨ File (or click the Insert File button) as shown in Figure 7-20.

   Selecting Insert ⇨ Item will attach another message to your new message, whereas selecting Insert ⇨ Object will add an object into the body of your message rather than as a separate attachment.

4. As shown in Figure 7-21, choose the file you wish to attach. You may need to search in the Look in list box to locate the correct folder.

5. Click the Insert button to insert the file into your message.

Insert File button

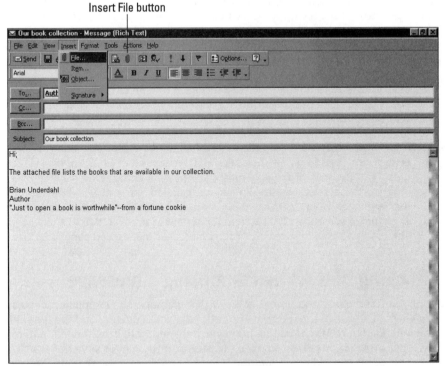

Figure 7-20: You can attach a file to your message by selecting File from the Insert menu or by clicking the Insert File button (the paperclip).

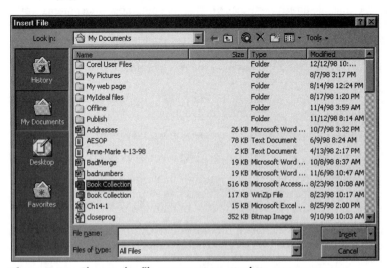

Figure 7-21: Choose the file you want to attach to your message.

Tip   You can also drag and drop file attachments quickly from Windows Explorer (or the Desktop) onto your message window.

You can attach more than one file to the same message, although you should remember that file attachments may greatly increase the overall size of the message. It's often more prudent to send several smaller messages rather than one huge message. That way you'll have far less to resend if a mail delivery problem occurs.

Sending an e-mail message that includes an attachment is no different than sending any other e-mail message. When you click the Send button, Outlook places the message in your Outbox until the next time you connect to the mail server. If the attachments are large, it will take quite a bit longer for the message to be sent to the mail server — especially if you use a slow connection like a modem.

Sending a file while using Microsoft Office

If you're working on a document in one of the Microsoft Office applications, there's no need to switch to Outlook simply because you want to send the document file to someone else. All the Office applications enable you to send the current file as either a message attachment or as the body of the message itself.

In most cases, you'll probably want to send Office documents as file attachments rather than as the message body. Sending the document as a file attachment enables the recipient to open and use the document in the correct Office application. Sending the document as the message body enables the recipient to open and view the message even if he or she does not have Microsoft Office installed on his or her system, but it does not allow the recipient to use the document as if it were the original file. To better understand the differences, consider the case of a complex Excel worksheet that includes numerous formulas along with the data. If you send the worksheet as an attachment, the formulas remain active in the document, and the recipient can add new data and can see the recalculated results. If you send the worksheet as the message body, all the results are static, so any changes the recipient makes won't change the results. On the other hand, the recipient won't need a copy of Excel to view the results, either.

To send an Office document from within an application, follow these steps:

1. Open the document within the application that you used to create the file.

2. Select File ➪ Send To ➪ Mail Recipient, as shown in Figure 7-22.

   You may see additional choices on the File ➪ Send To menu. In the figure, the additional choices provide methods of sending the file as an attachment, routing the file to one or more recipients so several people can collaborate on a project, or sending the file to an Exchange Server folder so that it is available to everyone who has been granted access to the folder.

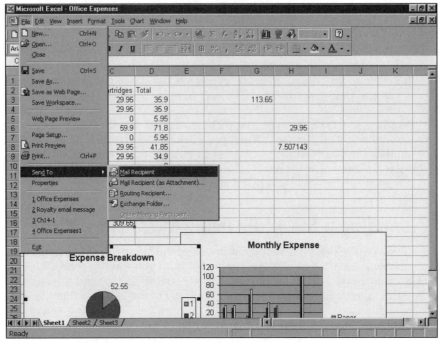

Figure 7-22: Choose the method of sending your file.

3. If you see a message similar to the one shown in Figure 7-23, choose the correct radio button to send the document in the desired format and click OK to continue.

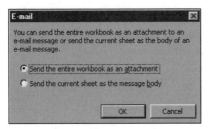

Figure 7-23: Choose the correct message format option to suit your needs.

4. Address your message as you would any other e-mail message. You may also wish to include a brief message so that the recipient understands the purpose of the file you are sending.

5. Click the Send button to place the message in the Outbox.

Messages you send from within an Office application are really no different than messages that you create and send from within Outlook itself. The message recipient will not be able to tell whether you created the message in Outlook and then added an attachment, or if you started in one of the other Office applications and used the File ➪ Send To command. Therefore, you should choose whichever option is most convenient for you.

Organizing Your E-mail

A little organization can go a long way towards making life a lot easier. If your telephone book weren't organized so that the records were in alphabetical order, you probably wouldn't find the book too useful for looking up phone numbers, would you? If the addresses on your street were assigned randomly without being organized into ascending order, making deliveries to your neighborhood would be pretty hard, too. You can probably think of many more examples where a bit of organization really helps out in daily life.

Organizing your e-mail messages can help out a lot, too. You probably don't just place everything that comes into your office into one big pile. It's more likely that you organize the chaos by separating different projects into different folders. That way it's easier to find everything that relates to the Prior Lake project — you don't have to sift through everything from the Lake Tahoe and Lake Hiawatha projects and check out each piece of paper each time. There's no reason you can't apply this same reasoning to your e-mail message organization within Outlook.

Organizing e-mail with personal folders

By default, Outlook places all incoming messages into the Inbox folder. This may work okay at first, but eventually you'll probably find that this causes one little problem — you can't find messages quite as easily as you'd like. Even worse is the likelihood that if you're trying to find all the messages that relate to a particular project you'll inadvertently pass over one or more critical messages.

The easy way around this problem is to create new folders that you use to organize your messages. When a message about a specific project arrives, you can simply move the message to the project folder. In Chapter 8, you'll even learn how you can instruct Outlook to automatically move certain messages as they arrive.

Creating a folder

Creating new folders is easy. If you've used Windows Explorer to create new folders on your computer, you'll find that creating Outlook folders is very similar.

To create a new Outlook folder, follow these steps:

1. Right-click a folder in your Outlook folder list, as shown in Figure 7-24. It's best to right-click the folder that you want as the parent of the new folder, but this is not absolutely necessary.

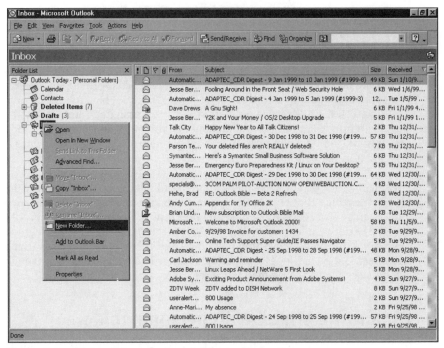

Figure 7-24: Right-click an Outlook folder to display the pop-up menu.

2. Select New Folder from the pop-up menu to display the Create New Folder dialog box.

3. Select the location for the new folder from the *Select where to place the folder* list box. The folder you select will be the parent of the new folder.

4. Select the type of folder content from the *Folder contains* list box. Normally, you'll want to choose Mail Items in this list box because you'll probably be storing messages in the new folder.

5. Enter a name for the folder in the Name text box. The Create New Folder dialog box should now look similar to Figure 7-25.

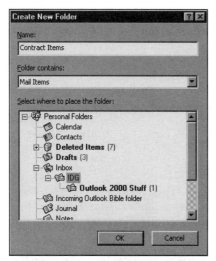

Figure 7-25: Enter the information for the new folder in the Create New Folder dialog box.

6. Click OK to create the new folder.

You can manually move items to your new folder either by right-clicking the item and choosing Move to Folder from the pop-up menu or by dragging and dropping selected items. Messages will retain the same read or unread status when they are moved between folders. If you move messages that you have not yet read, Outlook will show the destination folder in bold. In addition, the number of unread items in each folder is shown just to the right of the folder name in the folder list.

Sharing a folder

Unless you work in total isolation, there are probably times when you need to share documents with other people. You likely already share many of your e-mail messages by forwarding messages or by including certain people in the Cc field of your messages. Outlook provides another option—shared folders.

Shared folders are folders that enable other people to view the contents of the folder. In previous versions of Outlook folder, sharing was pretty limited. You could only share folders on an Exchange Server mail system, and then only with other users on that same system. Outlook 2000 provides a newer form of shared folders that are called *net folders*. These are simply folders that you can share with other Outlook 2000 users regardless of their location.

Note Although Outlook 2000 will seem to allow users of older versions of Outlook to share net folders, in reality everyone must be using Outlook 2000, or they will never see updates to the shared folders. Outlook will only generate *synchronization requests* for Outlook 2000 users, and without these automatic updates, users won't receive new folder items in the shared folder.

To share a folder that you've created, follow these steps:

1. Select the folder in the folder list. You cannot share the Inbox itself, but you can share folders that you have created yourself.

2. Select File ➪ Share ➪ This Folder.

3. You'll use the Net Folder Wizard to set up the sharing of the folder, as shown in Figure 7-26. *Pay special attention to the notice that there is no encryption used to protect the contents of shared folders.* Click Next to continue.

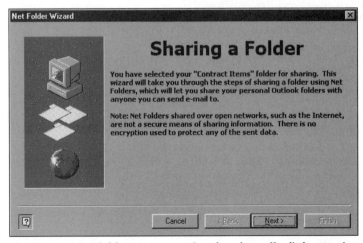

Figure 7-26: Net folders are convenient but they offer little security.

4. Click the Add button to choose the people who will share the net folder. Do not include yourself in the list — you automatically have access to the folder.

5. Click the Permissions button to display the Net Folder Sharing Permissions dialog box, shown in Figure 7-27.

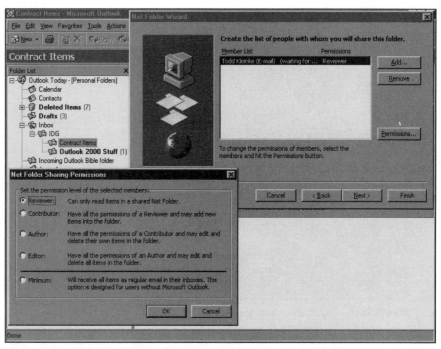

Figure 7-27: Choose what each person can do in the shared folder.

6. Select the permission level for each member. You can set different permission levels for different people.

7. Click OK to return to the Net Folder Wizard.

8. Click the Finish button to finish setting up the net folder.

Once you have created a net folder, Outlook will send out subscription requests to the people you have selected to share the folder. Members must accept the request in order for them to access the shared folder. Depending on the permission level that you set for each member, a member may have complete access to the items in the folder or he or she may be more restricted. Members who have a permission level that enables them to create or modify folder items will have their changes included in the shared folder that all members see.

You may need to adjust the schedule for shared folder updates. To do so, right-click the folder and select Properties. Click the Sharing tab, as shown in Figure 7-28, and choose the new sharing settings.

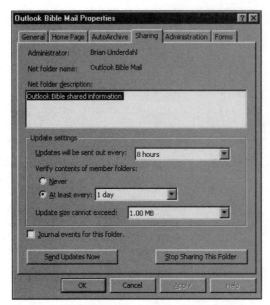

Figure 7-28: Adjust the sharing properties to change the update schedule.

If you need to change the members of the shared folder, select the folder in the folder list and choose File ➪ Share ➪ This Folder to reopen the Net Folder Wizard.

Summary

In this chapter, you learned some e-mail techniques that go beyond the basics of e-mail messages. You learned to use the message format options, how to apply advanced message options, how to send file attachments with your messages, and how to organize your e-mail.

In the next chapter, you'll learn about advanced e-mail concepts that can really make Outlook work for you.

✦   ✦   ✦

Advanced E-mail Concepts

◆　　◆　　◆　　◆

In This Chapter

Using rules to filter
your e-mail

Using certificates

Using faxes

Using distribution lists

Using remote mail

Getting to know
Outlook forms

◆　　◆　　◆　　◆

As powerful and easy to use as Outlook e-mail already
seems, there are a number of advanced tools that we
have not yet covered. You can, for example, set up rules in
Outlook that filter your e-mail messages so those messages from
your boss receive special handling or that automatically send
junk mail directly to the Deleted Items folder. If you have a need
for tight security, you can obtain and use a digital identification
certificate. You can set up Outlook to automatically handle your
faxing needs. You can set up a distribution list to easily send
messages to a specified group of people. For those times when
you may only want to retrieve certain messages and leave all
others on the server, you can use Remote Mail. Finally, you can
customize Outlook using forms. All these topics are covered in
this chapter.

Using Rules

Rules are sets of instructions that you create to tell Outlook
how to handle certain types of messages. Rules are sometimes
called filters, and in fact many famous people use a "bozo
filter" to screen out crank messages that are sent by strange
people. You can set up your own rules to give special handling
to important messages and to send junk mail directly to the
Deleted Items folder without it ever appearing in your Inbox.

You can set up rules for handling both incoming and outgoing
e-mail messages. Most of the time, of course, you'll only
concern yourself with incoming messages. Still, it's nice to
know that you can automate both if necessary.

Although it's really quite easy to set up rules, Outlook has a few
rules that have been set up and are ready to use immediately. In
the following sections, you learn first about setting up rules of
your own and then about how you can use the junk e-mail lists
that are built into Outlook.

Junk mail — or *spam,* as it is generally called — can be a major headache for anyone who has an e-mail account. If you want to control junk mail, you may be tempted to respond to the junk mailers — especially if the junk mail includes a notice that you can be removed from their mailing list by responding to a specific e-mail address using the word "REMOVE" (or something similar) in the subject line. Don't ever fall for this — it's one of the oldest tricks in the junk mailer's bag of tricks. Responding in any way to junk mail simply confirms that your e-mail address is valid and is almost certain to land you on even more junk mail lists. Use Outlook rules to trash the junk mail and you can just ignore it!

Using the Rules Wizard

Outlook provides a *Rules Wizard* to help you set up your own rules for handling e-mail messages. This Rules Wizard steps you through the entire process so that creating or modifying rules is really simple and straightforward.

To use the Rules Wizard to set up an e-mail message-handling rule, follow these steps:

1. Select Tools ➪ Rules Wizard. This will display the Rules Wizard dialog box.

2. Click the New button to begin creating a new rule.

3. Select the general type of rule from the *Which type of rule do you want to create?* list box, shown in Figure 8-1. As you select different types of rules, the description box provides a brief description of the rule.

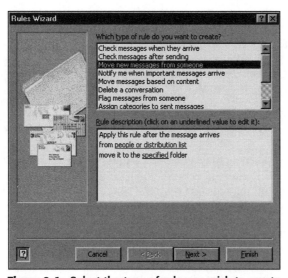

Figure 8-1: Select the type of rule you wish to create.

4. Click Next to continue.

5. Scroll through the *Which condition(s) do you want to check?* list box and choose the items that you want to apply to this rule.

Keep in mind that all the conditions that you choose must be met before the rule will be applied. If you were to choose both the *where my name is in the To box* and the *where my name is in the Cc box*, for example, the rule would only apply if your name were in both the To and the Cc boxes. The more conditions you specify, the less likely it is that any message will meet the full set of conditions. It's generally better to set as few conditions as possible — you can always go back later and add additional conditions if you discover that the rule is too broad.

6. Once you have applied all the necessary conditions to the rule, click each of the underlined items in the Rule description list box in turn. This will enable you to edit the item, as shown in Figure 8-2.

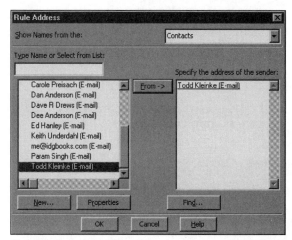

Figure 8-2: Select the values (names) to replace each underlined item in your rule at a time.

7. The choices you must make will vary depending on the type of value you are editing. To get to the dialog box shown in Figure 8-2, the underlined value called "people or distribution list" shown in Figure 8-1 was clicked. Select the names of the message senders and click the From button. When you have selected all the items for the selected value, click OK to continue.

8. If there are additional underlined items, click each in turn and choose the values. When you have completed your selections, the Rules Wizard dialog box should look something like Figure 8-3, with no remaining underlined items that need to be specified.

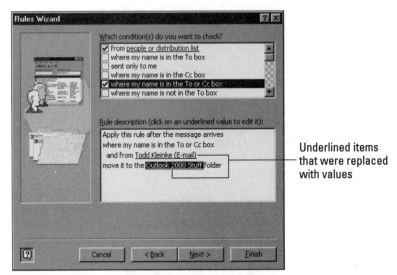

Underlined items
that were replaced
with values

Figure 8-3: Make certain that you have specified the
values for all underlined items before continuing.

9. Click the Next button to continue.

10. Choose any additional actions for this rule from the *What do you want to do
with the message?* list box, as shown in Figure 8-4.

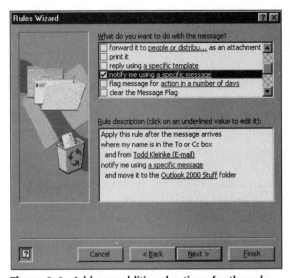

Figure 8-4: Add any additional actions for the rule.

11. Notice that specifying additional actions generally adds additional underlined items to the Rule description list box. Click the new underlined items to edit them, as shown in Figure 8-5. In this figure, the underlined item labeled "a specific message" is being replaced with the actual message that you want to appear. Click OK when you are done specifying the text in the Notification Message dialog box.

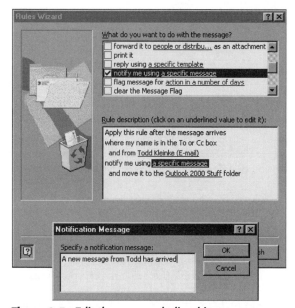

Figure 8-5: Edit the new underlined items.

12. Click the Next button in the wizard to continue.

13. If necessary, select any exceptions to the rule using the options in the *Add any exceptions (if necessary)* list box. If you add exceptions, you may need to edit additional underlined items that appear in the Rule description list box.

14. Click the Next button to continue.

15. Enter a descriptive name in the *Please specify a name for this rule* text box. The name you enter should clearly identify the rule — especially if you plan on specifying a number of rules in the future.

16. If you want to apply the new rule to existing messages, select the *Run this rule now on messages already in "Inbox"* checkbox. Selecting this option is a good way to check the operation of your new rule.

17. Make certain the *Turn on this rule* checkbox is selected. You can deselect this checkbox if you don't want the rule to apply immediately, but you'll have to remember to apply the rule later. The Rules Wizard dialog box should now look something like Figure 8-6.

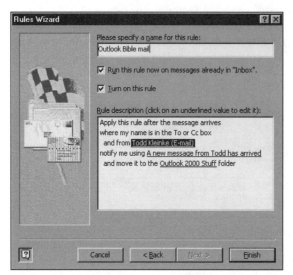

Figure 8-6: Verify that the rule description appears to be correct.

18. Click the Finish button to complete the creation of your new rule.

19. Click OK to close the Rules Wizard dialog box.

If you set up a number of rules for handling your messages, you may discover that some of those rules conflict with each other. As an example, consider what would happen if you set up a rule that displayed a special message telling you that an important message had arrived whenever someone marked their message as important. In addition, suppose you decided that you wanted to forward all incoming messages from your former girlfriend to your attorney without reading them yourself. If your former girlfriend marked her messages as important, which rule would apply? The answer is simple—Outlook applies rules starting at the top of the list of rules as they appear in the Rules Wizard dialog box. To change the order in which the rules are applied, you can use the Move Up and Move Down buttons in the Rules Wizard dialog box.

Keep in mind that more than one rule can apply to the same message. If the rule notifying you of important messages appears before the rule forwarding your ex-spouse's messages to the attorney, both rules would likely be triggered by messages she sends to you. If you move the forwarding rule up above the important message notification rule, then the message would be forwarded before the important message notification rule could be applied.

Using the junk e-mail list

Because junk e-mail is such a common problem, Outlook already has rules in place to handle junk mail. You simply have to turn those rules on to begin using them.

Outlook actually defines two classes of junk e-mail messages — junk messages and adult content messages. In both cases, those classes of messages are defined by keywords that Outlook looks for in the messages. Microsoft does not specify what keywords are used to identify junk messages and adult content messages, because this would make it easier for senders to circumvent Outlook's junk e-mail rules. You should note, however, that no keyword search could identify all junk and adult content messages. It is possible for some of these types of messages to slip through even if you have applied the rules.

Because no simple keyword search can be 100% effective, Outlook can also maintain lists of people who send junk or adult content e-mail messages. By adding someone to one of these lists, you are telling Outlook to apply the junk or adult content e-mail message rules to all messages that you receive from that person — whether those messages include the keywords or not.

The Outlook junk or adult content e-mail message lists are not used unless you specifically turn these features on. To begin using these features, follow these steps:

1. Select Tools ➪ Organize (or click the Organize button on the Outlook toolbar) to display the Inbox organizer.

2. Click the Junk E-Mail item at the bottom of the list of organizer tools, as shown in Figure 8-7.

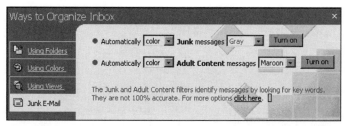

Figure 8-7: Use the Inbox organizer to turn on the junk or adult-content e-mail filters.

3. Select either *color* or *move* from the action list box for each of the two categories.

4. Select the color or the destination for the selected category.

   If you selected a destination folder other than Deleted Items, you will have to specify the location of the folder. If the folder does not exist, Outlook will create the folder for you.

5. Click the Turn on button to apply the rule. Figure 8-8 shows the Inbox organizer with junk messages set to be sent to the Deleted Items folder.

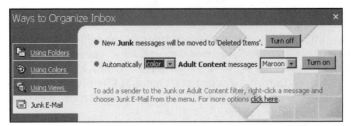

Figure 8-8: Click the Turn on button to apply a rule and the Turn off button to deactivate it.

6. Click the Organize button to close the Inbox organizer.

7. To add someone to the junk or adult content e-mail message lists, select a message from that person and choose Actions ➪ Junk E-mail ➪ Add to Junk Senders List.

Once you have specifically added someone to either the junk or adult content e-mail message lists, all messages they send to you will be handled according to the rules you have specified. To remove someone from one of those lists, follow these steps:

1. Click the Organize button to again display the Inbox organizer.

2. Click the Junk E-Mail item.

3. Click the underlined *click here* link.

4. Click either *Edit Junk Senders* or *Edit Adult Content Senders* to display the appropriate list. In Figure 8-9, the Edit Junk Senders dialog box is displayed.

Figure 8-9: Edit the junk or adult content e-mail message lists to add or remove people from the list.

5. Add, edit, or delete items from the list as necessary.

6. Click OK to continue.

7. Click the Organize button to close the Inbox organizer.

Caution   All messages from someone that you add to the junk or adult content e-mail messages lists will be treated the same regardless of their content. If someone only occasionally sends you offensive messages, you may find that it is more effective to use the Rules Wizard to create a special filter that applies to messages from that person.

Using Certificates

Certificates — or digital IDs — are a form of digital identification that you can use to send and receive secure e-mail messages. When you obtain and use a digital ID, message recipients can verify messages that they receive with your name on them are actually from you. In addition, if someone sends you their digital ID, you can send securely encrypted messages that only your intended recipient will be able to read.

Note   As of this writing, the United States prohibits the export of truly secure forms of encryption. By federal law, American companies cannot export encryption products that use over 40-bits of encryption, because they are classified as munitions. For domestic purposes, however, 128-bit encryption is commonly used. Each extra bit of encryption doubles the effort required to break a message's encryption, so if you really need to be certain that your messages are secure, you will definitely want to select domestic rather than export encryption levels when you have the option.

To obtain a digital ID, follow these steps:

1. Select Tools ➪ Options to display the Options dialog box.
2. Click the Security tab, shown in Figure 8-10.
3. Click the *Get a Digital ID* button to connect to the Internet and choose a certificate authority.
4. Follow the instructions you see on your screen for supplying the necessary information and obtaining your certificate. The exact procedures will vary according to which of the certificate authorities you select.
5. Once the certificate has been sent to your computer, you can install the certificate and begin using it.

After your certificate has been issued, you should again open the Security tab of the Options dialog box. Click the *Setup Secure E-Mail* button to display the Change Security Settings dialog box. Enter a descriptive name for your security settings and click the Choose button next to the type of security you want to use. For example, if you want to use a digital signature to positively identify your e-mail messages, click the Choose button next to the Signing Certificate text box. Figure 8-11 shows the Change Security Settings dialog box after a typical certificate has been obtained and installed.

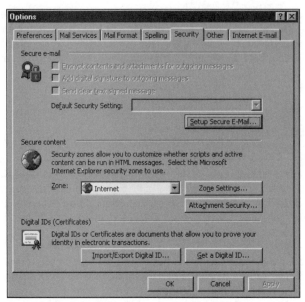

Figure 8-10: Use the Options dialog box Security tab to obtain a digital ID and set up secure e-mail.

Figure 8-11: Set up your secure e-mail options after your certificate has been issued.

Tip If you use more than one PC, you can share the same certificate between those systems. Use the *Import/Export Digital ID* button on the Security tab of the Options dialog box to export the certificate to a password-protected file that you can later import to your other computer.

To use message encryption, you will need to know the message recipient's digital ID. To send your digital ID so that someone can send you an encrypted message, make certain the *Add digital signature to outgoing messages* checkbox on the Security tab of the Options dialog box is selected. You must exchange messages that include digital IDs before you can send encrypted messages.

Using the Faxing Service

Long before e-mail became a popular method of sending messages, faxing made it possible for people to send messages virtually instantly over ordinary telephone lines. Faxes remain a common form of communication even in today's connected world. One reason for this is simple — you don't need a computer or even access to the Internet to send a fax.

Outlook has two different faxing options. The one that is available to you depends on the e-mail configuration that you have selected. If you choose the Internet Only e-mail option, you have to use the Symantec Fax Starter Edition faxing option. If you choose the Corporate or Workgroup e-mail option, you can use Microsoft Fax as your faxing service. Both types of fax service provide similar functions. The following discussions will show how to use Microsoft Fax — if you use Symantec Fax Starter Edition, you'll find the options are quite similar. To learn more about choosing your e-mail configuration, see Chapter 4.

Sending and receiving faxes

Virtually all modern modems also incorporate the capability to send and receive faxes. To your modem there is really very little difference between making a call to another computer or to a fax machine.

When you install a fax service such as Microsoft Fax, the fax service shows up as a new printer that is installed on your system. To send a fax, follow these steps:

1. Prepare your document and then choose Microsoft Fax (or Symantec Fax) from the Print dialog box, shown in Figure 8-12. In most applications, you can display the dialog box by selecting File ➪ Print.

2. Click the OK button to "print" your fax. You'll then see a few additional dialog boxes that step you through the process of preparing to send a fax.

3. If necessary, select your location and click Next.

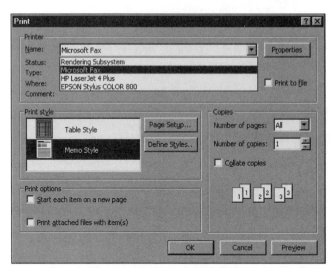

Figure 8-12: Choose Microsoft Fax as the printer to send a fax.

4. Enter the name and fax number of the recipient. You can send multiple copies of the same fax by specifying several recipients. If you have stored fax numbers in your Outlook Contacts list or a personal address book, you can click the Address Book button to select the recipients.

5. If you want to include a cover page, select it as shown in Figure 8-13. Cover pages may not be necessary for documents that include all necessary routing information such as a letter that you have prepared in Word, but they can be very important if the document you are faxing could be difficult to understand on its own.

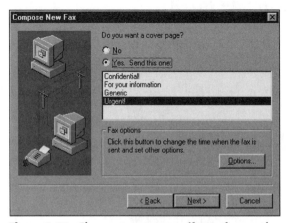

Figure 8-13: Choose a cover page if your fax needs one.

6. Click the Options button to display the Send Options for this Message dialog box, shown in Figure 8-14. You can use this dialog box to select when the fax will be sent and the message format.

The message format is especially important if you are sending a fax to a computer rather than to a standard fax machine. If you click the *Editable, if possible* radio button and the receiving system is a computer running compatible faxing software, your document will be sent as a document file rather than as a fax image file. This will allow the fax recipient to open and edit the document if they have the correct software for that document type. If you do not want the recipient to be able to edit the document, select *Not editable* so that the message is sent as a fax image — just as if it had been sent from a standard fax machine.

Figure 8-14: Choose the options for sending your fax.

7. Click OK to close the Send Options for this Message dialog box.

8. Click Next to continue.

9. Enter a subject and any cover page notes that you would like to include.

10. Click Next to continue.

11. Click the Finish button to send your fax. If you chose to defer the fax for later, your fax will wait until the time you specified it to be sent. Otherwise, the fax will be processed and sent in a few moments. Processing a fax message may take some time — especially for large and complex documents.

Caution   Whenever you change printers—such as when you send a fax—the new printer will generally remain selected. The next time you attempt to print a document, you may discover that your computer will try to initiate another fax. It's always a good idea to check your printer selection after you've sent a fax and reselect your standard printer if necessary.

Receiving a fax using an Outlook fax service is almost as easy as receiving an e-mail message. When an incoming fax arrives, Outlook will treat the fax as if it were an incoming e-mail message. The fax will appear in the Inbox as a new unread message that you can open like any other message.

Setting faxing options

Using the fax service to send or receive faxes is pretty simple. You may, however, need to set certain fax options to make the fax service work just the way you want.

For example, to receive incoming faxes successfully, remember the following important points:

✦ Outlook must be running in order to receive a fax.

✦ The fax service must be configured correctly to receive an incoming fax. Select Tools ➪ Services to display the Services dialog box. Double-click the fax service to display its Properties dialog box. Click the Modem tab and choose Properties to set the answer mode options.

✦ If you need to share the fax line with voice calls, don't set the fax service to automatically answer incoming calls. Use the manual option to display a dialog box so that you can choose to answer the call as a fax or as a voice call.

✦ If you want to be able to receive faxes when you aren't at the computer, set the fax service to automatically answer incoming calls.

To learn more about setting the fax service options, see Chapter 4.

Using Distribution Lists

If you ever work on projects that include a number of different people, you'll easily be able to appreciate the purpose of *distribution lists*. A distribution list is a group of people that you specify as the recipients of certain messages or meeting requests. What sets a distribution list apart from simply choosing the recipients when you send the message is that you create and name a distribution list in advance, and then you select the distribution list rather than the individuals when you address the message.

Have you ever prepared a message that you wanted to send to a number of different people and then later discovered that you forgot to address the message to one of the intended recipients? That is something that is very easy to do — especially if there are a large number of people who should be receiving the message. A distribution list is the easy answer to eliminating that problem.

Note   Outlook normally treats a distribution list as if it were a single address. In a few instances, however, it becomes necessary to split out the individuals within the list. For example, if you wish to check the availability of potential meeting participants who are part of a distribution list, Outlook must break down the distribution list into its individual members. Once Outlook breaks down a distribution list in this manner, all further processing of the meeting request (or any other type of message) must be done on an individual basis.

Creating a distribution list

You can create multiple distribution lists that serve different purposes. If necessary, some of the same people may show up in more than one of your lists. You might, for example, create a distribution list that includes all the department managers, another that includes the inside sales staff, another for the customer service department, and so on. In addition to these individual lists, you might have another distribution list that includes all of the employees. When you send out an important message, you could simply choose the correct distribution list to make certain that the correct group would receive the message.

To create a distribution list, follow these steps:

1. Select File ⇨ New ⇨ Distribution List. You can also click the down arrow at the right edge of the New button and select Distribution List from the drop-down menu.

2. Enter a descriptive name for the distribution list in the Name text box.

3. Click the Select Members button to display the Select Members dialog box.

4. Select each member from the left list and click the Add button to add them to the distribution list on the right, as shown in Figure 8-15.

5. Click OK to close the Select Members dialog box. The Distribution List dialog box should now look something like Figure 8-16.

6. If you need to add additional distribution list members, click the Add New button and enter the required information in the Add New Member dialog box. You might use this option to add new distribution list members who you did not want to add to your contacts list.

7. If you need to remove someone from the list, select the name in the list and click the Remove button. Outlook does not ask for confirmation before deleting the selected entry.

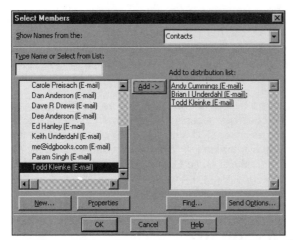

Figure 8-15: Select the members of your distribution list.

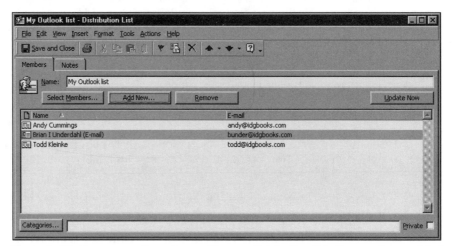

Figure 8-16: You can continue to modify your distribution list after you have added members.

8. Click the Categories button if you want to assign this distribution list to an Outlook category. You might want to use this option to help organize your contacts.

9. If you want to add notes about the distribution list, click the Notes tab and enter your comments there.

10. Click the Save and Close button to save your distribution list and close the dialog box.

Using a distribution list

A distribution list makes sending messages to a group of people very easy, and it all but eliminates the problem of forgetting to include someone in the message distribution. You simply choose the correct distribution list, and all members of that list automatically are included.

To use a distribution list to address a new message, follow these steps:

1. Begin a new message as you normally would—by clicking the New Mail Message button, for example.

2. Click the To button to open the Select Names dialog box.

3. Select the distribution list (shown in bold) and click the To button, as shown in Figure 8-17. You can add additional message recipients if necessary.

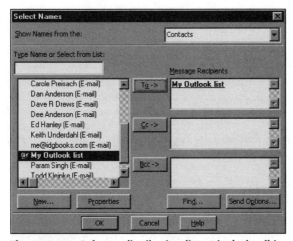

Figure 8-17: Select a distribution list to include all its members as message recipients.

4. Click OK to close the Select Names dialog box.

5. Complete your message and click the Send button.

Caution

When you send a message using a distribution list, Outlook expands the list and shows each recipient's address in the message header. If some of the message recipients do not wish their e-mail address to be known to the other message recipients, it would be better to send the message to those recipients privately or to use the Bcc address box for their e-mail address. Outlook does not provide a method of suppressing the recipient list directly.

Using Remote Mail

Outlook normally handles e-mail messages in a rather straightforward manner. Whenever Outlook connects to the mail server, any messages that are in your Outbox are sent to the mail server, and any incoming messages are downloaded and then deleted from the mail server. This routine ensures that your mail server is not overloaded with old messages that you have already downloaded, and that there will be room for new messages as they arrive.

There may be times, however, when this normal routine doesn't quite meet your needs. Suppose, for example, that you must take a business trip while you are waiting for an important e-mail message from one of your customers. You need to respond to that message as quickly as possible, so you take along your laptop computer so that you can log in and check your messages on the road. Because you'll have to dial a long-distance number to access your ISP, you'd rather not bother downloading the 50 other messages that may arrive in your mailbox in addition to the one important message. Those messages can wait until you return home. How can you download the one important message and ignore those others?

The answer is to use *Remote Mail* — a set of Outlook tools that enable you to find out what messages are available and then send and receive just the ones you want. Remote Mail connects to the mail server, downloads the message *headers* — the information about the sender and subject of each message, and then disconnects so that you can make your decisions about which messages to retrieve offline. After you have marked the messages you wish to retrieve, you can reconnect to the mail server and download just those messages you marked, leaving the remaining messages on the server for later retrieval.

Connecting and downloading headers

Using Remote Mail is a little different than using the normal Outlook mail services. When you use Remote Mail, you first connect, download the message headers, mark the messages you want to retrieve, and then connect again to download the actual messages. You can work with Remote Mail using Outlook's menus, but it's usually a bit easier to display the Remote Mail toolbar while you're working with Remote Mail.

To use Remote Mail, follow these steps:

1. Select Tools ➪ Remote Mail ➪ Remote Tools to display the Remote Mail toolbar (you must be in a mail folder to do this).

2. Click the Connect button to display the Remote Connection Wizard, shown in Figure 8-18.

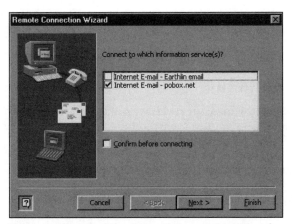

Figure 8-18: Open the Remote Connection Wizard and select the mail server.

3. In this case, two information services are set up on the system. Make certain that the correct mail server is selected by placing a check in the checkbox for any information service that you need to check.

4. Click Next to continue.

5. Select which actions you want Remote Mail to perform when it connects to the selected service. As Figure 8-19 shows, you can choose to retrieve new message headers and which messages you wish to send.

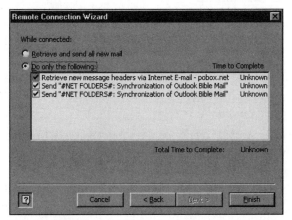

Figure 8-19: Choose the actions you want Remote Mail to perform.

6. Click the Finish button to complete the selected tasks. Remote Mail will connect to the mail server, download the message headers, and send the messages as you instructed.

Marking items for action

Once you have downloaded the message headers, you can decide what you want to do about each of the messages. You use the Remote Mail tools to *mark* message headers to indicate the desired action.

To mark and process the message headers, follow these steps:

1. If any message headers were on the server, Outlook will show the items in the Inbox. Double-click the item you wish to retrieve to display the Remote Item Header dialog box, shown in Figure 8-20. Alternatively, you can use the buttons on the Remote Mail toolbar to mark items for action.

Figure 8-20: Choose how you wish to handle the messages that Remote Mail found on the server.

2. Select the action you want Remote Mail to perform on the selected item:

- Select *Mark to retrieve this item* to retrieve the message and delete it from the mail server.

- Select *Mark to retrieve a copy of this item* to retrieve the message and leave the original on the mail server.

- Select *Mark to delete this item from the server* to delete the message from the mail server without retrieving it.

- Select *Unmark this item* to remove any marks you've added to the item. This will leave the item on the mail server.

3. Click the Connect button to again display the Remote Connection Wizard.

4. Make certain the correct mail service is selected.

5. Verify that the correct actions are selected.

6. Click Finish to connect and download the selected messages.

Once you have downloaded the messages that you marked to retrieve, those messages will appear in your Inbox just as they would if you had clicked the Send/Receive button. Outlook will remove the message headers that you marked and replace them with the actual messages.

Summary

This chapter has covered a lot of ground. First, you learned how to use rules to filter your e-mail messages. Next, you saw how to make your messages secure by using digital IDs to verify your identity. You learned how to use the Outlook fax services and how to create distribution lists so you can send a single message to a group of people. Finally, you learned how to use Remote Mail to manage your e-mail messages when it might not be convenient to use the shotgun approach.

The next chapter heads off in a different direction—there you learn all you need to know about using Outlook as a contact manager. You'll never have another good excuse for not having someone's e-mail address or for forgetting your sister's birthday!

✦　　✦　　✦

Microsoft Outlook 2000 as a Personal Information Manager

Microsoft Outlook is far more than a simple e-mail program. In Part III, you learn to use Outlook as a personal information manager so that you can get far more done with less effort. You see how you can use Outlook to maintain your address book, your schedule, and your to-do list. You see how Outlook automatically keeps track of your activities and provides you with electronic "sticky notes." Finally, you learn how to use Outlook to keep up with Internet newsgroups.

Managing Your Contacts

If you have used Outlook primarily as an e-mail program, then you have missed much of what makes Outlook so useful and powerful. Outlook is also a great manager of contacts — Outlook can help you keep track of all of those addresses, phone numbers, Web sites, and various other bits of information that you need constantly. Using Outlook to keep a record of all that information easily beats the old "write it on the back of the business card" method that passes for organization on far too many desktops.

Using Outlook to track your contacts doesn't have to be an all-or-nothing affair. If you have a tattered old address book, there's no reason you can't continue to use it while you gradually add people to your Outlook Contacts list. You can even start by just adding e-mail addresses as you send and receive messages. Of course, to get the full benefit of Outlook's contact management capabilities, you'll want to begin storing your contact information in Outlook as soon as possible. This chapter shows you how to use the Outlook Contacts list — once you see how easy and useful this is, you can proceed at your own pace.

An Overview of Contacts

People often think of contacts in a business context, but there's no reason why your definition has to be that narrow. In addition to business contacts, you probably keep in touch with both family and friends. Keeping track of address and phone number changes for those people is just as much a chore as is the task of keeping track of that information for your business associates. In fact, you likely keep track of even more information about family and friends than you do for business contacts. Who can remember all those birthdays and anniversaries without ever making a mistake?

Note Outlook has the capability to work with the older Windows Address Book (also called Personal Address Book) in addition to the Contacts list that is built into Outlook. The Contacts list has many more capabilities for managing your contacts than do the Address Books, so only the Contacts list will be covered in this chapter. You may wish to use the File ⇨ Import and Export command to import your old Address Book into the Outlook Contacts list before continuing with this chapter.

What are contacts?

Just what are *contacts*, anyway? In the context of Outlook, contacts are essentially the records that you keep about people. Figure 9-1 shows a typical Outlook contact card that records some of the types of information that you might keep on someone.

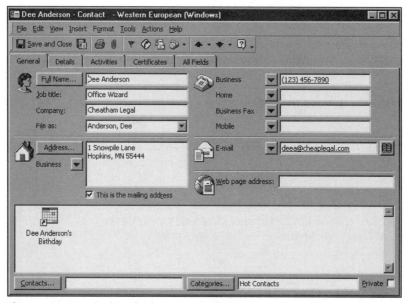

Figure 9-1: A typical Outlook contact includes a number of pieces of useful information about someone.

If you have trouble thinking of a contact as the information that you know about someone, it might be a little easier to think about how Windows deals with *objects*. Almost everything you see in a Windows program can be considered an object. A simple text box is an example of an object that you've dealt with numerous times. That simple object — the text box — has *properties* that define the object. A text box might have a font property that describes the font that is used to display information in the text box. It might also have other properties such as size, color, and so on. You aren't normally made aware of those properties, but the information that makes up those properties is what makes the object useful. The same applies to your contacts—the information you know about someone such as their name, phone number, e-mail address, and so on is how you define that person. If you don't have any information about someone, you have no way to define them.

What are the new Outlook contact features?

With each new version, Outlook has added a number of new features that make the program more powerful and easier to use. To get the most out of the contact-related features in this latest version of Outlook, it will be handy to have a quick look at what's new. Here's a brief synopsis of what's new about managing your contacts in Outlook:

✦ *Address mapping* displays a map that shows where a contact is located within the United States. This feature uses the Internet to access the Microsoft Expedia Web site when you click the *Display Map of Address* button while you have a contact open. At this Web site, you'll have the option to get driving directions to the contact's location or current local weather conditions, or to print a copy of the map.

✦ *Contact activity tracking* helps you keep track of all e-mail, tasks, appointments, Journal entries, and documents related to a contact. If you add someone's birthday or an appointment with them to your Outlook Calendar, that information will also show up in their contact information card. This makes it much easier to find all the information that relates to someone, because it is all linked together.

✦ *Distribution lists* can be customized so that it is easier to send messages or schedule events that involve groups of people. You'll find this feature greatly reduces the work and possibility of errors when you need to make certain that a number of people are kept informed about projects or events.

✦ *Enhanced mail merge* helps you to create more powerful mail merge lists by allowing you to use a filtered list that is a subset of your Contacts list. This makes possible for you to use the information in your Contacts list more effectively so that you can keep all of your contact information in one place.

✦ *Merge contact information* helps you maintain your contacts by checking to see if a new contact you add might be a duplicate. If a new contact is a duplicate, you have the option to automatically merge the new information with the existing contact entry. This is especially useful if you currently have contact information in several different formats and want to bring all your contacts together in the Outlook Contacts list for easier management.

✦ *QuickFind contact* makes it much easier to locate a contact from anywhere in Outlook. The Outlook toolbar now includes a handy *Find a Contact* text box that you can use to find people even if you don't know their complete name. Outlook will find the closest matches for what you do know so you can quickly choose the correct contact.

✦ *vCards* are the electronic versions of business cards you can use to send contact information over the Internet. You can attach a vCard in your outgoing e-mail messages so that people you correspond with always have your correct contact information.

Although each of these new or enhanced features is contact related, some of them really add most of their utility to other areas of using Outlook. For example, vCards are most often used as attachments to e-mail messages and were covered in Chapter 7. Distribution lists are also used very effectively when sending e-mail messages, so they were covered in Chapter 8. Mail merging is covered in Chapter 18. The remaining new contact-related features are discussed at various points in this chapter.

Viewing Your Contacts

The Outlook Contacts folder enables you to easily create, view, or modify your contacts. As Figure 9-2 shows, you have several options for viewing the Contacts folder. The default view — Address Cards — represents a pretty good compromise between showing just enough information to be useful and showing so much information that you are constantly scrolling in an attempt to locate people.

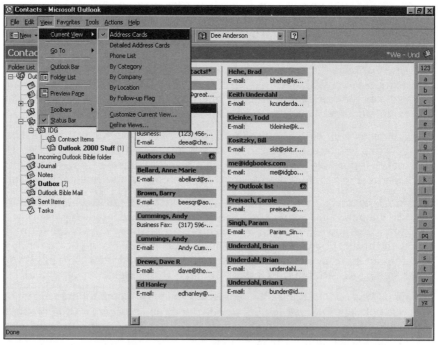

Figure 9-2: The Contacts folder provides easy access to all your contacts.

Regardless of the view you select for the Contacts folder, Outlook uses a standard form to display the detailed information about each of your contacts. In the following sections, you learn how to use each part of the Contact form to manage your contacts.

Understanding the General tab

The Contact form has a number of parts — too many to view on a single screen. In these sections, you learn about the elements of the General tab of the Contact form, shown in Figure 9-3. To display this tab, double-click one of the entries in your Contacts folder. The General tab is displayed by default.

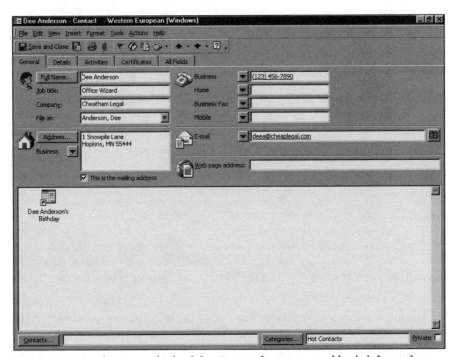

Figure 9-3: Use the General tab of the Contact form to record basic information about your contacts.

Name options

The first piece of information that you're likely to enter about any of your contacts is their name. Contact records would, after all, be pretty useless without including the person's name.

Outlook uses the information that you type in the Full Name and Company text boxes to create the range of entries that are available in the File as list box. As Figure 9-4 shows, you have several options to select from once you have entered both a name and a company for the contact.

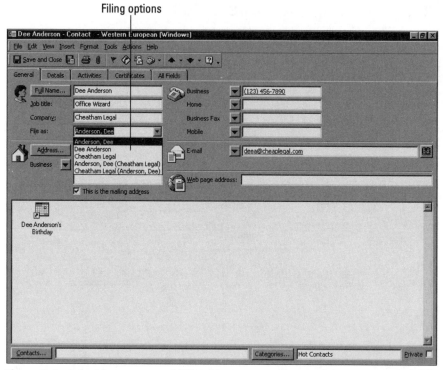

Figure 9-4: Select how you would like this contact to appear in your Contacts folder.

If you don't enter a company name, the File as list box will only show two choices — last name, first name, or first name and then last name.

> **Tip**   Choose the same File as format for all your contacts. Otherwise, some entries may be filed according to the first name and others may be filed by last name.

You can enter the contact's name by simply typing it in the Full Name text box or by clicking the Full Name button and using the separate text boxes in the Check Full Name dialog box. The only real advantage in using the Check Full Name dialog box is that this dialog box has drop-down list boxes for title and suffix. Unless you assign an unusual title or suffix to someone's name, Outlook should have little trouble understanding most names you might enter in the Full Name text box.

The entries in the Job Title and Company text boxes are optional, but Outlook will use them if they are available. For example, if you send a fax and include a cover page, Outlook will use these entries to help identify the intended fax recipient on the cover page.

Address options

The Address text box is used to hold the contact's addresses. As Figure 9-5 shows, Outlook has a provision for storing three different addresses for each contact.

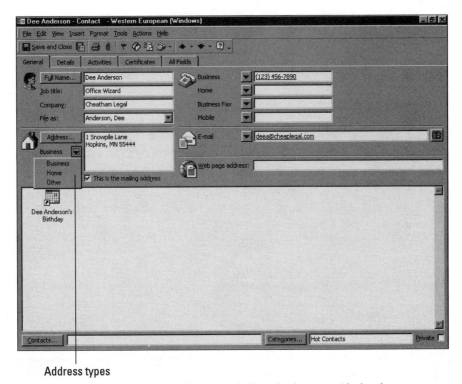

Address types

Figure 9-5: Select the type of address by clicking the button with the down arrow to the left of the Address text box.

You can also click the Address button to display the Check Address dialog box if you would rather use separate text boxes for each element of the address. You may want to use this dialog box to create address entries for foreign addresses, since the dialog box includes a Country/Region list box.

If you enter more than one address for a contact, be sure that you select one of the addresses as the mailing address by clicking the *This is the mailing address* checkbox. Only one address should be designated as the mailing address, but you may need to include a shipping address as the *Other* entry if the shipping and mailing addresses are not the same.

Phone number options

To the right of the name area in the Contact form are some very interesting text boxes. Like the Address text box, the four phone number text boxes are actually multipurpose text boxes. As Figure 9-6 shows, each of these text boxes can hold information from quite a variety of different fields.

Phone number types

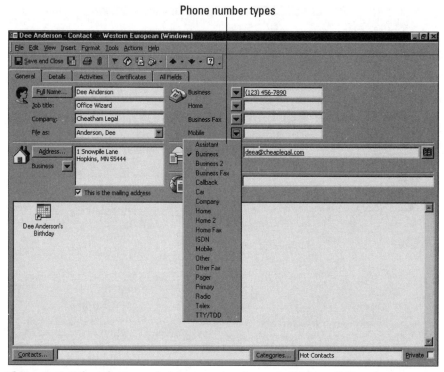

Figure 9-6: Select the type of phone number for each field by clicking the button with the down arrow to the left of the text box.

Although only four phone number text boxes are displayed at one time, you can actually enter as many of the different types of numbers as necessary. Simply click the down arrow to select a different field to be displayed and enter the associated number. Outlook will store as many of the different numbers as you enter. To view the number that is stored in a field, choose to display that field in one of the text boxes.

E-mail address options

Just as people often have a number of different telephone numbers, multiple e-mail addresses are also becoming fairly common. The e-mail text box accommodates this reality by being linked to three different e-mail address fields—just as the address and phone number text boxes link to multiple fields. You can click the down arrow to the left of the e-mail text box to choose which of the e-mail address fields is displayed in the text box.

To the right of the e-mail address text box is a button that displays the Select Name dialog box. If you click this button, you can choose the contact's name from the list of names in your Contacts folder. Although this may sound useful at first glance, this option essentially offers what would be known as a *circular reference* in a spreadsheet. If your Contacts list already has an e-mail listing for this contact, it would likely be shown in the e-mail address text box of the Contact form, so there would be no need to select it from the list. If you haven't already entered an e-mail address for this contact, it's also unlikely that you would be able to select the nonexistent entry from the list.

Rest of the General tab

The remaining elements of the General tab of the Contact form enable you to enter further useful information about the contact. Here's a brief look at these elements:

✦ The *Web page address* text box enables you to enter the URL of a Web site that you want to associate with this contact. Although this address would most commonly be the contact's Web site, you may also choose to display a different Web site address. For example, you might choose an address such as www.idgbooks.com so that you could easily locate the latest books from your favorite computer book author.

✦ The *notes* text box is really a multi-use area. You can enter notes about the contact, or you can show links to Calendar-related events for this contact. You might use this area to remind yourself about the contact's food preferences so that you could select the correct type of restaurant when inviting the contact out for a business lunch.

✦ The *Contacts* text box enables you to link this contact with other contacts, such as the contact's assistant, so you would know who to call if you couldn't reach the contact in an emergency.

✦ The *Categories* text box enables you to classify your contacts into groups so it is easier to locate specific types of contacts. If you combine business contacts with family and friends in your Outlook Contacts folder, you could use categories to help you organize these different groups.

✦ The *Private* checkbox makes it possible to hide this contact record from others if you share your Contacts folder. You might want to use this to hide the fact that you've been in touch with a management recruiter who has been trying to find a better position for you.

Understanding the Details tab

The Details tab of the Contact form provides additional text boxes that you can use to add more detailed information about a contact. Figure 9-7 shows the Details tab.

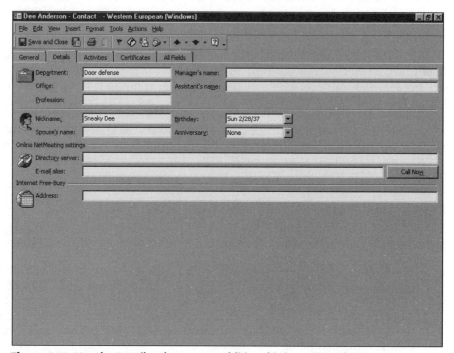

Figure 9-7: Use the Details tab to enter additional information about a contact.

You should be able to figure out the function of most of the text boxes on the Details tab simply by reading the label on the text box. You may, however, need a little clarification of the items associated with Microsoft NetMeeting settings.

NetMeeting is an application that enables you to hold online meetings with one or more people via the Internet. A NetMeeting meeting may consist of several elements including the following:

✦ Text-based chat, which enables each participant to type their comments for all the other participants to see.

✦ A *whiteboard,* which enables participants to illustrate points using an electronic slate on which you can draw simple images.

✦ Application sharing, which enables all participants to view and use a program that may only be installed on one of the participant's computers.

✦ Audio conferencing, which enables the participants to discuss subjects as if they were participating in a telephone conference call.

✦ Video conferencing, which enables the participants to see each other.

Of course, which of those elements are available depend on a number of factors. Video cameras are necessary to enable the video conferencing features, and fast access to the Internet is necessary to really make any of the features usable. Attempting to use a high-bandwidth feature such as video conferencing over slow dial-up connections would likely be nothing more than an exercise in futility!

To use NetMeeting, each of the participants must connect to the same directory server. This is a computer on the Internet that provides the link between each of the meeting participants. Because there are many different NetMeeting servers, it is important that all meeting participants coordinate so that they use the same server. You use the Directory server text box to specify which server the contact uses.

Once you are connected to a directory server, you must specify a name that the other participants can recognize so that you will all be able to join the same meeting. You use the E-mail alias text box to specify the name for the contact so that NetMeeting can locate the meeting participants.

Clicking the Call Now button connects you to the specified NetMeeting server and attempts to locate the contact on that server.

Understanding the Activities tab

The Activities tab of the Contact form shows all outstanding Outlook items that are related to the selected contact. These may include such items as Journal entries, contact records, open documents, e-mail messages, notes, phone calls, or upcoming activities. Figure 9-8 shows the Activities tab.

The Activities tab is one place where you'll really start to appreciate just how useful and powerful Outlook's contact management features really can be. Not only can you see a listing of all the open items for the contact, but you can easily open any of those items by double-clicking the item. You don't have to hunt through your Calendar, Tasks list, Inbox, Drafts folder, and so on to see what might need to be done. All you need to do is open the Contact form and have a quick look at the Activities tab. You can select which types of items should appear by making a selection from the Show drop-down list box.

Tip   You can quickly sort the items on the Activities tab by clicking a column heading.

Understanding the Certificates tab

The next tab of the Contact form is the Certificates tab. Figure 9-9 shows the Certificates tab.

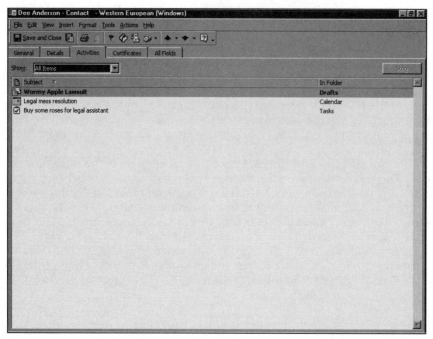

Figure 9-8: Use the Activities tab to locate all open items relating to a contact.

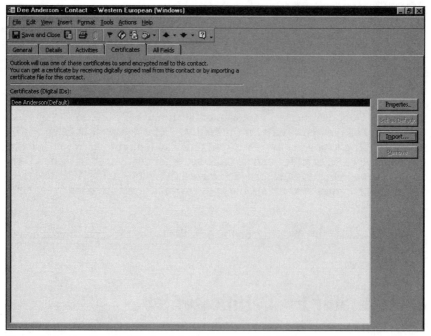

Figure 9-9: Use the Certificates tab to manage digital IDs for a contact.

Certificates are digital IDs that can be used to positively identify someone when they send an e-mail message. Certificates can also be used to encrypt messages so that only the intended recipient can read the message.

Note   You must have someone's digital ID in order to send them an encrypted message. The easiest way to obtain someone's digital ID is for them to send you a digitally signed message.

It's important to remember that certificates generally have a limited life span. When a certificate expires, it can no longer be relied upon as a valid identification. If you have obtained more than one certificate for someone, you may have to remove obsolete certificates from the list on the Certificates tab, or you may have to select one of the certificates to set as the default certificate. You can click the Properties button to view the information about a selected certificate — that way you can check to see whether the certificate is still valid.

Most certificate authorities provide personal certificates at no charge. To learn more about obtaining your own digital identification, see Chapter 8.

Understanding the All Fields tab

Outlook can track an incredible amount of information about your contacts. Using standard database terminology, each of your contacts is one record, and each piece of information about that contact is stored in a field. The Outlook Contacts database has far too many fields to completely display all of that information on any tab of the Contact form. That's why the Contact form includes the All Fields tab — so that you can see whatever information you want about a contact. Figure 9-10 shows the All Fields tab of the Contact form.

Rather than simply attempting to show every field on the All Fields tab, Outlook enables you to select the types of fields you would like to see from the Select from list box. In the figure, *Frequently-used fields* was selected to show the most common fields that are in the database. No matter which set of fields you choose to display, the fields will be listed in alphabetical order sorted by the name of the field.

The All Fields tab is also the location where you have the opportunity to create new fields or to modify the properties of some existing fields. You generally cannot modify fields that are standard Outlook fields, but you can change certain properties for fields that you created earlier. To add a new field, click the New button to display the New Field dialog box, shown in Figure 9-11. To modify a field that you had created earlier, you would click the Properties button to display the Field Properties dialog box — which is identical to the New Field dialog box except for the dialog box title.

Once you have entered a name for the new field, you can select a field type and format. Different field types have different available formats, so choose the type first. You should choose a field type that is compatible with the type of data that you intend to store in the field. For example, if you wanted to add a Date Hired field, you would choose Date/Time. Click the OK button to finish creating the new field.

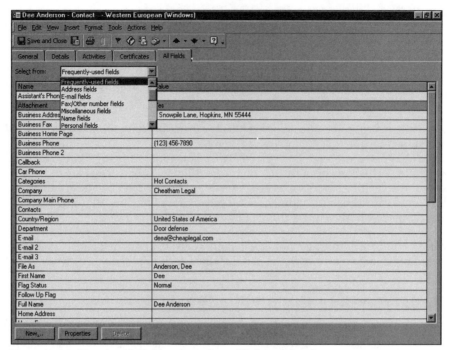

Figure 9-10: Use the All Fields tab to view all information for a contact.

Figure 9-11: Use the New Field dialog box to add your own fields to the Outlook Contact database.

Creating Contacts

Your Outlook Contacts list is only useful once you've added people to the list. Creating contacts is pretty easy, and Outlook provides several different methods to make the task even easier. In the following sections, you learn how to use several of these methods.

Importing contacts

The easiest way to create your Contacts list is really not to create the list at all. Instead of creating a list from scratch, you may be able to import a list that exists in a different format.

Outlook can import contact information in several different formats. If you were using another program that included contact information when you installed Outlook, you were probably given the option to import that information during the installation process. If you decided not to import the information at that time or if you now have new data that you could import, you can choose to import that information at any time you like.

Tip   If someone sends you vCard files, you can use Outlook's import capabilities to add the vCard information easily to your Contacts list.

To import data into your Outlook Contacts list, follow these steps:

1. Select File ⇨ Import and Export to display the Import and Export Wizard, shown in Figure 9-12.

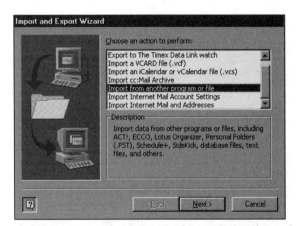

Figure 9-12: Use the Import and Export Wizard to quickly import existing data into your Outlook Contacts list.

2. Choose the type of information you wish to import. It's a good idea to scroll through the list to see if one of the choices mentions the source program in the description. Choosing the correct type of import greatly increases the chances of success.

3. Click Next to continue.

4. Depending on the type of import you selected, you will next need to select the source program. You may also need to choose the types of information that you wish to import, as shown in Figure 9-13.

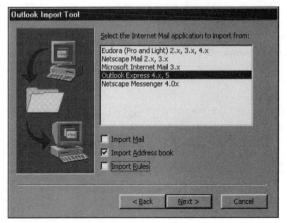

Figure 9-13: Select the source program and any import options.

5. Click Next to continue.

6. You may have additional choices to select, as shown in Figure 9-14.

   If you have a choice for the destination, choose the Outlook Contacts Folder radio button, shown in the figure. The Outlook Contacts folder has additional capabilities that are not available in the Personal Address Book.

   Choose how Outlook should handle duplicates. You may want to base your choice on which database contains the most recent information. If you choose to import duplicate records, you should check for duplicates immediately after performing the import and correct any errors that your find.

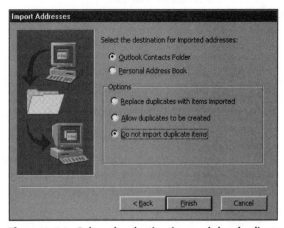

Figure 9-14: Select the destination and the duplicate import options.

7. Click Finish to complete the task. When the data import is completed, Outlook will display a summary to inform you of the number of records that were successfully imported.

You can repeat the import process as often as necessary. If you have contact data from several sources, you can use Outlook to consolidate all of the information in one central location by importing from each source in turn.

Caution   If you are importing data from several sources, be especially careful with your choice of duplicate handling options. Keeping track of duplicate records that exist in many different locations can be very difficult — keep all of your contact information in Outlook to prevent future confusion over which records are correct.

Creating contacts manually

You probably won't be lucky enough to be able to import all the contacts that you'll need to track in your Contacts list. Indeed, you'll probably end up creating a large number of contact records yourself. Fortunately, this is a simple process that won't take much time at all.

To begin creating a new contact record, follow these steps:

1. Open the Contacts folder.

2. Click the New Contact button to open a new Contact form, as shown in Figure 9-15. Alternatively you can select File ➪ New ➪ Contact or Actions ➪ New Contact to open this form.

3. Enter as much or as little information as you need for the new contact. At a minimum, you must enter the contact's name, but all other information is optional.

4. Click the Save and Close button to save the information on the new contact and to close the Contact form.

Tip   Remember that Contact form text boxes that show a down arrow to their left are multipurpose fields. You can select a different field to display in the text box by clicking the down arrow and choosing a field name from the list.

Once you have created contact records, you can easily reopen those records for editing. Double-click a contact in the Contacts folder to open the Contact form so you can edit the selected record.

Creating contacts while viewing an e-mail message

If you receive an e-mail message from someone who isn't already in your Contacts list, you can easily add him or her to the list with just a few clicks of your mouse. This will ensure that you can later send them a message and be certain of having the correct e-mail address.

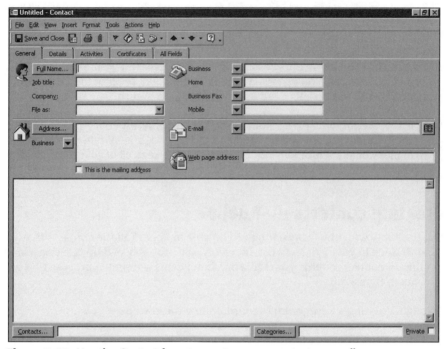

Figure 9-15: Use the Contact form to create a new contact manually.

Tip

You can add any person who is shown in a message header to your Contacts list the same way you add the sender. This includes anyone in the To, Cc, or Bcc address boxes.

As Figure 9-16 shows, the quickest method of adding someone who is listed in an e-mail message header to your Contacts list is to right-click their name and choose Add to Contacts.

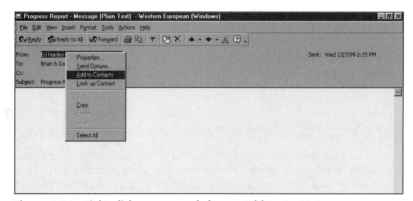

Figure 9-16: Right-click a name and choose Add to Contacts.

When you select Add to Contacts, Outlook will open the Contact form so that you can add additional information if necessary. If it turns out that the contact you are trying to add is a duplicate, Outlook will display the Duplicate Contact Detected dialog box, shown in Figure 9-17. If the new contact is really a duplicate, it's usually best to select *Update new information from this contact to the existing one* so that you don't create multiple records for the same person. Updating the existing record is generally a good idea, because the older record may not have the most current e-mail address.

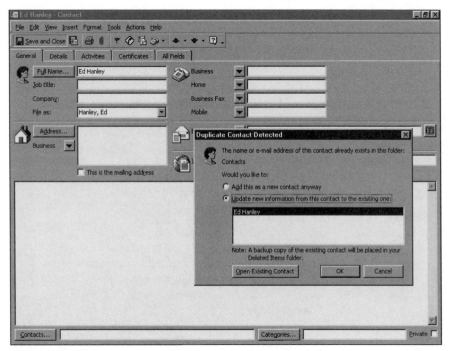

Figure 9-17: If the new contact seems to duplicate an existing contact record, you can choose to update or duplicate the record.

Using Contacts

Once you have a fairly complete Contacts list, you'll begin to appreciate how useful this list can be. You may even start to wonder why you took so long to begin tracking your addresses in such an efficient way. (Chapter 18 describes how your Outlook Contacts list can be even more useful by providing information that can be used in other applications such as the programs in Microsoft Office.)

Composing an e-mail message from contacts

The most obvious use of your Contacts list is probably for making certain that the e-mail address is correct when you compose and send a new e-mail message. Entering e-mail addresses manually can be a real exercise in frustration — especially because mail servers don't tolerate any errors. If you mistype a single character in an e-mail address, your message won't be delivered — or, perhaps worse, it will be sent to the wrong person!

Outlook helps you use your Contacts list records to correctly address e-mail messages in several ways. As Figure 9-18 shows, when the Contacts folder is open, the Outlook toolbar includes a *New Message to Contact* button. If you click this button, Outlook will open the New Message form with the selected contact already added to the To text box.

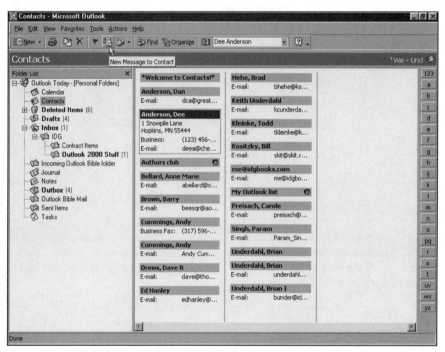

Figure 9-18: Click the *New Message to Contact* button to begin a new e-mail message to the selected contact.

Although the *New Message to Contact* button is convenient if you are working in the Contacts folder, you probably won't begin most new e-mail messages from the Contacts folder. It's more likely that you'll click the New Mail Message button and be greeted by an empty New Message form. If so, you can still use the entries in your Contacts list to quickly and accurately address the message.

Each address text box on the New Message form has an identifying button to the left of the text box. If you click this button, Outlook will display the Select Names dialog box, shown in Figure 9-19. Double-click a name to add it to the appropriate address box in the Select Names dialog box. You can also click the To, Cc, or Bcc button to add the selected address to an address box. Click OK to close the Select Names dialog box and return to the New Message form with the names added to the correct address boxes.

┌ Click these buttons to select names from the Contacts list

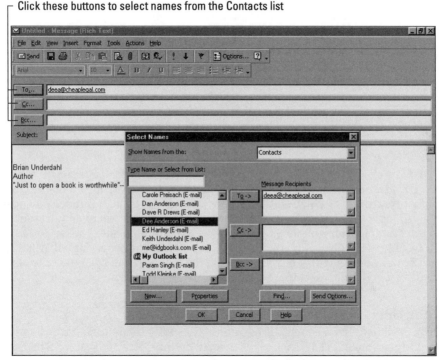

Figure 9-19: Use the Select Names dialog box to add addresses from your Contacts list to new messages.

Searching contacts

As your Contacts list grows, you may find that it is more difficult to locate specific information than you would like. This can be especially true if you aren't consistent in choosing the same File as format for each record. Outlook has the potential to use five different File as formats. In addition, you may need to find information that is somewhat hidden — such as which of your contacts are located in Nevada.

There are several different ways to search for information in your Outlook Contacts folder. The following sections show you these methods.

Using QuickFind

The fastest way to locate a contact is to use the QuickFind feature. As Figure 9-20 shows, you can find people using this method even if you are only sure about part of their name.

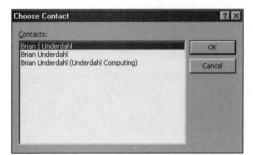

Figure 9-20: Use QuickFind to quickly locate contacts.

To use the QuickFind feature, enter as much of the contact's name as you're sure of in the *Find a Contact* text box and press Enter. This text box appears on the Outlook toolbar regardless of which Outlook folder is currently open. If Outlook can positively identify the contact based on the name you typed, it will open the associated Contact form for that contact. If your entry was somewhat ambiguous, Outlook may not be able to positively identify the contact. If this is the case, Outlook will display the Choose Contact dialog box as shown in the figure so you can select the correct contact from the short list that is displayed.

Using Find

If you need to locate a contact using information other than the contact's name, you'll need to use something a bit more advanced than the QuickFind feature. The Find tool searches the name, company, address, and category fields to locate contacts.

To use the Find tool, follow these steps:

1. Begin by clicking the Find button on the Outlook toolbar. This displays the Find Items in Contacts box.

2. Enter the search phrase in the Look for text box.

3. Click the Find Now button to search for matching records. As Figure 9-21 shows, Outlook hides any contact records that do not match the specified search criteria.

4. Click Clear Search or the Find Items in Contacts box close button to again display all your contact records.

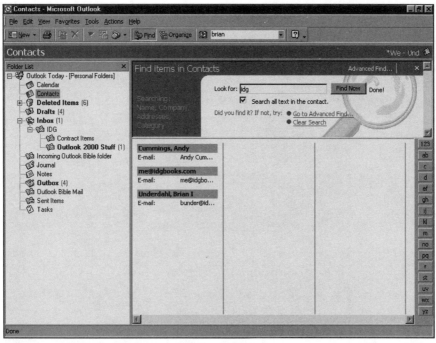

Figure 9-21: Use Find to locate contacts using the name, company, address, and category fields.

Using Advanced Find

Sometimes even the Find tool isn't specific enough. That's when you need to try the Advanced Find tool so that you can specify a broad range of selection criteria. This tool enables you to specify a search that is extremely specific. Not only can you search for a single word or phrase, but you can combine several criteria. If you want to search for all contacts who work in law firms in Nevada or California, you can use Advanced Find to locate them. If you want to find all contact records that were created during the past month, Advanced Find will help you do that, too. Figure 9-22 shows the Advanced Find dialog box that you can display by clicking Advanced Find.

Tip

Use Advanced Find to locate contact records that were modified when you imported information from another source. That way you won't have to manually search all the records to see if any records were incorrectly updated.

Be cautious in specifying the criteria for an advanced find. Use as few qualifiers as possible. Remember that each additional condition you specify makes it that much more difficult for any of the contact records to satisfy all the conditions. You could easily create a set of conditions that exclude all contact records — even the ones you are trying to locate.

Click here to conduct an Advanced Find

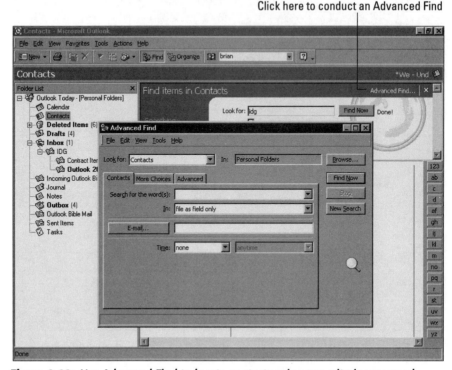

Figure 9-22: Use Advanced Find to locate contacts using any criteria you need.

Viewing address maps

Outlook incorporates one very handy feature that may be a surprise to you. For contacts who are located within the United States, Outlook can connect to the Microsoft Expedia Web site and show you a map that shows where the contact is located. You can even obtain directions for driving to the contact's location!

If you click the *Display Map of Address* button while you have a contact open, as shown in Figure 9-23, Outlook will attempt to connect to the Microsoft Expedia Web site and display a map with the contact's address designated by a map pin. You may need to confirm that you wish to connect to the Internet if you aren't already connected when you click the button.

Tip

While you are viewing the map, you can use the zoom in and zoom out controls located next to the map to change the level of detail that is displayed.

If the Expedia Web site is unable to positively identify the address, you will be given the option to select from other address possibilities that appear to be similar to the specified address. You may be able to determine that one of these is the correct address — especially if you can see that your contact record contains an obvious misspelling.

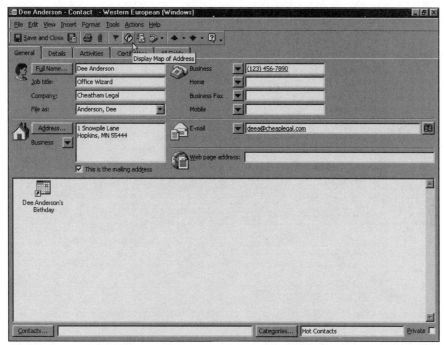

Figure 9-23: Click the *Display Map of Address* button to view a map of the contact's location.

Using the AutoDialer to make a phone call

Outlook has another feature that is intended to make working with your contacts just a little easier. The program includes a built-in AutoDialer to dial a phone number using your computer's modem. Not only that, but you can have Outlook keep track of phone calls by recording the date, time, and duration in the Outlook Journal.

Note

Using the Outlook AutoDialer requires that your modem share the same telephone line that you use for voice calls. You may find this quite inconvenient, because you will not be able to make a voice call and use the modem at the same time. Since you can use more than one modem with your computer, you may find that this provides an excellent way to use an old modem that is too slow to be practical for Internet access. You can connect the old modem to your voice line and designate it as your AutoDialer modem. No matter how slow the old modem is, it will be plenty fast if all it has to do is dial phone numbers for your voice calls.

Figure 9-24 shows the drop-down menu that appears when you click the down arrow to the right of the AutoDialer button. This button appears on the Outlook toolbar whenever the Contacts folder or a Contact form is open. If you simply click the AutoDialer button, Outlook will dial the number that is at the top of the drop-down menu. You can also display the AutoDialer menu by selecting Actions ➪ Call Contact.

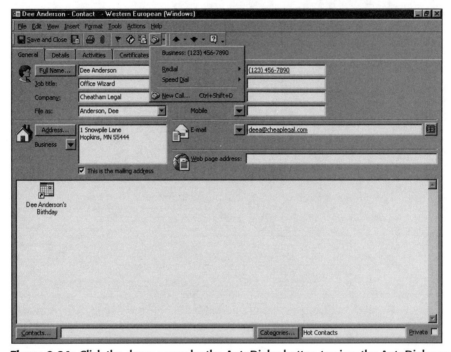

Figure 9-24: Click the down arrow by the AutoDialer button to view the AutoDialer menu.

If you need to track your telephone calls — perhaps for billing purposes — you can use Outlook to automatically log calls made using the AutoDialer. Outlook logs calls using the Outlook Journal, which is covered in detail in Chapter 13.

To log calls you make using the AutoDialer, follow these steps:

1. Click the down arrow next to the AutoDialer button (or select Actions ➪ Call Contact) to display the AutoDialer menu.

2. Select New Call to open the New Call dialog box.

3. Select the contact to call in the Contact text box, as shown in Figure 9-25. If no contacts are listed in the Contact box, enter the contact name in the box.

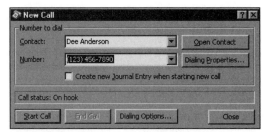

Figure 9-25: Use the New Call dialog box to log calls you make using the AutoDialer.

4. Select the *Create new Journal Entry when starting new call* checkbox. This will cause Outlook to create an entry in the Journal when the call begins.

5. Click Start Call to dial the contact and begin the call log.

6. Click End Call to stop the call log and record the ending time of the call.

Outlook can only record the date, time, and duration of your phone calls. If you need to add additional notes to the call log, you'll need to open the call log and add your notes manually. See Chapter 13 for more information on using the Outlook Journal.

You can also set up the Outlook AutoDialer to include a list of phone numbers in the Speed Dialer. Click the Dialing Options button and add the numbers to the Speed Dial list. You can then choose the numbers you've added from the AutoDialer menu.

Summary

Outlook is a very powerful contact manager. In this chapter, you learned how to use Outlook's Contacts list to create, view, and manage all those addresses, phone numbers, and personal details that you need to track. You also learned that Outlook enables you to do advanced tasks such as locate the precise location of your contacts automatically by using the Microsoft Expedia Web site.

The next chapter shows you how to use Outlook's Calendar to manage your time, schedule your activities, and coordinate your schedule with others.

✦   ✦   ✦

Managing Your Calendar

It would be almost impossible to live in today's world and not have a calendar. How else would you keep track of when jobs need to be done, when bills need to be paid, and when you get to go on vacation? What about planning that big family reunion that's a year and a half away? The Outlook Calendar can help you do all these tasks and much more. Unlike paper calendars, the Outlook Calendar never goes out of date or needs a refill.

In this chapter, you learn how to use the Outlook Calendar as your daily calendar. You also see how you can share the Outlook Calendar so that group planning becomes much easier. You also learn how to save an Outlook Calendar as a Web page so that it can be shared on the Internet.

Understanding the Outlook Calendar

You've probably seen many different calendars in dozens of different formats. But have you ever considered what a calendar really is? We use calendars to represent the passage of time and to allow ourselves to plan for events that will occur on specific dates. We need calendars for these purposes because calculating dates is so complex.

Consider for a moment the facts that you think you know about time. A day is equal to 24 hours, a week is 7 days, a month is usually about 30 days, and a year is typically 365 days. In reality, only one of these is an exact figure. Days aren't exactly 24 hours long, months can be anywhere from 28 to 31 days, and we have leap years almost every fourth year to adjust the length of the year. All these adjustments are necessary because we expect certain events to line up neatly with our calendar. If we just settled on a fixed calendar, we'd soon find that winter was beginning in June this year, and we'd need to find a totally different method of planning for seasonal events.

Printers have made a big business out of producing paper calendars. You can't just reuse last year's calendar, so most people get new calendars each year. That's one reason why an electronic calendar such as Outlook's Calendar is so useful—it doesn't need to be replaced on New Year's Day. Figure 10-1 shows the Outlook Calendar.

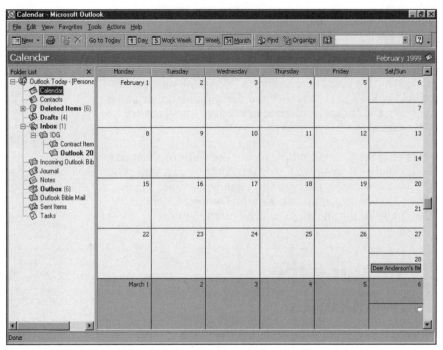

Figure 10-1: The Outlook Calendar never goes out of date.

How is the Outlook Calendar useful?

Any calendar is useful for keeping track of what day it is. The Outlook Calendar does this, of course, but it can also do a lot more for you. Here are just a few of the ways you may find the Outlook Calendar pretty useful:

✦ If you add someone's birthday to your Outlook Calendar, their birthday will appear on the same date every year. If you're not very good at remembering birthdays, the Outlook Calendar can make you look like a truly thoughtful person—although you still have to buy the birthday cards yourself.

✦ If you have a bill that is due on the same date each month, the Outlook Calendar can easily remind you when to get out the checkbook.

✦ If you are the events planner for an organization, you can use the Outlook Calendar to track events so that two events don't conflict. You also can publish the event schedule on your Web site so members can check for last minute updates.

✦ If you want to plan an around-the-world trip next year, you can easily view next year's dates on the Outlook Calendar. If you were using a paper calendar, you might have some difficulty obtaining printed calendars that show dates far enough in advance.

✦ If you work an unusual schedule, you can customize Outlook's Calendar view to show your schedule and even print out weekly planner sheets to match your needs.

As you use the Outlook Calendar, you'll find even more ways that you can use it to make your life just a little easier.

Understanding the new Calendar features

Outlook has several new or enhanced features that make the Outlook Calendar more useful than it was in earlier versions of Outlook. Here are some of the important improvements:

✦ Internet calendars — *iCalendars* — make it easier to share schedules over the Internet. You can publish your Outlook Calendar information to a Web site for other Internet users. You can also send and receive meeting requests and responses over the Internet in the iCalendar format. Since iCalendar is an Internet standard, the people whom you share iCalendar information with don't need Outlook as long as they use an iCalendar-compatible calendar program.

✦ You can now expand distribution lists when you are scheduling meetings. This enables you to select the meeting participants using a distribution list that you have created, but to remove selected people from the list. Using a distribution list not only is handy, but also makes it less likely that you'll make an error and forget to include someone. Distribution lists are discussed in Chapter 8, and meeting planning is discussed in Chapter 11.

✦ If you're using Microsoft Exchange Server, resources such as meeting rooms can be set up to accept and decline meeting invitations automatically. That way you'll be able to plan a meeting, invite participants, and reserve the meeting space all at the same time.

✦ You can now save a Calendar as a Web page — in HTML format — so that it can be published to the Internet or sent in an e-mail message. Because any Web browser can view Web pages, people won't need Outlook to view your Outlook Calendar.

Viewing the Calendar

The Outlook Calendar can look like many different types of calendars. You'll probably find that different views are useful for different purposes. You may be surprised to learn that the Outlook Calendar can also look nothing like any calendar you've ever seen in the past. These unique views make it much easier to perform certain tasks and to understand just what is in the Calendar.

Accessing different Calendar views

Choosing the Outlook Calendar view can be a little confusing. That's because you choose the Outlook Calendar views in two different places depending on just what you want to accomplish.

To choose the actual calendar view, you use the View ⇨ Current View menu, shown in Figure 10-2. This menu enables you to select the types of views you would normally associate with a Calendar or some of the unique Outlook Calendar views that focus more directly on what is on your Calendar.

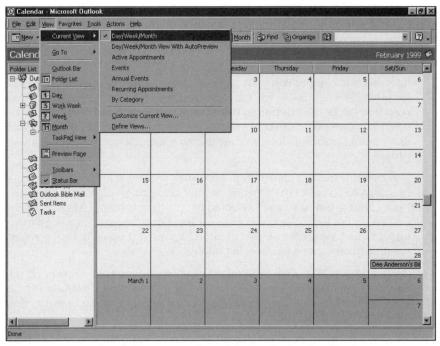

Figure 10-2: Use the View menu to change the Outlook Calendar view.

To choose a variation on the Day/Week/Month view, you use the time period buttons on the Outlook toolbar, as shown in Figure 10-3. These variations display the types of Calendar views that people normally think of when they think about calendars.

Time period buttons

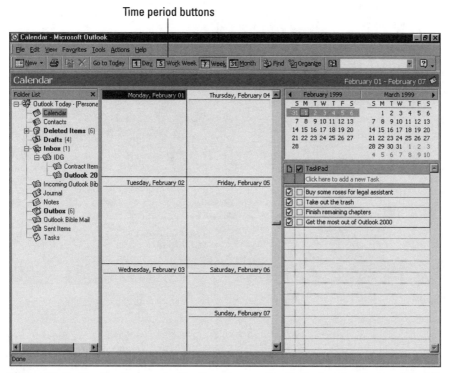

Figure 10-3: Use the time period buttons to vary the Outlook Calendar Day/Week/Month view.

Understanding Calendar view types

Because Outlook has so many different ways to display the Calendar, it's important to understand how the views differ and why you may want to use some of them. In the following sections, you see each of the views and learn why each view is useful.

Day view

The Day view displays a detailed schedule for one day, as shown in the example in Figure 10-4. In this view, you can easily see which time periods during the day are scheduled and which are currently free. You can view other times of the day by scrolling up or down using the scroll bar. Click the Day button on the Outlook toolbar to change to Day view.

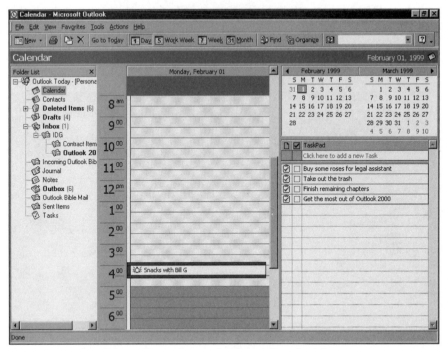

Figure 10-4: Use the Day view to see a detailed daily schedule.

When you display the Day view, Outlook shows the current date by default. You can view a different day by clicking a date in the monthly calendars shown in the upper-right section of the Calendar view. To display a date in a month that is not currently shown, click the arrows that are just above the monthly calendars. The left arrow displays earlier months, and the right arrow displays later months.

Tip   You can always return quickly to the current date by clicking the Go to Today button on the Outlook toolbar.

See "Customizing Calendar views" later in this chapter for more information on setting the start and end times for the workday.

Work Week view

The Work Week view is similar to the Day view, except that Outlook attempts to show the schedule for Monday through Friday on one screen, as shown in Figure 10-5. This view is handy when you need to plan events for your entire work week, but because each day has such a narrow slot available, it's difficult to view the details of any event. Click the Work Week button on the Outlook toolbar to display the Work Week view.

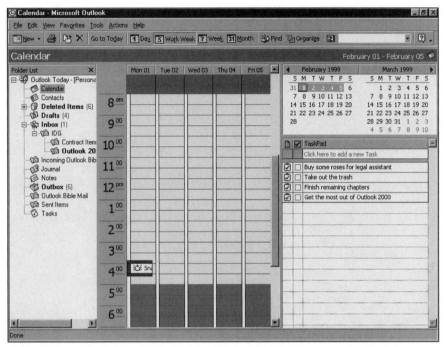

Figure 10-5: Use the Work Week view to see a detailed work week schedule.

Navigation in the Work Week view is similar to navigating in the Day view. The only real difference is that you can choose a particular day of the week by clicking in the appropriate column. If you choose a different date in one of the small calendars, Outlook will show you the workdays for the week you select.

See "Customizing Calendar views" later in this chapter for more information on setting your workdays.

Week view

The Week view displays the entire week, as shown in Figure 10-6. Unlike the Work Week view, the Week view does not attempt to show a detailed schedule for each day, but rather simply lists the scheduled events for each day. Click the Week button on the Outlook toolbar to display the Week view.

To view a different week, you can use the scroll bar to change the display one week at a time. Alternatively, you can click within a week in one of the small calendar displays to go directly to that week.

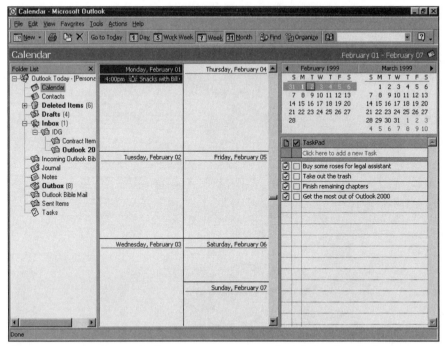

Figure 10-6: Use the Week view to see an events schedule for the week.

By default, Outlook condenses the blocks used to display both Saturday and Sunday. As you'll learn in "Customizing Calendar views" later in this chapter, you can set Outlook to give each day the same size block.

Month view

The Month view is the Outlook Calendar view that looks the most like a traditional calendar. As Figure 10-7 shows, the Month view enables you to easily see anything that is on your schedule for the entire month, since both the small calendars and the TaskPad are removed from the display when you switch to Month view. Click the Month button on the Outlook toolbar to display the Month view.

You can use the scroll bar to view different dates, but if you wish to view a date that is more than a few months off, it is easier to use the Go To Date dialog box. Select View ➪ Go To ➪ Go to Date to display the Go To Date dialog box and then enter a date in the Date box. Click OK to display that date.

Tip   Press Ctrl+G to quickly display the Go To Date dialog box.

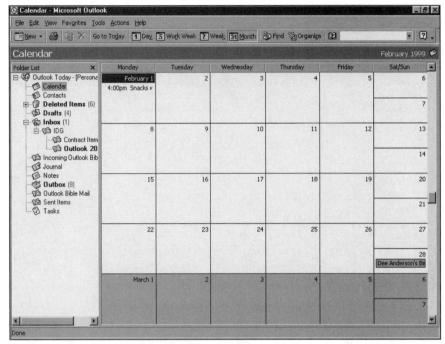

Figure 10-7: Use the Month view to see an events schedule for the entire month.

AutoPreview view

On Outlook's View ➪ Current View menu, you'll find both Day/Week/Month and Day/Week/Month View With AutoPreview listed as options. These two choices are identical except that the second displays the first line of an event's description when you pause the mouse over the item, as shown in Figure 10-8.

You can select any of the standard day, work week, week, or month choices when you choose the Day/Week/Month View With AutoPreview view. Navigation is identical whether you choose AutoPreview or not. Choosing the Day/Week/Month View With AutoPreview view does make it slightly easier to find specific events because you don't have to open the events to see a brief description of them.

Active Appointments view

The Active Appointments view shows your appointments and meetings starting with today's date as shown in Figure 10-9. You display this view by selecting View ➪ Current View ➪ Active Appointments.

Pause mouse over item

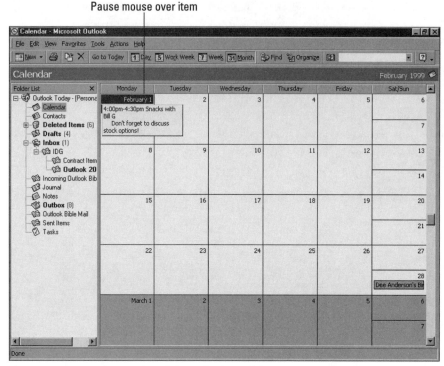

Figure 10-8: Use the Day/Week/Month View With AutoPreview view to see the first line of an event's description.

The Active Appointments view separates your appointments and meetings by how often they reoccur. That enables you to easily see which appointments happen on an ongoing basis and which ones are set for a single time.

You may have numerous appointments in each recurrence category. To make it a little easier to concentrate on specific categories, click the small box that appears just to the left of the word *Recurrence*. If this box shows a minus sign, the category is fully expanded. If it shows a plus sign, the category is collapsed to provide more room to view the remaining categories.

Note   *Appointments* are activities that you plan that do not involve inviting other people (or reserving resources if you use Exchange Server). *Meetings* are appointments that involve inviting other people (or reserving resources). *Events* are activities that last a full day or longer.

Events view

The Events view shows the current year events that are on a schedule, as shown in Figure 10-10. You display this view by selecting View ➪ Current View ➪ Events.

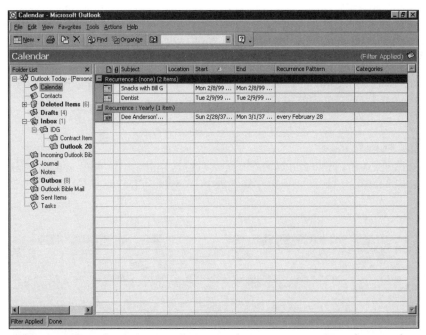

Figure 10-9: Use the Active Appointments view to see your upcoming meetings and appointments.

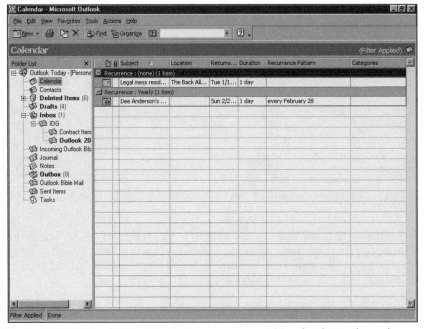

Figure 10-10: Use the Events view to see your activities that last a day or longer.

Your events list is also separated into recurrence categories, but unlike the active appointments list, the events list includes current year events that have already passed. Items that might be included on your events list include such things as vacations, trade shows, and business trips that last a full day or longer.

Tip   To change an event into an appointment or meeting, remove the check from the All day event checkbox in the Event form.

Annual Events view

The Annual Events view shows the annual events that are on your schedule as shown in Figure 10-11. You display this view by selecting View ➪ Current View ➪ Annual Events.

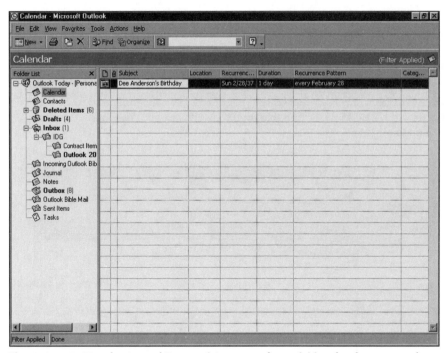

Figure 10-11: Use the Annual Events view to see the activities that happen each year.

Annual events include such things as birthdays, anniversaries, life insurance payments, and anything else that you might need to remember each year. If you've ever forgotten an important date such as your spouse's birthday, the Annual Events view can be just the thing to keep you out of hot water in the future!

Recurring Appointments view

The Recurring Appointments view shows the ongoing appointments that are on a schedule, as shown in Figure 10-12. You display this view by selecting View ➪ Current View ➪ Recurring Appointments.

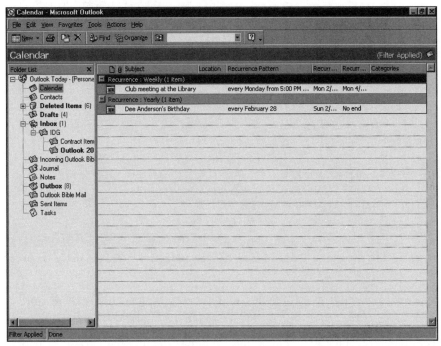

Figure 10-12: Use the Recurring Appointments view to see the activities that happen on a regular basis.

You probably have a number of recurring appointments even if you've never quite thought of them that way. For example, if you belong to a club that meets every month, you probably block out the meeting time mentally even if you don't show it on your calendar. There's no reason why you shouldn't include such things on your Outlook Calendar. That way you won't inadvertently schedule something else for the same time. Remember that you can always choose to ignore items that are shown on your Outlook Calendar, but if you haven't included something, it's likely you'll eventually schedule something else for the same time.

By Category view

The By Category view shows the items on your schedule broken down by category, as shown in Figure 10-13. You display this view by selecting View ➪ Current View ➪ By Category.

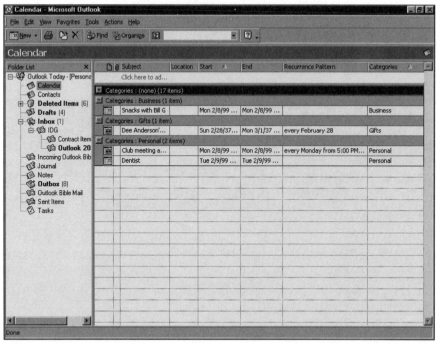

Figure 10-13: Use the By Category view to see your activities broken down by category.

You can use categories to organize almost everything in Outlook. Categories make it a lot easier to separate items into groups so that you can determine their importance. For example, if you need to make time in your schedule to accommodate an important customer, you may decide that certain categories of activities are more expendable than others. (In Chapter 11, you learn more about creating appointments and assigning categories.)

Tip

If none of the predefined categories are quite right, you can create your own categories to classify Outlook items.

Customizing Calendar views

As you use the Outlook Calendar, you may discover that certain little things simply annoy you. For example, weekends may be very important to you, so you may not like the way Outlook condenses the display of Saturdays and Sundays. Or perhaps your work day starts at an earlier hour than the 8 a.m. start time that Outlook shows. Fortunately, it's very easy to change these as well as a number of other Outlook Calendar settings.

You can choose to customize a single Outlook Calendar view, or you can open a dialog box that allows you to work with any of the views. In the following steps, you learn how to work with any view. If you only want to modify the current view, select View ➪ Current View ➪ Customize Current View and skip to Step 5.

To customize Outlook's Calendar views, follow these steps:

1. Make certain the Outlook Calendar folder is open.

2. Select View ➪ Current View ➪ Define Views to display the Define Views for "Calendar" dialog box, shown in Figure 10-14. You'll use this dialog box to select the views you wish to customize.

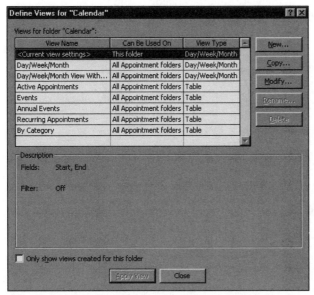

Figure 10-14: Use the Define Views for "Calendar" dialog box to select the views to modify.

3. Select the view that you wish to customize. As you select different views, the Description box will show the current settings for the selected view.

4. Click the Modify button to open the View Summary dialog box, shown in Figure 10-15. Depending on the view that you have selected to modify, some of the options in the View Summary dialog box may be unavailable.

5. Click the Fields button to display the Show Fields dialog box, shown in Figure 10-16.

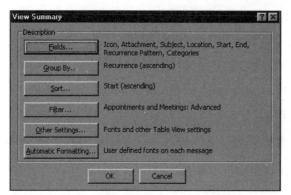

Figure 10-15: Use the View Summary dialog box to customize a view.

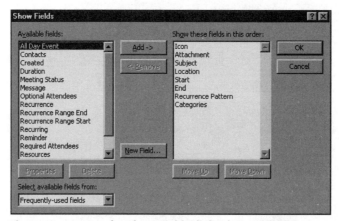

Figure 10-16: Use the Show Fields dialog box to choose which fields are shown in the view.

6. Choose the fields that you want to include in the view. You may want to add certain fields that will help you better understand the activities that are shown in the view, or remove fields that you don't use in order to present a cleaner display.

7. Click OK to close the dialog box when you have completed your changes.

8. Click the Group By button to display the Group By dialog box.

9. Choose the fields that you want to use for grouping the activities that are shown in the view.

10. Select Ascending or Descending to choose the sort order for the selected field.

11. Choose the Expand/collapse defaults setting you prefer. You may want to choose *As last viewed* so that Outlook will remember how the view appeared when you last closed the view.

12. Click OK to close the dialog box when you have completed your changes.

13. Click the Sort button to display the Sort dialog box.

14. Choose the sort order settings you prefer. Sort order settings differ from the Group By settings in that Outlook does not separate sorted items into individual groups.

15. Click OK to close the dialog box when you have completed your changes.

16. Click the Filter button to display the Filter dialog box, shown in Figure 10-17.

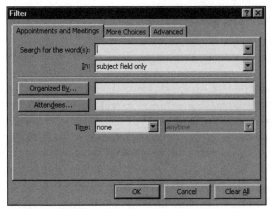

Figure 10-17: Use the Filter dialog box to choose which items are shown in the view.

17. Select the settings that will display the activities you want to see in this view. For example, you may want to view only those activities that will start within the next seven days if your calendar of events is extremely full.

18. Click OK to close the dialog box when you have completed your changes.

19. Click the Other Settings button to display the Other Settings dialog box.

20. Choose the settings you prefer. If you are modifying one of the Day/Week/Month views, you can choose the settings for condensing weekends as well as the start and end times for the work day.

21. Click OK to close the dialog box when you have completed your changes.

22. Click the Automatic Formatting button to display the Automatic Formatting dialog box, shown in Figure 10-18.

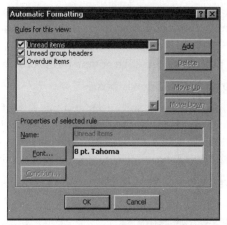

Figure 10-18: Use the Automatic Formatting dialog box to choose how you want Outlook to display items in this view.

23. Choose the settings you prefer. For example, you may want to change the font for overdue items to a larger size in a brightly contrasting color so that those items draw your immediate attention.

24. Click OK to close the dialog box when you have completed your changes.

25. Click OK to close the View Summary dialog box.

26. Choose another view to modify or click the Close button to close the Define Views for "Calendar" dialog box.

Rather than modifying an existing view, you may want to experiment by copying a view and then making your changes to the copy. That way you'll be able to create a custom view without losing the original.

Tip   If your changes have made a real mess out of a view, select the view in the Define Views for "Calendar" dialog box and click the Reset button to revert to the original settings.

Sharing Your Calendar with Others

It's pretty likely that you have a number of reasons to share a calendar with other people. If you work as part of a project team, it's important that the team members have access to the project schedule so that everyone knows when tasks are due. If you are an officer in an organization, you may want to be able to share committee schedules with the other officers so everyone knows when meetings are scheduled.

If you are organizing a large family reunion, you may want an easy way to keep everyone informed of the activities that you're planning. These are just a few of the countless reasons why you may want to share your Outlook Calendar.

Previous versions of Outlook required that you and everyone you wanted to share an Outlook Calendar with be connected to an Exchange Server. This was a rather severe limitation that made the feature pretty useless for the vast majority of Outlook users. Now Outlook has enabled everyone to share their Outlook Calendar using Net Folders. Rather than requiring that you have access to an Exchange Server, Outlook now enables you to share your Outlook Calendar over the Internet.

Because Net Folders share unencrypted information over the Internet, there could be some security issues if you are dealing with sensitive or confidential information. You may want to create a separate folder under the Outlook Calendar folder for the items you intend to share. Then you could share the separate folder rather than your complete Calendar folder.

To share your Outlook Calendar using Net Folders, follow these steps:

1. Select File ⇨ Share ⇨ Calendar to display the Net Folder Wizard, shown in Figure 10-19.

Figure 10-19: Use the Net Folder Wizard to share your Outlook Calendar.

2. Click Next to continue.

3. Click the Add button to display the Add Entries to Subscriber Database dialog box, shown in Figure 10-20.

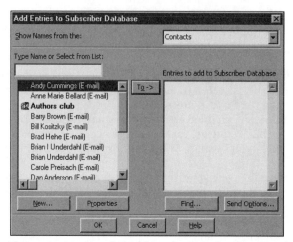

Figure 10-20: Use the Add Entries to Subscriber Database dialog box to select those who will share your Outlook Calendar.

4. Select the people who you wish to share your Outlook Calendar and click the To button to add them to the list. The subscribers should be using Outlook 98 or 2000 — otherwise they will not be able to fully participate in sharing the Outlook Calendar.

5. Click OK to close the Add Entries to Subscriber Database dialog box and return to the Net Folder Wizard.

6. Select one or more of the subscribers and click the Permissions button to display the Net Folder Sharing Permissions dialog box, shown in Figure 10-21.

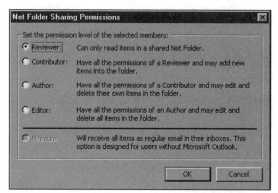

Figure 10-21: Use the Net Folder Sharing Permissions dialog box to specify how subscribers will share your Outlook Calendar.

7. Select the level of activity that you will allow the selected subscribers.

8. Click OK to close the Net Folder Sharing Permissions dialog box and return to the Net Folder Wizard.

9. Click Next to continue.

10. Enter a description for the folder.

11. Click Next to Continue.

12. Click Finish to close the Net Folder Wizard and send out the subscription requests.

When you share your Outlook Calendar as a Net Folder, Outlook first sends out subscription requests to the people whom you've selected to share the Calendar. Once they accept the request, their response is returned to Outlook, and periodic synchronization requests are sent out to their computer. Outlook uses those synchronization requests to update the remote Calendar folders and to update your shared Calendar folder if you've assigned anyone permission to make changes.

Saving Your Calendar as a Web Page

Outlook provides another way to share your Outlook Calendar — as a Web page. Saving your Outlook Calendar as a Web page means that you can share that Calendar with anyone who has a Web browser. You could, for example, use the Outlook Calendar to create a monthly event calendar for an organization and then display that calendar on your group's Web site. The members would be able to easily view the upcoming schedule just by visiting the Web site.

To save your Outlook Calendar as a Web page, follow these steps:

1. Open the Outlook Calendar folder.

2. Select File ➪ Save as Web Page to display the Save as Web Page dialog box, shown in Figure 10-22.

3. Select the starting and ending dates.

4. Make certain the *Include appointment details* checkbox is selected if you want the Web page to include information about the listed events.

5. Select the *Use background graphic* checkbox if you want to include an image behind the calendar. You can use the Browse button to locate the image file you want to use.

6. Enter a title for the calendar.

7. Specify a name for the calendar file.

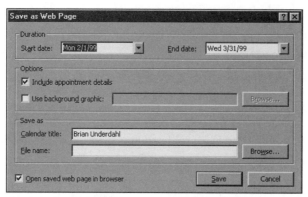

Figure 10-22: Use the Save as Web Page dialog box to save your Outlook Calendar in HTML format.

8. Click Save to save the file. If you haven't used this feature before, you may need your Outlook 2000 CD-ROM to install the Save as Web Page feature. Figure 10-23 shows how the calendar appears when it is opened in Internet Explorer.

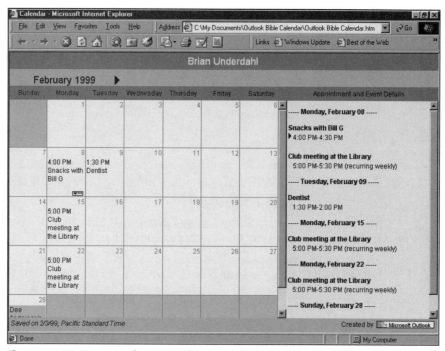

Figure 10-23: Once you have saved your Outlook Calendar as a Web page, it can be opened in any Web browser.

Notice in the figure that when your Outlook Calendar is saved as a Web page, visitors can view the event details as well as the calendar. If you had not selected the *Include appointment details* checkbox, visitors would be limited to those details that could be shown in the calendar itself.

Tip   If you choose to include a background graphic, it is best to use one that is quite light. Otherwise, visitors may have a difficult time viewing the text on the calendar.

Summary

This chapter has provided you with a comprehensive overview of the Outlook Calendar. You've learned about using the various options for viewing the Calendar, sharing your Calendar with others, and saving your Calendar as a Web page.

The next chapter continues the coverage of the Outlook Calendar by showing you how to use the Calendar for scheduling your time. You'll learn how to create appointments, schedule meetings, and make Outlook remind you of important events.

✦   ✦   ✦

Scheduling Your Time

T he Outlook Calendar is very adept at replacing the paper calendar that you might have hanging on your wall, but it's even more useful once you start using it for scheduling. Scheduling isn't just something that is used by busy executives. If you've ever had to look at your calendar to make certain that you would be free for dinner on a certain night, or tried to plan for a vacation so that you could attend a special event, you've used scheduling. If you've ever had to rearrange your schedule so that you could make an appointment for a haircut, you've used scheduling.

In this chapter, you learn how to use the Outlook Calendar to schedule your appointments and meetings. You also learn how to use both NetMeeting and the NetShow services with the meetings that you schedule in Outlook. Maybe even more importantly, you learn how you can have Outlook remind you of events so you'll never again forget that important birthday or anniversary!

Understanding Scheduling

When you use Outlook to schedule your time, you create events that appear on the Outlook Calendar. Outlook uses the term *appointment* to denote events that last less than a full day and don't require scheduling anyone else's time. *Meetings* are similar to appointments except that they do require coordinating your schedule with someone else's schedule. *Events* are simply appointments that last 24 hours or longer.

Note   If you use Exchange Server, Outlook can also schedule resources such as meeting rooms or video equipment just as it schedules meetings. Because scheduling a resource is really no different from scheduling meeting participants, you can use the same techniques to schedule a resource as you use to schedule meeting participants.

Scheduling is really just the task of allocating available time. Time is something that everyone measures the same way, so it's quite possible to schedule a meeting for 10 a.m. Monday and expect that everyone will know when they are to arrive at the meeting. Of course, just because everyone agrees on a schedule is no guarantee that they'll be there on time, but that's one problem that Outlook can't solve.

There are many ways to use Outlook's scheduling capabilities to help manage your time. Here are a few ideas:

✦ If you belong to an organization that holds meetings on a regular basis, you may want to include those meetings on your Outlook Calendar so that you'll always make certain to reserve the time to attend.

✦ If you need to meet with several important clients, you may want to figure out a schedule that allows you to minimize your time away from the office by keeping your travel time to a minimum. You can use the Outlook Calendar to see which days you would be able to visit with more than one client on the same day.

✦ If you're working with a team on a project, you could use Outlook to plan a meeting by automatically finding the next available free block of time for the meeting on everyone's Outlook Calendar.

✦ If you're planning a vacation, you can allocate the time on your Outlook Calendar so that no one schedules an important meeting that you must attend during the time you're planning on being away.

✦ You can add events such as birthdays and anniversaries to your Outlook Calendar and then set Outlook to remind you well in advance so that you can buy a gift or card.

No matter what types of events and activities you need to schedule, the Outlook Calendar can help make scheduling your time a lot easier and more efficient. You'll soon find that using Outlook to manage your schedule can be a real improvement over trying to manage your schedule manually.

Creating an Appointment

To begin scheduling your time, you can start by creating appointments. Appointments are the easiest activity to schedule because they don't require that you coordinate your schedule with anyone else's schedule—at least not in Outlook. Most appointments, of course, do involve other people, but you aren't responsible for making sure they have free time in their schedule for the appointment.

To create a new appointment in Outlook, follow these steps:

1. Open the Outlook Calendar folder.

2. Select the day of the appointment in the calendar. This step is actually optional, but may save you some time because you won't have to choose the date after you open the Appointment form.

3. Select File ➪ New ➪ Appointment (or click the New Appointment button) to open a blank Appointment form, as shown in Figure 11-1.

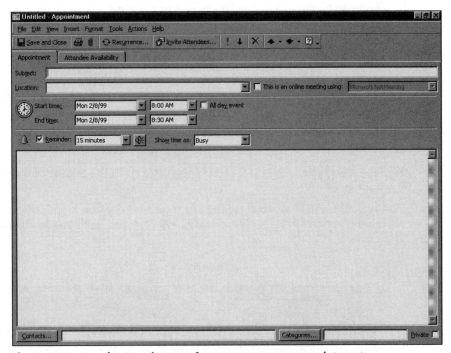

Figure 11-1: Use the Appointment form to create new appointments.

4. Enter a brief description of the appointment in the Subject text box. Only the first part of this description will show in the Outlook Calendar, so don't use this space to write the "great American novel."

5. If necessary, enter the appointment location in the Location text box.

6. Select the date and time of the appointment. If this is an all day event, such as a birthday, select the *All day event* checkbox rather than a time.

7. If you would like to be reminded in advance, select the Reminder checkbox and then choose how far in advance you'd like to be reminded of this appointment.

8. To choose the sound file that is played, click the Reminder Sound button to display the Reminder Sound dialog box, shown in Figure 11-2.

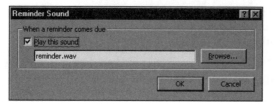

Figure 11-2: Choose a sound file to play as a reminder
of this appointment.

9. Click the Browse button if you want to select a different sound file.

Tip

You can use the Windows Sound Recorder to record your own reminders that
Outlook can play to remind you of appointments.

10. Click OK to close the Reminder Sound dialog box.

11. Add any special notes you want in the text box in the middle of the Appointment form.

12. Click Save and Close to close the form and save the new appointment. The new appointment will appear on your Outlook Calendar, as shown in Figure 11-3.

New appointment

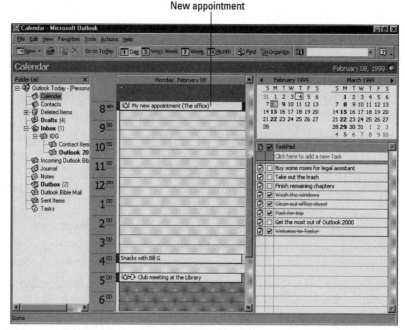

Figure 11-3: Choose the date of the appointment to view the appointment
on your schedule.

To edit an existing appointment, double-click the appointment to again open the Appointment form. Always remember to click Save and Close to save any changes when you close the form.

If you need to change the time of an appointment, you can reopen the Appointment form and adjust the time settings. Another way to adjust the time is to drag the start or end time as shown in Figure 11-4. You can drag to adjust the time in half-hour increments — unless you specify a different time interval (as discussed in Chapter 10).

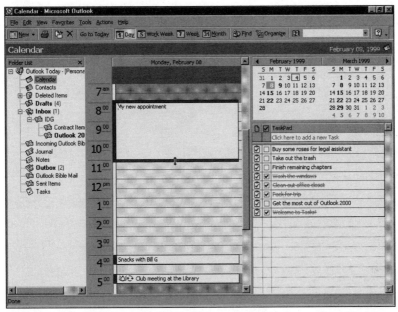

Figure 11-4: Drag the start or end time to adjust the time or length of the appointment.

If you need to move an appointment to a different date, there's no need to start over. You can simply choose a different date in the Appointment form, or you can drag the appointment to a new date, as shown in Figure 11-5. In this case, the appointment was dragged from Monday, February 8th to Friday, February 12th. You'll need to change to Week or Month view to drag an appointment to a new date.

You can also designate that an appointment is a recurring one. See "Setting Meetings as Recurring" later in this chapter for more information on this subject.

Appointment dragged from here . . .   . . . to here

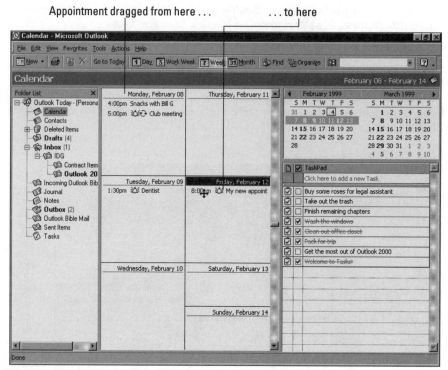

Figure 11-5: Drag an appointment to a new date to move the appointment.

Creating a Meeting

Creating a meeting in Outlook isn't really all that different from creating a new appointment. There is, of course, the complication of coordinating the schedules for the meeting participants, but Outlook automates most of that process. When you set up a meeting, Outlook can automatically check the availability of participants who use Outlook to schedule their time. You don't have to spend time calling to find out when people will be available because Outlook will find a time for you.

In the following sections, you learn how to use Outlook to set up a meeting. Since meetings are quite similar to appointments in so many ways, we'll concentrate primarily on those settings that are unique to creating a meeting.

Beginning a new meeting

Setting up a new meeting is slightly more complicated than setting up an appointment. One complicating factor is that because meetings involve multiple people, the meeting location is considerably more important than it is for an ordinary appointment. If you set up an appointment to visit your dentist, it's probably pretty clear that the appointment will take place in the dentist's office. With a meeting, things may not be quite so clear, and you'll want to specify all the details so that there is no chance of confusion.

To start a new meeting, follow these steps:

1. Select File ➪ New ➪ Meeting Request to display the Meeting form, as shown in Figure 11-6.

   Notice that the selected meeting time conflicts with other items on the Calendar. This conflict will be resolved later.

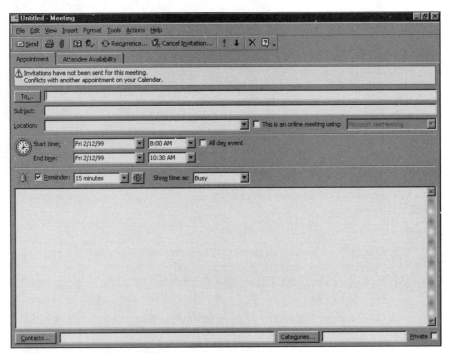

Figure 11-6: Use the Meeting form to plan a new meeting.

2. Enter the meeting description in the Subject text box.

3. Choose a location for the meeting. Later, you will learn how to plan an online meeting.

4. Click the Attendee Availability tab, as shown in Figure 11-7. You could wait with this step until you have designated the other meeting attendees, but because you already know that there is a conflict with your schedule, you may as well correct that conflict first.

Conflict indicated here

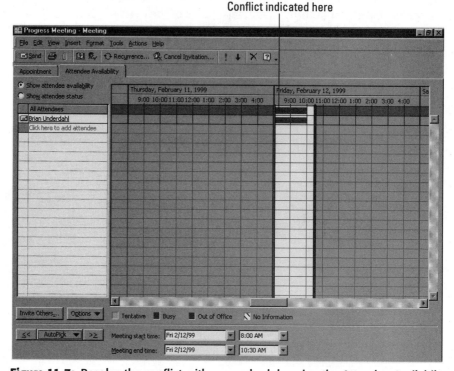

Figure 11-7: Resolve the conflict with your schedule using the Attendee Availability tab.

5. Click the >> button to have Outlook choose the next open time slot for the meeting. Alternatively, you can click the << button to schedule the meeting for an earlier time slot. Figure 11-8 shows that Outlook found an available time by setting the meeting for two hours later than the originally scheduled time.

6. Click the Appointment tab to continue setting up the meeting.

7. Click the To button to display the Select Attendees and Resources dialog box. Notice that your name will already be listed in the Required box. This indicates that you are one of the people who is vital to the success of the meeting.

8. Add the additional attendees to the appropriate boxes. If you are using Exchange Server, you may also be able to reserve resources such as meeting rooms if those resources have their own schedules available on the server. Figure 11-9 shows the completed entries.

No conflict here

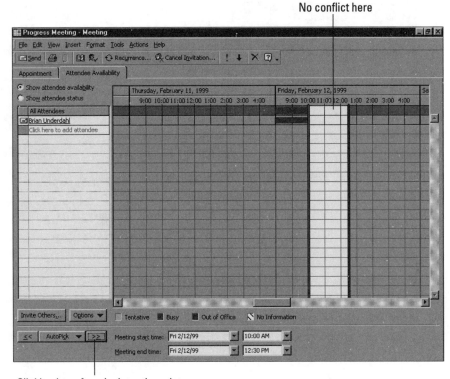

Clicking here found a later time slot

Figure 11-8: Click the >> button to find the next available time for the meeting.

9. Click OK to close the Select Attendees and Resources dialog box and return to the Meeting form.

10. Click the Send button to send the meeting requests.

After you click the Send button, Outlook will send an e-mail message to each attendee inviting them to the meeting. If the attendees are using Outlook to manage their schedule, Outlook will also check their schedule to see if the proposed meeting time seems to be available. If the meeting conflicts with some of the schedules, Outlook can suggest an alternative time that may work better just as it did in moving the meeting time so that it would not conflict with your schedule.

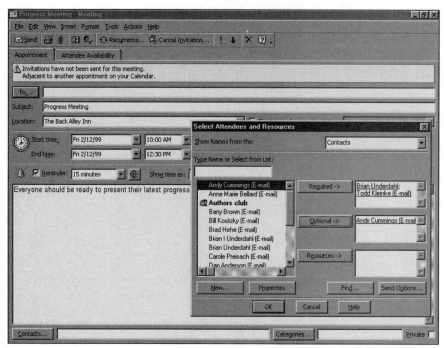

Figure 11-9: Select the people you want to invite to the meeting.

Viewing attendee availability

Once the meeting requests have been sent out and the responses returned, you can check on the status of the attendees. You can also manually set the status for attendees who responded in person or with a phone call rather than through e-mail.

To view or update the availability of the meeting attendees, follow these steps:

1. Double-click the meeting in the Outlook Calendar to open the meeting's form.

2. Click the Attendee Availability tab.

3. Click the *Show attendee status* option button, shown in Figure 11-10.

4. Click in the Response box to set the attendee's status.

5. Click in the Attendance box to change an attendee from required to optional (or to a resource). You cannot change the setting for the meeting organizer.

6. If you need to adjust the meeting schedule, click the *Show attendee availability* radio button.

7. Use the << or the >> button to select a new time that fits everyone's schedule.

Click here to view attendee status

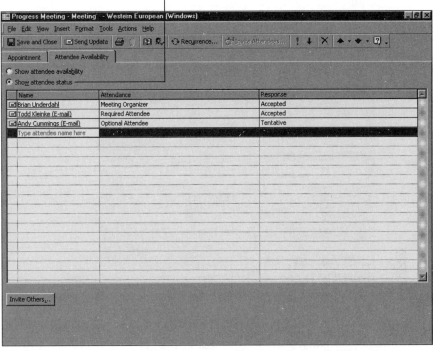

Figure 11-10: View or set attendee status on the Attendee Availability tab.

8. If you changed the meeting time, click the Send Update button to send a message to the attendees informing them that the meeting schedule has changed.

9. Click the Save and Close button to save any changes that you made and close the Meeting form.

Adding additional attendees

Planning a meeting can take some carefully coordinated efforts. Often it is necessary to make certain that a few people can attend before you invite the rest of the crowd. This may be the case if you were planning a meeting and wanted to be sure that your speakers could be there first. There wouldn't be much point in inviting everyone to hear a speaker if you weren't positive that the speaker could attend!

If you need to invite additional attendees once you've set up a meeting, follow these steps:

1. Double-click the meeting in the Outlook Calendar to reopen the Meeting form.

2. Click the Attendee Availability tab.

3. Click the Invite Others button to open the Select Attendees and Resources dialog box, shown in Figure 11-11.

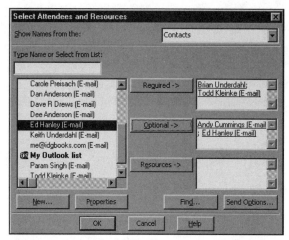

Figure 11-11: Add additional meeting attendees as necessary.

4. Add any additional people to the lists.

5. Click OK.

6. Click the Send Update button to send out the new invitations.

If you plan on inviting people to a meeting in two stages, make certain that you invite all the required attendees the first time. Optional attendees can be invited later without adversely affecting the meeting.

Specifying recurring meetings

A *recurring* meeting is one that takes place two or more times. Some recurring meetings have a limited duration, whereas others may go on indefinitely. A good example of a recurring meeting would be the Executive Committee meeting for an organization. This type of meeting might be held on the same day each month — such as the second Friday of each month.

You can change the status of any appointment or meeting into that of a recurring one. To set up the recurrence schedule, follow these steps:

1. Double-click the meeting or appointment in the Outlook Calendar.

2. Click the Recurrence button to display the Appointment Recurrence dialog box, shown in Figure 11-12.

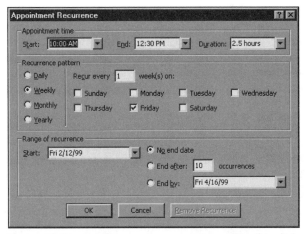

Figure 11-12: Set the recurrence options using this dialog box.

3. Set the appointment time options.

4. Choose the appropriate recurrence pattern options. Note that the dialog box will display different options depending on which of the Daily, Weekly, Monthly, or Yearly radio buttons you select. If you choose Monthly or Yearly, you can choose either a specific date—such as the 12th day of the month—or a specific day—such as the second Friday.

5. Choose the range of recurrence options. You can set a starting date and the duration. For example, you can set the meeting to go on indefinitely by choosing the *No end date* radio button.

6. Click OK to close the Appointment Recurrence dialog box.

7. Click Save and Close to close the Meeting form and save your changes.

If you've set a meeting reminder, Outlook will remind you before each occurrence of the recurring meeting.

Tip   To change a meeting back into a single meeting, open the Appointment Recurrence dialog box and click the Remove Recurrence button.

Integrating with NetMeeting and NetShow

It's becoming more and more common for people to work together even though they are physically many miles apart. The Internet has made it possible to communicate with people almost anywhere in the world. Outlook can leverage these facts by enabling you to schedule and hold online meetings using Microsoft NetMeeting or Microsoft NetShow Services.

NetMeeting is an online collaboration service that enables users to conference via audio, video, chat, whiteboard, and application sharing. NetShow Services are a method of delivering streaming audio and video presentations over the Internet. NetMeeting is a conferencing solution in that it allows two-way interaction. NetShow Services are intended as a one-way content delivery solution—almost like a TV broadcast.

To set up an online meeting using NetMeeting or the NetShow Services, follow these steps:

1. Open the Meeting form for the online meeting. This can be an existing meeting or a new meeting.

2. Select the *This is an online meeting* checkbox. Outlook will add an additional section to the Meeting form for the online meeting details, as shown in Figure 11-13.

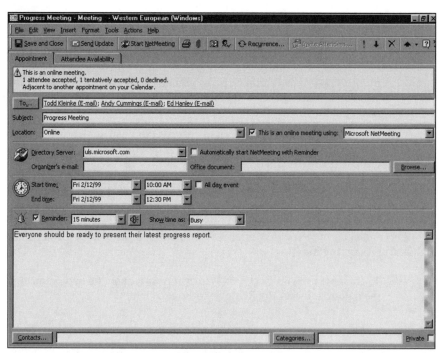

Figure 11-13: Set the online meeting options.

3. Select either Microsoft NetMeeting or NetShow Services as appropriate for your meeting.

4. Select the directory server that you want to use. Each attendee must use the same directory server. If you are using NetShow Services, specify the event address.

5. To have Outlook start NetMeeting (or NetShow Services), select the *Automatically start NetMeeting with Reminder* checkbox.

6. If you want the meeting to begin with a document shown on the attendees' screens, enter the filename in the Office document text box.

7. Click the Send Update button to send out e-mail updates to the attendees.

Because NetMeeting requires considerable bandwidth for acceptable performance, you probably won't want to use advanced features such as video conferencing if you connect to the Internet via a modem. An ISDN connection is really the minimum speed connection that will allow NetMeeting to work very well.

Summary

In this chapter, you learned how to use the Outlook Calendar to manage your schedule. You learned how to create appointments and how to schedule meetings. You saw how Outlook can automatically take over the task of finding available time slots that will fit into everyone's schedule. Finally, you saw how you could set up an online meeting so that people in remote locations can attend a meeting without traveling hundreds or thousands of miles.

The next chapter shows you how to use the Outlook task list to help you keep track of your to-do items.

✦   ✦   ✦

Tracking Tasks

Whether or not you keep a formal list of tasks that you need to accomplish, you likely have your own informal to-do list. It may be something as uncomplicated as just remembering that you need to clean out your garage some time, but everyone has things they need to do.

The Outlook Tasks list is intended to help bring a little organization into the chaos of trying to keep track of those things that you need to get done. You may not feel that you need anything quite so formal as the Outlook Tasks list, but how many times have you forgotten to do something important? Wouldn't it have been handy to have a gentle reminder so you could be just a bit more efficient at completing your tasks?

This chapter will show you how to make the Outlook Tasks list an important yet unobtrusive part of your daily routines. You see how organizing your to-do list can actually make life a little easier by making certain you do those things that are really important to you.

Understanding Tasks

The last chapter demonstrated how to schedule appointments and meetings. At first glance, you might think that tasks could also be scheduled on your Outlook Calendar. There is, however, a very important difference between tasks and those items that you schedule — tasks can be very difficult to schedule.

Consider this example. Suppose you have a garage and a new car. Your garage is too full of junk to leave room for parking your car. You know that winter is coming in a few months, and you'd like to be able to have your car in the garage during the winter. To do this, you'll have to spend a day cleaning out the garage. You could just schedule a garage cleaning day, but what if it turns out that the day you picked several weeks in advance was just too nice to spend inside your filthy old garage? Wouldn't it make more sense to simply place the garage cleaning on a list of things to do and set a specific date when you wanted to be done with the job? That way you would have a constant but gentle reminder of the task, but you could do it when the mood struck you.

Tasks don't all require a specific due date. The garage-cleaning task had a due date because you knew that you wanted it done before the bad weather arrived. Other tasks don't have that kind of urgency. Taking out the trash is an example of a task that needs to be done, but doesn't require setting of a specific date—when the trash can is full it needs to go out, no matter how long it has been since it last went out. The Outlook Tasks list can easily handle both types of tasks—those with a due date and those without one.

Figure 12-1 shows the Outlook Tasks list with several examples of both open-ended tasks (those that show "None" as the due date) and those with specific due dates.

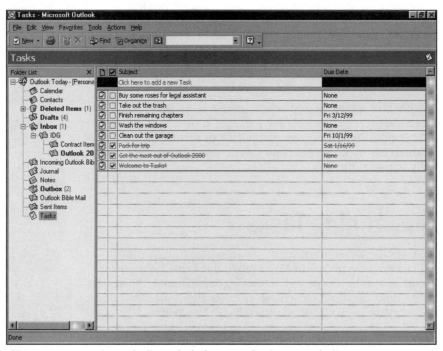

Figure 12-1: Use the Tasks list to help keep track of your to-do list.

The Outlook Tasks list can take on several different appearances. If you display the Outlook Calendar in Day, Work Week, or Week view, the Tasks list shows up in the form of the TaskPad—a condensed view of the Tasks list. If you open the Outlook Today folder, a list of tasks appears, along with a synopsis of your appointments and a total of your active message. As Figure 12-2 shows, you also have quite a few options available on the View ➪ Current View menu for viewing your Tasks list in the manner that is most useful to you.

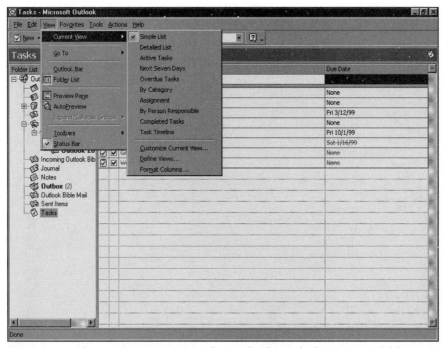

Figure 12-2: Choose the view options that make the Tasks list most useful for your purposes.

Tip Click a column heading in the Tasks list to sort the tasks.

Creating a Task

Adding a new task to your Tasks list is quite easy. In most cases, you can create a new task directly in the Tasks list without even opening the Task form. In fact, depending on how extensively you use the Tasks list, you may find that the simplest method completely serves your needs.

To create a new task in the Tasks list, follow these steps:

1. Open the Tasks Folder.
2. Click at the top of the Tasks list where you see the words *Click here to add a new task*.
3. Type the subject of the task, as shown in Figure 12-3.
4. If you need to set a due date, click the Due Date box and then click the down arrow at the right edge of the box to display a calendar, as shown in Figure 12-4.

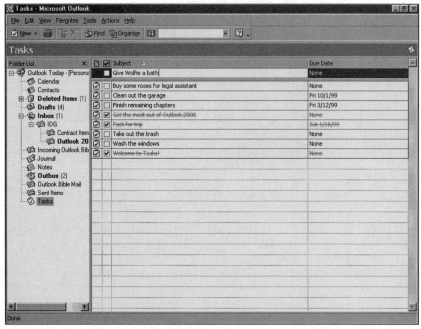

Figure 12-3: Click at the top of the Tasks list to add a new task.

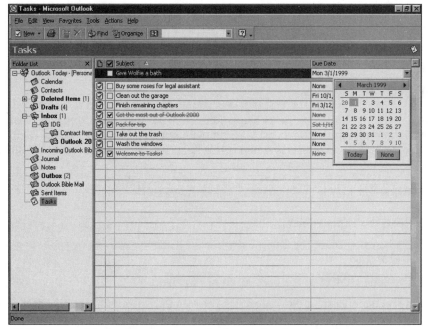

Figure 12-4: Click the down arrow to display a calendar so that you can select a due date.

5. Click a date in the calendar to select the date. If necessary, you can display different months using the right and left arrows at the top of the calendar.

6. Press Enter to add the new task to your Tasks list.

Once a task appears in your Tasks list, there's nothing that's quite so satisfying as seeing the task completed. You've probably noticed that the second column of the Tasks list includes a checkbox in front of each task. To mark a task as completed, you click in the task's checkbox. Outlook shows completed tasks in a lighter color and with a line drawn through the task subject.

Note

Outlook leaves completed tasks in your Tasks list. This enables you to reopen a task by removing the check from the completed checkbox. But leaving completed tasks in the Tasks list also makes it harder to see which tasks remain to be done. When tasks are truly completed, you can remove them from the Tasks list by selecting the completed tasks and clicking the Delete button on the Outlook toolbar.

Setting Task Options

Some tasks are more complicated than others. Although you may be able to handle most tasks very simply using the Tasks list, others are best handled by opening the Task form so that you can access the complete range of task options. You don't have to use all the available options, of course. Still, it's handy to know which options are available so that you have an idea how they may be useful to you.

To open the Task form and set the various options, follow these steps:7

1. Open the Tasks Folder if it is not already open.

2. Double-click a task to display the Task form for that task.

3. To choose a due date or a start date for the task, click the down arrow at the right of the appropriate text box, as shown in Figure 12-5. You may want to specify a start date for those tasks that cannot be started before a specific date. For example, in most cases you could not begin filing your income tax return before the end of January. At the same time, it would be pretty easy to figure out that the due date for that task would probably be April 15th.

4. Click the down arrow at the right of the Status list box, as shown in Figure 12-6, to choose a description of the task's status. Because the Status box is a list box, you must choose one of the options that is shown in the list.

5. Choose Low, Normal, or High in the Priority list box. Setting the task priority is a good way to help you organize your tasks. In most cases, you'll want to complete high-priority tasks first, and leave low priority tasks for last.

6. Use the up and down arrows next to the % Complete spin box to indicate how much of the task you've completed. This is especially useful for tasks that will require several work sessions to complete, or for tasks where you'll need to report on your progress from time to time.

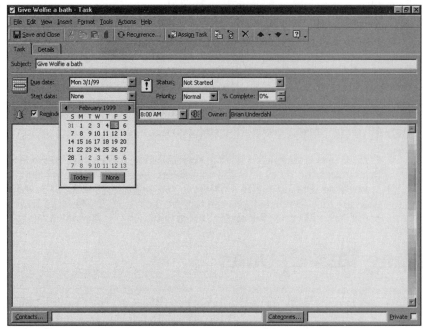

Figure 12-5: Use the Due date and Start date text boxes to specify dates for the task.7

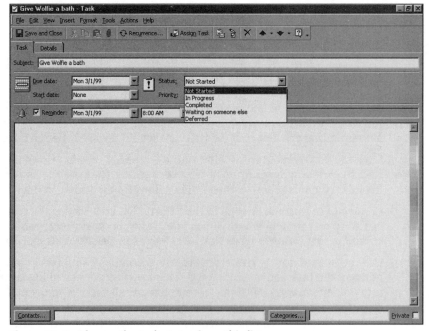

Figure 12-6: Choose the task status from this list.

7. If you want Outlook to give you a reminder that the task is due, make certain the Reminder checkbox is selected.

8. Choose a date and time that you wish to be reminded of the task. By default, Outlook issues reminders at the beginning of the work day, which is generally 8:00 a.m. unless you have specified different working hours.

9. Click the Reminder Sound button to display the Reminder Sound dialog box. You can use this dialog box to select the sound that Outlook plays to remind you that the task is due. Don't forget that you can record your own reminder sounds using the Windows Sound Recorder.

10. Enter any notes about the task in the large text box in the middle of the Task form. You can include anything you find useful here. For example, if you'll need some special supplies to complete this task, you might want to include a shopping list of those supplies.

11. If you need to link this task to someone in your Contacts list, click the Contacts button and choose them.

12. You can also click the Categories button to assign a category to the task. Outlook can then sort the tasks according to their assigned categories.

13. Click the Private checkbox to prevent people who share your Tasks list from seeing this task. Private tasks are only visible in your local Tasks list.

14. Click the Details tab, shown in Figure 12-7. You'll use this tab to add some additional information about the task.

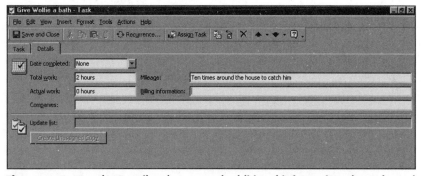

Figure 12-7: Use the Details tab to record additional information about the task.

15. If the task has been completed, enter the date in the Date completed text box.

16. Use the Total work text box to indicate the length of time you expect the task to require.

17. Use the Actual work text box to indicate the amount of time you have spent on the task. This information might be very important for billing purposes.

18. Add any further information necessary in the remaining text boxes.

19. Click the Save and Close button to save your changes and close the Task form.

To print the details of an open task, select File ➪ Print from the Task form menu. This will enable you to print all of the information that you've entered for the task. This might be very handy if the task details include special instructions or something like a necessary materials listing.

Tip To print the details of a task in the Tasks list, right-click the task and choose Print.

If you need to further edit an existing task, remember that you can easily open a task anywhere you see the task. This includes the Tasks folder, the TaskPad in certain Calendar folder views, and in the Outlook Today folder. In fact, since the tasks that are shown in the Outlook Today folder are actually links, simply clicking a task in the Outlook Today folder opens the Task form.

Assigning Tasks to People

One of the nicest things about being in charge is that sometimes you can assign a task to someone else. You may still be responsible for seeing that the job is completed satisfactorily, but someone else will be doing the actual work. In this section, you'll learn how to use the Outlook Tasks list to help you delegate your workload.

You can assign items on your Outlook Tasks list to another person. You might put this feature to good use if you are chairing a committee and need to make certain that a number of items central to the committee's success are completed in a timely manner. By creating the tasks in your copy of Outlook and then assigning those tasks to the committee members, you can track the progress and make certain that you are informed as each task is completed.

To assign a task on your Tasks list to someone else, follow these steps:

1. Open the Task form for the task you wish to assign, as shown in Figure 12-8.
2. Click the Assign Task button on the toolbar to begin assigning the task, as shown in Figure 12-9.
3. Click the To button to display the Select Task Recipient dialog box.
4. Select the person who will be assigned the task.
5. Click the To button.
6. Click OK to close the Select Task Recipient dialog box.
7. To keep a copy of the task in your Tasks list, make certain that the *Keep an updated copy of this task on my task list* checkbox is selected.
8. Make certain that the *Send me a status report when this task is complete* checkbox is selected so that you will be informed when the task is finished.
9. Click the Send button to send out an e-mail message requesting that the recipient accept the task assignment.

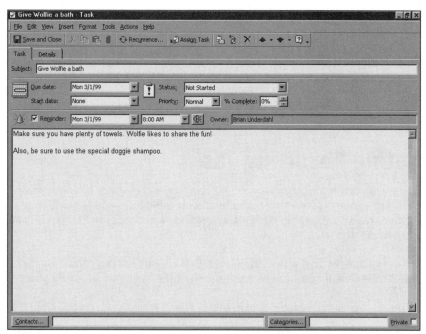

Figure 12-8: To assign a task to someone else, first open the Task form.

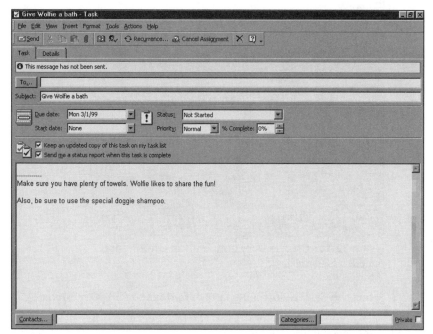

Figure 12-9: Outlook e-mails the task assignment to the person that you specify.

The person who receives the task assignment request can accept the assignment, decline the assignment, or assign the task to someone else. You will receive their response in an e-mail message.

Note   Accepting an assignment request means that you become the owner of the task. Only the task owner can make changes to a task. The person who assigned a task may receive updates regarding the task's status, but they can no longer modify the task.

Creating Recurring Tasks

Some tasks are recurring—you just can't get rid of them no matter how hard you try. For example, your dog probably needs a bath several times a year and your office trash container keeps getting refilled. You probably have other tasks that are recurring, too.

You can specify that a task in your Outlook Tasks list is a recurring task. When you do, Outlook will continue to remind you of the task for as long as you like.

To set a task as a recurring task, follow these steps:

1. Open the task that you wish to set as a recurring task.

2. Click the Recurrence button to display the Task Recurrence dialog box, shown in Figure 12-10.

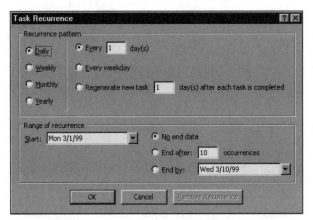

Figure 12-10: Use the Daily button to set a recurrence pattern based on days.

3. Select the daily recurrence pattern options to suit your needs:

   • If you want reminders for this task every so often, select the *Every x day(s)* radio button.

- If you want reminders for this task every day, select the *Every weekday* radio button.

- If you want Outlook to create a new task a specified number of days after this task is completed, select the *Regenerate new task x day(s) after each task is completed* radio button.

4. To set the recurrence pattern based on a weekly option, click the Weekly button, as shown in Figure 12-11.

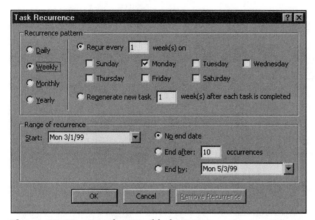

Figure 12-11: Use the Weekly button to set a recurrence pattern based on weeks.

5. Select the weekly recurrence pattern options to suit your needs:

- If you want reminders for this task every so often, select the *Recur every x week(s) on* radio button and then choose the days when you want the reminders.

- If you want Outlook to create a new task a specified number of weeks after this task is completed, select the *Regenerate new task x week(s) after each task is completed* radio button.

6. To set the recurrence pattern based on a monthly option, click the Monthly button, as shown in Figure 12-12.

7. Select the monthly recurrence pattern options to suit your needs:

- If you want reminders for this task every so often, select the *Day x of every x month(s)* radio button and then choose the days when you want the reminders.

- If you want reminders for this task on specific days each month, select the *The x x of every x month(s)* radio button and then choose the days when you want the reminders.

- If you want Outlook to create a new task a specified number of months after this task is completed, select the *Regenerate new task x month(s) after each task is completed* radio button.

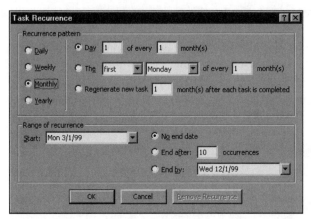

Figure 12-12: Use the Monthly button to set a recurrence pattern based on months.

8. To set the recurrence pattern based on a yearly option, click the Yearly button, as shown in Figure 12-13.

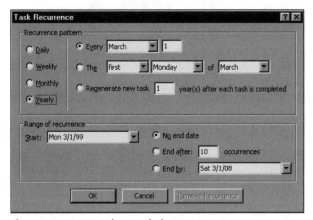

Figure 12-13: Use the Yearly button to set a recurrence pattern based on years.

9. Select the yearly recurrence pattern options to suit your needs:

- If you want reminders for this task every so often, select the *Every x x* radio button and then choose the dates when you want the reminders.

- If you want reminders for this task on specific days each month, select the *The x x of x* radio button and then choose the days when you want the reminders.

- If you want Outlook to create a new task a specified number of years after this task is completed, select the *Regenerate new task x year(s) after each task is completed* radio button.

10. Once you have set the recurrence pattern options, use the options in the lower section of the Task Recurrence dialog box to specify how long the task should repeat.

11. Click the OK button to close the Task Recurrence dialog box.

12. Click Save and Close to save your changes and close the Task form.

You can use recurring tasks for a number of useful purposes. One example might be to provide yourself a reminder that your life insurance premium is due every six months, or that your property taxes are due the first of each quarter. Rather than leaving these types of reminders constantly on your Tasks list, you can use one of the regenerate new task options to have Outlook create a new task when the time is right.

Summary

Doing tasks may sometimes be boring, but at least remembering what you need to do is one task that you can assign to Outlook. In this chapter, you learned about handling tasks in Outlook and how to set task options. You learned how you can use Outlook to assign tasks to other people and how to set a task as recurring.

In the next chapter, you'll learn about the Outlook Journal. You'll see how you can use Outlook to track the time that you spend working on projects and how the Journal can help you be better organized.

✦   ✦   ✦

Keeping Your Journal

If you ever need to keep track of the time you spend working on projects, you'll appreciate how the Outlook Journal can keep an automatic record of the documents you create and use. If you need to know how long you worked on that presentation, the Outlook Journal can tell you. If you need to track the time you spend on the telephone supporting certain customers, the Outlook Journal can tell you that, too.

In this chapter, you learn not only how to use the Outlook Journal's automatic tracking features, but also how you can add your own manual Journal entries. You see how you can use the Outlook Journal to view your work record several different ways so that you can make the most of the information that the Outlook Journal has recorded.

Understanding the Journal

You might do well to think of the Outlook Journal as being similar to a diary. Just as you might use a diary to keep track of things that you've done, the Outlook Journal keeps track of some of the things that you do on your PC. When you work on a Word document, for example, Outlook notes the date and time that you open and close the file. If you later open the same document file, Outlook updates the record to show the new date, time, and duration.

The Outlook Journal automatically tracks the usage data for Access, Excel, PowerPoint, or Word documents. In addition, the Outlook Journal tracks a number of the activities that you perform within Outlook itself — such as sending e-mail and meeting requests. To get the full benefit of the Outlook Journal's automatic document tracking features, you must use Microsoft Office applications to work on your documents. Outlook Journal does not automatically track documents you create using most other programs, but you can easily create your own manual Journal entries.

Figure 13-1 shows one example of how the Outlook Journal tracks certain activities. In this figure, Remote Mail was used several times to access the mail server.

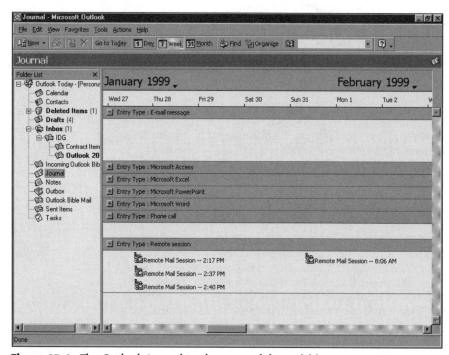

Figure 13-1: The Outlook Journal tracks many of the activities on your PC.

Entries in the Outlook Journal are more than just a log of your activities. Each *Journal entry* actually includes a number of details about the activity, as shown in Figure 13-2. In this Journal entry, the details show that first one message titled "Progress Report" was retrieved and then one new message header was then retrieved from the mail server. No errors were encountered and no messages were sent. To view a Journal entry, double-click the entry in the Outlook Journal event log.

Caution

If you work on an Office document—such as a résumé or personal letter—that you don't want anyone else to know about, you'll need to delete several links in order to hide the record of the document. First, the Office application itself keeps a record of the document at the bottom of the File menu. To remove this, you must select Tools ⇨ Options in the application and then remove the check from the *Recently used file list* checkbox on the General tab. Second, Windows keeps a record of your recently used documents as shortcuts in the \Windows\Recent folder. Remove the relevant shortcut from this folder. Finally, the Outlook Journal log contains a record of each time you worked on the document. You must select and then delete these entries to remove them from the log. It may be better simply to refrain from working on documents that you don't want other people to know about than to try and remove all record of that document from your PC.

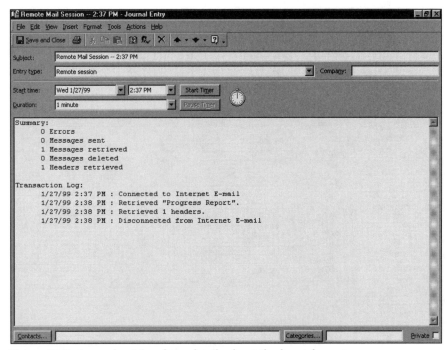

Figure 13-2: Journal entries show details about the logged event.

Although the Outlook Journal can automatically track quite a few different types of activities, it doesn't create Journal entries for everything you do on your PC. Often you must create Journal entries yourself if you want to keep a log of your activities. In some cases, Outlook can provide some assistance with beginning a Journal entry, but you'll have to handle some of the details yourself. For example, if you use the Outlook AutoDialer to call one of your contacts, Outlook can create a Journal entry that begins when you click the Dial button. But because Outlook has no way to determine when you complete the call, you'll have to stop the timer yourself. The Journal entry will then include the call duration as well as the information from the Contacts list.

Note   Because Journal entries contain links to your documents rather than copies of the actual documents, the Journal entries may reference documents that no longer exist on your system. The Outlook Journal does not have any way to record that files have been deleted, moved, or renamed.

Viewing the Journal

Because the Outlook Journal creates a record of your activities, the information that it contains is displayed in several formats that are considerably different from the formats used in the other types of Outlook folders. In the following sections, you get a chance to see each of the Outlook Journal display formats and learn why you might want to view the Outlook Journal in that format.

Using the By Type view format

The default Outlook Journal view is the *By Type* format, shown in Figure 13-3. In this type of view, the Journal entries are arranged in a timeline and are categorized by the document type. To select the By Type view, select View ➪ Current View ➪ By Type.

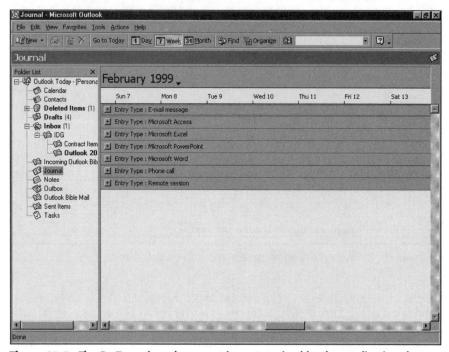

Figure 13-3: The By Type view shows entries categorized by the application that was used.

Each entry type is indicated by a title bar that shows the Journal entry type — Microsoft Word, for example. The left edge of the title bar includes a small box that you can click to expand or contract the type. A plus sign (+) in the box means that the type is collapsed, whereas a minus sign (–) indicates that the type is expanded. You may need to use the vertical scrollbar to see all of the Journal entry types.

When you expand a type, you can view any Journal entries for that type in the area just below the type's title bar. Outlook expands the Journal entry area just enough to display the entries, but you may be a little surprised to discover that no entries appear when you expand a type. The reason for this is that Outlook displays the entries as a timeline. If no entries for the selected type were created recently, you may need to use the horizontal scrollbar to find the most recent entries.

The By Type view is most useful if you want to find out which documents you worked on during a specific period. This view is not particularly useful for locating documents based on any other criteria. You wouldn't want to use the By Type view to try and locate all documents relating to a particular contact, for example.

Using the By Contact view format

The next Outlook Journal view is the *By Contact* format, shown in Figure 13-4. In this type of view, the Journal entries are also arranged in a timeline and are categorized by the contact. To select the By Contact view, select View ➪ Current View ➪ By Contact.

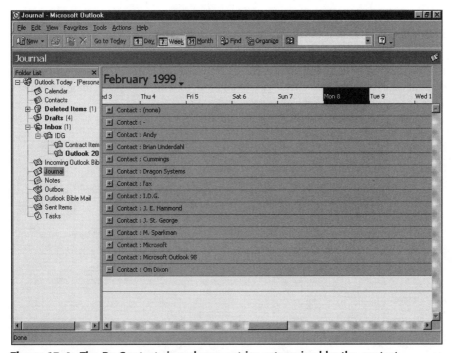

Figure 13-4: The By Contact view shows entries categorized by the contact.

Each entry type is indicated by a title bar that shows the contact name. Click the small box to expand or contract the type. You may also need to use the vertical scrollbar.

The By Contact view makes it quite easy to find all documents related to a specific contact. Any type of document, whether it is an Excel worksheet or an e-mail message, can appear in the list.

Caution Documents will only appear in the correct category in the By Contact view if the document is linked to the correct contact. This will be done automatically for items such as e-mail messages, but you must take care to see that Office documents are linked correctly. One way to ensure documents are correctly linked is to select the contact in the Outlook Contacts folder and then select File ➪ New ➪ Office Document.

To make the By Contact view truly useful, you may need to open the Category (none) category and then assign the existing Journal entries to specific contacts. To do so, double-click the Journal entry to open it, click the Contacts button, choose the contacts you wish to link to the entry, and click Save and Close to update the Journal entry.

Using the By Category view format

The next Outlook Journal view is the *By Category* format, shown in Figure 13-5. In this type of view, the Journal entries are also arranged in a timeline and are organized by the category that you assigned. To select the By Category view, select View ➪ Current View ➪ By Category.

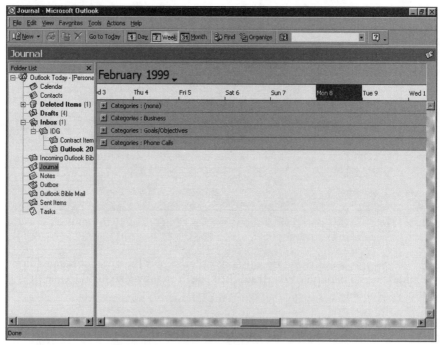

Figure 13-5: The By Category view shows entries organized using the categories you selected.

The By Category view can be very handy—especially if you create categories that break down the Journal entries by project. This view can also be almost useless unless you take the time to click the Categories button when you create documents. By default, Outlook doesn't assign any categories, so the usefulness of this view is totally dependent on your assigning the categories yourself.

You can assign categories using the existing categories, or you can create your own categories. As Figure 13-6 shows, you can click the Categories button at the bottom of the Journal Entry form to display the Categories dialog box (you'll find the Categories button at the bottom of many types of Outlook forms). You can choose from the list of available categories, or click the Master Category List button to display the Master Category List dialog box so that you can create your own categories. One very useful way to use these options would be to create categories for each project—such as an Outlook Bible category. That would enable you to assign the project's category to all documents relating to that project, and would make it very easy to locate everything relating to the project.

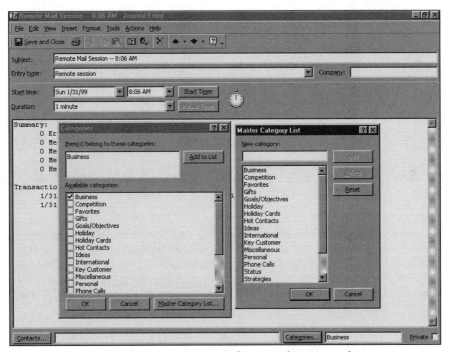

Figure 13-6: Create the categories you need to organize your projects.

Using the Entry List view format

The next Outlook Journal view may turn out to be the most useful of all. The Entry List view dispenses with the timeline view and instead displays all the Journal entries, as shown in Figure 13-7. To select the Entry List view, select View ➪ Current View ➪ Entry List.

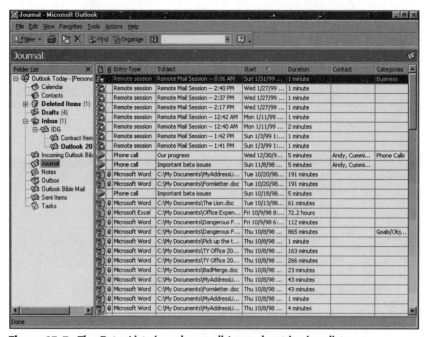

Figure 13-7: The Entry List view shows all Journal entries in a list.

Because the Entry List view does not use the timeline to display the entries, it's much easier to view the list of entries — you don't have to use the horizontal scrollbar to locate the items. By default, this view is sorted in descending order based on the start date, but you can quickly sort the list using any of the columns. Simply click a column heading to sort the list based on the entries in the selected column. Click a second time to reverse the sort order.

The paperclip icon in the second column of the Entry List view indicates that an entry is a document. If there is no paperclip icon, the entry is a log of an activity that occurred within Outlook — such as an e-mail message.

Because the Entry List view makes it easy to see all the Journal entries, you'll find this view is very helpful if you want to open Journal entries so that you can assign them to specific contacts or categories. Double-click an entry to open its Journal Entry form so that you can make any necessary changes. Click Save and Close to save your changes and return to the Outlook Journal.

Using the Last Seven Days view format

The Last Seven Days view looks quite similar to the Entry List view. Figure 13-8 shows the Last Seven Days view. To select the Last Seven Days view, select View⇨ Current View⇨Last Seven Days.

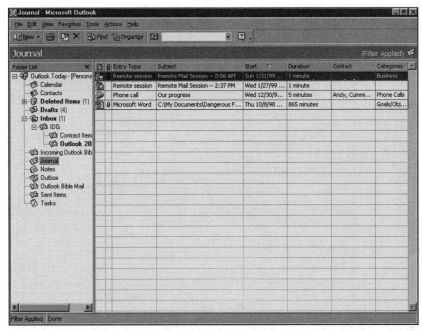

Figure 13-8: The Last Seven Days view shows the last week's Journal entries in a list.

If you look closely at the figure, you may notice that something doesn't look quite right. The dates shown for the Journal entries clearly span much more than a week. Why are these entries showing up in the Last Seven Days view? The answer is both simple and subtle. The dates that are shown are the *start* dates for the Journal entries—not the dates when the items were last accessed. What the Outlook Journal is displaying are the Journal entries that were created, accessed, or modified within the past week. Each of the Journal entries in the list were accessed in some way during the past week—even though the original Journal entries may have been created quite some time ago.

The Last Seven Days view is very useful when you need to locate items you've worked on recently—especially if you can't quite remember the filename.

Tip

> You can use the View⇨Current View⇨Customize Current View command to customize the Last Seven Days view to specify a different time period—such as the past month.

Using the Phone Calls view format

The final Outlook Journal view is the Phone Calls view as shown in Figure 13-9. This view singles out those Journal entries for phone calls. To select the Phone Calls view, select View ➪ Current View ➪ Phone Calls.

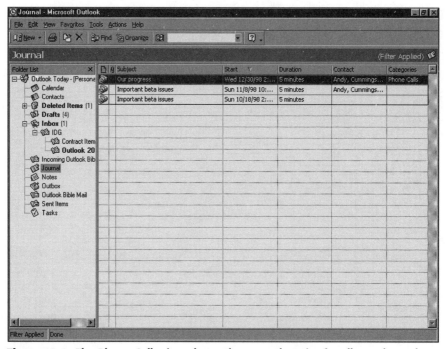

Figure 13-9: The Phone Calls view shows the Journal entries for all your logged phone calls.

Outlook will only create Journal entries for phone calls automatically if you use the Outlook AutoDialer to begin the call. You'll have to specify the duration yourself by entering the appropriate time in the phone call Journal entry. You can do so by actually entering a time or by clicking the Stop Call button.

Tracking your phone calls in the Outlook Journal may be more useful than you imagine. If you bill for your time, you can use the phone call Journal entries to keep track of the time you spend on billable calls. But even if you don't bill for your time, you'll find that phone call Journal entries make it easier to recall what was said in the conversation.

Tip

Remember to link your phone call Journal entries to the appropriate contacts so that it will be easier to find all entries relating to specific contacts.

Controlling Journal Data

The Outlook Journal records a lot of information automatically, but these automatic settings may not completely suit your needs. In the following sections, you learn how to control which types of information the Outlook Journal tracks. You also learn how to create your own entries for items that aren't tracked automatically.

Limiting Journal data

You may not want the Outlook Journal to automatically record all of the information that it does by default. You can easily control which information the Outlook Journal records so that the logs more closely meet your needs.

To select which items the Outlook Journal tracks, follow these steps:

1. Select Tools ➪ Options to display the Options dialog box.

2. Click the Journal Options button on the Preferences tab to display the Journal Options dialog box, shown in Figure 13-10.

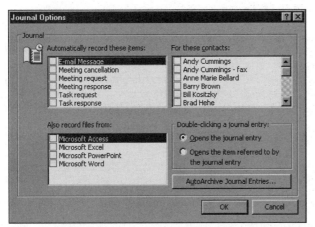

Figure 13-10: Use the Journal Options dialog box to select which items are recorded automatically.

3. Select the Outlook events that you wish to record from the *Automatically record these items* box.

4. Select the Microsoft Office documents you wish to track in the *Also record files from* box.

5. Select the contacts you wish to track in the *For these contacts* box. You can choose, for example, to track e-mail messages from certain contacts and ignore those from other contacts.

6. Choose the action that you want to occur when you double-click a Journal entry in the Outlook Journal. It's usually best to open the Journal entry rather than the document—otherwise it will be more difficult to edit the information in the Journal entry. You can always open the items referenced in a Journal entry from within the Journal entry itself.

7. If you wish to change the way Outlook handles old Journal entries, click the *AutoArchive Journal Entries* button and select the settings you prefer.

8. Click OK to close the Journal Options dialog box.

9. Click OK to close the Options dialog box.

If you change the Outlook Journal options, be sure to select all the items that you wish to record. If you add a check to any of the checkboxes in the Journal Options dialog box, Outlook will stop using the default settings and only record those items that you specifically selected.

Caution   Don't forget that limiting the information that is recorded in the Outlook Journal does not prevent Windows or the application you are using from keeping a record of documents you work on.

Adding Journal entries manually

If you occasionally use programs that don't create automatic Journal entries, you may still wish to keep a record of the fact that you've worked on a project. This would be especially true if you need to track the time you've spent for billing purposes, but you may want to keep these records simply to help keep things organized. Fortunately, you'll find that creating your own Journal entries manually is a simple process.

To create Journal entries manually, follow these steps:

1. Select File ➪ New ➪ Journal Entry to display a blank Journal Entry form, as shown in Figure 13-11.

2. Enter a descriptive subject for this Journal entry.

3. Choose the type of entry.

4. If necessary, enter a company name.

5. To link this Journal entry to a contact, use the Contacts button and choose the contact.

6. To assign a category, use the Categories button and choose a category.

7. To link this Journal entry to a file, drag and drop the file into the note area. You'll probably find that Windows Explorer is the easiest tool to use for dragging and dropping a file.

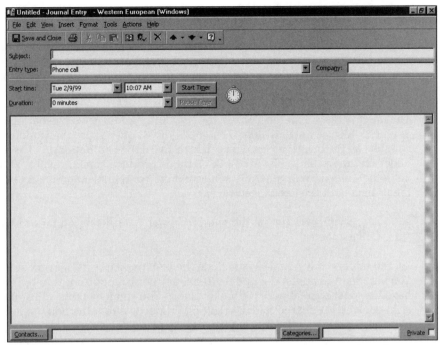

Figure 13-11: Use the Journal Entry form to create your own Journal entries manually.

8. Specify a starting date, time, and duration.

9. Alternatively, click the Start Timer button to begin logging the time you spend.

10. Click the Pause Time button to stop logging the time.

11. Click the Save and Close button to save your Journal entry.

You can later reopen your new Journal entry just the same way you open any other Journal entry. If you did not change the default double-click setting, you can simply double-click a Journal entry to open it. Regardless of the double-click setting, you can always open a Journal entry by right-clicking it and choosing Open from the pop-up menu.

Tip   If you can't remember which entry type you chose for a manual Journal entry, select View ⇨ Current View ⇨ and choose Entry List or Last Seven Days as appropriate.

Sharing Journal Information

Because the Outlook Journal keeps track of activities using a timeline, you may find that the Outlook Journal is one of the most useful of Outlook's folders to share. If you are working on a project with several people, a shared Outlook Journal may be just the thing that you need to make certain everyone is on track.

The most universal method of sharing the Outlook Journal is by sharing the folder as a net folder. If you and all of the people you want to share the Outlook Journal with use an Exchange Server, you can also share the Outlook Journal as a public folder on the Exchange Server. Both methods produce similar results, although the net folder approach is generally somewhat easier to implement unless everyone in the project uses the Exchange Server.

Cross-Reference   See "Sharing Folders" at the end of Chapter 7 for details on how to share your Outlook Journal.

Shared folders may not always include the latest updates from every subscriber. You may want to adjust the update frequency if it is important that the subscribers have the most current information available. You can make this adjustment by right-clicking the shared folder, selecting Properties from the pop-up menu, and choosing options on the Sharing tab.

Summary

The Outlook Journal is a very handy tool for tracking activities and documents on your PC. In this chapter, you learned how to use the Outlook Journal to automatically track many of these things, and how to create manual Journal entries when necessary. You learned how to change the way the Outlook Journal displays items so that you can more easily find what you need. Finally, you learned that you can easily share your Outlook Journal with others.

The next chapter shows you how to use Outlook's Notes. If you've ever used those little paper sticky notes to remind yourself about something, you'll appreciate the fact that Outlook Notes can fill in quite nicely — they don't get buried on your desktop, and they don't end up filling up your trashcan.

✦   ✦   ✦

Taking Notes

Notes are probably the Outlook feature that people use the least. In some ways, that's a little hard to understand, especially when you realize that almost everyone has those sticky paper notes all over their desk. Outlook Notes can easily replace those paper sticky notes, and they won't get buried under all the other paper on your desktop.

In this chapter, you learn how to use Outlook Notes. You have a chance to see if using Notes can help make your desktop just a bit less cluttered and your life just a bit more organized.

Understanding Notes

If you've ever written yourself a reminder on one of those little paper sticky notes, you're already familiar with the concept behind Outlook Notes. They're perfect for all those quick little things that you need to jot down, such as a phone number, a name, an address, the title of a book someone just told you about, or whatever you need to jog your memory.

Outlook Notes have several advantages over those paper sticky notes:

✦ Paper sticky notes are easily lost — especially if there's a lot of paperwork covering your desk. Outlook Notes, on the other hand, are easy to find. If they're closed, you'll find them in the Outlook Notes Folder. If they're open, they'll appear right there on your computer screen — even if Outlook is minimized.

✦ Paper sticky notes have a limited amount of space for you to write your note. but Outlook Notes can expand to hold as much text as you need.

✦ Paper sticky notes can be hard to read — especially if you have sloppy writing. Outlook Notes are always easy to read — the text is just as clear as any other text on your monitor.

✦ Paper sticky notes must be refilled when the pad runs out, but Outlook Notes are always available in a free, endless supply.

Figure 14-1 shows a typical Outlook Note.

Tip   If you need to store several pieces of text and have them available while you're creating a document, you may want to paste those clips onto Outlook Notes. Unlike the Windows Clipboard, the text on your Notes won't be replaced when you copy something new to the Clipboard. You can easily cut, copy, and paste text to and from Notes.

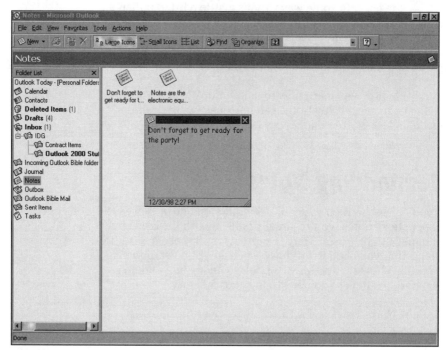

Figure 14-1: Use Outlook Notes in place of those paper sticky notes that are easily lost on your desktop.

Creating and Editing Notes

Paper sticky notes wouldn't be nearly as popular as they are if they weren't so darn convenient to use. You just grab the pad, jot a quick note, and stick it someplace where you'll find it when you need it. Outlook Notes are just about as easy to create as those paper sticky notes. Outlook Notes are even better than a paper sticky note if you need to edit what's on the note—you don't have to throw away the old note and start over because you ran out of space!

To create a new Outlook Note, follow these steps:

   1. If necessary, open Outlook.

2. If you intend to create several Notes, open the Notes Folder. This is optional, but if the Notes Folder is open, you can click the New Note button to begin a new Note without wading through Outlook's menus.

3. Select File ➪ New ➪ Note to display a new, blank Note, as shown in Figure 14-2.

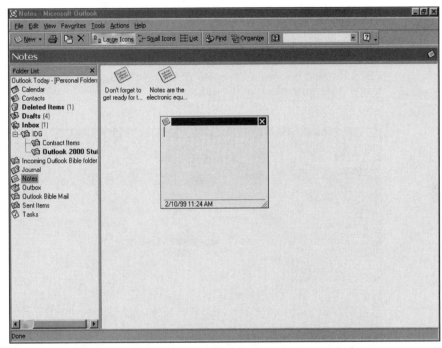

Figure 14-2: Use a Note to give yourself a handy onscreen reminder.

4. Type the text of your Note.

5. Click the Close button if you want to close the Note. Otherwise, you can click outside the Note to leave the Note open on your screen.

6. Click the Note icon on the Windows taskbar to view open Notes that are covered by other windows.

Tip Right-click in an open Note to display a pop-up menu that you can use to cut or copy text from the Note and place in the Windows Clipboard, or to paste text from the Windows Clipboard into the Note.

Windows treats open Notes almost as though they were separate programs. You can view the text of an open Note even if the Outlook window is minimized. Any open Notes are closed when you close Outlook, however.

The same thing that makes paper sticky notes so convenient — their small size — also makes them hard to edit; they don't have much room for corrections. Unless you write your notes in pencil, making corrections on a paper sticky note usually means crossing out the incorrect information and trying to find room for the replacement text. Often this means starting over with a new paper sticky note.

Editing an Outlook Note couldn't be easier. Here's how to edit an existing Outlook Note:

1. Open the Outlook Notes folder.

2. Double-click the Note you want to edit.

3. Type the new text, as shown in Figure 14-3. If you want to replace existing text, select the text you want to replace before you begin typing so that your new text will take the place of the old text.

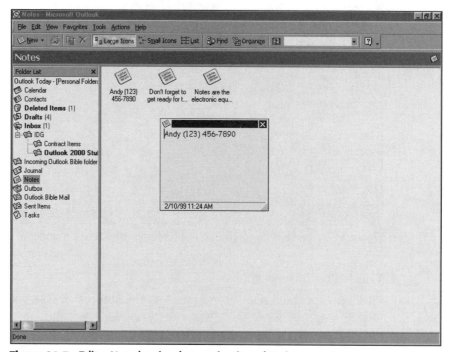

Figure 14-3: Edit a Note by simply opening it and typing your text.

4. Close the Note or leave it open as you please.

Tip   If a Note is already open, just click within the Note to begin editing the Note.

You may have noticed that the only type of Note content that has been mentioned is text. The reason for this is quite simple—Notes can't hold anything except text. If you were to copy any nontext item to the Windows Clipboard, you wouldn't be able to paste it into a Note. This means that you cannot, for example, place a picture within a Note.

Using Note Options

Because Outlook Notes are so simple, they don't really require a lot of options. There are a few small changes that you can make, however, and they are discussed in the following sections.

Specifying a color

You can use five different colors for your Notes. Whether you choose colors for simple aesthetic reasons or to specify different types of notes is up to you. Outlook treats all Notes equally regardless of the color.

To choose a color for a Note, follow these steps:

1. Open the Note.
2. Click the Note icon in the upper-left corner of the Note.
3. Select Color, as shown in Figure 14-4, and choose the color for the Note.

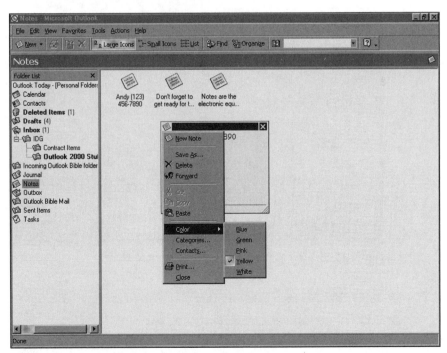

Figure 14-4: You can choose from five colors for your Notes.

As you'll see in "Specifying Note default options" shortly, you can also choose a default color for your Notes.

Specifying a category

You can assign categories to your Notes if you want to organize them. This will enable you to view your Notes by category—which may be especially useful if you create a large number of Notes.

To assign a category to a Note, follow these steps:

1. Open the Note.
2. Click the Note icon in the upper-left corner of the Note.
3. Select Categories to display the Categories dialog box, shown in Figure 14-5.

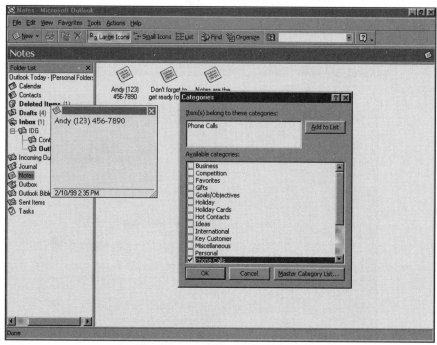

Figure 14-5: You can choose categories for your Notes.

4. Add a check to each category that you wish to assign to this Note.
5. Click OK to close the Categories dialog box.

Tip   Remember that you can click the Master Category List button to create your own custom categories.

Specifying a contact

You can also link a Note to a contact. Anything that you link to a contact will be accessible from their Contact form. You might find this feature handy if you need to create a Note that you want open on your desktop, because a Note takes up far less room than the Contact form.

To link a Note to a contact, follow these steps:

1. Open the Note.

2. Click the Note icon in the upper-left corner of the Note.

3. Select Contacts to display the Contacts for Note dialog box.

4. Click the Contacts button to display the Select Contacts dialog box, shown in Figure 14-6.

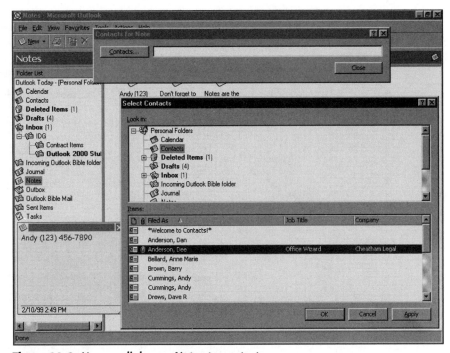

Figure 14-6: You can link your Notes to contacts.

5. Select the contacts you wish to link to this Note.

6. Click OK to close the Select Contacts dialog box.

7. Click Close to close the Contacts for Note dialog box.

Tip   You can assign several contacts to the same Note if necessary.

Specifying Note default options

If you use Outlook Notes a lot, you may decide that you would like your Notes to look just a bit different. For example, if you often create very short Notes, you may want to choose a smaller default size so that you don't have to drag the Note borders to minimize the space that they occupy on your desktop.

To set the defaults for all new Notes, follow these steps:

1. Select Tools ⇨ Options to display the Options dialog box.

2. Click the Note Options button on the Preferences tab to display the Notes Options dialog box, shown in Figure 14-7.

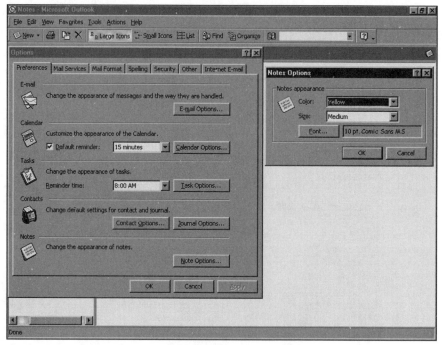

Figure 14-7: Choose the Note default settings your prefer.

3. Select the default color from the drop-down Color list box.

4. Select the default size for your Notes from the drop-down Size list box. Don't forget that you can resize a Note no matter what default size is chosen.

5. Click the Font button if you want to change the font settings. If you like, you can easily choose different fonts, sizes, attributes, and colors.

6. Click OK to close the Notes Options dialog box.

7. Click OK to close the Options dialog box.

Changing the default settings won't affect any of your existing Notes.

Specifying timestamp options

Outlook normally adds the date and time that a Note was created to the bottom of each Note. In most cases, you'll probably appreciate having this reminder of the age of the Note, but if you don't want the date and time shown, you can deselect this option. Unlike most Note options, however, this option is well hidden.

To control the display of the date and time on your Notes, follow these steps:

1. Select Tools ⇨ Options to display the Options dialog box.

2. Click the Other tab.

3. Click the Advanced Options button to display the Advanced Options dialog box, shown in Figure 14-8.

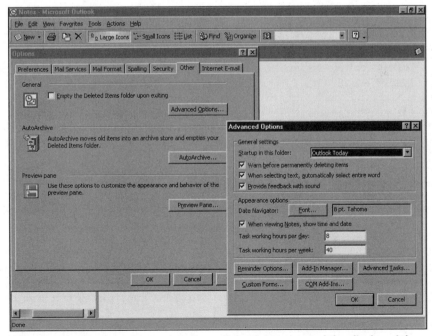

Figure 14-8: Use the Advanced Options dialog box to control the display of the date and time on Notes.

4. To hide the date and time display, remove the check from the *When viewing Notes, show time and date* checkbox.

5. Click OK to close the Advanced Options dialog box.

6. Click OK to close the Options dialog box.

If you change the setting for the time and date display, Outlook will use the new setting for all Notes — new or old. If you later choose to redisplay the time and date, Outlook will remember the dates and times for your existing Notes.

Viewing Your Notes

If you create a lot of Notes, you'll eventually find that you need a little organization in order to keep track of them. Outlook provides this organization in the form of different views of the Notes Folder. In the following sections, you learn how these different views may be useful to you.

Using the Icon views

There are actually three different views that you can display using the View ⇨ Current View ⇨ Icons command. When you choose this command, Outlook adds three buttons to the toolbar. The Large Icons button displays each Note using a large Note icon and the first few words of the Note. The Small Icons button displays your Notes using a small Note icon followed by the text of the Note, as shown in Figure 14-9. The List button displays your Notes almost identically to the way they are displayed using the Small Icons button. The difference between these two views is that Small Icons view often includes a scrollbar at the bottom of the window so that by scrolling you can read more of the text of the message.

Because the Large Icons view displays the largest number of your Notes onscreen at one time, you may wish to use this view if you need to locate a particular Note — especially if you haven't used categories or colors to organize your Notes.

Using the Notes List view

The Notes List view is quite similar to the Small Icons view except that more of the Note text is displayed on the screen. Figure 14-10 shows the Notes List view. To display this view, select View ⇨ Current View ⇨ Notes List.

Because the Notes List view shows more of the Note text onscreen, you may find this view particularly useful in helping jog your memory as you try to locate a specific Note. Of course, you'll also have to scroll more using this view, because each Note takes up so much more of your screen space.

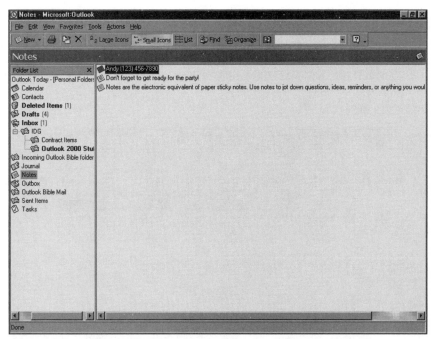

Figure 14-9: The Icon views display your Notes in alphabetical order.

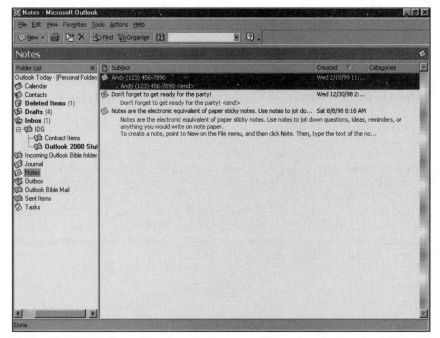

Figure 14-10: The Notes List view displays your Notes showing much of their text.

Using the Last Seven Days view

The Last Seven Days view is virtually identical to the Notes List view, except that the view will only include those Notes created in the past week. Figure 14-11 shows the Last Seven Days view. To display this view, select View ➪ Current View ➪ Last Seven Days.

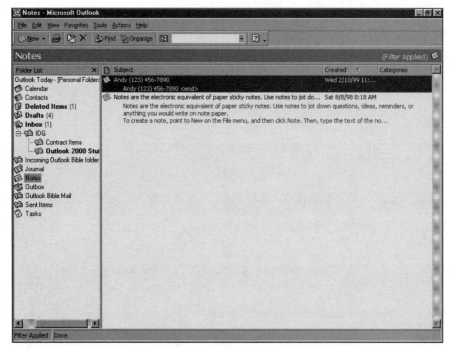

Figure 14-11: The Last Seven Days view displays your Notes created during the past week.

Note   As the figure shows, Outlook displays the default Note that Outlook creates to explain Notes, even though this Note is clearly more than a week old. You can delete this Note if you like.

You'll find the Last Seven Days view very useful if you create a lot of Notes and need to find one of your more recent ones. You probably won't want to use this view as your default view, however, because you'll quickly lose track of important Notes once they have been around for over a week.

Using the By Category view

The By Category view organizes your Notes by the categories you assign to them. Figure 14-12 shows the By Category view. To display this view, select View ➪ Current View ➪ By Category.

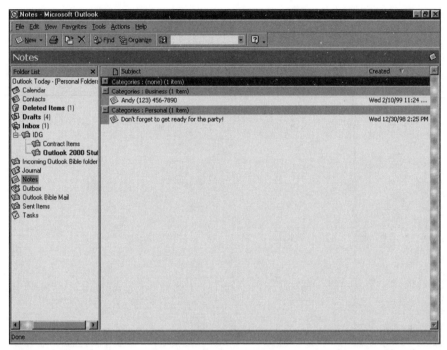

Figure 14-12: The By Category view displays your Notes using the categories that you assign.

Note

If you open a Note and assign a category to the Note, Outlook does not apply the change until you close the Note. If you've opened a Note in the By Category view and then assigned a category to the Note, Outlook won't update the view until you close the Note.

In the By Category view, Outlook displays a title bar for each category that you have assigned to a Note. At the left edge of the title bar, you'll see a small box with a plus sign (+) or a minus sign (–). You can click the plus sign to expand the category display or the minus sign to collapse the category.

Using categories to organize your Notes can be an excellent way to make certain you can find related Notes. Because you can create your own categories, you can easily organize your Notes by project.

Using the By Color view

The final Outlook Notes view is the By Color view, shown in Figure 14-13. In this view, your Notes are grouped using the five available Note colors. To display this view, select View ➪ Current View ➪ By Color.

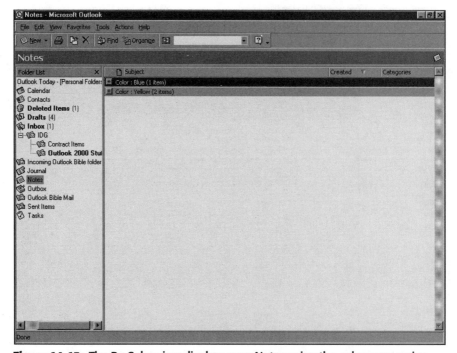

Figure 14-13: The By Color view displays your Notes using the colors you assign.

Like the By Category view, Outlook displays a title bar with a small box at the left edge for each color that you have assigned to a Note. You can click the plus sign to expand the color display or the minus sign to collapse the color.

With only five colors available, the By Color view offers far fewer organizational options than the By Category view. Still, if you only need a few Note groups, organizing them by color does offer one large advantage — the different colors are easy to see in any view or even when a Note is simply open on the Windows desktop.

Summary

Outlook's Notes can be very handy. As a replacement for those paper sticky notes, Outlook Notes offer several advantages. In this chapter, you learned how to create and edit Notes, how to use the available options, and how to use the Note views to help you organize your Notes.

In the next chapter, you learn how to use Outlook to view newsgroups on the Internet. You also see how you can use Outlook to search through the thousands of newsgroups to find topics of interest.

✦　　✦　　✦

Using Newsgroups

Outlook is a tool that manages information. In this chapter, you learn about using Outlook to manage information that you can find in *newsgroups* on the Internet. You may not even realize that this vast source of information exists, but even if you do, you probably aren't aware that you can use Outlook to access it.

Outlook's support for Internet newsgroups is one of the least obvious features of the program. You've probably noticed that Outlook uses folders to organize the various types of information — such as e-mail messages, contacts, and your Calendar. A quick glance at the Outlook folder list, however, doesn't reveal a Newsgroup folder. That won't stop you from accessing newsgroups — it just makes this chapter all the more important if you want to get the most out of Outlook.

What Is a Newsgroup?

Newsgroups are a part of the Internet, but you may not even be aware they exist. They are places where people get together online to share all sorts of information. In most newsgroups, people post questions and comments, and other people join in with an answer, another question, or a comment. You can often learn quite a bit just by looking at the messages in a newsgroup, even if you don't post any messages yourself.

Caution

Newsgroups contain a wide range of information. Not all of the information posted in newsgroups is necessarily accurate. (This applies to the Web as a whole, by the way.) Although most people who post messages in newsgroups are probably trying to provide useful information, it's quite likely that you'll also encounter people who get their kicks by intentionally misleading people whenever possible. You must be the ultimate judge of the accuracy of the information that you receive from newsgroups. If possible, try to verify important information using a different source before relying on possibly suspect advice from someone in a newsgroup.

Tens of thousands of newsgroups exist on the Internet. No one can give an accurate count of the newsgroups because the number is constantly changing. You'll find that there are several newsgroups devoted to almost any subject that might interest you. Each newsgroup has its own unique flavor that results from the blend of characters that frequent the newsgroup. If you don't care for one newsgroup, you can probably find a different one that better suits your needs.

Unfortunately, newsgroups also have some unpleasant aspects:

✦ Most newsgroups that are not *moderated* — meaning that there is someone in charge who monitors the messages that are posted — seem to be heavily infested with ads for get-rich-quick schemes and pornography.

✦ *Flames* — insults — are a common form of communication in many newsgroups. Some people seem to feel that the anonymous nature of the Internet makes it perfectly acceptable to be an absolute bore. These people often use language in newsgroups that they would never use in normal conversation. Unfortunately, there isn't a whole lot you can do except to ignore the flames and hope that the bozos will eventually grow up.

✦ Allowing your e-mail address to appear in newsgroups is almost like asking to have your Inbox swamped with *spam* — junk e-mail messages. Many junk mailers use special programs that search through newsgroup postings looking for e-mail addresses. The garbage they send out typically has nothing to do with the newsgroup subject — they're just hoping that a few of the hundreds of thousands of junk e-mail messages they send out will produce a positive response.

 Tip

One way to prevent at least some of the junk e-mail messages from reaching your Inbox is to set up and use a separate online e-mail account when you need to post messages in newsgroups. For example, you can get a free online e-mail account from Microsoft by going to www.hotmail.com or by clicking the Hotmail link that appears on the Microsoft Web site. (Other free e-mail accounts are available from RocketMail, Yahoo!, Infoseek, Lycos, and a host of others.)

With all the negative things that I've said about newsgroups, you may be wondering why anyone would ever bother visiting them. There are several reasons why you may find newsgroups useful:

✦ Newsgroups are often the best source of information you can find about a subject. For example, a manufacturer's tech support department may deny that a piece of hardware or software has any problems. You've probably heard "you're the only person who's reported that problem" just a few too many times. In a newsgroup, you may find out the solution to the problem that the manufacturer says doesn't exist.

✦ Newsgroups can be great places to see what people are thinking about a subject. Where else can you see the thoughts and opinions of people from around the globe so quickly and without government intervention or censorship?

✦ Newsgroups may provide the only source of information about certain subjects. If you want to know where you can find a front axle for a 1939 Ford 9N tractor or how to prepare lutefisk, you'll probably have better luck in the newsgroups than just about anywhere else.

✦ A newsgroup may be the only place where you can find other people who are interested in many obscure subjects. Because newsgroups tend to draw people with deep interest in their subjects, you'll probably find the real experts if you frequent the right newsgroups.

Preparing to Use Newsgroups

Although newsgroup messages bear some resemblance to the e-mail messages that appear in your Outlook Inbox, there are a number of important differences between the two types of messages. Newsgroup messages aren't generally sent to your e-mail address. Rather, those messages are *posted* to a message board so that anyone can read the messages and any replies. Also, the sheer volume of newsgroup messages means that you have to deal with those messages differently than you deal with your e-mail messages.

Rather than downloading all the newsgroup messages to your computer, you first download the list of available newsgroups. Next, you pick the newsgroups that look interesting and download a group of message headers from that group. Finally, you select individual messages that you want to read and download those messages. Although this may sound like a cumbersome set of steps, it's the only practical method of dealing with the gigabytes of newsgroup messages. Even the fastest modem would never be able to download every newsgroup message—new messages are always being posted faster than you would be able to download them.

Setting up newsgroups

The first time you access newsgroups, you'll need to download the entire list of newsgroup names. Depending on the speed of you connection, this process could take as long as fifteen minutes. After the first time you have downloaded the newsgroup list, you won't need to download the whole list again, so future newsgroup access will be much faster than the first time you connect.

Outlook actually uses the Outlook Express Newsgroup Reader to provide you with access to the newsgroups. You won't really notice too much difference, except that you'll have a second program running alongside Outlook.

Note   Just as you must specify which mail server Outlook should access to send and receive e-mail messages, you'll need to specify which news server to access for newsgroups. Your ISP will provide this information. The server you want will be called either the news server or the NNTP server—these two are the same thing.

To access the newsgroups from Outlook, follow these steps:

1. Select View ➪ Go To ➪ News. This will open the Outlook Newsreader window, as shown in Figure 15-1.

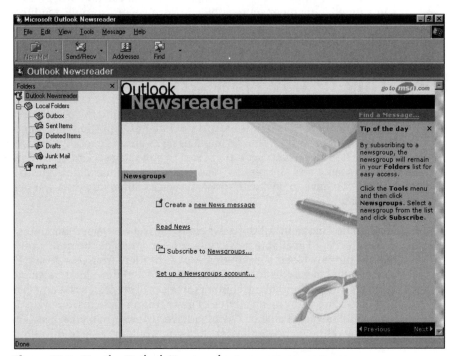

Figure 15-1: Use the Outlook Newsreader to access newsgroups.

2. You should be prompted to connect to the Internet.

3. Click the Read News link to connect to the news server. If you have not subscribed to any newsgroups, you'll probably see a message similar to the one shown in Figure 15-2.

4. Click Yes to continue. If this is your first time accessing the news server, you will have to wait while the newsgroup names are downloaded.

5. When the Newsgroup Subscriptions dialog box is displayed, as shown in Figure 15-3, wait until your modem indicator lights in the System Tray stop flashing and the newsgroup names are displayed. You will then be ready to continue.

At this point, you can subscribe to newsgroups, as described in the next section, or skip ahead to the following section on viewing newsgroup messages. You don't have to subscribe to newsgroups to read and post messages, but subscribing may make it easier to access your favorite newsgroups.

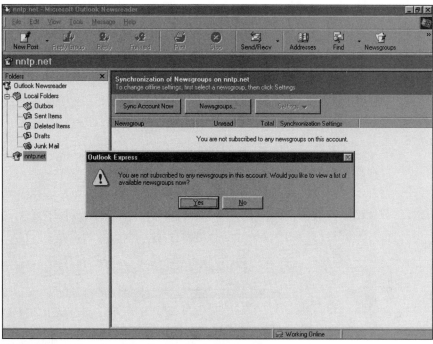

Figure 15-2: Download the list of newsgroups.

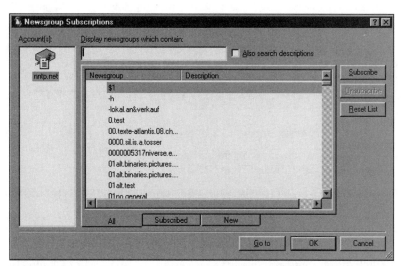

Figure 15-3: The Newsgroup Subscriptions dialog box shows the list of available newsgroups.

Subscribing to newsgroups

Subscribing to newsgroups offers you one big advantage—you don't have to search through the thousands of available newsgroups to find your favorites. When you subscribe to a newsgroup, that newsgroup appears on your folder list in the Outlook Newsreader. You can then go directly to that newsgroup by selecting it from the folder list.

To subscribe to a newsgroup, follow these steps:

1. Select the newsgroup that interests you in the Newsgroup Subscriptions dialog box, shown in Figure 15-4.

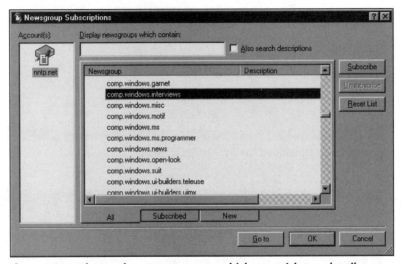

Figure 15-4: Choose the newsgroups to which you wish to subscribe.

2. Click the Subscribe button to add the newsgroup to your subscriptions.

3. Click the Subscribed tab to view the list of newsgroups to which you've subscribed, as shown in Figure 15-5.

4. If you wish to subscribe to additional newsgroups, return to the All tab and repeat Steps 1 and 2.

5. If you want to remove a newsgroup from your subscription list, select the newsgroup on the Subscribed tab and click the Unsubscribe button.

6. Click the OK button to close the Newsgroup Subscriptions dialog box. Your subscribed newsgroups will appear in the folder list, as shown in Figure 15-6.

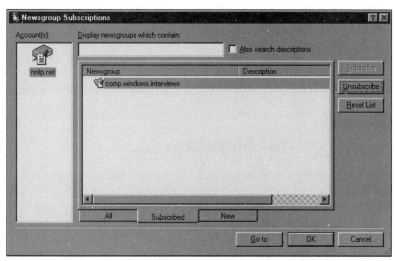

Figure 15-5: View the newsgroups to which you have subscribed on the Subscribed tab.

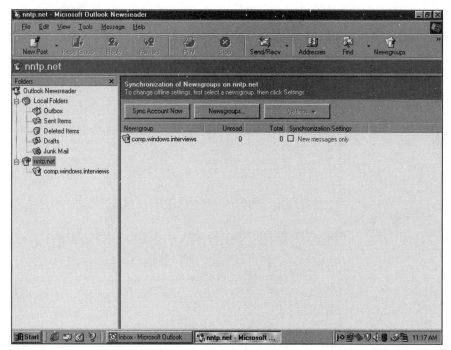

Figure 15-6: Newsgroups to which you have subscribed appear in the folder list for easy access.

Once you've subscribed to a newsgroup, you can view the messages contained in that newsgroup by selecting the newsgroup in the Outlook Newsreader folder list.

Note   Subscribing to a newsgroup is not like subscribing to a magazine. Newsgroup subscriptions don't cost anything, and you can cancel your subscriptions at any time. No message is sent to anyone indicating that you've subscribed to the newsgroup.

Viewing Newsgroup Messages

The method you use to view newsgroup messages varies depending on whether you've subscribed to the newsgroup. If you've subscribed to a newsgroup, you can simply select the newsgroup in the folder list. Viewing messages in nonsubscribed newsgroups is only slightly more complicated, as you see in the following section.

Viewing messages

To view the messages in newsgroups that you've subscribed to, select the newsgroup in the Outlook Newsreader folder list, shown in Figure 15-7. Click the message you wish to read in the upper pane, and the message text will appear in the lower pane.

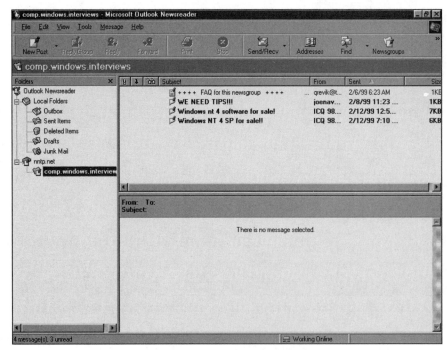

Figure 15-7: Select a subscribed newsgroup to view the list of messages.

Notice the list of messages includes a column at the far right that indicates the size of the message. Some messages, especially those that include attachments, can be quite large. If you select a very large message, the Outlook Newsreader may seem to freeze for a few minutes while the message is downloaded. Watch the modem indicators in the System Tray to see all of the activity that is occurring.

To view the message in any newsgroup, even those to which you are not subscribed, follow these steps:

1. Click the Newsgroups button on the Outlook Newsreader toolbar to display the Newsgroup Subscriptions dialog box.

2. If necessary, confirm that you wish to connect.

3. Select the newsgroup, as shown in Figure 15-8.

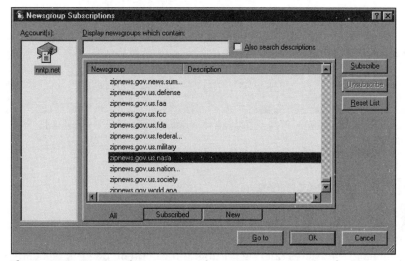

Figure 15-8: You can view messages in any newsgroup using the Newsgroup Subscriptions dialog box.

4. Click the Go to button to download the message headers for the newsgroup.

5. Select a message to download and read the message.

If you have downloaded the message headers for a newsgroup but haven't subscribed to the newsgroup, you'll see a message similar to the one in Figure 15-9 when you select a different folder in the Outlook Newsreader Folder List. You can choose to subscribe to the newsgroup by selecting Yes. Select No if the newsgroup turns out to be one that doesn't interest you enough to return to it.

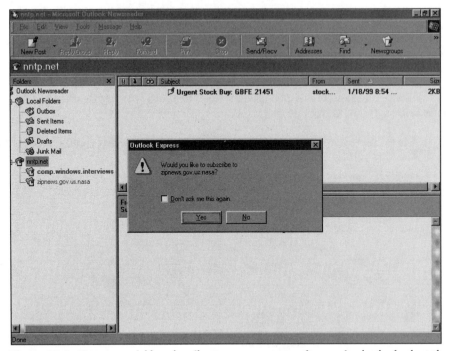

Figure 15-9: You can quickly subscribe to a newsgroup after you've had a look at the messages.

Filtering messages

One of the biggest problems you're likely to encounter in newsgroups is that many—if not most—newsgroup messages don't really apply to the newsgroup topic. You may find messages that are promoting get-rich-quick schemes, advertisements for Web sites offering pornographic content, bogus stock market advice, and many other off-topic messages. Because of this, it may be difficult to sort through and find the message that you really want to read.

The Outlook Newsreader provides you with several ways to filter newsgroup messages. You can create a quick filter that simply deletes messages from specified people. You can also create a more complex filter that processes newsgroup messages based on content.

Caution   No rule that you can create for filtering newsgroup messages can possibly be 100 percent effective in blocking every message that you might find offensive. You must also use a little common sense and realize that if you are truly offended by the messages that appear in certain newsgroups, you may be better off avoiding those newsgroups entirely. This also applies to rules that you might create to prevent family members from seeing certain types of messages—ultimately you must take personal responsibility for what you or your family views on the Internet. The Internet was never intended as a children's playground.

To create a rule for filtering newsgroup messages, follow these steps:

1. Select Tools ➪ Message Rules ➪ News to open the New News Rule dialog box, shown in Figure 15-10.

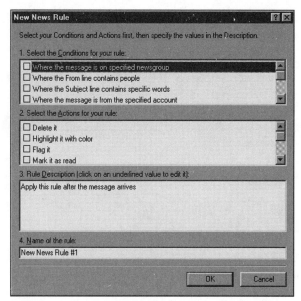

Figure 15-10: Use the New News Rule dialog box to create rules for filtering newsgroup messages.

2. In the *Select the Conditions for your rule* box, select the conditions that you want to trigger this rule. You can select more than one condition, but remember that messages must meet every condition before the filter will apply. It may be better to create additional rules that use narrow sets of conditions than to try to create a multiple-condition rule that may fail if one condition cannot be met.

3. In the *Select the Actions for your rule* box, select the actions you want to occur when a message meets the filtering conditions. In most cases, a single action will be adequate.

4. Once you have added all the conditions and actions, click each of the underlined values in the *Rule Description* box to edit the value, as shown in Figure 15-11.

5. Click OK to close the dialog box that you use to specify the values. The name of this dialog box may vary according to the type of value you are entering.

6. Continue replacing each of the underlined values until you have completed the rule. Depending on the complexity of your rule, you may have several values to replace.

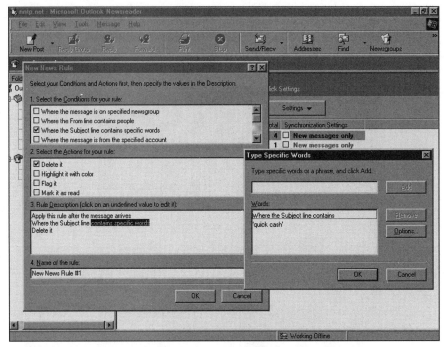

Figure 15-11: Edit the underlined values to specify the filter values.

7. Type a descriptive name for the rule in the *Name of the rule* text box. It's probably not a good idea to accept the default name, because you'll want to be able to locate specific rules if you later decide they need modifications.

8. Click OK to close the New News Rule dialog box and display the Message Rules dialog box, shown in Figure 15-12.

9. If you have more than one rule defined, you can use the *Move Up* and *Move Down* buttons to change the order in which the rules are applied. The order in which rules are applied can be very important. Rules nearer to the top of the list are applied before those lower on the list. Make certain that the rules appear in order of most important to least important.

10. To temporarily disable a rule without removing it, remove the check from the checkbox to the left of the rule name.

11. To add an additional rule, click the New button and repeat the steps for creating a new rule.

12. To modify an existing rule, select the rule and click the Modify button. Again, follow the same steps you used to create a new rule.

13. Click the Apply Now button to display the Apply News Rules Now dialog box, shown in Figure 15-13. You'll use this dialog box to select rules that you want to apply immediately to specified folders.

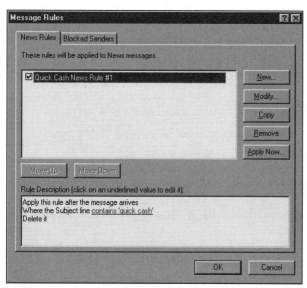

Figure 15-12: Use the Message Rules dialog box to apply your rules.

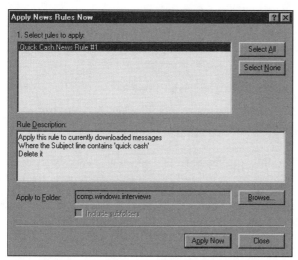

Figure 15-13: Use the Apply News Rules Now dialog box to specify where to apply your rules.

14. Select the rules that you want to apply.

15. Select the newsgroup folder that you want to filter by clicking the Browse button and choosing the folder.

16. Click OK to return to the Apply News Rules Now dialog box.

17. Click Apply Now to filter the messages in the specified folder using the selected rules.

18. Click OK to confirm that the rules were applied.

19. If you wish to filter additional newsgroup folders, use the Browse button and the Apply Now button to apply the rules to those folders.

20. Select Close to close the Apply News Rules Now dialog box.

21. Click OK to close the Message Rules dialog box.

Rules that you create to filter newsgroup messages will apply to future messages that you download from the newsgroups. Unless you use the Apply News Rules Now dialog box, your rules will not be applied to existing messages.

You can also create a quick rule to block messages from a specific sender. This will place the sender on the blocked senders list and prevent any future messages from that sender from reaching you.

To add someone to the blocked senders list, follow these steps:

1. Open a newsgroup folder that contains a message from the sender you wish to block.

2. Select a message from that sender.

3. Select Message ➪ Block Sender to display the Edit Sender dialog box, shown in Figure 15-14.

4. Select the types of messages you wish to block.

5. Click OK to add the e-mail address to the blocked senders list.

6. Click OK to confirm the message that appears.

The blocked senders list only applies to future messages. Any existing messages that you have downloaded already will not be filtered.

Tip   Use the blocked senders list to avoid receiving messages from people who have decided to engage in a flame war with you. The best way to deal with people who are attempting to incite you is to simply ignore them. Sending a heated reply generally succeeds only in escalating the conflict.

If you create rules for filtering the newsgroup messages, it's a good idea to test those rules by using the Apply News Rules Now dialog box. It's also a good idea to keep your rules as simple as possible. Rules that are too restrictive can prevent you from seeing important messages that just happen to fit the filter. It's usually better to allow a few items you don't want to slip by your rules than to miss things simply because your rules are too extreme.

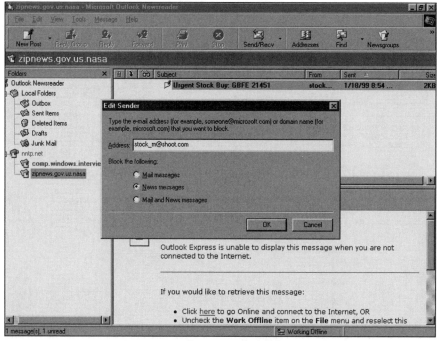

Figure 15-14: You can block messages from specific e-mail addresses.

Following message threads

Very few newsgroup messages are very useful by themselves. What makes newsgroup messages useful and interesting are the answers, comments, and questions posted in response to the original message. This group of related messages is known as a *message thread*. By following a message thread, you can find out a lot more about the subject than you would from any single message.

Figure 15-15 shows a typical newsgroup with a number of different messages that you can read. Notice some messages include a small box at the left edge of the Subject column. This box indicates that the message is a thread and that there are replies to the message. If the box contains a plus sign (+), as do several in the figure, you can click the box to expand the list of replies. If the box contains a minus sign (−), the message thread has been expanded so that you can see the replies.

You can view a newsgroup message by selecting it from the list of messages. Viewing a message thread works the same way — you simply select the message that you wish to view. The difference between threaded and nonthreaded messages is very minor. As the figure shows, messages are normally sorted by the date they were sent. This default sort order would, however, make it very hard for you to follow a message thread. That's why newsgroup messages use message threads — to make it easier for you to see replies.

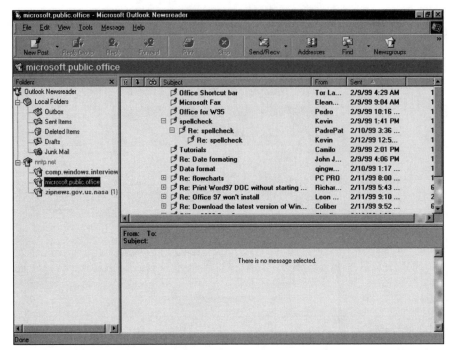

Figure 15-15: You can view messages and any responses in the message thread.

Although it is easy to see the related messages in an existing message thread, you'll probably see a lot of interesting newsgroup messages that have not yet generated a full range of responses. For example, suppose you visit a newsgroup and discover that someone has just posted a very interesting question. You want to know what responses the question generates. You could simply visit the newsgroup regularly and search for the original question to see if there are any replies, but you would have to remember each of the questions that interested you so that you could do your search. Fortunately, the Outlook Newsreader provides a better way to keep track of an ongoing conversation.

As Figure 15-16 shows, you can have the Outlook Newsreader watch for new messages in a message thread. Simply select the message that you want to track and then select Message ➪ Watch Conversation. The Outlook Newsreader will place an eyeglass icon in front of the message header to indicate that the conversation is being watched. When new messages arrive in the thread, you'll be notified so that you can read those responses.

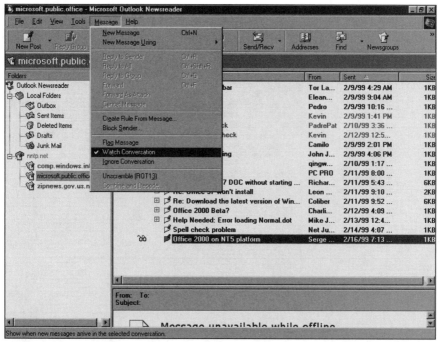

Figure 15-16: You can watch messages to see when responses appear in the message thread.

Viewing the new messages

If you've found an interesting newsgroup, you probably want to update the message headers for that newsgroup often enough so that you can see what new messages have been posted. You can, of course, view the current message headers in any newsgroup by choosing the newsgroup in the Newsgroup Subscriptions dialog box and clicking the Go to button. If you haven't subscribed to a newsgroup, that is the only way to update the messages for the newsgroup. If you have subscribed to a newsgroup, there's an easier way to update the messages. You can have the Outlook Newsreader *synchronize* — update — newsgroups that you've subscribed to.

To synchronize the messages for your subscribed newsgroups, follow these steps:

1. Click the news server folder in the Outlook Newsreader folder list.

2. To change the synchronization settings for a newsgroup, select the newsgroup and then click the Settings button, as shown in Figure 15-17.

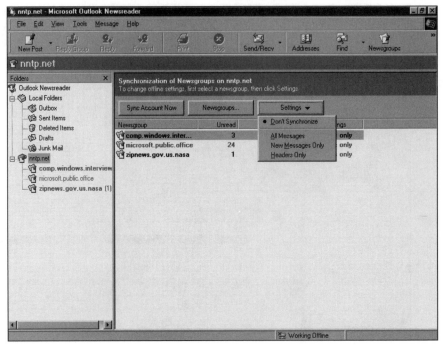

Figure 15-17: Choose the settings for updating your newsgroup subscriptions.

3. Choose the method for updating the messages for this newsgroup.

4. Click the Sync Account Now button to update each of your newsgroup subscriptions according to your selected settings. If you aren't currently connected to the Internet, you may have to respond to prompts to connect.

Subscribing to newsgroups and then synchronizing the messages in those newsgroups is one of the best ways to keep track of new messages that may interest you. When you add in the ability to watch certain conversations, you can be ensured of knowing about what's new in your favorite newsgroups.

Tip   Although the Outlook Newsreader can help you keep track of your favorite news-groups, it's not really designed to look for every message that might be of interest in hundreds or thousands of newsgroups at the same time. For that, you may want to check out an intelligent agent such as NewsMonger. You can find out more about this software at www.techsmith.com, where you can also download a trial version.

Posting to Newsgroups

Eventually, you'll decide that simply reading the messages in your favorite newsgroups is interesting, but that it would be even more fun to add your own messages. Adding a message to a newsgroup is known as *posting* a message to the newsgroup. Posting newsgroup messages isn't much different from creating and sending e-mail messages, except that the message recipient is the newsgroup rather than an individual.

Different newsgroups have different customs. As a newcomer — *newbie* — to a newsgroup, it's always a good idea to hang around for a while to learn those customs before you blindly post a message that the newsgroup regulars view as stupid or lazy. For example, if you barge in and post a message like "I don't have the time to read the old messages so can someone tell me in detail how I should set up my computer to make my software and hardware work correctly," don't expect a friendly response. The people who visit newsgroups and offer their help to others are generally nice people, but they don't have to be nice to you — especially if you act like a world-class boor!

Posting a new message and replying to an existing message are virtually the same. When you post a new message, you need to come up with a descriptive subject line that will make people want to read your message, but otherwise there's no important difference between a new posting and a response.

To post a new message, follow these steps:

1. Open the newsgroup where you want to post the message.

2. If you are replying to a message, select the message for which you want to post your reply.

3. Click the Reply button to post a reply or the New Post button to begin a new message subject. Figure 15-18 shows the New Message form that appears when you click the New Post button.

4. If this is a new message, enter a subject line. Try to be as brief and descriptive as possible. Remember that many people will only see the first few words of the subject line.

Caution Although the New Message form does allow you to specify more than one newsgroup for posting your message, such *cross-posting* is generally frowned upon. If you can't take the time to locate the correct newsgroup for your posting and simply try the shotgun approach, you won't be welcomed in most newsgroups.

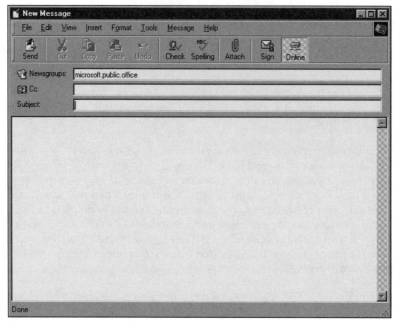

Figure 15-18: Posting newsgroup messages is very similar to creating and sending e-mail.

5. Enter the text of your message. If you are replying to an earlier message, it is common to include enough of the text of the previous message so that people can understand your response without opening the earlier post.

6. Click the Spelling button to check your spelling once you've finished typing your message.

7. If you want to include a file attachment, click the Attach button and choose the file.

8. If you want to use a digital ID so that people who read the message can be sure it was you who sent the message, click the Sign button and choose the digital certificate you wish to use. See Chapter 8 for more information on using certificates.

9. When you are done creating the message, click the Send button.

10. You may have to click the Send/Recv button to post the message. If you are working *offline* — not connected to the Internet — you will need to connect in order to post your message.

Although you may see a quick response to new postings if a newsgroup is particularly active, it's more likely that you'll have to wait a day or two in most newsgroups. While you're waiting, you may want to search for existing postings that address the same or a similar subject.

Caution Be careful about the type of information that you post in newsgroups. Remember that there is no guarantee that the people who read newsgroup messages have your best interests at heart. Posting your address or phone number is never considered to be a wise idea.

Summary

Newsgroups can be a very interesting and useful part of the Internet. The Outlook Newsreader makes it possible for you to read and post your own messages to those newsgroups. In this chapter, you learned how to use the Outlook Newsreader to access the tens of thousands of newsgroups and how to subscribe to your favorite newsgroups.

The next chapter shows you how to make Outlook work more effectively for you by customizing the program to meet your needs.

✦　　✦　　✦

Getting the Most out of Microsoft Outlook 2000

P A R T

IV

✦ ✦ ✦ ✦

In This Part

Chapter 16
Customizing Outlook 2000

Chapter 17
Using Folders Effectively

Chapter 18
Integrating with Other Applications

✦ ✦ ✦ ✦

Microsoft Outlook is a powerful tool, but with a little extra thought it can be even more useful for you. In Part IV, you learn how to customize Outlook to suit your needs. You learn how to make the best use of your Outlook folders, and you learn how to combine Outlook with other applications so that your computer does more of the work than you do.

Customizing Outlook 2000

◆ ◆ ◆ ◆

In This Chapter

Customizing Outlook

Organizing your Outlook folders

Using Web integration

◆ ◆ ◆ ◆

By now, you've probably used Outlook enough to discover that there are a number of little things about the program that you would change if you could. In this chapter, you learn how to make many of those changes and customize Outlook so that it suits your needs a bit better.

In addition to changing the appearance of Outlook, some changes that you can make may have more fundamental effects on your use of Outlook. In this chapter, you also see how you can make some of these types of changes — such as taking charge of the security settings so that you won't have to worry about an e-mail macro virus damaging your computer.

Customizing Outlook

Most of the changes you can make to Outlook primarily affect Outlook's appearance. That is, even if you change the number of days of calendar events that are displayed in the Outlook Today folder, Outlook won't really work any differently than with the default settings. It's true that you'll see a different number of days in the display, but Outlook will still remember all the events that are outside the display range. As a result, you don't have to be afraid to experiment. If you don't care for the results, you can always return Outlook to its original settings.

Some of the Outlook customizations that you see in the following sections have been briefly touched on in earlier chapters. Here, however, you learn more about the changes that you can make that more directly affect how you use Outlook — especially now that you likely have more experience with the program.

Customizing Outlook Today

It's likely that the first thing you see when you open Outlook is the Outlook Today folder. You'll want to know about the various options that are available for customizing Outlook Today so that it shows just what is most useful to you.

To begin customizing Outlook Today, open the View menu, as shown in Figure 16-1. This provides you with access to several interesting options:

✦ The *Go To* menu selection enables you to quickly open any Outlook folder. This option is most useful if you choose to hide the Outlook bar and the folder list. You'll also find this option provides you with access to the Outlook Newsreader, Internet Explorer, and NetMeeting.

✦ *Outlook Bar* is a toggle that controls the display of the Outlook bar. The Outlook bar provides point-and-click access to your folders using icons to represent the folders. As detailed later in the section "Customizing the Outlook bar," you can add your own shortcuts to the Outlook bar.

✦ *Folder List* is a toggle that controls display of the folder list. The folder list provides a Windows Explorer–type view of your Outlook folders. Displaying both the Outlook bar and the folder list is essentially redundant and uses considerable screen space.

✦ *Show Folder Home Page* is a toggle that displays the standard view of the Outlook Today folder. If you choose to turn this option off, you will not see the Calendar, Tasks list, or message list in the Outlook Today folder. Turning off this option makes the Outlook Today folder pretty useless.

✦ The *Toolbars* menu selection enables you to decide which of the Outlook toolbars are displayed. As discussed in the section "Customizing the toolbars," you can modify the toolbars to include the tools you prefer.

✦ *Status Bar* is a toggle that controls the display of the status bar at the bottom of the Outlook window. Removing the status bar provides slightly more room to display the items in the window and may be useful if your screen is quite small, you have a large number of items that show in your Outlook Today folder, or you run Outlook at less than full-screen. Remember, though, that the status bar performs several useful functions. The status bar provides information about the current folder and the status of actions that Outlook performs.

In addition to the options that appear on the View menu, you can click the *Customize Outlook Today* button to display the Customize Outlook Today form, as shown in Figure 16-2. This form enables you to change the way the Outlook Today folder displays information from the other Outlook folders. Most of the options on the Customize Outlook Today form should be pretty familiar to you by now. One of the options, however, deserves special consideration. If you prefer to have a different Outlook folder active whenever you open Outlook, deselect the *When starting, go directly to Outlook Today* checkbox. If you deselect this option, Outlook will remember which Outlook folder was active when you last closed Outlook, and reopen the same folder the next time you start Outlook. Click the Save Changes button to close the Customize Outlook Today form and return to Outlook Today.

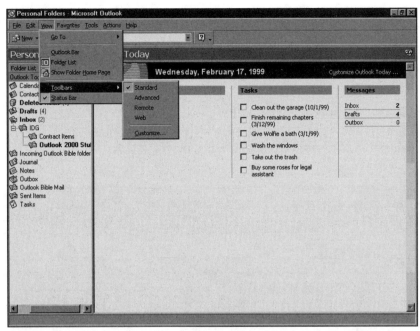

Figure 16-1: Use the View menu to access several Outlook Today options.

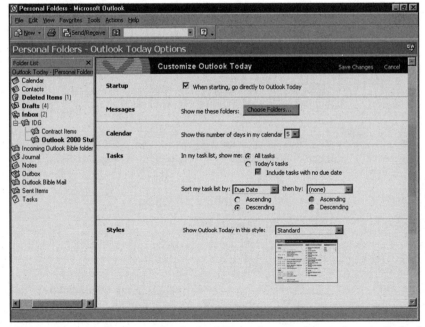

Figure 16-2: Use the Customize Outlook Today form to change the way Outlook Today displays information.

If you would rather specify the folder that Outlook opens by default, you'll have to dig a little deeper into Outlook's options. To explicitly specify the default Outlook folder, follow these steps:

1. Select Tool ⇨ Options to display the Options dialog box.

2. Click the Other tab.

3. Click the Advanced Options button.

4. Click the down arrow at the right of the *Startup in this folder* list box, shown in Figure 16-3. Choose the folder from the list.

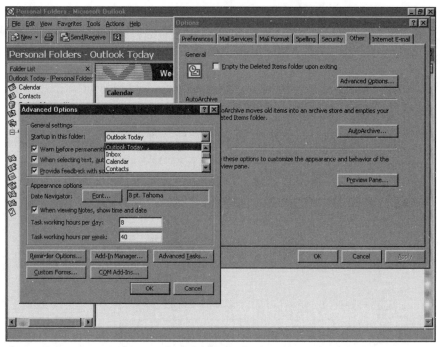

Figure 16-3: You can choose which folder Outlook starts up by default.

5. Click OK to close the Advanced Options dialog box.

6. Click OK to close the Options dialog box.

Customizing the menus

Outlook 2000 shares a feature with the other applications in Office 2000 that you may find quite useful or totally annoying. When you open an Outlook menu, only some of the menu's commands will appear on the menu. After a short delay, the remaining menu items will appear; but while you're waiting, it's quite easy to become confused and move on to another menu, thinking that you may have opened the wrong menu. To further complicate matters, commands that you seldom use are moved off the main menus to make way for commands you use more often.

If you find these constantly changing menus confusing, the following steps show you how to change this behavior.

Note   Changing these menu settings affects all Office programs, not just Outlook.

1. Select Tools ➪ Customize to display the Customize dialog box, shown in Figure 16-4.

Uncheck this

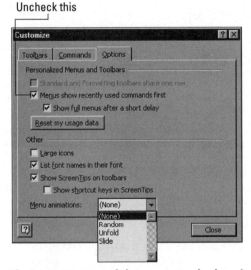

Figure 16-4: Control those constantly changing menus.

2. To display the full menus immediately, deselect the *Menus show recently used commands first* checkbox.

3. If you decide to keep the short menus, choose whether to automatically show the full menus after the menu has been open for some time:

   • Select *Show full menus after a short delay* to have the full menu drop down automatically.

   • Deselect *Show full menus after a short delay* to have the full menu drop down only when you click the down arrow at the bottom of the menu.

4. If you decide to keep the short menus, you can click the *Reset my usage data* button to have Outlook return to the original set of menu options. Because Outlook will otherwise show only those commands that you've used recently, this button resets the menus to the way they appeared when you first installed Outlook.

5. To animate the menus, select one of the animation options in the *Menu animations* list box.

6. Click Close to close the Customize dialog box.

Tip   Be sure to reset the usage data or display full menus before allowing other people to use Outlook. Otherwise, they may be confused by the missing commands on the Outlook menus.

Customizing the toolbars

Outlook's menus aren't the only parts of the user interface that can change automatically. As you use the toolbars, tools that you use the least often can move off the toolbar to make room for other buttons that you use more often. Needless to say, this can be somewhat confusing, too.

Outlook has several toolbars. In most cases, the toolbars adapt to the type of folder that is being displayed. You can choose to display additional toolbars by selecting View ➪ Toolbars and then choosing the toolbars you want to see. Although this changes the selection of toolbars, it does not change the way Outlook adds and removes toolbar buttons automatically.

You can choose additional tools to add to the toolbars by clicking the More Buttons arrow that appears at the right side of each toolbar. This displays the Add or Remove buttons option, as shown in Figure 16-5, so that you can choose which buttons to display.

Any of the buttons that have a check to the left of the button name in the list of buttons will appear on the toolbar. You can add buttons by placing a check in front of their name. You can also choose Reset Toolbar to return the toolbar to the default settings.

In addition to changing the tools that are shown on the toolbars, you can change the toolbar locations. At the left edge of each toolbar is a vertical bar that acts as a handle so that you can drag the toolbar to a new location. Although you cannot place a toolbar and the Outlook menu on the same row, you can place multiple toolbars onto the same row.

Tip   To maximize the space in the Outlook window without removing important functionality, you can drag a toolbar down to create a floating toolbar. You can even dock a toolbar along the left edge of the Outlook window.

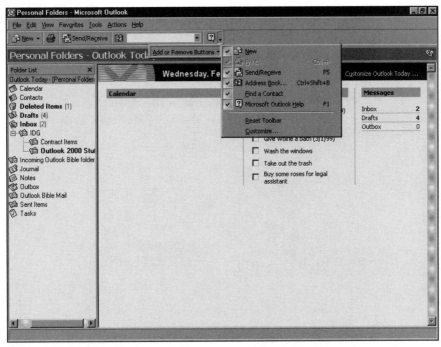

Figure 16-5: Choose the buttons that appear on the toolbars.

If none of the Outlook toolbars has quite the mix of tools that you need, you can create your own toolbars. To create a custom toolbar, follow these steps:

1. Select View ➪ Toolbars ➪ Customize to display the Customize dialog box, shown in Figure 16-6.

2. Click the New button.

3. Enter a name for your toolbar.

4. Click OK to return to the Customize dialog box.

5. Drag tools from any of the toolbars onto your toolbar. Hold down Ctrl as you drag to copy a tool button rather than move it.

6. Click Close to close the Customize dialog box. You can only customize a toolbar when the Customize dialog box is open.

7. Drag your toolbar to dock it in the desired location (or simply leave it floating anywhere on the screen).

If you forget to hold down Ctrl as you drag buttons, you'll probably want to reset the tools on toolbars that you used as the source for buttons for your custom toolbar.

A customized toolbar

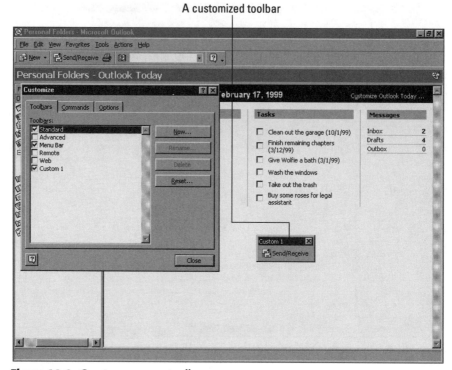

Figure 16-6: Create your own toolbars.

Caution Although you can create your own toolbars to completely replace Outlook's toolbars, remember that your toolbars won't automatically adjust for different types of Outlook folders. It's usually best to create custom toolbars that complement rather than replace Outlook's toolbars.

Customizing the Outlook bar

If you prefer to use the Outlook bar rather than the folder list, you can add your own shortcuts and groups to the Outlook bar. You can also change the size of the Outlook bar icons. Figure 16-7 shows the pop-up menu that appears when you right-click the Outlook bar. You use this menu to customize the Outlook bar.

You may have noticed something that looks a little unusual in the figure. Rather than showing Outlook folders, Outlook is showing the items from the My Computer folder. You can browse the folders on your computer by selecting the correct group of shortcuts on the Outlook bar.

You can add a new shortcut by selecting Outlook Bar Shortcut from the pop-up menu. Figure 16-8 shows the Add to Outlook Bar dialog box that you use to select the folder you wish to add as a new shortcut.

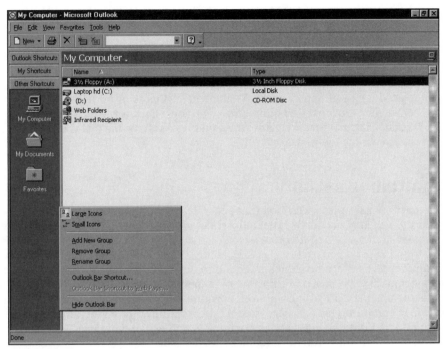

Figure 16-7: You can also customize the Outlook bar.

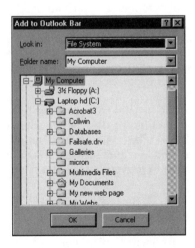

Figure 16-8: You can add new shortcuts to the Outlook bar.

When you are adding a new shortcut to a folder, you can select either File System or Outlook in the Look in list box. If you select File System, you can then choose any of the folders that are available on your computer or on your network. If you select Outlook, you can choose any of Outlook's folders.

Note   Although you can add shortcuts to both Outlook and File System folders to your Outlook bar, you cannot have both types of folders open in Outlook at the same time. This means that you cannot drag and drop items between Outlook and File System folders. It is possible to use the Edit ➪ Copy command to copy an item that is in an Outlook folder and then use Edit ➪ Paste to paste it into a File System folder. Unfortunately, this won't accomplish much that is of any value, because the pasted item will appear as an "Outlook Item" that is of no use in any program other than Outlook. Going the other direction — from a File System folder to an Outlook folder — simply creates a new message with the file that you copied as an attachment to the message.

Controlling security

One part of customizing Outlook that generally gets little attention is the area of security. You may not realize that a potential security threat even exists. However, even e-mail messages that you receive could cause problems if you aren't careful.

Computer viruses are programs intended to do you some harm. Oh, it's true that many computer viruses don't do a lot of immediate damage, but by the simple fact of taking up space on your computer, even the most benign viruses are harmful. The first computer viruses were executable programs. For a long time, most people assumed that data files — such as documents and e-mail messages — couldn't contain viruses. Unfortunately, that's no longer true.

The problem with data files is that they're often more than just data files. Many programs use a *macro language* that enables the user to include some automation in their documents. In Office 2000, that macro language is Visual Basic for Applications (VBA). Programs that are written in VBA are part of a document, so documents can now be just as destructive as ordinary programs. If a document contains macros that are executed by the application that opens the document, the macro program within the document runs pretty much like any other program on your computer.

Because Outlook uses VBA for automation, it's quite possible for someone to send you an e-mail message that includes VBA code that could be destructive when it runs on your system. To counteract this, you should take control of the Outlook security settings and make certain macros contained in e-mail messages cannot run without your approval. That way, you'll be able to prevent e-mail message macro viruses from harming your computer.

To set the Outlook security level, follow these steps:

1. Select Tools ➪ Macro ➪ Security to display the Security dialog box, shown in Figure 16-9.

2. Choose the security level that you prefer. Unless you really like to live dangerously, do not select Low.

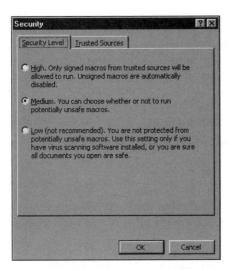

Figure 16-9: Make certain that you decide which macros run on your system.

3. Click the Trusted Sources tab to display the list of certificates that are available on your system. If you have someone's digital ID but do not want to assume that e-mail they send will be safe, select them from the list and click Remove.

4. Click OK to close the Security dialog box.

Caution

No matter which security level you choose, macros from anyone who appears on your Trusted Sources list will run automatically. If you want the highest level of protection against potential problems, remove everyone from the Trusted Sources list.

Organizing Your Outlook Folders

If you use Outlook a lot, you probably have a huge amount of information stored in your Outlook folders. Of course, just having a lot of information isn't very useful — you also need to be able to find the information that you need. One of the best ways to make certain information is accessible is to organize that information. In the following sections, you learn about one of the ways that Outlook can help you organize the information in your Outlook folders.

What is the Organize feature?

You've probably noticed the Organize button on the Outlook toolbar, but you may not have used it yet. The Organize button displays a small window just above the folder contents pane. In the Organize window, you'll find tools that can help you organize the items in your Outlook folders using several different options.

The organizational options that are available in Outlook include the following:

✦ *Categories* — This option enables you to place selected items into existing categories such as business, hot contacts, key customer, and so on. You also have the option to create new categories on the spot. You can later view the items that you've placed in each category, making it easy to find specific types of records based on their assigned category.

✦ *Colors* — This option enables you to make specific messages stand out by using a contrasting color. You might, for example, have Outlook show all messages that come from your boss in green, and all messages from a special customer in red.

✦ *Folders* — This option enables you to move selected items to a specific folder. It also enables you to create a rule that moves new messages from certain people into a special folder. This option would be very useful if you wanted all e-mail messages from specific customers to automatically be moved to folders that you have created for each customer. Such a setup would help you keep track of all messages from those customers, because you wouldn't have to search through your mail folders — you could look directly in the customer-specific folder.

✦ *Junk E-Mail* — This option enables you to either move or color junk or adult content messages as they arrive. You'll find this quite useful if you receive a lot of e-mail messages that you would just as soon have Outlook automatically delete or highlight so that you can quickly find and deal with them yourself.

✦ *Views* — This option enables you to quickly change the view of the current folder. You might, for example, want to use a view like *Flagged for Next Seven Days* to quickly see which items you need to deal with immediately before you take off on a suddenly arranged business trip.

Using the Organize feature

Each Outlook folder displays the Organize button on the toolbar and an Organize option on the Tools menu. In each case, selecting the Organize tool displays the Organize pane just above the folder contents pane. Even so, you'll find that the type of Outlook folder that is displayed will control which of the Organize options are available. Table 16-1 shows the Organize options available for each of Outlook's standard folders. New folders that you create will display the same set of options as the folder that is closest to the type of your new folder.

<table>
<tr><td colspan="2" align="center">Table 16-1
Organize Options in Outlook Folders</td></tr>
<tr><td>*Folder*</td><td>*Options*</td></tr>
<tr><td>Calendar</td><td>Categories, Views</td></tr>
<tr><td>Contacts</td><td>Categories, Folders, Views</td></tr>
</table>

Folder	Options
Deleted Items	Colors, Folders, Junk E-Mail, Views
Drafts	Colors, Folders, Junk E-Mail, Views
Inbox	Colors, Folders, Junk E-Mail, Views
Journal	Categories, Views
Notes	Folders, Views
Outbox	Colors, Folders, Junk E-Mail, Views
Sent Items	Colors, Folders, Junk E-Mail, Views
Tasks	Categories, Folders, Views

The following sections will show you a little about each of the organizational options.

Using categories to organize

When you use categories to organize your folders, you select the items that you want to assign to specific categories and then choose the category. Figure 16-10 shows the Using Categories option for the Calendar folder.

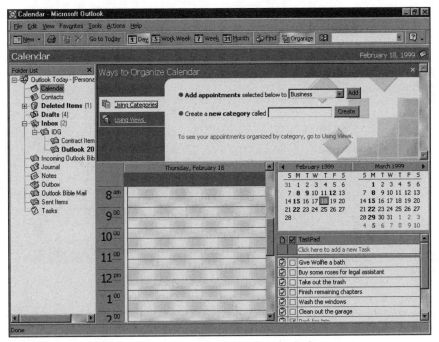

Figure 16-10: Use categories to organize items into logical groups.

To use this option, follow these steps:

1. Open the folder you want to organize.

2. Click the Organize button.

3. Select Using Categories.

4. Select the items that you wish to assign to a category.

5. Either select an existing category from the drop-down list box and click the Add button, or enter a new category name in the text box and click Create.

6. Repeat Steps 4 and 5 as necessary until you have finished assigning items to categories.

Using colors to organize

When you use colors to organize your folders, you specify that messages to or from specific people should be highlighted in a color that you select. You can also specify that messages that were sent only to you are highlighted in color. Figure 16-11 shows the Using Colors option for the Deleted Items folder.

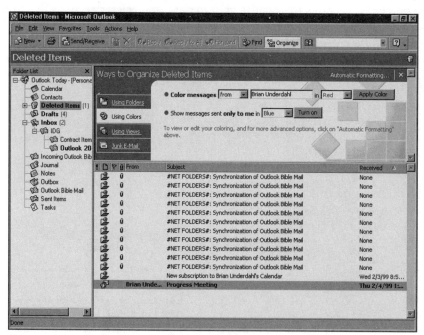

Figure 16-11: Use colors to make specific messages stand out.

To use this option, follow these steps:

1. Open the folder you want to organize.

2. Click the Organize button.

3. Select Using Colors.

4. Select either *from* or *sent to* in the first list box.

5. Specify the name in the second box. The easiest method of doing this is to select a message from the person that you want.

6. Select the color from the drop-down list box.

7. Click the Apply Color button to color all the matching messages as you have specified.

8. To also color messages that were addressed only to you, choose a color in the lower drop-down color list box and click the Turn on button.

Using folders to organize

When you use the Using Folders option to organize your folders, you move items to specific folders. You can also create a rule that automatically moves new items to a specific folder. Figure 16-12 shows the Using Folders option for the Inbox folder.

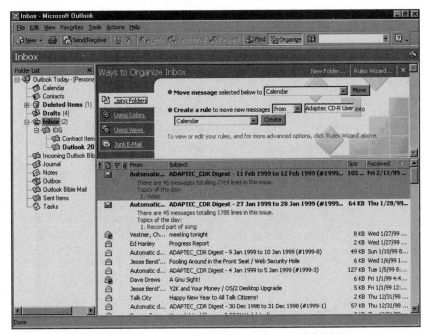

Figure 16-12: Use folders to move specific items to special folders.

To use this option, follow these steps:

1. Open the folder you want to organize.

2. Click the Organize button.

3. Select Using Folders.

4. Select items that you want to move or that you want to use as an example for a new rule.

5. To move the selected items immediately, select the destination folder from the upper drop-down list box and click Move.

6. To create a new rule, select either *from* or *sent to* from the middle drop-down list box.

7. Select the destination folder from the lower drop-down list box.

8. Click the Create button to create the new rule.

> **Tip**
>
> If you wish to create a new rule and move existing items, create the new rule first so that you can use an existing item as a sample. Once you have created the new rule, you can move the existing items.

Using Junk E-Mail to organize

When you use the Junk E-Mail option to organize your folders, you move or color junk or adult content items. Figure 16-13 shows the Junk E-Mail option for the Sent Items folder.

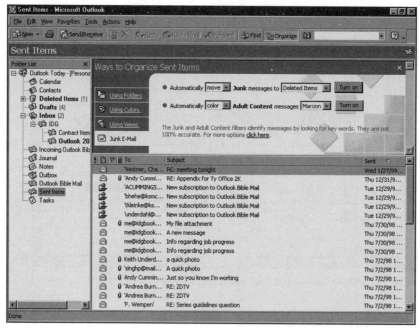

Figure 16-13: Use the Junk E-Mail option to move or color junk and adult content messages.

To use this option, follow these steps:

1. Open the folder you want to organize.

2. Click the Organize button.

3. Select Junk E-Mail.

4. Select either *move* or *color* as the option for junk messages.

5. Select the destination folder or the color for junk messages.

6. Click the Turn on button to apply the rule for junk e-mail messages.

7. Select either *move* or *color* as the option for adult content messages.

8. Select the destination folder or the color for adult content messages.

9. Click the Turn on button to apply the rule for adult content e-mail messages.

Tip

> Click the underlined *click here* link to edit the junk and adult content senders lists or to visit the Outlook Web site so that you can update Outlook's junk e-mail and adult content filters.

Using views to organize

When you use views to organize your folders, you change the way the items in the folder are displayed. Figure 16-14 shows the Using Views option for the Tasks folder.

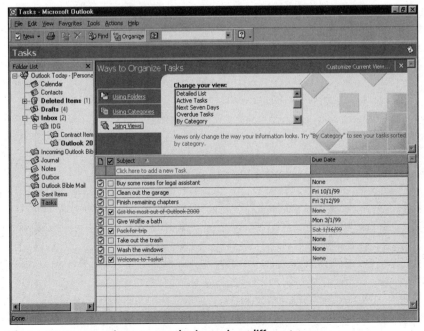

Figure 16-14: Use views to see the items in a different way.

To use this option, follow these steps:

1. Open the folder you want to organize.

2. Click the Organize button.

3. Select Using Views.

4. Select the view you want to try.

Using different views doesn't change any of the items in your folders, but you may want to try the Using Views option after you've used one of the other options to see what effect the other options had.

Integrating with the Web

As the Internet has become more a part of everyday life, we've come to expect that using the Internet should be an easy task. In this latest version of Outlook, you can use the Internet in many ways that greatly simplify a lot of the things that you do, such as visiting Web sites and sending Web pages with e-mail messages.

If you select View ➪ Toolbars ➪ Web to display the Web toolbar, you can enter a Web page address and visit a Web site without ever leaving Outlook. Figure 16-15 shows a popular Web site as viewed in Outlook.

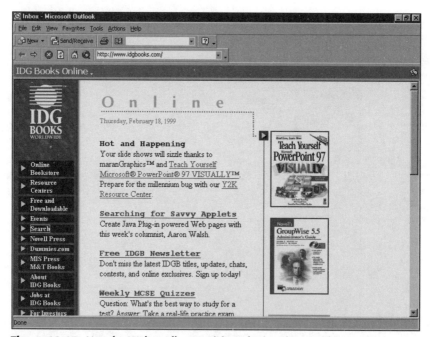

Figure 16-15: Use the Web toolbar to visit Web sites from within Outlook.

While you're viewing a Web page, you can easily send that Web page to someone as part of an e-mail message. Simply select Actions ➭ Send Web Page by E-Mail, as shown in Figure 16-16. You can even do this after you've gone offline, as long as you visited the Web page during the current session — if Outlook can still show the Web page without reconnecting to the Internet, you can send the page.

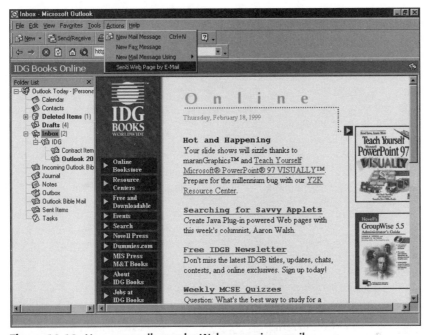

Figure 16-16: You can easily send a Web page via e-mail.

If you often visit the same Web site, you can add a shortcut to the Web site to your Outlook bar. Select File ➭ New ➭ Outlook Bar Shortcut to Web Page. This will add the shortcut to the bottom of the My Shortcuts group on the Outlook bar. Clicking the new shortcut will open the Web page.

Tip   You don't have to be online to add an Outlook bar shortcut to a Web page. Use the Web toolbar to display the Web page, and add the shortcut offline.

You can also assign a Web page as the home page for an Outlook folder. Doing so will display the contents of the Web page rather than the folder's contents. You can switch between the folder view and the Web page view by selecting View ➭ Show Folder Home Page. You may find this feature useful if you've created your own Web page, and it includes a number of important Web page links so that you can quickly visit Web pages related to a project.

Summary

Customizing Outlook is the best way to make certain Outlook works the way that best suits you. In this chapter, you learned how to customize Outlook, how to use the Organize feature to make working with Outlook items a bit easier, and how to use Outlook with the Internet.

In the next chapter, you learn how to use folders in Outlook more effectively.

✦   ✦   ✦

Using Folders Effectively

Anyone who has used Windows has certainly been exposed to the concept of folders, so Outlook's folder system shouldn't seem too unusual. Outlook uses folders to organize the different types of information that you can track in the program. But the information in Outlook is somewhat different from the information you store in your Windows Explorer folders, so Outlook's folders have some differences from those other types of folders, too.

In this chapter, you learn a lot more about how to use Outlook's folders effectively. You learn about the different types of folders and how you can manage and share the information contained in those folders. You also learn how to ensure Outlook makes the best use of the space it needs for your information storage needs.

Understanding Folders

If you really want to understand Outlook's folders, it's probably good to start with some of the basics. That way you'll have a better understanding of what you can and cannot do with Outlook folders and their contents.

+ Although the Outlook folder list displays the Outlook folders in a view that looks very similar to the way that Windows Explorer displays the folders on your hard drive, you cannot use Outlook folders and standard folders interchangeably. That is, you use Outlook folders in Windows Explorer, and you cannot directly exchange items between Outlook folders and Windows Explorer folders.

+ Each type of Outlook folder is intended to hold specific types of items. In most cases, you must store Outlook items — such as Calendar events and e-mail messages — in the proper type of folder.

✦ Outlook folders are more closely related to an Access database than to almost anything else on your system. A single file—normally called Outlook.pst—contains all the Outlook folders and the items that those folders contain. This file is usually encrypted and can only be opened using Outlook.

✦ When you delete items from your Outlook folders, Outlook does not automatically recover the space that those items were using. As detailed in the section "Using the Deleted Items folder" later in this chapter, you must explicitly tell Outlook to recover that lost space if you don't want your Outlook.pst file to waste space on your hard disk.

✦ You can share Outlook folders, but only with people who are also using Outlook. In some cases, you can share certain information with non-Outlook users, but that sharing is limited to sending the information via an e-mail message.

What are folders used for?

Outlook's folders store all of the information that you keep within Outlook. But even more than simply storing information, Outlook's folders help you to organize that information logically. You don't, for example, have to look through the Inbox folder to find a copy of an e-mail message that you've sent to someone. Messages that you've sent are moved to the Sent Items folder.

You are not limited to the ten folders that Outlook creates by itself. As Figure 17-1 shows, you can create your own Outlook folders to organize your Outlook items to suit your needs.

Tip   Drag the right side of the folder list pane to expand the pane so that you don't need to use the horizontal scrollbar to view the entire folder tree.

In the figure, the Outlook folder list is being used to select the active Outlook folder. You can also use the Outlook bar to access your Outlook folders, but remember that you must explicitly create Outlook bar shortcuts to folders that you create. You can also use the View ➪ Go To ➪ Folder command to display the Go to Folder dialog box, shown in Figure 17-2. The folder list is usually the most convenient method of selecting Outlook folders, but you may want to hide both the folder list and the Outlook bar if you normally display Outlook in a small window on your Windows desktop.

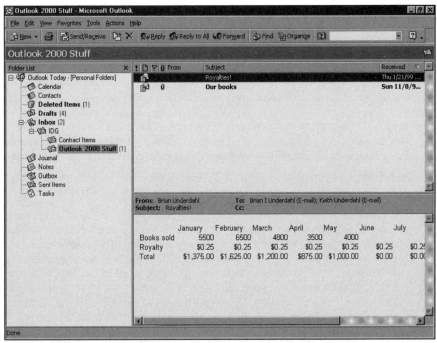

Figure 17-1: Use Outlook folders to organize your information.

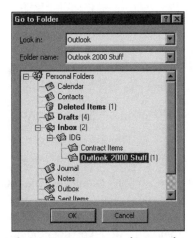

Figure 17-2: You can also use the
Go to Folder dialog box to navigate
your Outlook folders.

Understanding folder types

You can create and use several types of Outlook folders. Each of these different types of Outlook folders can also contain several categories of folders — with each category being the type of information that you can store within those folders.

Here are the main types of folders that you can use with Outlook:

✦ *Personal Folders* are the most common type of Outlook folder. Personal Folders are those folders located completely on your computer. Personal Folders are also personal — they aren't generally shared with other people.

✦ *Net folders* are the newest type of Outlook folder. Net folders enable you to share Outlook information with other Outlook users via e-mail over the Internet or your local network.

✦ *Offline folders* are a type of folder that enable you to use information from a Microsoft Exchange Server even if you are not currently connected to the server. You can work with the information in an offline folder and then synchronize that information later with the information on the Exchange Server. Offline folders are very similar to Personal Folders except that they synchronize the information between your local system and the Exchange Server. Offline folders are available only if you connect to an Exchange Server.

✦ *Public folders* are a type of folder that enable you to share information with other people who are also connected to your Exchange Server. Public folders provide similar functionality to net folders except that Public Folders are usually considered a bit more secure, because only those people who have access to your Exchange Server can access your Public Folders.

Understanding folder categories

Each type of Outlook folder can contain several categories of folders. The folder category is based on the type of information that you wish to store in the folder. You've seen each of these folder categories in earlier chapters, but the following list provides a quick review of them:

✦ *Calendar* folders contain schedule items, such as appointments and meetings.

✦ *Contacts* folders contain information on people, such as e-mail and mailing addresses.

✦ *Journal* folders contain information on activities that you've performed on your computer, such as the length of time that you worked on specific documents.

✦ *Mail* folders contain incoming or outgoing messages, such as e-mail and faxes.

✦ *Notes* folders contain reminders that you create for yourself. The items in these folders are often compared to paper sticky notes.

✦ *Tasks* folders contain information on your to-do list.

Creating Folders

You can create new Outlook folders to suit your needs. If, for example, you are starting a new project and expect the project to generate quite a few messages, you may want to create one or more folders specifically for the messages relating to that project. In most cases, you'll probably create your new folders within your Outlook Personal Folders list. You likely don't need the extra complication of having multiple sets of Personal Folder files, but in the following sections, you learn about some special circumstances that may make extra Personal Folder files worth the effort.

Adding new folders

You can add folders wherever you like in the Outlook folder tree. In most cases, you'll probably want to keep related items together, but there's no reason that you can't place your folders where they make the most sense to you.

One strategy is to place new folders under existing folders that hold the same type of information. In this case, you may place folders for incoming messages under the Inbox folder, and move messages from the Inbox to the appropriate folders as they arrive.

You may also consider an alternative way to organize your new folders. Rather than creating new folders under the existing Outlook folders, you may want to create a project folder that is on the same level as Outlook folders, like the Inbox. Then you could create subfolders under the project folder for project-related messages, Calendar items, notes, and so on. In this model, you would find it very easy to organize the items for a project, because they would all be in folders under the project folder.

Finally, you might even consider using a completely separate Personal Folder file for each project. Although this is by far the most complicated way to organize your Outlook items, it does offer some real advantages. A separate Personal Folder file is easy to open and close as needed, is perfect when you want to be able to separately archive everything relating to specific projects, and can easily be transferred between different computers if necessary.

Regardless of the organizational strategy that you choose, creating new Outlook folders is pretty quick and easy. To create new folders, follow these steps:

1. In the folder list, right-click the folder that you want as the parent for the new folder. Although you can start in any folder, choosing the parent folder reduces the chance that you'll accidentally place the folder in the wrong location.

2. Select New Folder, as shown in Figure 17-3.

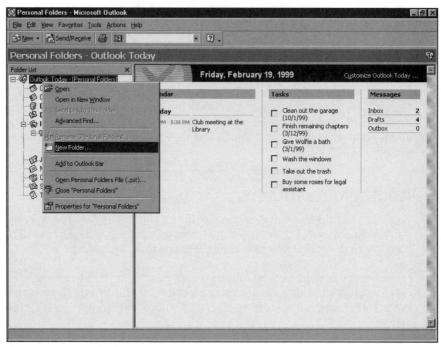

Figure 17-3: Select New Folder from the pop-up menu to create a new folder.

3. In the *Name* text box, enter a descriptive name for the folder. (Remember, names that are too long can be difficult to view in the folder list.)

4. Click the down arrow next to the *Folder contains* list box and choose the type of items that you will place in this folder, as shown in Figure 17-4. If this is a master project folder that will later contain additional subfolders for the project-related items, you can choose any item type, because you may not be storing anything in the master folder.

5. If you did not select the correct location for the new folder, choose the location in the folder tree that is displayed in the *Select where to place the folder* list box (this list box is hidden behind the drop-down list in Figure 17-4).

6. Click OK to close the Create New Folder dialog box and create the new folder.

If you need to create additional folders, repeat the same steps.

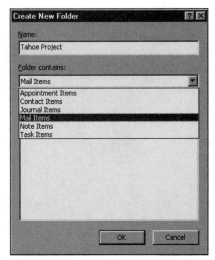

Figure 17-4: Select the type of item you'll store in the folder.

Customizing your new folders

If you are creating a master project folder, you'll probably want separate subfolders for messages that you receive and messages that you send. This is not, however, something that Outlook requires. If you choose to keep both messages that you receive and messages that you send in the same folder, you will be able to tell which messages were ones that you sent by looking at the From column. Your name will appear in the From column for messages that you sent.

Of course, knowing that you sent a message is important, but you probably would like to know to whom the message was sent. For that, you'll need to customize your new folder so that it better serves the dual purpose of a folder for both sent and received items.

To customize the folder to show additional information, follow these steps:

1. Open the folder that you wish to modify.
2. Right-click the column headings in the folder contents pane.
3. Choose Field Chooser from the pop-up menu as shown in Figure 17-5.

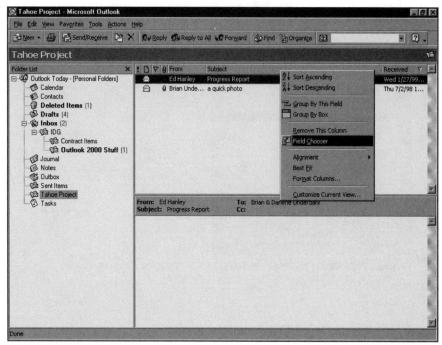

Figure 17-5: Select the Field Chooser to choose which fields are displayed in the folder.

4. Drag the To field from the Field Chooser dialog box to the location where you would like the new field to appear in the column headings. In Figure 17-6, the To field is being dragged to a position between the From and Subject fields.

5. Add any additional fields that will be useful in this folder view.

6. To remove fields you don't need, drag them from the column headings and drop them onto the Field Chooser dialog box.

7. Click the Close button to close the Field Chooser dialog box.

8. If necessary, drag the right edge of a field's column heading to adjust the width so that you can view the information in the column. You can adjust the width to fit the widest entry by double-clicking the right column border.

Figure 17-7 shows the new folder with the added To field. In this case, both the From and To columns were adjusted to show more of the information in the fields.

The To field being dragged

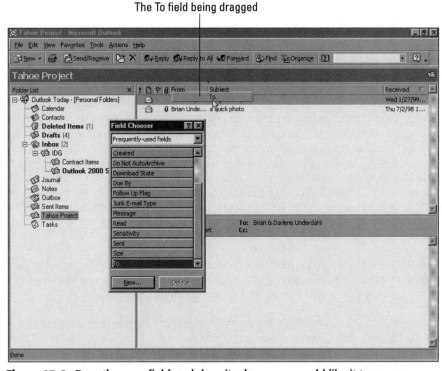

Figure 17-6: Drag the new field and drop it where you would like it to appear.

The added To field

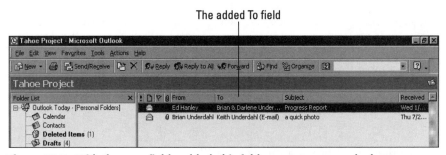

Figure 17-7: With the new fields added, this folder can now serve dual purposes.

You can also use the options available on the View ➪ Current View menu to further customize your new folder. For example, if you select Format Columns, you can choose the display format for the columns in the view. If you select Customize Current View, you can choose such properties as the default sort order, how the records are grouped, and any filters that will be used to choose the items to display.

Creating additional Personal Folders

You already know that Outlook uses a Personal Folder file to store Outlook's information on your computer. You may not realize that you can create additional Personal Folder files and that you can have more than one Personal Folder file open at the same time.

Why would you want to do this? One very good reason for having multiple Personal Folder files is that this is one of the easiest ways to move items between copies of Outlook on two different computers. Suppose, for example, that you use both a desktop and a laptop computer. You normally use Outlook on your desktop system to manage all your e-mail messages, but when you go on a business trip, you take your laptop system so that you can send and receive messages on the road. When you get back to the office, you have some important e-mail messages on the laptop system that you would like to move to your desktop computer. A separate Personal Folder file that you share between the laptop and desktop system is a very simple and efficient way to handle this task.

Another reason for having multiple Personal Folder files is so that you can organize multiple projects more easily. You can create a separate Personal Folder file for a project and then keep all the project-related items in that file.

Caution   Outlook's Personal Folder files aren't intended for multiple user access. If you have a Personal Folder file open on one computer, you should close the file before you can open it on a different computer. Otherwise, you might encounter problems if both computers attempt to modify the file contents.

Creating a new Personal Folder file is easy, but certainly there are a few potential pitfalls. If you wish to share a Personal Folder file between two computers, you'll probably want to place that file in a location that's just a bit easier to find than the default location—in the folder \Windows\Local Settings\Application Data\ Microsoft\Outlook. This folder may be a good and safe location for your mail Personal Folder file, but it's not exactly the first place you would think of looking if you couldn't remember the entire pathname.

To create a new Personal Folder file, follow these steps:

1. Select File ⇨ New ⇨ Personal Folders File to display the Create Personal Folders dialog box, shown in Figure 17-8.

2. Choose the location for the new file. You may want to click the My Documents button so that the file is saved in your my Documents folder, because this is a folder that is generally quite easy to locate on any Windows-based PC.

3. Enter a descriptive name in the File name text box. If you are creating multiple Personal Folder files, be sure to use a name that will enable you to quickly identify a specific Personal Folder file when you want to open the file.

4. Click the Create button to display the Create Microsoft Personal Folders dialog box, shown in Figure 17-9.

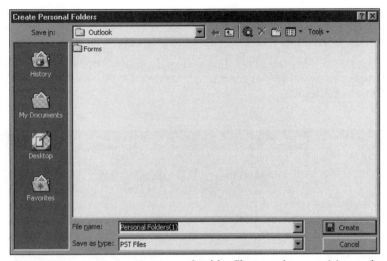

Figure 17-8: Create a new Personal Folder file to make organizing and sharing Outlook data a bit easier.

Figure 17-9: Control the access to your new Personal Folder file.

5. Type a name for the new Personal Folder file in the Name text box. This is the name that will appear in the Outlook folder list. It's a good idea to make this name unique so that you can easily identify the new folders.

6. Choose a level of encryption for this file. In most cases, you can accept the default, as this makes the file unreadable by programs other than Outlook, but also allows the file to be compressed so that it uses less disk space.

7. Enter a password in both password text boxes if you want to limit access to those who know the password.

8. Select the *Save this password in your password list* checkbox if you want your system to remember the password so that you don't need to enter it. It's usually best not to select this option if you truly need password security.

9. Click OK to close the dialog box and apply your settings. Figure 17-10 shows the new Personal Folder file named "Virginia City Project" opened in the Outlook folder list.

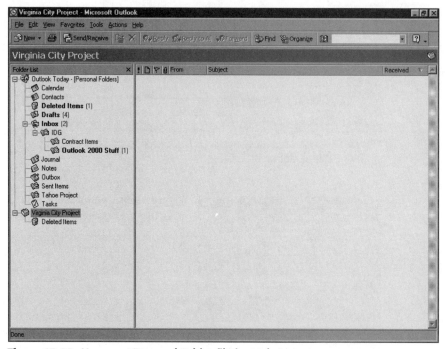

Figure 17-10: Your new Personal Folder file is ready to use.

Caution   You cannot change the type of encryption after a Personal Folder file has been created. If you need to use a specific type of encryption, be sure to select it while you are creating the file.

You'll have to create your own folders as needed. You can drag and drop folders and their contents between different Personal Folder files, or you can create new folders as described earlier in "Adding new folders."

When you no longer need to use a Personal Folder file, you can close the file by right-clicking the file and choosing the Close option from the pop-up menu, as shown in Figure 17-11. You'll want to do this if you intend to open the same file on another computer.

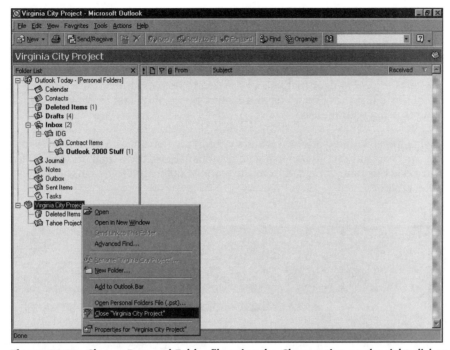

Figure 17-11: Close a Personal Folder file using the Close option on the right-click menu.

To open a Personal Folder file, select File ⇨ Open ⇨ Personal Folders File (.pst) from the Outlook menu. You can easily open a file that is located on your network as long as you have access to the folder where the Personal Folder file is located. You must have full access to the folder if you want to make any changes in the file.

Managing Items within the Folders

It's probably a reasonable guess that most Outlook users don't really manage the items in their folders too well. If you take a look at your Inbox, it may contain hundreds of e-mail messages that you've received. Your Sent Items folder is likely just about as bad. Finding any particular item in all of that chaos can be the equivalent of trying to find a needle in the haystack — far too difficult when a little organization can help so much.

Moving items

In Chapter 8, you learned how to use the Rules Wizard to set up rules for handling messages. You saw that you could create a rule that automatically placed messages from someone into a specific folder. Now that you know how to create new folders and, more importantly, new Personal Folder files, you can see how those rules could be very effective in helping you automate the management of projects within Outlook.

You don't, however, have to use rules to move items in Outlook. Often you'll probably find that it's just easier to do some tasks manually. Moving existing messages to new folders that you've created to help organize your Outlook items is one of those tasks that could be automated, but is often just as easy to do in a few minutes using your mouse.

Moving items within Outlook's folders couldn't be easier. As Figure 17-12 shows, you can drag and drop items using your mouse. Here, the e-mail message titled "Our books" is being dragged from the Outlook 2000 Stuff folder to the Tahoe Project folder.

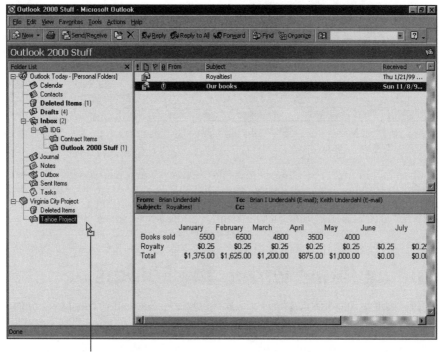

Dragging a message from one folder to another

Figure 17-12: Drag and drop works the same in Outlook as it does in Windows Explorer.

If you want to make a copy of an item that you're dragging rather than moving the item, hold down the Ctrl key while you release the left mouse button. Holding down the Ctrl key adds a plus sign (+) to the mouse pointer, and this indicates that the selected objects will be copied rather than moved.

Tip   You can move or copy multiple objects at the same time. Hold down the Ctrl key while you select individual items or the Shift key while you select a contiguous range of items. Release the key and then drag the selection to the new location — using the Ctrl key just before releasing the mouse button to copy items instead of moving them.

If you have a lot of folders or if you just can't quite get the hang of dragging and dropping, Outlook provides an alternative method for moving selected items. Right-click items that you've selected and choose Move to Folder from the pop-up menu to display the Move Items dialog box, shown in Figure 17-13. Choose the destination folder and click OK to move the items.

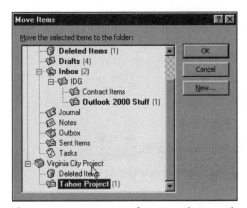

Figure 17-13: You can also move items using the Move Items dialog box.

You can also use the Cut, Copy, and Paste commands on the Edit menu to move and copy items. These commands work the same within Outlook as they do within other Windows applications, but there is one thing you need to watch out for. If you copy an item from an Outlook folder and then try to paste it into a Windows Explorer folder, you may be surprised by the result. Rather than creating the readable copy of a message that you might expect, you'll create a file that is listed in Windows Explorer as an "Outlook Item." Unfortunately, this Outlook Item will only be readable within Outlook. The next section shows you how to create a file that contains the message text in a format that can be read by many different programs.

Saving items as text files

To save the text of a message in a text file so that the text will be readable in other programs, you have a couple of options. You can open the message in Outlook, select the text, copy the text to the Clipboard, switch to the other application, and then paste the text into your new document. Alternatively, you can save the message as a text file directly from Outlook.

To save an Outlook message as a text file, follow these steps:

1. Select the message that you want to save as a text file.

2. Select File ⇨ Save As to display the Save As dialog box, shown in Figure 17-14.

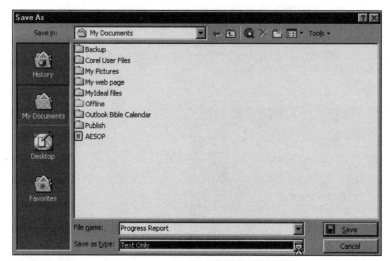

Figure 17-14: You can save Outlook messages as text files for use in other programs.

3. Choose the location for saving the file.

4. Enter a name for the file — Outlook will automatically add the .txt file extension.

5. Click the Save button.

Saving a message as a text file offers an advantage over copying the text using the Clipboard. When you save a message as a text file, Outlook includes the message header in the text file so that you can see who sent the message, when it was sent, who the message was sent to, and the subject line.

Sharing Folders

Sharing Outlook folders is an excellent way to share information. When you share Outlook folders, everyone has access to the latest information. You don't have to remember to send out individual messages to the people who are sharing the folder — they automatically receive any new information that appears in the shared folder.

You can share several different types of Outlook folders. In past versions of Outlook, sharing was somewhat difficult and limited to those users who were connected to a Microsoft Exchange Server. Outlook 2000 has broadened the range of users who can share Outlook folders by allowing all Outlook users to share folders.

Note   In order to fully share Outlook folders, all users must generally be using the same version of Outlook. Older versions of Outlook will have limited capabilities for sharing data from Outlook 2000.

Sharing Personal Folders

Each Outlook user has a set of Personal Folders. These folders are the ones that appear in your Outlook folder list under the title "Personal Folders." As you learned earlier in the section "Creating additional Personal Folders," you can create new Personal Folder files as needed.

Personal Folder files are intended to be just that—*personal*. These files aren't meant for multiuser access, so sharing your Personal Folders isn't a simple case of allowing someone else access to your files. In fact, if you open the same set of Personal Folder files on two different PCs at the same time, you're likely to see an error message on one or both of the PCs eventually. You may even need to close Outlook and restart your computer to resolve the problem.

Even though you shouldn't try to open the same set of Personal Folders on two computers at the same time, there's no reason why you can't open the same Personal Folder file on two different computers at different times. You may want to do this to synchronize items between Outlook on your desktop system and Outlook on your laptop system.

To open a Personal Folder file that is located on another computer on your network, follow these steps:

1. Select File ⇨ Open ⇨ Personal Folders File (.pst) to display the Open Personal Folders dialog box.

2. Click the down arrow next to the Look in list box, shown in Figure 17-15.

3. Choose the location of the remote file. If you aren't sure of the correct location, you may want to click the Tools button and use the Find command to locate the .pst files on your network.

4. Select the Personal Folder file you wish to open, as shown in Figure 17-16.

5. Click OK to open the file.

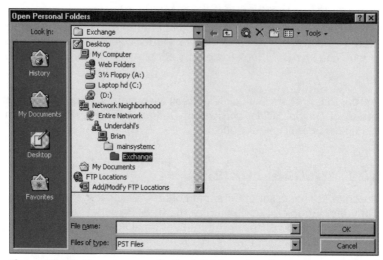

Figure 17-15: You can open Outlook folders elsewhere on your network.

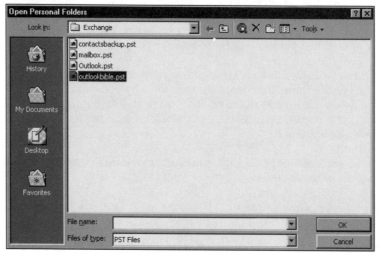

Figure 17-16: Select the file that you want to open.

Caution   If you are opening a Personal Folder file that is on another computer, make certain the same file is not open at the same time on both computers. The best way to do this is to close Outlook on the remote system while you work with the file on your computer. Close the file as soon as possible to avoid conflicts.

Sharing net folders

Net folders, like the Public Folders that were available to Exchange Server users in earlier versions of Outlook, were designed to be shared. You can use these types of shared folders for many different purposes. Members of a project team could share a folder that automatically sends everyone the latest project updates. Members of a club could use shared folders as a method of posting the latest event calendar.

When you share a folder, you have the ability to control access to the shared folder. You can grant some people very limited access that only allows them to read the folder contents, while you grant other people increased levels of access. Some people may need to add items to the shared folder, but should not have the right to edit other people's contributions. A few people may need even more access. Outlook enables you to set whatever access level is necessary.

See "Sharing Folders" at the end of Chapter 7 for details on how to share your net folders.

Once you set up a shared net folder, Outlook will send out subscription requests to the designated subscribers. These requests are sent as e-mail messages. Those who respond with a message accepting the subscription will be added to the folder's subscription list.

Outlook adds a copy of the shared folder to each subscriber's Outlook folder list. What happens next depends on the permission levels that you granted:

✦ Minimum-level subscribers are sent folder updates as e-mail messages. The frequency of these messages depends on how often the shared folder contains new items.

✦ Reviewer-level subscribers are sent folder updates as synchronization requests. These requests are sent at the intervals that you specify in the Properties dialog box for the shared folder.

✦ Higher-level subscribers are also sent folder updates as synchronization requests, but they receive two such requests at each update. One request sends new information, and the other collects any new items the subscriber has added to the folder.

Outlook can only do so much in controlling submissions to a shared folder. Even if you have the ability to post messages, you may need permission from someone in your organization to actually do so.

To add a new message to a shared folder, select File ➪ New ➪ Post in This Folder. This will display the Discussion form, shown in Figure 17-17. When you have completed the form, click the Post button to place the message in the folder.

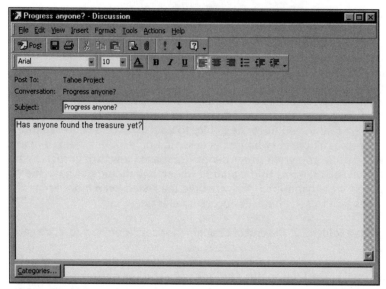

Figure 17-17: Post messages to the shared folder to share them with the subscribers.

Shared folder security

Any time you share information with other people, there exists the possibility that the information may end up available to people other than the intended recipients. Public folders on an Exchange Server are slightly more secure than net folders — if only because fewer people have access to the folders on an Exchange Server.

If you need to share sensitive information, you may want to consider the fact that shared folders don't use encryption to protect your data. Net folders are generally shared across the Internet, and this means the potential for snooping may exceed your personal comfort level. If so, here are some options you may wish to consider:

✦ Use a separate program such as WinZip or PGP to encrypt the items you place in the shared folders. The subscribers will need to know the correct password to open the items, so anyone who does not know the password will not have access to them. You can find these programs on the Internet.

Tip   You can find WinZip at www.winzip.com and PGP at www.pgp.com.

✦ You may want to avoid using the shared folders for any sensitive information. You can still use the shared folders, but limit what you place in them.

✦ You may want to forego shared folders entirely. You could exchange digital IDs with the other participants and then use a personal distribution list, as discussed in Chapter 8, to distribute encrypted messages. Although this would be far more work and far less convenient than using shared folders, it would afford considerable security for your most sensitive messages.

Using the Deleted Items Folder

An important part of using your folders effectively is to make certain that you do a little housecleaning from time to time. Each item that you store in your Outlook folders takes some room. Although most items take a very small amount of space, eventually you may build up hundreds or thousands of things in your Outlook folders.

Even if you aren't concerned about the amount of disk space that is used by your Outlook data, you probably should be concerned about the amount of time that you spend searching for important messages. If your Inbox has a thousand messages, you might take a bit longer than you would like trying to find that important message that your boss sent you a couple of weeks ago.

The Deleted Items folder is a lot like the Recycle Bin on your Windows desktop. When you delete items from other Outlook folders, those items are moved to the Deleted Items folder as a means of giving you a second chance. If you discover that you've deleted something in error, you can recover it from the Deleted Items folder — as long as you haven't already emptied the Deleted Items folder.

Deleting items

You probably have a lot of old messages that you no longer need. Perhaps you have exchanged a series of messages with someone, and each time one of you replied to the earlier message, you included the earlier message text in your response. You could easily delete the earlier messages and keep the final one. You might have received several dozen e-mail messages touting some get-rich-quick scheme — why would you want to keep them?

In most cases, deleting old messages is quite simple. You select the messages that you want to delete and then click the Delete button on the Outlook toolbar. The selected messages are quickly moved to the Deleted Items folder where you can deal with them later.

Sometimes, though, you may only want to delete part of a message. Suppose you're working on a project and someone sends you an important project-related message that includes a large file attachment. You probably save the attachment for use on your computer, so keeping the attachment with the message effectively doubles the space that is used on your hard disk. You could just delete the entire message, but you can recover that lost space without removing the message — only the unneeded attachment.

Here's how you can remove the file attachment and keep the message:

1. Double-click the message to open it.

2. Right-click the attachment and choose Remove, as shown in Figure 17-18. Some types of attachments will show a slightly different pop-up menu than the one shown in the figure. If you don't see Remove on the menu, choose Clear or Cut.

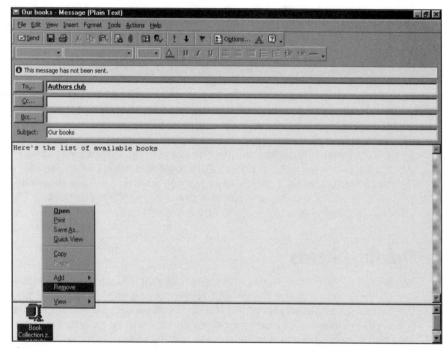

Figure 17-18: Remove attachments that you've saved to save disk space.

3. Click the Close button. Outlook will display a message similar to the one shown in Figure 17-19.

Figure 17-19: Save your changes to eliminate the attachment.

4. Click Yes to save your changes and close the now much smaller message.

Caution

> When you remove an attachment from a message, Outlook does not place the attachment in the Deleted Items folder. Make certain you have saved the attachment or that you do not need the attachment before removing it from a message.

Purging deleted items

Moving items to the Deleted Items folder cleans up your other Outlook folders, but it does not eliminate the wasted space that is used by those items. You need to empty the Deleted Items folder to truly eliminate the items that you've deleted.

Figure 17-20 shows one way to empty the Deleted Items folder. Right-click the Deleted Items folder and choose Empty "Deleted Items" Folder from the pop-up menu.

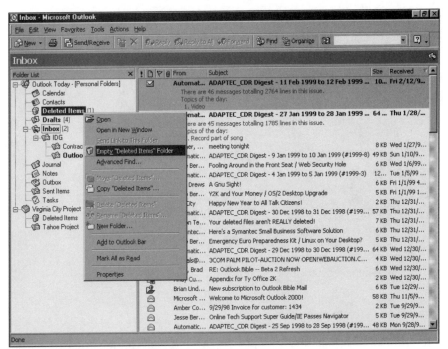

Figure 17-20: Empty the Deleted Items folder to finally remove the items you deleted earlier.

You can also use the Tools ➪ Empty "Deleted Items" Folder command to clear out the Deleted Items folder.

If you want to selectively remove items from the Deleted Items folder, first open the Deleted Items folder. Then select the items you wish to eliminate and click the Delete button. Choose Yes to permanently delete the selected items.

You can also tell Outlook to automatically empty the Deleted Items folder whenever you close Outlook. Follow these steps to automate the process:

1. Select Tools ➪ Options to display the Options dialog box.

2. Click the Other tab.

3. Select the *Empty the Deleted Items folder upon exiting* checkbox, as shown in Figure 17-21.

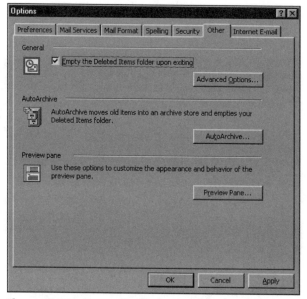

Figure 17-21: Automatically empty the Deleted Items folder whenever you close Outlook.

4. Click OK to close the dialog box.

If you choose to automatically empty the Deleted Items folder when you close Outlook, you'll be asked to confirm that you want to do so when you exit from Outlook. Even so, this is a good way to make certain that your Deleted Items folder doesn't fill up with useless old messages that you no longer need.

Compacting Outlook folders

Even though you delete items from your Outlook folders and clear out the Deleted Items folders, your Personal Folder file can continue to grow. The reason for this is that Outlook does not automatically recover the space that was used by items that you've deleted. You must tell Outlook to *compact* your Personal Folder file to recover that space.

To compact your Personal Folder file, follow these steps:

1. Select Tools ➪ Services to display the Services dialog box.

2. Select Personal Folders from the list of services.

3. Click the Properties button to display the Personal Folders dialog box, shown in Figure 17-22.

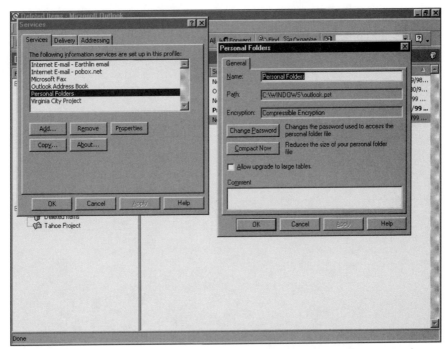

Figure 17-22: Reduce the space used by your Personal Folder file by compacting the file.

4. Click the Compact Now button to remove the wasted space. If you haven't selected this option for some time, you may have to wait a few minutes for the task to complete.

5. Click OK to close the Personal Folders dialog box.

6. Click OK to close the Services dialog box.

Be sure to compact your Personal Folder file regularly — especially if you've just eliminated a lot of old files from your Outlook folders.

Summary

Using your Outlook folders effectively is a good way to help you organize your Outlook data. In this chapter, you learned how Outlook's folders work, how to create folders, and how to manage the items in your folders. You learned several ways to share Outlook folders. Finally, you learned how to eliminate wasted space by using the Deleted Items folder and by compacting your Personal Folder files to recover space that Outlook wouldn't do on its own.

In the next chapter, you learn how to use Outlook along with the other applications on your computer. You see how you can be more effective and save yourself a lot of work by using applications together.

✦   ✦   ✦

Integrating with Other Applications

Computers are a wonderful and complex tool. Unlike a simple tool such as a hammer, a computer is intended to handle many very different tasks. This versatility is the result of the broad range of software that is available for modern computers.

Outlook, of course, is one of those pieces of software that you use to enable your computer to perform certain tasks. But Outlook is just one piece of software, and it has a limited set of capabilities — Outlook can't do everything that you may want to do with your system. For a lot of those other things, you need additional software with capabilities quite different from the ones you'll find in Outlook.

In all likelihood, your copy of Outlook came as a part of Microsoft Office. But even if it did not, you probably have software that provides word processing functions, other software that manages database information, and software that handles calculations. You probably have many other applications on your computer, too. All these different pieces of software may seem totally independent of each other, but as you learn in this chapter, you may want to use some of them to complement each other. You might, for example, want to use the contact information that you have in Outlook to help you create perfectly addressed letters using your word processor. You also might want to send a spreadsheet file that you're working on as an e-mail message. These are just a small part of the benefits you can gain from integrating Outlook with some of the other applications on your computer.

Integrating Outlook with Office

As you would probably expect, Outlook works very well with the other applications that are a part of Microsoft Office. If you want to use your Outlook Contacts list to start a new letter in Word, you'll find a command right on the Outlook menu to begin the process. In fact, if you want to share information between applications, Outlook is ready both to provide information to other programs and to use information that is provided by other programs.

Strictly speaking, much of this two-way data sharing can be thought of as common to many different programs. It's often quite easy to share data between programs provided by different software manufacturers. You don't have to use Word, Excel, or Access to share information with Outlook. Of course, because Microsoft would like you to use their products, they've made it just a bit easier to share information between the programs of Microsoft Office than with other programs.

One way to share information between programs is to use *linking* or *embedding* to place an object from one program into a document in another program. Linking places a link in your document so that changes in the original object are reflected in your document. Embedding places a static copy of the object into your document. Linking offers the advantage of smaller document size and always up-to-date content, but embedding offers the advantage of having everything combined into a single package.

You might include a chart from an Excel worksheet in an e-mail message to show your team members how expenses have really increased over the past year. Or you might use a PhotoDraw image to illustrate an important point about how your new building proposal will fit in with the existing structures in the neighborhood. The possibilities are really endless.

Here's a quick example of how you might place an Excel chart into an e-mail message:

1. Create the chart in an Excel worksheet.

2. Select the object that you wish to use in your e-mail message. In this case, you would select the chart of monthly expense.

3. Select Edit ➪ Copy to copy the object to the Windows Clipboard.

4. Switch back to Outlook. If the taskbar is visible, you can click the Outlook icon on the taskbar, or you can use Alt+Tab to switch between applications.

5. Click the New Mail Message button to display a new Message form.

6. Enter the addresses and subject line.

7. Type your message.

8. Select Edit ➪ Paste Special to display the Paste Special dialog box, shown in Figure 18-1. You could simply choose Edit ➪ Paste, but this won't enable you to choose the link option.

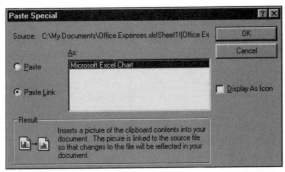

Figure 18-1: You can insert objects into your documents using different options.

9. Choose Paste to embed the object or Paste Link to link the object. In an e-mail message there isn't likely to be too much practical difference between the two, but in other types of documents the differences could be important.

10. Once you have selected how you want to paste the object, you may be able to select the object type. Generally the types shown at the top of the list will retain the closest to the object's original appearance.

11. Click OK to paste the object as shown in Figure 18-2.

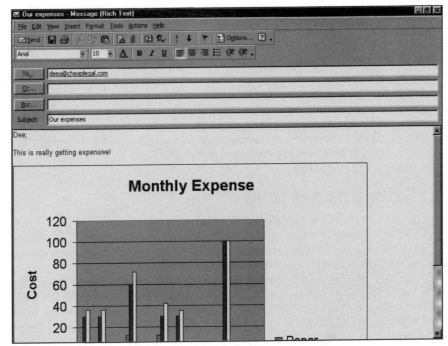

Figure 18-2: Inserted objects become a part of your document.

12. Click Send to send the e-mail message.

Tip   Don't use plain text as the message format if you wish to place objects into the message. You can only paste text into a plain text message.

As you use Outlook and the other applications on your computer, it's a good idea to think about how you might share information between different applications. Don't make the all too common mistake of thinking that information can only be used in documents created in the application where the data resides. As you'll see in several additional examples in this chapter, you can almost always find a way to reuse data without going through the work of reentering it in a new program.

Creating a Mail Merge

A *mail merge* is the process of creating form letters, mailing labels, envelopes, or a catalog from a set of related information. There are several ways to create a mail merge document. You can either use your Outlook Contacts list to create these documents or you can create them from lists of information that you have in other applications.

Choosing the source for your data can affect what you can do with mail merge:

✦ If you have all the names and addresses in Contacts, Outlook will be the easiest program to use because you won't have to export the information to another application.

✦ Outlook, however, doesn't offer some advanced capabilities that you'll find in other Office programs. If you need to do things like automatically separate the mail merge documents into individual zip codes to take advantage of special mailing rates, you may want to use Excel or Access to do the mail merge.

✦ If you need to produce a very large set of mail merge documents, such as thousands of form letters, you may want to use Access. This would be especially true if you have a huge database and need to be able to select a subset of the records for a particular need.

Getting names from contacts

If you already have the names that you wish to use for your mail merge in your Outlook Contacts folder, creating a mail merge directly from Outlook is a pretty simple process. Before you begin, however, you should put a little thought into what information the mail merge will use.

When you do a mail merge, Outlook provides you with two options. You can create a mail merge using only the selected records, or you can create one from all the contact records that are shown in the current view. Unless you have applied a filter to the current view, Outlook will include all your contact records in the view.

Although you may want to create a form letter to send to each of your contacts, it's more likely that you'll want to use a subset of the contact records. Suppose, for example, that you have assigned categories to each of your contacts. If you want to send a form letter to your relatives, you could create a view that only shows those contacts in the family category. You can learn more about filtering your contacts in Chapter 9.

To create a mail merge using records in your Contacts list, follow these steps:

1. Open the Contacts folder.

2. If you want to use a subset of the records in the mail merge, do one of the following:

   • Open a view that filters the records so that only the subset of records is shown.

   • Select the records that you wish to use. Hold down Ctrl as you select each record to add it to the selection.

3. Select Tools ➪ Mail Merge to display the Mail Merge Contacts dialog box, shown in Figure 18-3.

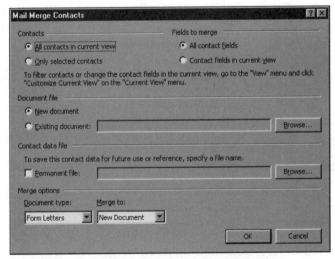

Figure 18-3: Use the Mail Merge Contacts dialog box to produce a mail merge from contact records.

4. Select which records to merge:

   • Choose *All contacts in current view* if you have applied a filter to select a subset of records or if you want to use all your contacts.

   • Choose *Only selected contacts* if you selected the subset of records manually before beginning the mail merge.

5. Select which fields to include:

- Choose *All contact fields* if you want the mail merge to include all of the contact information.

- Choose *Contact fields in current view* if you want the mail merge to include only those fields that are displayed in the current view.

6. Choose whether you want to create a new document or use an existing one. To use an existing document, you can locate the document via the Browse button.

7. Select the *Permanent file* checkbox and specify a filename if you want to save the mail merge data for future use. You might want to choose this option to provide a permanent record of the contacts that you used for this mail merge. Normally, though, you'll want to perform a new mail merge each time you need the information so that you don't accidentally use outdated information.

8. Select the type of mail merge document from the drop-down Document type list box, shown in Figure 18-4:

- *Form letters* are documents that include merged information along with additional text that you specify.

- *Mailing labels* are documents that contain multiple labels on each sheet. These are generally printed on peel-off label stock in standard sizes.

- *Envelopes* are similar to mailing labels, except that the addresses are printed directly on standard size envelopes.

- *Catalogs* are similar to mailing labels, except that they are usually printed on plain paper and are intended for uses such as membership lists.

Figure 18-4: Choose the document type appropriate for your needs.

9. Choose the destination from the drop-down Merge to list box, shown in Figure 18-5:

- *New Document* produces a document file that you can further edit as needed before printing.

- *Printer* sends the merged document directly to the default system printer.

- *E-mail* creates e-mail messages and places them in your Outbox.

- *Fax* sends the merged document directly to the fax service.

Figure 18-5: Choose the correct destination for the merged documents.

10. If your current view includes any distribution lists, they will not be incorporated in the mail merge. Click OK to confirm the message regarding this if it appears.

11. Once Word opens, click the Insert Merge Field button to add fields to the document. Remember to include spaces and punctuation as necessary.

12. Enter any additional text as necessary to complete your document. Figure 18-6 shows an example of a form letter that is almost ready to merge with the contact information from Outlook.

13. Click the Merge button to display the Merge dialog box, shown in Figure 18-7.

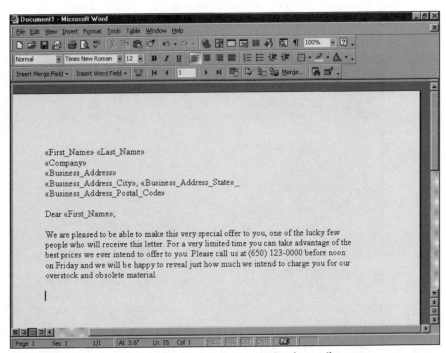

Figure 18-6: Complete your document to prepare for the mail merge.

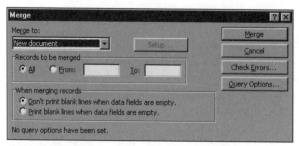

Figure 18-7: Select the final mail merge options.

14. Make certain the *Don't print blank lines when data fields are empty* radio button is selected. This will prevent your completed document from looking like something is missing when a record does not contain data in one of the merge fields.

15. Click Merge to perform the merge. Figure 18-8 shows an example of a completed form letter with the contact information substituted for the merge fields. If you chose to merge to the printer, fax, or e-mail, the completed mail merge documents will be directed to the correct destination rather than to documents.

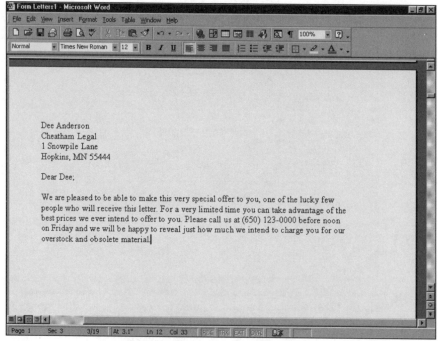

Figure 18-8: Your completed mail merge will replace the merge fields with the information from your Contacts list.

16. Print and save your mail merge documents as necessary.

Caution

Mail merge documents often contain nasty surprises such as missing or misplaced information. It's a good idea to practice using mail merge in advance to make certain that your mail merge works as you expect. In addition, it's always a good idea to take a quick look through the merged documents before you print and mail them. You may find that you need to do some additional tune-up of the master mail merge document before it is really ready to produce the documents that you want.

Getting names from Office applications

Mail merges don't have to depend on Outlook for the information that is included in the merge. You may have a table of names in a Word document, an Excel worksheet, or an Access database that contains the data for the mail merge. If so, you can perform the mail merge in almost the same way as when you use your Outlook Contacts list. The primary difference is that you must direct Word to the correct data source.

To perform a mail merge using data from a source other than your Outlook Contacts list, follow these general steps:

1. Open Word.

2. Select Tools ⇨ Mail Merge to display the Mail Merge Helper dialog box, shown in Figure 18-9.

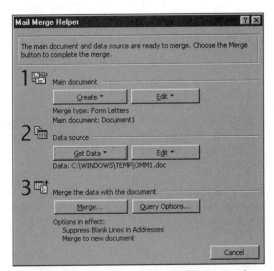

Figure 18-9: You can use the Mail Merge Helper to merge data from sources other than Outlook.

3. Select the type of document and create the master mail merge document as you did earlier.

4. Click the Get Data button and choose the type of data source. Most often you'll use the Open Data Source option and choose the source.

5. Click the Merge button and complete the mail merge the same way as when Outlook was the data source.

Although the preceding steps are rather general, once you've created a mail merge using your Contacts list, you'll easily see what needs to be done at each step. Because the Outlook Contacts list is really a very comprehensive database of contact information, the main difference you're likely to notice when you use a different data source is that you probably won't have nearly as many merge fields you can choose from for your document.

Sending an E-mail from an Application

Outlook's messaging capabilities make it very easy for you to open Outlook and create a new e-mail message. Although this is certainly not a difficult task, switching between applications can be a distraction — especially if you're deep into a project and discover something important that you need to send out immediately. You've probably experienced this yourself. You're working on a spreadsheet or a report and decide that you should send off a copy to someone else. So you switch over to Outlook and click the New Mail Message button, address the message, and begin to type your message. Then you click the Insert File button and realize that you can't remember the correct filename. And even if you can remember the name of the file that you want to send, you aren't absolutely certain that you saved your latest revisions to the file. You switch back to the original program, click the Save button, note the filename, and switch back to your e-mail message. You complete the message and send it off, but you're frustrated by all the time that you've wasted.

Even if you've never thought about it before, you're probably starting to realize that it might be just a bit easier if you could send a document as an e-mail message without all that switching back and forth. Not only would it be less distracting to your train of thought, but you wouldn't have to try and remember the name of the file that you want to send, nor just exactly where you saved it.

You can send an e-mail message directly from any Office application as well as from many other Windows programs. The process is very similar in most applications, so the following example will show you how to send an Excel worksheet from within Excel.

To send a document directly from an application, follow these steps:

1. Open the document that you wish to send. In some programs, you must name the document by saving it before you can send it as an e-mail message.

2. Select File ➪ Send To to display the Send To menu, shown in Figure 18-10. Different applications may have different sets of options on the Send To menu, but most will include a Mail Recipient option.

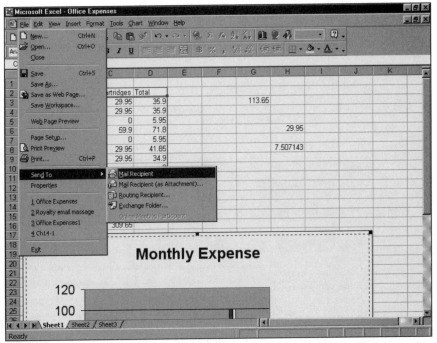

Figure 18-10: You can send a document from within the application that created it.

3. Choose the option you prefer:

- *Mail Recipient* generally sends the document as a file attachment, but in Office 2000 applications, you can choose to send the document as an HTML page.

- *Mail Recipient (as Attachment)* specifies that you wish to send the document as a file attachment to a text message.

- *Routing Recipient* sends the file to a specified group of people and returns it to you when everyone has finished adding their changes.

- *Exchange Folder* sends the file to an Exchange Server folder, where it will be available to all authorized users of that folder.

- *Online Meeting Participant* sends the file to someone who is participating with you in an online meeting using NetMeeting.

4. If you selected Mail Recipient in an Office 2000 application, you'll next see a message similar to the one shown in Figure 18-11. Choose the format that best suits your needs and click OK.

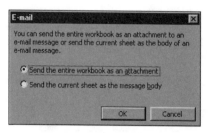

Figure 18-11: Choose the proper document format.

5. Select the message recipients.

6. Enter any additional text and set any message options as necessary. Figure 18-12 shows the message ready to send.

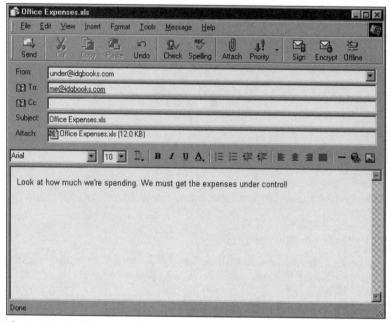

Figure 18-12: Complete the message just as you would if you were sending it from Outlook.

7. Click the Send button to send your message.

What happens after you click the Send button may depend on several factors. If Outlook is running, the message should be sent to your Outbox. If Outlook is not running, the message may be sent immediately using Outlook Express, or you may be prompted to select a messaging profile—depending on the application that you used to create the e-mail message. To prevent confusion, it's usually best to make certain Outlook is running before you decide to send an e-mail message.

Importing and Exporting Data

Your computer is probably worth a fraction of what the data it contains is worth to you. If you think about all the time and effort that you've put into entering information into various programs, documents, and databases, it's pretty easy to see how valuable that information may be. As important as that data may be, it's not very useful if you can't use the information the way you need to.

Outlook handles many different types of data. You may have several sources of data that you would like to use in Outlook, and you may have a number of places where your Outlook data might also be useful. The key to making all of this data more useful is to import and export the information so that you can use it where you need it.

Note

Outlook can import more types of data than it can export. If you need to use data from another program in Outlook, or use Outlook data in another program, you may encounter situations where neither program seems to support the other's format. If so, look for another format that both programs support — such as dBASE, comma-separated values, or even tab-separated values. If you cannot find a common format, you may be able to use Word, Excel, or Access to handle the format conversion.

Importing information into Outlook

There are several types of information that you may wish to import into Outlook. Typically, though, these fall into a few categories:

✦ Contact information such as e-mail addresses

✦ vCard electronic business cards

✦ vCalendar scheduling information

✦ Messages stored in Personal Folder files

To import data into Outlook, follow these steps:

1. Select File ➪ Import and Export to display the Import and Export Wizard, shown in Figure 18-13.

2. Select the type of information that you wish to import. If you aren't sure which option to choose, select each option and read the description in the lower part of the dialog box.

3. Click Next to continue.

4. Choose the type of file you wish to import, as shown in Figure 18-14. The choices will vary according to your selection in Step 2. In this case, Personal Folder File is selected.

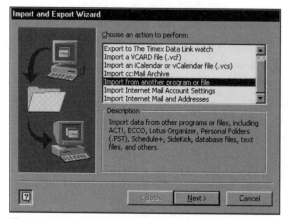

Figure 18-13: Use the Import and Export Wizard to bring data into Outlook.

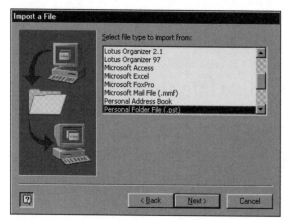

Figure 18-14: Choose the type of file you wish to import.

5. Click Next to continue.

6. Select the name of the file that you wish to import, as shown in Figure 18-15.

7. Choose any options for the import. These will vary according to the type of file that you are importing, but the options shown in Figure 18-15 are fairly typical when you are importing contact information.

8. Click Next to continue.

9. If you are importing from a Personal Folder file, choose which folders you wish to import, as shown in Figure 18-16. If you are importing data from other types of sources, you probably won't have to make this selection.

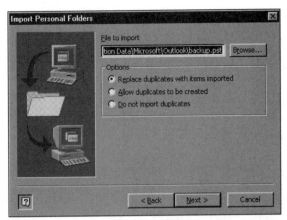

Figure 18-15: Specify the name of file you wish to import.

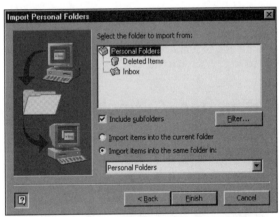

Figure 18-16: Choose which folder information to import and where to place that information.

10. If you only wish to include certain items, click the Filter button to display the Filter dialog box, shown in Figure 18-17.

11. Specify the set of conditions that will filter the records and only import those that meet your needs.

12. Click OK to apply the filter and close the Filter dialog box.

13. Click the Finish button to import the data.

Other types of data sources will involve different sequences of steps, but the import process will be similar in all cases. You must choose the type of data, the source file, and how to handle duplicates.

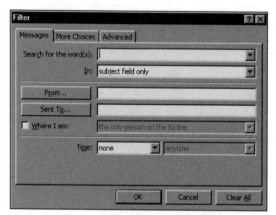

Figure 18-17: Create a filter if you want to selectively import information.

Tip

If you import a large number of contact records into Outlook, be sure to review Chapter 9 to learn how to assign categories to your contacts. Assigning categories will make it much easier for you to manage your contact records — especially if you have a lot of people listed in your Contacts folder.

Exporting information from Outlook

Just as you can import data into Outlook from several different formats, you can also export Outlook data into a number of formats. Sometimes, though, the way that Outlook exports data may leave something to be desired. Fortunately, there are alternatives that may work better in some cases.

To export data from Outlook, follow these steps:

1. Select File ⇨ Import and Export to display the Import and Export Wizard.

2. Select the type of export. In most cases, you'll want to choose the *Export to a file* option.

3. Click Next to continue.

4. Choose the type of file you wish to create, as shown in Figure 18-18. Most of the format options are best suited for exporting contact information.

5. Click Next to continue. If this is the first time that you have exported data to a particular format, you may need to insert your Outlook CD-ROM so that the correct export filter can be installed.

6. Select the folder that you wish to export, as shown in Figure 18-19. If you choose a folder other than Contacts, you may not be pleased with the results — especially if you hope to save messages. See "Saving Outlook Messages" later for a better way to save your message text.

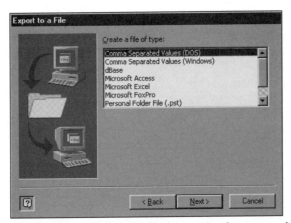

Figure 18-18: Choose the file format for the exported data.

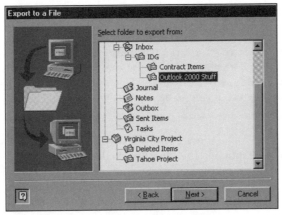

Figure 18-19: Choose the folder to export.

7. Click Next to continue.

8. Specify a name for the exported data file.

9. Click Next to continue.

10. Verify the actions to be performed, as shown in Figure 18-20, and then click the Finish button to export the data.

Tip

Be sure to open the exported data file to verify the contents before you delete the data within Outlook. You may discover that the exported data is incomplete or unusable, and it is far better to determine this while you can still recover the information in Outlook.

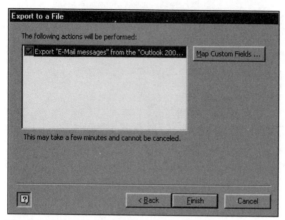

Figure 18-20: Verify that Outlook will export the information that you expect to export.

Saving Outlook messages

If you look at data that you've exported from Outlook, you may be somewhat less than thrilled with the results. The reason for this is that data you export is generally saved in a database type of format, and this may not be what you intended — especially if you were trying to save a message for use in another program.

When you want to save a message, there's another way to do so that will generally produce better results than exporting the message. Follow these steps to save a message as a text file:

1. Select the message that you wish to save.
2. Select File ➪ Save As to display the Save As dialog box, shown in Figure 18-21.
3. Choose the destination for the file.
4. Enter a filename for the message. By default, Outlook will use the message subject as the filename.
5. Click Save to save the file.

When you save a message as a text file, Outlook includes the message header information at the top of the text file. This makes it very easy for you to see the information such as who sent the message, the message date, the recipients, and the subject line. Following all of this, you'll see the message text.

Caution   Saving a message as text does not save any message attachments. Be sure to save any important attachment separately.

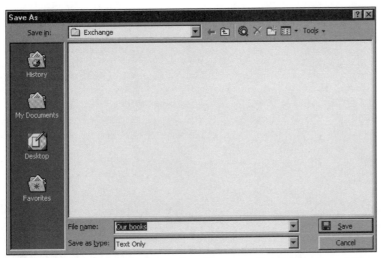

Figure 18-21: Save a message rather than exporting it if you want the message text to appear in a file.

Summary

Outlook is a very capable program, but that doesn't mean you have to use it in isolation. Indeed, as you learned in this chapter, Outlook works very well with other programs. You saw that Outlook integrates very well with the other programs in Microsoft Office. You also learned how to use Outlook's Contacts list to produce form letters using mail merge. You saw that sending e-mail from within other applications is sometimes easier than switching back to Outlook, and you learned how to share data between Outlook and other programs.

In the next part of this book, you learn the basics of developing your own applications within Outlook.

✦   ✦   ✦

Basics of Microsoft Outlook 2000 Development

Part V focuses on developing custom applications using Outlook 2000 and its related technologies. After getting a general overview of the different types of applications you can create with Outlook, you learn about the elements of a simple Outlook form and how to create one. You also learn the specifics behind each of the various form controls and how to use them, and what custom fields are and when they are appropriate.

Outlook 2000 Application Types

So that you may grasp the full potential of Outlook 2000 application programming, this chapter provides you with an understanding of the different types of applications that you can create. You learn about the various Outlook 2000 client applications, Outlook 2000 Office applications, Outlook 2000 Web applications, and LOBjects (Line of Business Objects), which consist of various third-party solutions that utilize these same technologies.

Outlook 2000 Client Applications

The most common Outlook application can be categorized as an Outlook client application. The client applications consist mainly of forms, which provide the user interface, and postings routed between folders, which provide the content. Although the degree of customization is vast, forms can be classified into three categories:

- ✦ Message forms
- ✦ Post forms
- ✦ Built-in forms

Outlook 2000 Forms Designer

The Outlook 2000 Forms Designer (OFD) is the tool that programmers use to customize the three types of forms. Once the forms have been customized, the Outlook 2000 Forms Designer publishes the form so that it may be used within Outlook. All the buttons, drop-down menus, tabs, fields, and other elements that make up a form are created with this tool. In order to get a general understanding of each different form type, we will show you the elements of the forms as seen within the Outlook 2000 Forms Designer.

Cross-Reference Although this chapter will provide a general overview of the Outlook 2000 Forms Designer, Chapter 21 provides detailed insight into the tool by demonstrating specifics on customizing forms.

The Outlook 2000 Form Designer can be accessed by selecting Tools ⇨ Forms ⇨ Design a Form. This opens the Design Form dialog box, as shown in Figure 19-1.

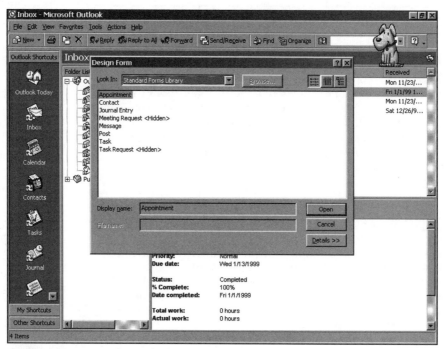

Figure 19-1: Access the Outlook 2000 Forms Designer by selecting Tools ⇨ Forms ⇨ Design a Form.

The forms you see displayed in the Design Form dialog box are part of the Standard Forms Library, as you can see in the Look In drop-down menu. The Look-In drop-down menu enables you to access both personal and public folders.

Tip When opening a form in Design view within the Outlook 2000 Forms Designer, it's a good idea to get in the habit of holding the Shift key down as you open the form (that is, as you click the Open button). By holding the Shift key down, you will prevent the running of any code that is supposed to be triggered as the form opens.

Message forms

Let's begin by taking a look at the message form. The message form is used when composing an e-mail message. This form can be opened via the Design Form menu box by selecting the message form, as described previously.

Tip   Alternatively, this form can be opened in the Outlook 2000 Forms Designer by opening a standard e-mail message from the Inbox, and then selecting Tools ➪ Forms ➪ Design This Form.

An example of the message form opened in the Outlook Forms Designer is shown in Figure 19-2.

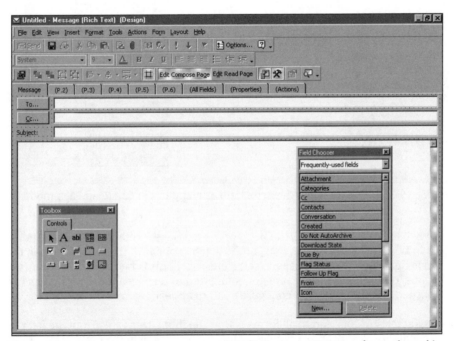

Figure 19-2: This message form appears in Edit Compose Page mode, as viewed in Outlook 2000 Forms Designer.

It's important to note that the Edit Compose Page button on the toolbar is selected. This means the form appears in particular this format when a user is composing an e-mail message. In addition to the Compose mode, the message form can also appear in a second mode — Read mode. Figure 19-3 shows the same form in Edit Read Page mode; note how the form has changed to reflect what a user will see when reading an e-mail message. Also note that the addressing fields are disabled in Edit Read Page mode.

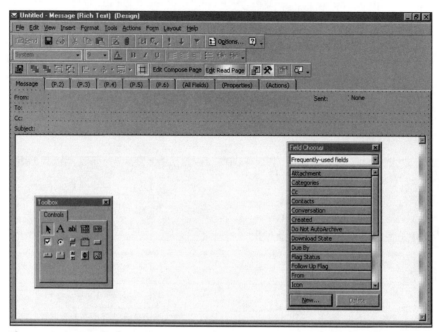

Figure 19-3: Here's the same message form as it appears in Edit Read Page mode.

As you can see in Figure 19-3, the body of the message form includes nine different tabs in Design view. However, none of these tabs appear to the end user when the form is being used to compose or read a message. This is because the contents of all the tabs, other than Message, are not configured to display after the form has been published. Details on how to configure a tab to appear are covered in Chapter 21.

A characteristic common to all forms is that the first seven tabs (from the left) have the capability to appear in a published form. However, only the first six tabs provide you with the ability to customize the form's interface. Figure 19-4 demonstrates how tabs (P.2) through (P.6) are blank to allow for additional functionality on a single form.

The (All Fields) tab, shown in Figure 19-5, provides a listing of fields supported within the form. The drop-down menu at the top of the tab allows you to show only the fields that you want to see. The New button at the bottom of the window for this tab allows you to add user-defined fields. A user-defined field is a category of data that you define to allow for the storage of data that is not already defined by Outlook 2000.

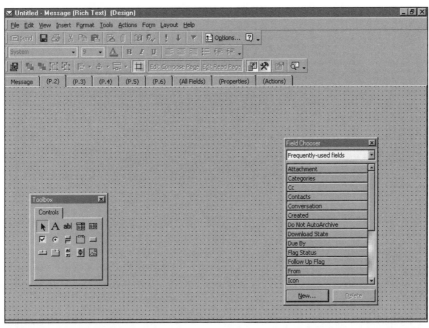

Figure 19-4: Blank tabs are designed to support additional form functionality.

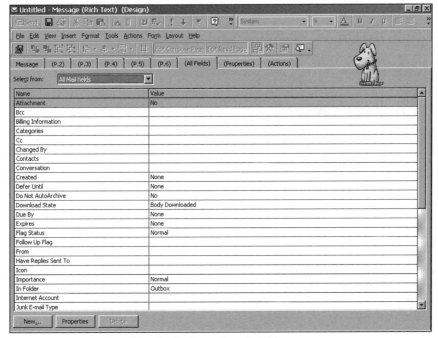

Figure 19-5: The All Fields tab displays all mail fields.

The (Properties) tab, shown in Figure 19-6, is also common to all form types and is used to specify attributes for a particular form. In addition, the (Properties) tab displays information regarding relationships with Contacts and Categories, as well as additional relational information.

Cross-Reference   The (Properties) tab is discussed in greater detail in Chapter 23.

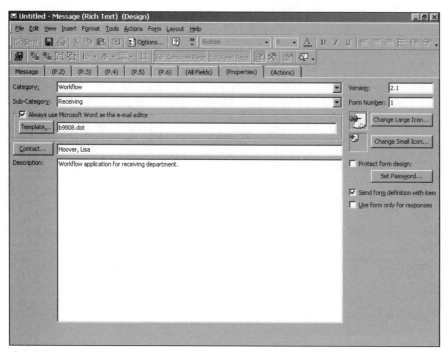

Figure 19-6: Use the (Properties) tab to specify information for a particular form.

The (Actions) tab, shown in Figure 19-7, displays information regarding the behavior of the form. Specifically, this tab identifies the various options regarding how the data behind the form is stored and/or transmitted.

Post forms

Post forms are another type of form used within the Outlook 2000 Forms Designer. Post forms are used to "post" information to a specified folder. An example of a post form, as viewed in the Outlook 2000 Forms Designer in Edit Compose Page mode, is shown in Figure 19-8.

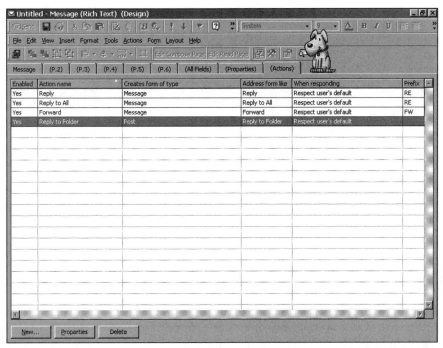

Figure 19-7: The (Actions) tab shows options for how the form data is stored and/or transmitted.

Note that the post form is very similar to the message form touched on earlier. The major differences between the two forms are in the addressing sections. Whereas the message requires an e-mail address for its destination, the post form requires a folder name. You access the post forms the same way you do message forms.

Figure 19-8: This post form appears in Edit Compose Page mode.

Figure 19-9 shows the post form in Edit Read Page mode. As with the message form, the only real difference between the post form in Edit Compose Page mode and in Edit Read Page mode is in the addressing section. The remaining tabs of the post form—that is, (P.2), (Properties), and so on—are similar to the corresponding tabs in the message form and serve the same purposes.

Figure 19-9: Here's the same post form as it appears in Edit Read Page mode.

Built-in forms

Built-in forms refer to the other forms that make up a portion Outlook 2000's user interface. For example, the Contact form that opens when you add a person in the Contacts section of Outlook 2000 (see Figure 19-10) is considered a built-in form.

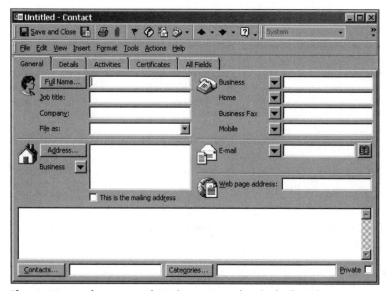

Figure 19-10: The Contact form is an example of a built-in form.

Other examples of built-in forms include the following:

✦ Appointment form

✦ Journal Entry form

✦ Task form

Caution

You can open these forms and others, located in the Standard Forms Library, in Design view. However, although Outlook 2000 will allow you to open a form in Design view, some forms do not have the option of being published under a different name after you customize them. For example, the Task Request form may not be customized and used within your application. In addition, Outlook 2000 Office Document forms, which are covered later in this chapter, may be opened within the Outlook 2000 Form Designer, but the form containing the Office document may not be customized.

Examine the Contact form in the Outlook 2000 Forms Designer, as shown in Figure 19-11, and notice that it has many of the same characteristics found in the other form types.

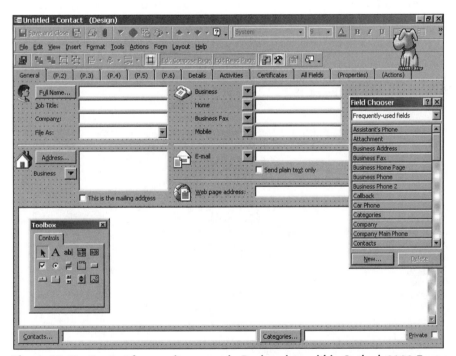

Figure 19-11: Contact form as it appears in Design view within Outlook 2000 Forms Designer

Some of the differences worth noting on the Contact form are the additional tabs (Details, Activities, and Certificates) and the Full Name button functionality. Specifically, subwindows providing additional details open when the Full Name button is selected. Similar features, such as the Address and Call Now features, are scattered throughout the form.

Tip

The main purpose of providing programmers access to the built-in forms within Outlook 2000 is to save them time in developing their own forms. For instance, suppose a programmer needs to track tax-related information for an accounting firm. In addition to the taxpayer's tax ID, number of dependents, and marital status, the application would likely need to store other personal information, such as the home address, spouse's name, and profession. Because much of this information is already stored in the Contact form, it makes more sense to customize the Contact form, rather than start from scratch with a standard post form.

Outlook 2000 Office Applications

The applications within Office 2000 have been designed to be tightly integrated. As a result, Office applications within Internet Explorer 5.0, Word 2000, Excel 2000, and PowerPoint 2000 provide their own functionality within Outlook 2000.

For instance, you can forward a Web application from within Internet Explorer by accessing the URL for the application and selecting Send Page from the Mail button menu, as shown in Figure 19-12.

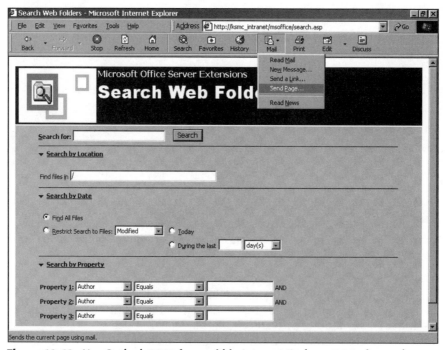

Figure 19-12: Use Outlook 2000 from within Internet Explorer 5.0 to forward an application.

As you can see in Figure 19-13, address information is inserted above the application, so it can be forwarded via e-mail.

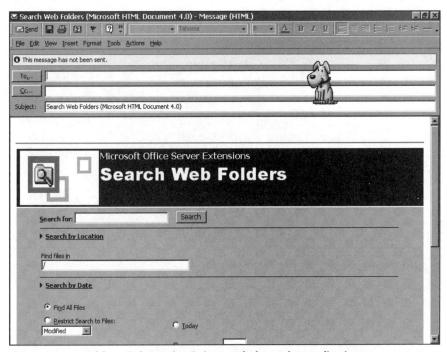

Figure 19-13: Address information is inserted above the application.

This same functionality is also inherent in Word 2000, in Excel 2000, and, as shown in Figure 19-14, in PowerPoint 2000. Outlook is accessed within these applications by selecting Send To ➪ Mail Recipient from the File menu. This functionality, however, is not a part of Access 2000.

In addition to sending Office 2000 documents as the text of an e-mail message, documents may be posted to a personal or public folder within Outlook 2000. To post a document to a folder, select File ➪ Send To ➪ Exchange Folder and specify the folder you would like to post the document to. This type of functionality could be appropriate in a document-tracking application.

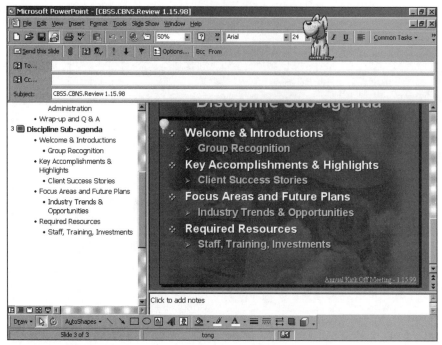

Figure 19-14: Outlook can also be used within PowerPoint 2000.

Outlook 2000 Web Applications

As Outlook continues to mature, it and the applications it integrates with become more and more closely tied to the Internet. As a result, Outlook 2000 utilizes and functions with a wide range of Internet technologies. As the Internet matures, Outlook 2000 will continue to utilize the technology wherever it can.

Collaborative discussions via Web folders

In addition to the tight integration of its applications, Office 2000 also supports collaborative discussions through the use Web folders. Before moving on, you need to understand what Web folders and collaborative discussions are.

Through the use of a Web server running Internet Information Server (IIS) 4.0 with Office Server Extensions installed, organizations will be able to easily share Office 2000 documents, anywhere around the world. Through the use of Web folders, such items as Word documents, Excel spreadsheets, PowerPoint presentations, and HTML documents may be accessed and edited through Internet Explorer 5.0. Figure 19-15 demonstrates a Web folder being used in place of a traditional file server.

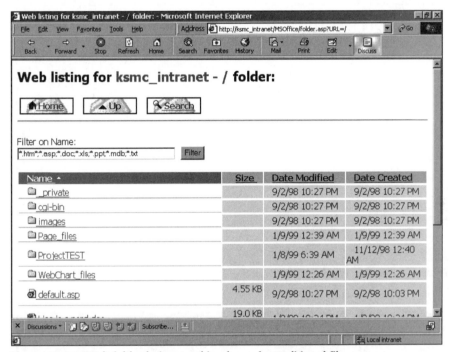

Figure 19-15: Web folder being used in place of a traditional file server.

Web folders will become a common tool used within corporate intranets and extranets in the near future. In order to demonstrate how this tool works, let's take a look at a simple Word document stored within a Web folder. Word 2000 allows you to save documents in HTML format by choosing File ➪ Save as Web Page. Because this document was saved as a Web page, anyone with access to the Web server can view it (see Figure 19-16).

By clicking the Edit button on the Internet Explorer 5.0 toolbar, the document opens in Word 2000, as shown in Figure 19-17, to enable you to edit it, assuming you've been assigned appropriate rights. Any computer with Word 2000 installed will offer the capability to edit this document. The Office Server Extensions on the Web server make this possible.

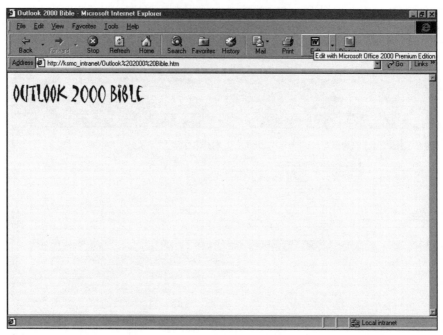

Figure 19-16: This Word document was published to a Web folder in HTML format.

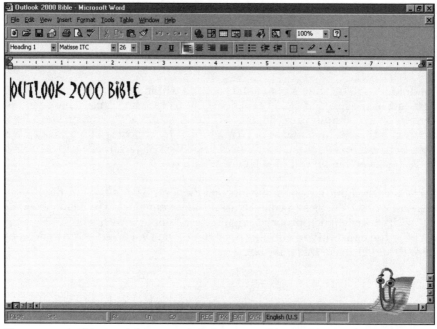

Figure 19-17: This Word document is being remotely edited by another user.

Messaging comes into play when we bring in the concept of collaborative discussion within a Web folder. In order to demonstrate a collaborative discussion, let's use the same Word document from the preceding example here. Clicking the Discuss button within Internet Explorer 5.0 opens a Discussion bar at the bottom of the screen. By selecting *Insert about the Document* from the Discussions menu in the lower-left corner, the dialog box shown in Figure 19-18 appears.

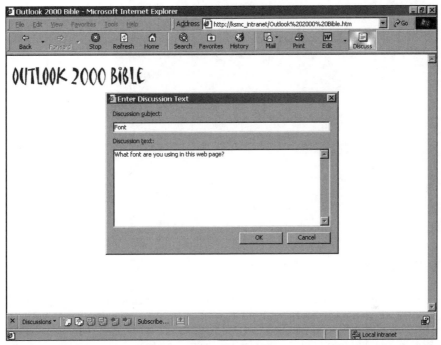

Figure 19-18: The Discussion Text dialog box can be used to add a comment to a document within a Web folder.

Once a comment is entered into the Discussion text field and the OK button is clicked, the discussion comment is saved for the other users to read, as shown in Figure 19-19.

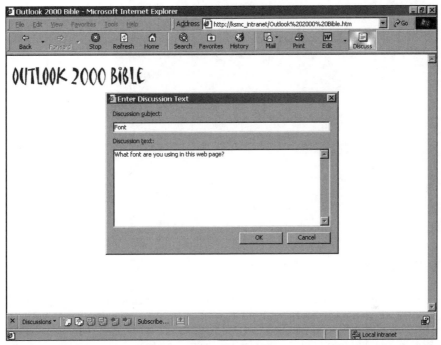

Figure 19-19: A discussion comment is displayed for others to see.

If you click the Subscribe button on the Discussion tool bar and supply your e-mail address, you will be notified when the document has been changed, deleted, moved, or any number of other options. You may also limit the notifications to appear when the change occurs, once a day, or once a week. The subscription options are shown in Figure 19-20.

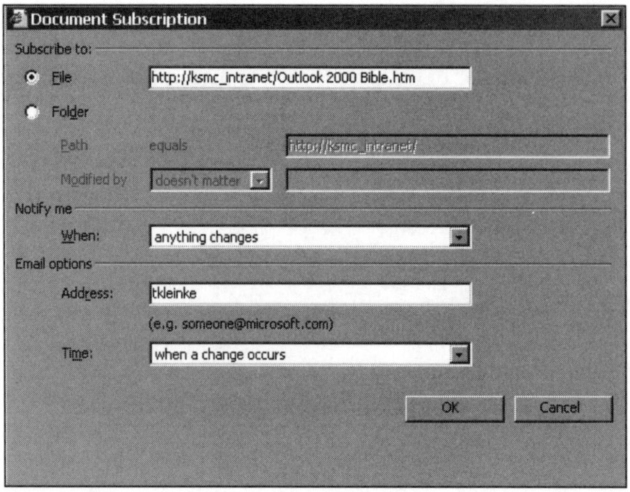

Figure 19-20: Use these subscription options for notification of change.

By clicking the drop-down menu next to the paper icon near the discussion comment, another user can reply to the comment, as shown in the example in Figure 19-21. After the other user's comment is posted, you would receive an e-mail notification that the document you subscribed to has been changed.

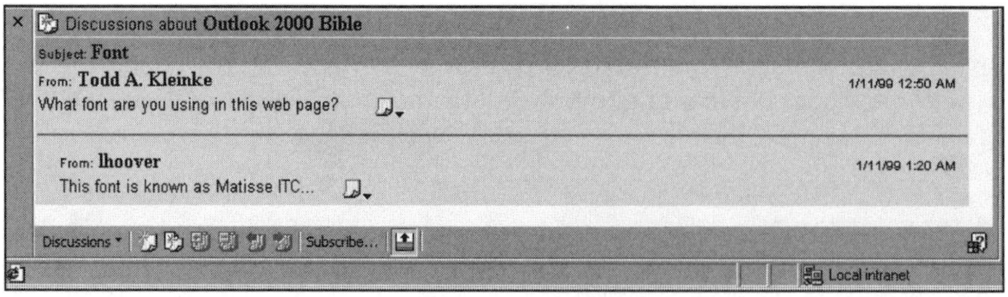

Figure 19-21: A reply has been made to the discussion comment.

The theory behind collaborative discussions is that people can work more efficiently in teams if the following conditions are met:

✦ A simple mechanism is provided for collaboration.

✦ Team members are allowed to collaborate at times that are convenient for each individual person.

Building your own Outlook Today page

In addition to the customization you can implement directly in the Outlook Today interface installed with Outlook 2000, you can build your own Outlook Today page. Because Outlook Today actually utilizes Internet Explorer 5.0, any functionality that can be built into a HTML document, Active Server page, XML page, or Dynamic HTML document can be utilized in your own Outlook Today page.

For example, many people choose to customize their Outlook Today to house information of interest to them. Through the same functionality contained within other Web sites, your Outlook Today page can display current weather forecasts, stock prices, or news headlines.

Other examples include Outlook Today pages designed specifically for a company or department. These pages enable companies to disseminate corporate-specific information in an interesting, nontraditional manner. The example presented in this chapter could be modified to provide such functionality.

On the CD-ROM

The CD distributed with this book contains the sample files used in the demonstration that follows. You may modify these files to customize your Outlook Today page, or you can create your own code. In addition, if you have problems accessing the HTML code using any of the methods described in the following text, you can simply use the OutTBib.htm file provided in the Chapter 19 folder on the CD-ROM. See Appendix A for details.

Begin by creating the following folder to store your custom Outlook Today files:

```
C:\OutlookToday\
```

Next, close Outlook 2000 and open Internet Explorer 5.0. In the address section, enter the following path:

```
res://C:\Program%20Files\Microsoft%20Office\Office\1033\outlwvw.dll/outlook3.htm
```

If you have the Microsoft Script Debugger installed, you may be prompted to debug the file, but select No if prompted. The error is a result of the page not being opened from within Outlook 2000. Depending on how your machine is configured, you may not receive an error message at all.

Note   Although Internet Explorer 5.0 is an integral part of Office 2000, you have the option to not install version 5.0 and use Internet Explorer 4.0 in its place. Although you may lose functionality in other areas within Office 2000, Internet Explorer 4.0 may be used to its fullest capability when building your own Outlook Today page.

Next, you need to right-click in the body of the document and select View Source, as shown in Figure 19-22. Alternatively, you may select View ⇨ Source.

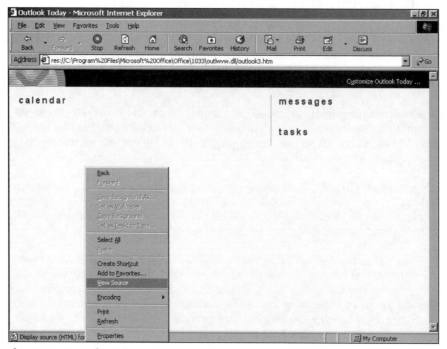

Figure 19-22: Select View ⇨ Source to view the source of the document.

The source code for the document should then be displayed in Notepad. From the Search menu in Notepad, select Find, and click Find Next to search for the following text:

    display:none

Change the text you find to read as follows:

    display:

Click Find Next again and make the same change. You should find three instances of display:none, all of which need to be changed to display:.

Now, save your changes in Notepad as follows:

```
C:\OutlookToday\OutTBib.htm
```

At this point, close Notepad and Internet Explorer 5.0.

Tip

When saving an HTML document in Notepad, make sure you display all file types (*.*) in the common dialog box, rather than the text file type (*.txt). Then, when you type in the filename, type the .htm file extension as well. If you fail to do so, the file will be saved as a text file, and it will not display properly in a Web browser.

Next, you need to edit the Registry in order to instruct Outlook 2000 to display your custom Outlook Today file. To edit the Registry, select Start ⇨ Run, enter **regedit** in the text box, and click OK.

Caution

Because Windows uses the Registry to store specific information regarding the behavior of applications, you should use extreme care when viewing and/or editing this information. The authors of this book assume no responsibility for any problems that may arise on your PC, so edit the Registry at your own risk.

Figure 19-23 shows the HKEY_CURRENT_USER key within the Registry Editor.

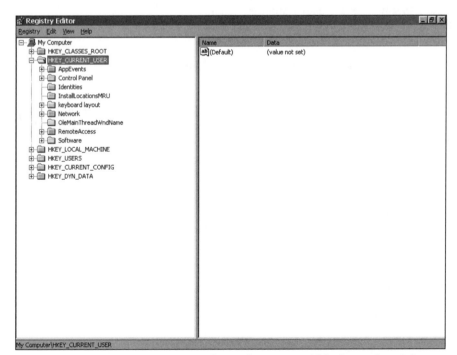

Figure 19-23: HKEY_CURRENT_USER key as it appears within the Registry Editor

Under the HKEY_CURRENT_USER Registry key, go to the following path:

```
HKEY_CURRENT_USER/Software/Microsoft/Office/9.0/Outlook/Today/
```

Right-click the Today folder and select New ⇨ String Value.

Name your new string value as follows (case-specific):

```
Url
```

Once the string value is created, right-click `Url` and select Modify. The Edit String dialog box will open, as shown in Figure 19-24. Enter the following path in the dialog box and click OK: **file://C:\OutlookToday\OutTBib.htm**.

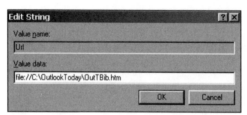

Figure 19-24: Enter the path in the Value data field of the Edit String dialog box.

Once this is complete, you should close the Registry by selecting Registry ⇨ Exit.

In order to verify the changes, open Outlook 2000 and select Outlook Today. If you right-click the Outlook Today icon and select Properties, the configuration for Outlook 2000 should appear. On the Home Page tab, under Address, you should see a path pointing to your custom Outlook Today file, as shown in Figure 19-25.

Click OK or Cancel to close the dialog box.

Now that you've configured Outlook 2000 to display a specified HTML file, you may customize as you wish. The file may be created and edited in Notepad, FrontPage 2000, Visual InterDev, other Office 2000 applications, or whatever other tool you choose.

The sample Outlook Today HTML file included on the CD is displayed in Figure 19-26. This example displays user-specific information, such as the Calendar, Messages, and Tasks, as well as integrates streaming media posted on the corporate intranet to inform employees of corporate news.

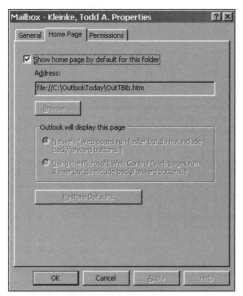

Figure 19-25: This dialog box shows the path to a custom Outlook Today file.

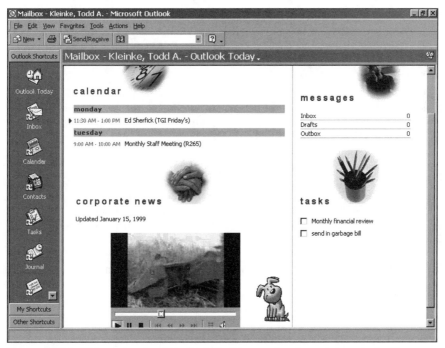

Figure 19-26: This customized Outlook Today page has been integrated with a corporate intranet.

Other examples of information that may work well within a custom Outlook Today interface include the following:

✦ 401(k) stock quotes

✦ Weather forecasts

✦ Scrolling news announcements

✦ Hyperlinks to departmental intranet Web folders

✦ Pictures of new employees

✦ Corporate calendar

✦ Financial forecasts

As you can see, the possibilities are endless.

Integrating Outlook 2000 with your intranet

In addition to incorporating your company's intranet into the Outlook Today page, it may also make sense to devote an entire Outlook bar group to intranet navigation, as demonstrated in Figure 19-27.

 Cross-Reference Chapter 16 provides details on creating custom Outlook bar groups.

Outlook Web access

Companies may wish to implement Outlook Web Access (OWA) if they have employees who do a great deal of traveling, but have Internet access on the road. OWA provides an Outlook 2000 interface embedded within a browser by integrating an Exchange 5.5 Server with a Web server running Internet Information Server 4.0.

If a company standardizes on Internet Explorer as the browser, a wide variety of custom applications may be designed in a secure environment using OWA. In addition, the customization of these forms is simple when compared to other alternatives. The Exchange 5.5 installation CD contains tools, such as the Exchange Forms Wizard, to aid in the creation of custom OWA forms. The Exchange Forms Wizard is shown in Figure 19-28.

If you would like more information on OWA, visit the Microsoft Exchange Web site at www.microsoft.com/exchange.

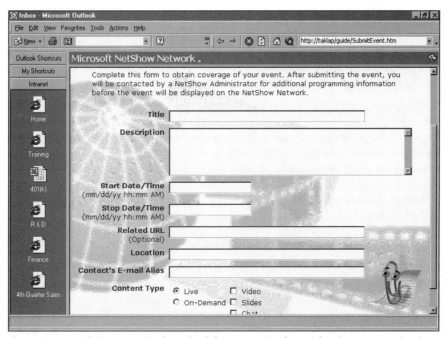

Figure 19-27: This customized Outlook bar group is devoted to intranet navigation.

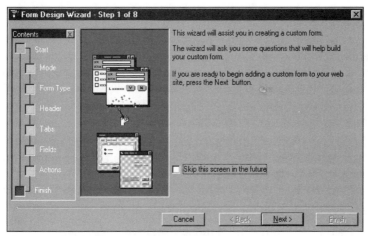

Figure 19-28: Exchange Forms Wizard

LOBjects

The capabilities of Outlook 2000 can be dramatically extended through the use of third-party components. Because these components frequently serve industry-specific functions, they are often referred to as *Line Of Business Objects*, or *LOBjects*.

LOBjects are sets of components designed to work together to accommodate a particular business need. Typically, these sets of components are available as enhancements to Outlook 2000 and are utilized as part of a collaborative solution effort. Therefore, LOBjects go beyond the standard functionality within Outlook 2000, but maintain the same reusability characteristics.

Examples of types of LOBjects could include components specific to the following lines of business:

✦ Sales force automation (SFA)

✦ Supply chain management (SCM)

✦ Industry-specific needs

Currently, there are not a great deal of these types of components available on the market. However, independent software vendors (ISVs) and consulting firms will offer more and more LOBjects as the technologies progress.

Summary

In this chapter, you learned of the various types of applications that can be developed or integrated with Outlook 2000. Because Outlook 2000 offers a great deal of functionality that is common between a wide range of applications, the application is a practical tool to integrate into other applications, especially given the ease of integration. The chapter covered the following points:

✦ Four main groups of applications exist in Outlook 2000: Outlook 2000 client applications, Outlook 2000 Office applications, Outlook 2000 Web applications, and Line Of Business objects (LOBjects).

✦ Three types of forms are available in the Outlook 2000 client application group: message forms, post forms, and built-in forms.

✦ Forms are customized within the Outlook 2000 Forms Designer.

✦ Word 2000, Excel 2000, PowerPoint 2000, and Internet Explorer 5.0 can all host applications within Outlook 2000 forms. These applications are described as Outlook 2000 Office applications.

✦ Outlook 2000 Web applications integrate with the Internet as well as corporate intranets/extranets.

✦ Web folders integrated with SQL Server 7.0, Exchange 5.5, and Internet Explorer 5.0 offer collaboration through Web document discussions.

✦ Outlook Today can be customized to fit a wide range of individual needs by leveraging the Internet and the latest technologies utilized in Internet Explorer 5.0.

✦ LOBjects are sets of components designed to work together to accommodate a particular business need. They integrate and utilize the features of Outlook 2000.

✦   ✦   ✦

Creating a Simple Outlook Form

◆   ◆   ◆   ◆

In This Chapter

Accessing the
Outlook Forms
Designer

Manipulating forms

Adding controls

Using the Property
window

Adding fields
to a form

Using the Script
Editor

Publishing the form

◆   ◆   ◆   ◆

Most Outlook 2000 custom applications utilize custom forms. Perhaps you have a business problem concerning the capture of a very specific and unique set of data. Custom forms enable you to capture only the data you need, and control how the data is presented and where it is transmitted. But that's just the tip of the iceberg. You'll quickly learn that what you can do with Outlook forms is only limited by your imagination.

Accessing the Outlook Forms Designer

As mentioned in the previous chapter, the Outlook Forms Designer (OFD) is the tool used by application developers to create custom Outlook forms. There are three basic types of forms:

+ Message forms

+ Post forms

+ Built-in forms

All custom Outlook forms are variations of these three types of forms. A Message form is suitable for forms that are sent or routed among e-mail recipients. Post forms are used to write information to either a Personal Folder or private folder for the purposes of storing information. Typically, data is posted to a Public Folder, so the information may be shared. Use Outlook's built-in forms when you need the functionality already inherent in them; rather than re-create the wheel, it sometimes makes sense to expand on or add to existing functionality in these forms.

Choosing a form

In order to design a custom form, you need to open one of the three basic types of forms in Design view with the Outlook Forms Designer (OFD). To do so, select Forms ➪ Design a Form from the Tools menu.

Once the command is selected, the Design Form dialog box will open, as shown in Figure 20-1. From here, you can select the form you wish to edit from the Standard Forms Library. In addition, the dialog box enables you to browse through the Personal and Public Folders, Personal Forms Library, user templates in the file system, or any other Outlook module in order to find the form you're looking for.

Note Not all forms displayed in the Design Form dialog box may be edited. Specifically, those forms with the word "<Hidden>" after the title, as shown in Figure 20-1, may not be edited.

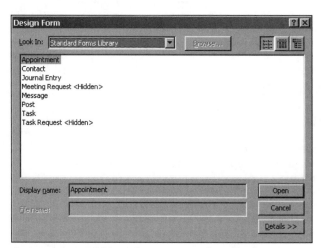

Figure 20-1: <Hidden> forms cannot be edited.

The following sections take you through the various steps of how to modify the Message form. To open the Message form, select Message and click the Open button. The Message form should then be displayed in Design view, as shown in Figure 20-2.

Tip Alternatively, a form can be opened in Design view within the OFD by opening the form you wish to edit, and then selecting Design This Form from the Tools menu. This method is shown in Figure 20-3.

Neither of these methods offers benefits over the other — just two different ways to perform the same task.

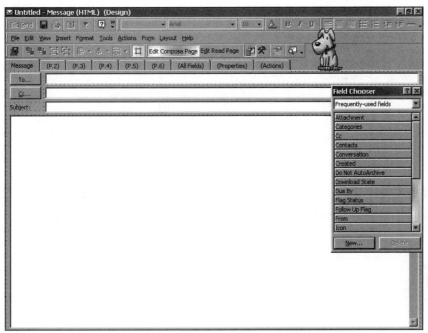

Figure 20-2: The Message form as it appears in Design view

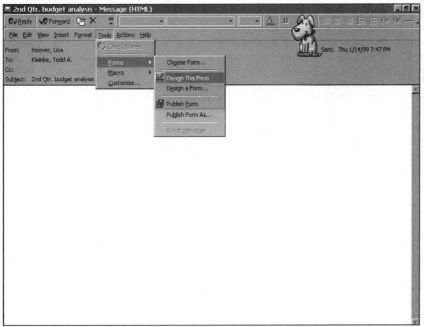

Figure 20-3: Outlook gives users an alternative method of viewing forms in OFD.

Manipulating the Form in the Design Window

Once you have the form opened in the Outlook Forms Designer, you're ready to make changes to it. You may want to acquaint yourself with the OFD by clicking the different objects within the form. When an object is selected, notice that you can move the object to a different location on the form. In addition, you can resize the object to the desired dimension. The objects shown in Figure 20-4, such as the text boxes, tabs, labels, and other objects, may all be manipulated. By manipulated, we are referring to how the size, color, border, and other attributes of the form components can be modified to portray a desired look and feel.

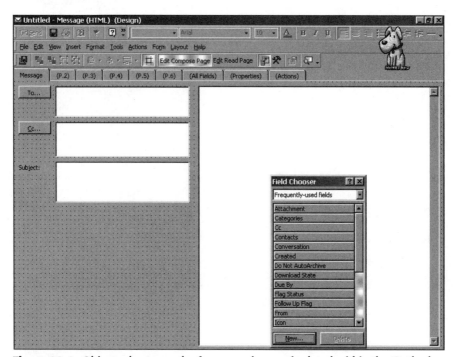

Figure 20-4: Objects shown on the form may be manipulated within the Outlook Forms Designer.

Tip   Because Outlook forms are often used to replace paper processes, it may make sense to format your Outlook form in a layout similar to the old paper form that it replaces. This softens the transition from paper to the electronic version for those users who have become accustomed to the paper form.

When the Message form is in Design view, notice that you have the option of displaying as many as six pages on one form. When replacing paper forms, Outlook form pages can provide substitutes for each page of a multipage paper form. Once again, this softens the transition from the paper process. Before a page will appear as part of the completed form, you must configure the page to be active. To do so, follow these steps:

1. Select the tab you wish to make active.

2. Select Form ➪ Display This Page. Notice that the parentheses are removed from the tab label.

3. Select Form ➪ Rename Page and type in the new label for the tab, as shown in Figure 20-5.

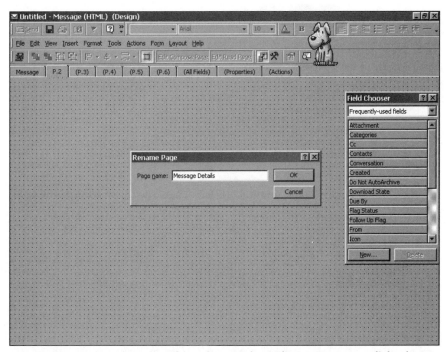

Figure 20-5: Activate a page within a form and use the Rename Page dialog box to rename it.

Once the form is published, the first two pages of this form will appear. (We discuss form publishing later in this chapter.) At this time, notice that the second page of the form (the P.2 tab), renamed Message Details, does not have any content. Why would you want a page with no content? Well, you wouldn't. That's why we're going to add some controls.

Adding Controls with the Toolbox

You add controls to a form within the OFD by using the Toolbox. The Toolbox is one of the most important tools within the OFD, because it is what you use to actually build the user interface. For this reason, it's important to learn each aspect of the Toolbox, which we cover in greater detail in the next chapter. However, for now it is only important to understand the general purpose behind the Toolbox. The Toolbox is shown in Figure 20-6.

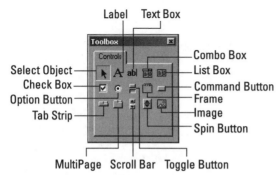

Figure 20-6: The Toolbox is used to build the user interface.

The Toolbox may or may not appear when you open your form in the OFD. If it doesn't, select Form ⇨ Control Toolbox. Alternatively, you may access the Toolbox by clicking the Toolbox menu icon (it's the one with the crossed hammer and wrench).

For the sake of simplicity, we're going to go through the steps for how to add the most basic control to a form — a label. Labels provide descriptions for other controls. Without a label, you would have no idea what the purpose of a control is.

The CD-ROM distributed with this book contains the sample file used in the demonstration discussed in this chapter. If you have problems with any of the steps described in the following text, you can simply use the file provided in the Chapter 20 folder on the CD-ROM. The name of the file is SimpleForm.oft. See Appendix A for details.

To add a label, do the following:

1. Click the label button on the Toolbox. The label button is the button with the letter *A* on it. Your cursor will change to a letter *A* with a cross next to it.

2. Next, click the form in a location you would like to create your label, hold the mouse button down, and draw a rectangle in the desired size.

3. Select the Label 1 text, which automatically appears in the label box, and then type your description, as shown in Figure 20-7.

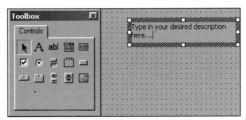

Figure 20-7: Type the desired description.

Using the Properties Window

The Properties window is used to modify how a control appears, define what data fields are accessed with the control, and specify any necessary validation. Using our example form, the following steps demonstrate changing the font of the label through the Properties window.

1. To modify the appearance of your label, right-click the label and select Properties from the menu.

2. Once the Properties dialog box opens, you may choose from the various options on the Display tab to modify the appearance of the label, as shown in Figure 20-8.

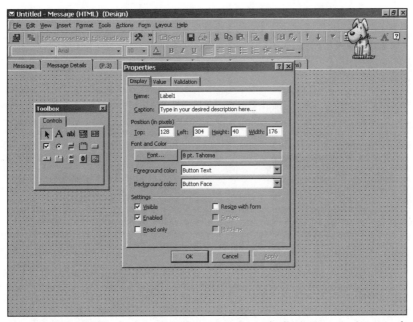

Figure 20-8: Modify the label's appearance through the various options on the Display tab of the Properties dialog box.

3. Change the font by clicking the Font button. The Font dialog box will appear. Make different font selections and click Apply to see changes in the label text. Click OK to return to the Properties dialog box.

Experiment with the other choices on the Display tab to get a feel for what each choice does. The Value and Validation tabs do not apply now, but are covered in Chapter 22.

Adding Fields to the Form

As you probably already know, a field represents a piece of information that is used within Outlook 2000. For example, in a Message form, the message recipient, the subject, and the message body data are all stored in separate fields. In addition to these fields, you also have the option of including additional standard fields or custom fields on your form. Although not the only method of adding a field, the easiest way to add a field to a form is through the Field Chooser window. The Field Chooser window displays a list of available fields to add to the form.

Although the Field Chooser may display by default when you open the Outlook Forms Designer, you can open the Field Chooser window by selecting Field Chooser from the Form menu if the window is not displayed.

To add a field to the form via the Field Chooser window, perform the following steps:

1. Choose a field category from the drop-down menu at the top of the Field Chooser window, as shown in Figure 20-9. Notice how the list of fields in the window changes as the field category changes. For this example, we'll use the All Mail Fields category.

Figure 20-9: The Field category drop-down menu lists fields that correspond to a particular category, such as All Mail Fields.

2. To add a field to the form, simply click the field on the Field Chooser window you wish to add, hold your mouse down, and drag the field onto the form. For this example, the Importance field was chosen, as shown in Figure 20-10. Notice your cursor changes to a letter *A* with a rectangle while you're dragging the field.

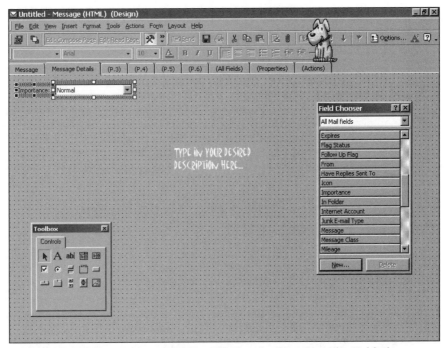

Figure 20-10: The Importance field is added to the form from the Field Chooser window.

3. If you click the drop-down arrow of the ComboBox, you'll notice that the Importance field has three possible choices specified—Low, Normal, and High (see Figure 20-11).

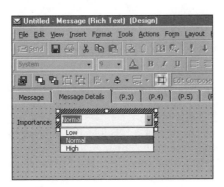

Figure 20-11: Drop-down menu choices are specified in the ComboBox.

Introduction to the Script Editor

The Script Editor is used to add functionality to the form through the use of VBScript. VBScript is a slimmer version of the Visual Basic programming language, hence the *VB* in VBScript. By creating VBScript functions and/or subroutines in the Script Editor, you specify certain pieces of code to execute when certain events occur.

An example of when you may want to use VBScript and the Script Editor is when you have a need to integrate a form with a database. Suppose you're creating a scheduling application that records the hours to be billed to your clients. In order for the billing application to function properly, it needs a client number. However, nobody knows the client numbers that correspond to the client without looking up the number. Through VBScript, you could program a drop-down list box to look up and display client names as they appear in the accounting system database. In addition, you could write code to look up the corresponding client number behind the scenes, and provide the proper client number to the billing application. Any functionality you can provide with VBScript can be implemented in an Outlook form.

Using VBScript with a command button

In order to demonstrate a simple subroutine within the Script Editor, the following steps show how to create a command button that will display a message when clicked:

1. Select Form ➪ View Code to open the Script Editor.

2. Make the Outlook Forms Designer window active, click the CommandButton control within the Toolbox, and create a command button on the form in the same manner the label earlier in the chapter was created.

3. By default, the command button should be named CommandButton1; however, we can confirm this from the Display tab on the Properties window. Therefore, right-click the command button, select Properties from the menu, and verify that the Name text box on the Display tab displays CommandButton1, as shown in Figure 20-12.

4. Now you're ready to enter some code. Make the Script Editor active and type the following code (exactly as shown below):

```
Sub CommandButton1_Click

MsgBox "This is a test."

End Sub
```

Your code will be saved along with the form, even if you close the Script Editor. Therefore, if you wish to save your code, you may do so by saving the form as you normally do. To test the code, run the form. To do so, select Form ➪ Run This Form. The form should open in Normal mode. At this point, select the Message Details tab and click the CommandButton1 command button. The message should appear, as shown in Figure 20-13. Click OK to close the message box and then switch back to the Message form design window.

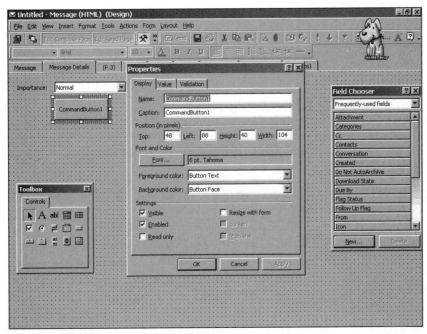

Figure 20-12: Name the Command button CommandButton1.

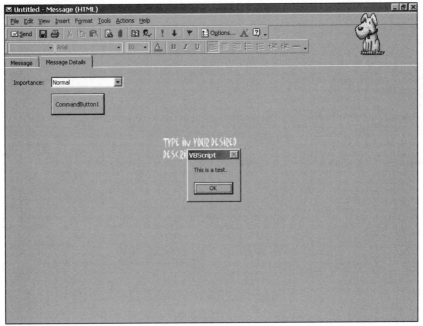

Figure 20-13: Clicking the command button to get the message generated by the code

Publishing the Form

At this point, there's only one more step involved in creating our simple form, and that is to publish it. To publish the form, select Forms ➪ Publish Form from the Tools menu.

As illustrated in Figure 20-14, you have the option of saving your form in your choice of folders. In this example, the form is published to the Personal Forms Library. If you intend to send your form to others, select Yes when a dialog appears that prompts you to determine whether to save the form definition with the item.

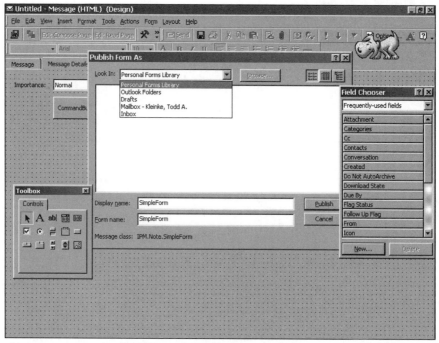

Figure 20-14: Specify publishing options in the Publish Form As dialog box.

This method of publishing a form works fine in a single-user environment. However, when distributing an Outlook 2000 form to multiple users, there are other factors to consider. These details are covered in Chapter 23.

Summary

In this chapter, you learned how to create a simple form in Outlook 2000. The chapter covered the following points:

✦ The Outlook Forms Designer (OFD) is used to design forms in Outlook 2000. You may select a standard form from which to develop a customized version, or choose to manipulate the current form you are viewing.

✦ When a form is in Design view within the Outlook Forms Designer, the form may be manipulated in a number of ways to suit your individual needs.

✦ The Controls Toolbox assists developers in providing additional functionality within a form.

✦ The Properties window is used to further customize and configure the controls on a form.

✦ The Field Chooser window enables developers to easily add fields with standard configurations to a form.

✦ The Script Editor utilizes VBScript to provide additional functionality, which includes, but is not limited to, integration with external databases.

✦ In a single-user environment, forms may be easily published to a number of folders; however, a greater deal of complexity is involved with distributing a form.

✦   ✦   ✦

Controls in Outlook Forms

◆ ◆ ◆ ◆

In This Chapter

Labels

Text boxes,
checkboxes,
combo boxes,
and list boxes

Frames

Option buttons,
spin buttons, and
command buttons

Messages

MultiPage and
TabStrip controls

Image controls

◆ ◆ ◆ ◆

This chapter covers the details behind each of the controls used in Outlook 2000 application development. Although we do not cover every detail for every control, we do highlight the important ones. Because these controls define the look and feel of your user interface, it's important to use the best control for the job. The success of your application is often a result of how easy it is to use. If an application is too difficult to use, the tasks it performs, no matter how sophisticated, are irrelevant. By familiarizing yourself with these controls and understanding when they're appropriate, you'll have the tools and knowledge you need to design a great application.

The CD-ROM distributed with this book contains the sample file used in the demonstration discussed in this chater. If you have problems with any of the steps described in the following text, you can simply use the file provided in the Chapter 21 folder on the CD-ROM. The name of the file is Chapter21Form.oft. See Appendix A for details.

Labels

Although we touched on the Label control in the last chapter, let's quickly review the basics of this control as well as dig a little deeper into its properties. For the examples in this chapter, begin with the Contact form opened in Design view within the Outlook 2000 Forms Designer.

1. First, open the Contact form in Design view. The easiest way to do this is to select Forms ⇨ Design This Form from the Tools menu.

2. If the Toolbox is not already shown, select Control Toolbox from the Form menu. Alternatively, you may click the crossed tools icon on the toolbar to access the Toolbox.

Once you have completed the preceding steps, your screen should appear similar to the one shown in Figure 21-1.

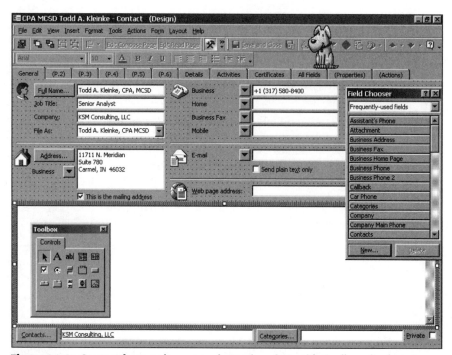

Figure 21-1: Contact form as it appears in Design view with Toolbox displayed

We want our example to expand the basic capabilities of the Contact form, so the controls added to the form will appear on a separate tab.

3. Rename and display the (P.2) page by selecting Rename Page from the Form menu. In the example, we used "1040 Details" for our description.

4. Click the Label button (featuring an icon with the letter *A*) in the Toolbox and draw a label onto the form page.

5. Right-click the label and select Properties from the pop-up menu.

6. In the Caption box, change the description of the label to whatever you like. In the example, we changed the caption to "Taxpayer Information", as shown in Figure 21-2.

7. Select a font and font size with the Font button, select foreground and background colors using the Foreground color and Background list boxes, and click OK. Once complete, your label should look similar to the one in Figure 21-3.

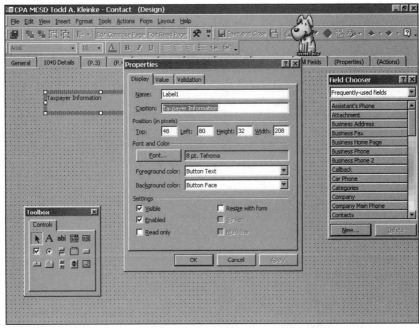

Figure 21-2: Changing the label caption from the Properties window.

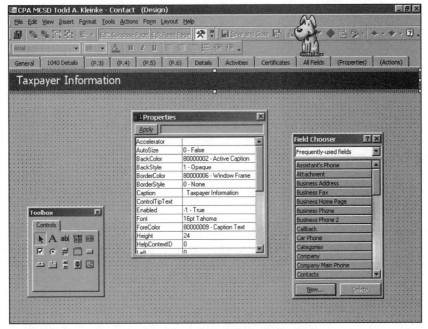

Figure 21-3: Format your label in the Properties dialog box.

8. In addition to the standard properties, you may want to utilize some of the functionality available to you through the Advanced Properties dialog box. To access the Advanced Properties dialog box, right-click the label and select Advanced Properties from the pop-up menu. The Advanced Properties dialog box is also displayed in Figure 21-3.

9. To specify an advanced property, select the property you wish to configure, edit the property in the field to the right of the Apply button, and click Apply. For example, Figure 21-4 shows the ControlTip Text property being modified. This property defines what control tip is displayed when the pointer hovers over the label (that is, the little yellow box that describes the control). Control tips add clarity to each part of the user interface.

Figure 21-4: Configure the ControlTip Text Advanced Property.

The best method of familiarizing yourself with the various options in the Advanced Properties dialog box is to simply play around with them. In other words, just go through each one of the properties therein and see what it does. Note, however, that the majority of the properties of the Label control relate to formatting, so you already know 90 percent of the Label control.

Text Boxes

In simple terms, text boxes are the fields that display the data. In addition to displaying the data, they enable you to input and edit data.

✦ The easiest way to create a text box is to drag and drop from the Field Chooser. If the Field Chooser is not displayed, you can select Field Chooser from the Form menu. Alternatively, you can click the Field Chooser icon on the toolbar. In the example shown later in Figure 21-5, the Job Title field was dragged onto the form from the Field Chooser.

✦ Alternatively, you can click the TextBox button on the Toolbox (the icon with "ab|" on it) and manually draw your field onto the form. If you decide to go this route, you need to specify which field your text box refers to by selecting from the list under the Choose Field button on the Value tab of the Properties dialog box. Keep in mind, if you manually draw a text box, you will need to manually draw its label. If you use the field selector, both are created at the same time.

As with the Label control, there are a number of different advanced properties you can configure to change the look and feel of your text box.

Frames

Frames refer to the etched lines you sometimes see on forms. In addition to enhancing the aesthetics of the form, frames help organize information on the form by grouping fields by category. To create a frame, do the following:

1. Click the Frame button in the Toolbox (the icon depicting a box with *XYZ* at the top) and draw your frame onto the form.

2. Right-click the frame, select Properties from the pop-up menu, and enter your description in the Caption field, as shown in Figure 21-5.

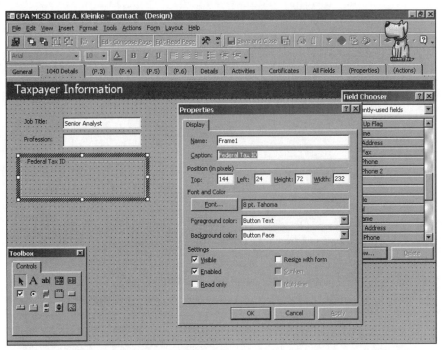

Figure 21-5: Create a frame by using the Frame tool in the Toolbox, and enter a caption for it in the Properties dialog box.

Tip

You may notice that the controls you drag into the frame do not appear if they were created before the frame. To alleviate this problem, select the control, right-click, and select Bring Forward from Order on the pop-up menu. This moves the control "to the top" so that when you drag the control into the frame, it shows up!

Option Buttons

Option buttons enable the user to specify certain information without having to type it in. Option buttons are appropriate when you want to present a limited number of choices to the user. For example, when you want users to specify their 1040 filing status, it makes sense to provide a list of the only four choices available. If users typed the filing status into a text box, variation in the data entered is inevitable. For instance, a user with married filing jointly status could type in "Married filing jointly", "married – jointly", "JOINTLY", or any other variation of the same. Running a query against data like this would be a nightmare!

1. To add an option button to your form, simply click the OptionButton button in the Toolbox and draw your radio button. The OptionButton button sports an icon of a circle with a black dot in the middle.

2. As with the other controls, the option button can be configured by right-clicking the drawn button and selecting Properties (or Advanced Properties) from the pop-up menu. This is demonstrated in Figure 21-6.

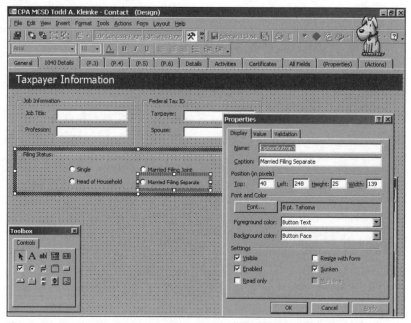

Figure 21-6: Use the OptionButton tool to create and configure option buttons.

Checkboxes

As you can imagine, checkboxes are pretty much the same thing as option buttons, except they're square. The only difference relates to the types of data that each displays. Option buttons are often part of option groups, which means that more than one option button can be tied to one field, but only one option button may be selected at any time. Checkboxes are typically one box per field, so the data stored in the field is typically of a yes/no nature.

1. To add a checkbox to your form, simply click the CheckBox button in the Toolbox and draw your checkbox. The CheckBox icon is a small box with a check in the middle.

2. As with objects created by the other controls, the checkbox can be configured by right-clicking the drawn checkbox and selecting Properties (or Advanced Properties) from the pop-up menu. This is demonstrated in Figure 21-7.

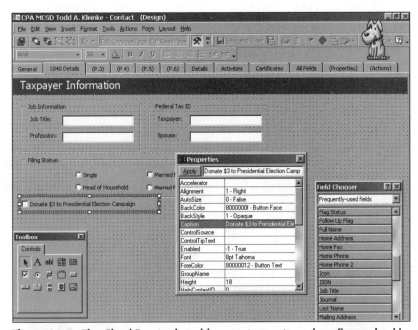

Figure 21-7: The CheckBox tool enables you to create and configure checkboxes.

Combo Boxes

Combo boxes look similar to text boxes, but have an arrow on the far right that drops down a list of choices from which the user may select. As with the option buttons, combo boxes are appropriate when you want to provide the user with a list of choices. The advantage a combo box has over option buttons is that you can specify far more choices in a small area. The disadvantage is that the choices are not displayed, except when the user makes a selection.

1. To create a combo box, select the ComboBox button from the Toolbox and draw the control onto the form. The ComboBox icon, located to the right of the TextBox icon, shows a miniature version of a combo box and its drop-down menu.

2. As with the other controls, the combo box is configured through either the Properties or Advanced Properties dialog box.

To demonstrate how to fill the combo box with possible values, let's look at how to create a custom field called Residency:

3. Select the combo box drawn on the form, right-click, and select Properties from the pop-up menu.

4. On the Value tab, click the New button to the right of the Choose Field button.

5. Type **Residency** in the Name field of the New Field dialog box and click OK.

6. In the Possible values field on the Value tab, enter **Alabama; Alaska; Arizona**, as shown in Figure 21-8, and click OK.

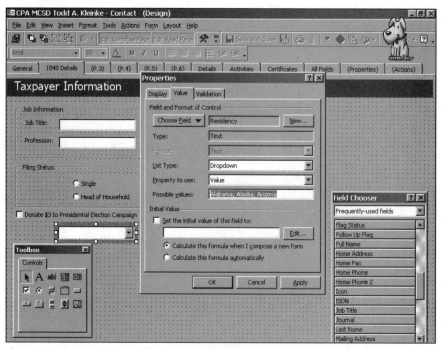

Figure 21-8: Specify possible values for a custom field combo box in the Properties dialog box.

List Boxes

List boxes are similar to combo boxes in that you specify the choices from which the user can choose. One difference is that a list box is larger. In addition, the user scrolls through the choices and selects the one he or she wants, rather than selecting from a drop-down list. The advantage over a combo box is that the choices are displayed, even after selection. However, the size could be a disadvantage.

1. To create a list box, select the ListBox button from the Toolbox and draw the control on the form. The ListBox icon looks similar to the ComboBox icon, but only shows two "items" for selection.

2. You define the selection choices in the same manner as for the combo box, as shown in Figure 21-9. See the section "Combo Boxes" for assistance.

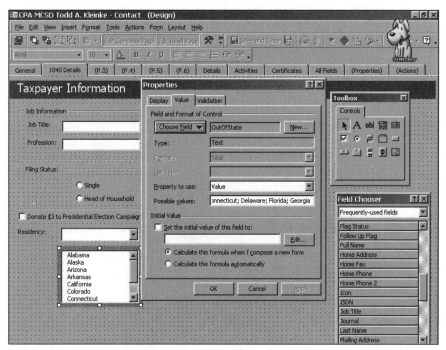

Figure 21-9: Specify possible values for a custom field list box in the Properties dialog box.

Multiple Pages

Multiple pages are good to use when you need to squeeze a lot of information into a small area. In fact, you've already been exposed to multiple pages earlier in this chapter. The example form has multiple pages — General, 1040 Details, Details, and so on. However, when we speak of the MultiPage control, we are referring to smaller pages being displayed on top of a larger one.

1. To create multiple pages on your form, click the MultiPage button in the Toolbox and draw the control on the form as you normally would. The MultiPage icon is the larger of the two icons that resemble a form with two tabs. (The smaller icon is for the TabStrip tool, discussed later.)

2. Once the pages are created, you may rename the page description by right-clicking the page tab and selecting Rename from the pop-up menu, as shown in Figure 21-10.

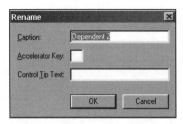

Figure 21-10: Rename a page on a MultiPage control by bringing up the Rename dialog box.

3. To add or delete a page from the MultiPage control, you need to right-click the page tabs and select Insert or Delete, respectively.

4. In addition, you can rearrange the order of your pages by right-clicking the tab page and selecting Move from the resulting pop-up menu. Then, choose a page from the Page Order dialog box and choose Move Up or Move Down to change the order (see Figure 21-11).

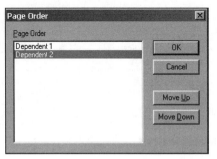

Figure 21-11: You can adjust the page order on a MultiPage control.

5. Once you have your new pages configured, you can add controls on top of the MultiPage control, just as you would on any other area of the form. For example, Figure 21-12 shows a text box added to the first page.

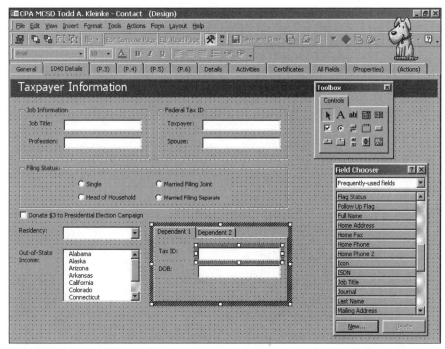

Figure 21-12: Specific controls can appear on each page of a MultiPage control.

Tab Strips

The TabStrip control is pretty much the same as the MultiPage control. However, there is one slight difference — the TabStrip control is designed to display the same controls on each tab, whereas the MultiPage control is designed to display different controls on each page. Although you may gain a small degree of performance by using the TabStrip control, the MultiPage control seems easier to use.

To use the TabStrip control, follow the same steps as described in the previous section for the MultiPage control. The TabStrip icon looks like the MultiPage icon, except that it is smaller. Note that you will need to add a VBScript subroutine or function if you want the control source of your controls to change when the tabs do. VBScript is covered in a bit more detail later in Chapter 26.

Image Controls

Image controls do exactly what their name implies — they display images. As you would expect, the control supports all popular image formats.

Caution   Although images can often bring excitement to an otherwise dull form, they also tax computer performance. The number and/or size of the images you include can drastically affect how quickly your form responds to user interaction.

1. To add an image to your form, click the Image button and draw a box where you would like your image to be displayed.

2. Right-click the box you've just drawn and select Advanced Properties from the pop-up menu.

3. Select the Picture property on the Advanced Properties dialog box and click the ". . ." button in the top-right corner of the form. Point to the image file you would like displayed in your form and click OK. An example is shown in Figure 21-13.

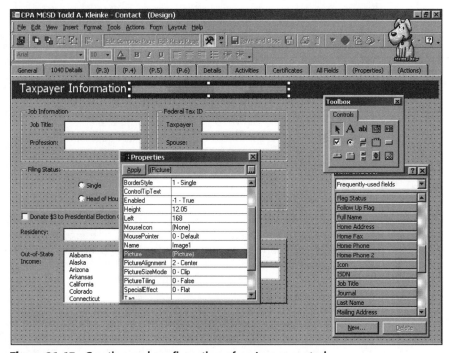

Figure 21-13: Creation and configuration of an Image control

Spin Buttons

Spin buttons usually work in conjunction with a text box. In such a case, the text box typically stores a numeric value, and the spin buttons are used to scroll through a set of numbers. Spin buttons are meant to be a convenience for the user, because it enables the user to manipulate the data by a click of the mouse. However, some users still prefer to have the option of typing a number into the text box.

1. Before you actually create the SpinButton control, you should create the text box that will store your values. You will be attaching a custom field to the text box, so create the field by using the TextBox tool in the Toolbox, rather than dragging and dropping a field from the Field Chooser. See the section "Text Boxes," earlier in this chapter, for details on creating a text box.

2. After your text box has been created, select it, right-click, and select Properties from the pop-up menu. Using the New button on the Value tab, create a new field called Exemptions, with Number as the field type (see Figure 21-14), and click OK to return to the Value dialog box.

3. Select the option button that says *Calculate this formula automatically*. When finished, click OK.

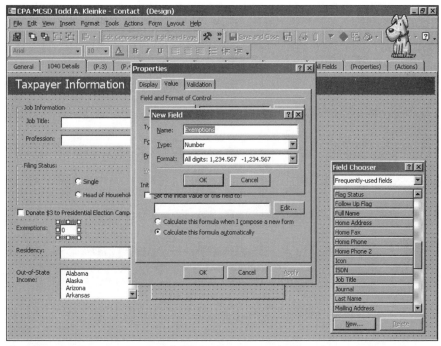

Figure 21-14: Create a custom field text box to attach the SpinButton control to.

4. Click the SpinButton button in the Toolbox menu and draw the control onto the form. Right-click the control you've just drawn and select Properties from the pop-up menu.

5. Click the Choose Field button on the Value tab, select Exemptions from the menu under the option *User-defined fields in folder,* and click OK.

Tip

You can verify that your form is functioning properly by selecting Run This Form from the Form menu.

Command Buttons

Command buttons are controls that require underlying VBScript to function. You could think of the command button as being similar to a key that starts a car engine, with the engine being, of course, the underlying VBScript function or subroutine. Although here we briefly touch on VBScript to demonstrate the command button, VBScript is not the focus of this chapter. We do, however, dig deeper into VBScript later in the book.

The first step is to actually create the command button:

1. Click the CommandButton button in the Toolbox and draw a button on the form. Right-click the drawn button and select Properties from the pop-up menu. On the Display tab, verify that the name of the control is CommandButton1, change the caption to read Test, and click OK.

2. You must access the Script Editor in order to write your VBScript, so select View Code from the Form menu.

3. In the Script Editor, type the following lines of code, as shown in Figure 21-15:

```
Sub CommandButton1_Click

    Dim varDate

    varDate = Date()

    MsgBox "The current date is " & varDate & "."

End Sub
```

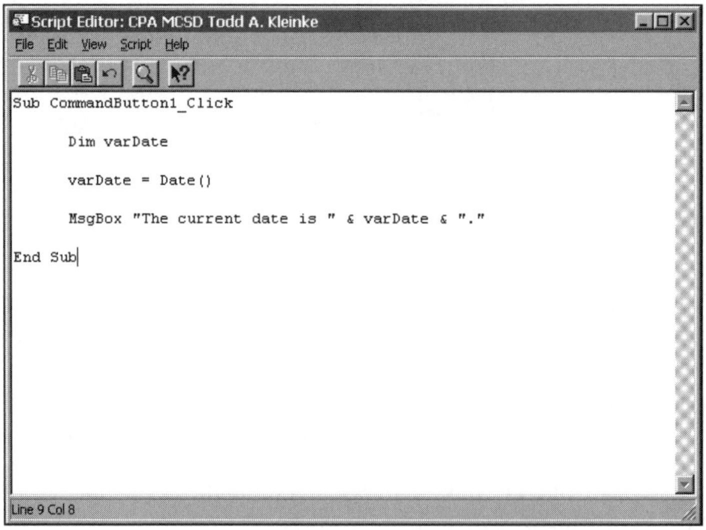

Figure 21-15: Enter your VBScript into the Script Editor.

4. Close the Script Editor window and select Run This Form from the Form menu. When you click the Test button, you should get a VBScript message informing you of the current date, as shown in Figure 21-16.

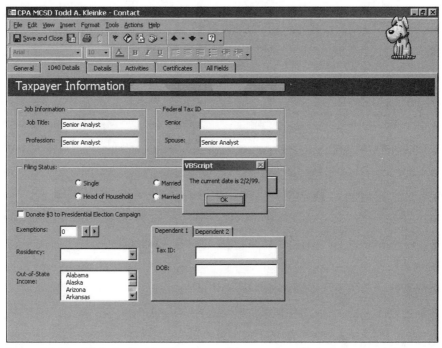

Figure 21-16: Click the Test button to see this message displaying current date.

Toggle Buttons

Toggle buttons are similar to command buttons, but can be less complex. Although you may define VBScript functions and subroutines behind toggle buttons, you may also treat toggle buttons as yes/no responses. Yes/no responses are feasible, because a toggle button has two states — pushed in or not pushed in. Therefore, a toggle button could be described as a command button that does pop back when clicked. Oftentimes, toggle buttons appear in pairs, so when one toggle button is pressed, the other is not, as in Figure 21-17.

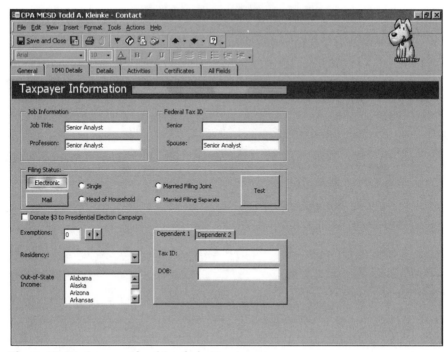

Figure 21-17: An example of toggle buttons

Summary

In this chapter, you learned the following details regarding the various controls used within the Outlook 2000 Forms Designer:

✦ Labels are used to describe the data employed by other controls. In other words, labels give meaning to the information stored within other controls. For example, "Price: $1.50" has much more meaning than just "$1.50". (In this case, "Price:" is the label.)

✦ Text boxes are probably the most commonly used control. In addition to displaying data, text boxes enable the user to enter new data, edit existing data, and delete unwanted data.

✦ Frames are the etched boxes you often see around groups of similar data. In addition to enhancing the appearance of the form, frames also aid in the organization of similar data controls.

✦ Option buttons are the radio-style buttons used to limit the number of choices to the user. Typically, multiple option buttons will be attached to a single field in what's called an option group.

✦ Checkboxes are similar to option buttons, but are square and usually apply to yes/no type replies.

✦ Combo boxes contain a list of values from which the user can choose. This offers an advantage over option buttons in that more options can be made available while taking up less space.

✦ List boxes also contain a list of values from which the user can choose. List boxes require a bit more space on the form, but can display optional values even after the user has made a selection.

✦ Multiple pages offer the flexibility of overlapping space; pages are accessed by their tabs and can contain different controls.

✦ Tab strips are similar to pages, but utilize the same set of controls on all tabs.

✦ Image controls display images and can require significant resources. This control should be used sparingly.

✦ Spin buttons provide an interface for scrolling through values in a text box.

✦ Command buttons launch VBScript functions or subroutines. The code behind command buttons is created in the Script Editor.

✦ Toggle buttons are similar to command buttons, but may interface with yes/no type data as well as VBScript code.

✦　　✦　　✦

Utilizing Custom Fields

Although a wide variety of fields already exist in Outlook 2000, chances are you may still need to add a few fields to your form to suit your individual needs. Adding custom fields to your form accommodates the processes and information unique to your organization. After all, isn't that what custom applications are all about?

Custom Form Fields

Before you jump right in and start adding a bunch of new fields to your form, it's a good idea to spend some time planning just what fields to add. You'll be glad you did.

Planning your custom fields

To get an idea of how you should plan for your application, you need to do some analysis. Here are some good questions to ask yourself before creating a form with multiple custom fields:

- ◆ What are the data elements that need to be captured in my form?
- ◆ Which of these fields already exist?
- ◆ How will my form interact with other Outlook 2000 folders, such as the Contacts folder?
- ◆ Can any of my custom data be grouped together?
- ◆ Will the custom data fields continue to accommodate business needs as the organization grows?

The time you spend planning up front will save you time down the road. Applications designed without a great deal of planning often need to be completely rewritten later, because the application no longer fulfills the business need. Although you cannot predict the future, you can design your application with the flexibility to grow with the organization.

For example, say you're developing a T-shirt order form that, among other attributes, enables a customer to specify a color. Because Outlook 2000 does not inherently contain fields for color attributes, you need to create custom fields. One approach would be to create three custom fields — a red field, a blue field, and a yellow field. However, this approach would make it difficult to expand the options in the future. These fields could be created as part of an option group, as shown in Figure 22-1.

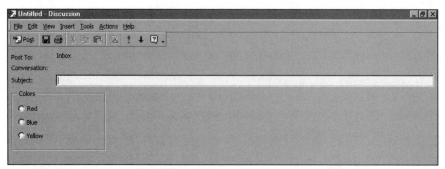

Figure 22-1: These custom fields are designed in a fashion that limits future growth.

Suppose you designed your form as shown in Figure 22-1. Now suppose that your company decides to offer 20 different colors, and your form needs to accommodate the change. Does it make sense to add 17 more custom fields to your application? Nope.

If the application were designed with one field, *color*, the application could easily accommodate a change in colors offered. Figure 22-2 demonstrates this method of accomplishing the same task.

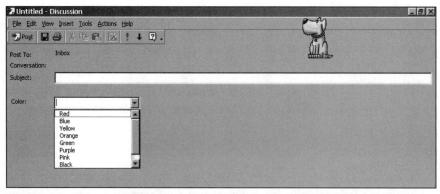

Figure 22-2: This custom field is designed with the flexibility to accommodate future needs.

By spending the time to plan our custom fields, we considered the possibility of more colors being added in the future. Therefore, rather than add 17 additional fields to this form, as well as 17 additional radio buttons and labels, we only needed to add the new choices to our combo box.

The CD-ROM distributed with this book contains the sample file used in the demonstration discussed in this chapter. If you have problems with any of the steps described in the following text, you can simply use the file provided in the Chapter 22 folder on the CD-ROM. The name of the file is Ch22.oft. See Appendix A for details.

Creating custom fields

Custom fields can be tied to any control that interacts with data. In addition, custom fields are typically created while you are configuring your control.

For information on creating and configuring controls, see Chapter 21.

To create a custom field, complete the following steps:

1. Make sure your form is in design mode within the Outlook 2000 Forms Designer.

2. Create a new control from your Toolbox menu, but make sure it is a control that enables you to interact with data. For this example, use a ComboBox.

3. Right-click the control and select Properties from the pop-up menu.

4. Select the Value tab.

5. Rather than choosing from the Choose Field drop-down menu to assign a field, click the New button in the upper-right corner of the Properties window.

6. Enter the name of your new custom field, as shown in Figure 22-3.

At this point, you should choose the appropriate type and format for your custom field. The Type menu specifies the type of data to be stored within the field. Because the field in this example will be storing words, the Text data type is appropriate. However, if you wanted to store a dollar amount, the Currency data type would be appropriate; if you wanted to store a date, the Date/Time data type would be appropriate, and so on.

For this example, select Text as the type and Text as the format, and then click OK to close the New Field dialog box.

The Format menu specifies how the data is presented within the field. When using the Text data type, you only have the option of using the Text format. However, certain data types, such as the Date/Time data type, enable you to choose from a number of formatting options. One value, stored as a Date/Time data type, could be displayed in a number of ways. Figure 22-4 gives you an idea of the numerous choices available in the format field.

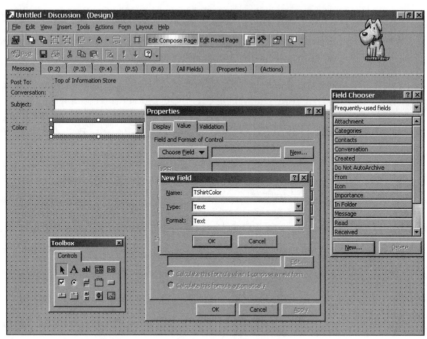

Figure 22-3: Enter the name of your new custom field.

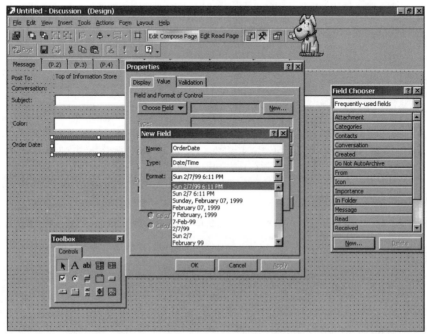

Figure 22-4: The Date/Time data type allows for numerous formatting choices.

Tip

Be sure to match the appropriate data type to the type of data you will be storing in your field. If you fail to do so, you may run into problems when calculating formulas or coding against the data. For example, currency formatted using the Text option will not function within a formula to calculate sales tax.

Experiment with the data types and the formats that each supports. You'll find there's a great deal of flexibility in regard to how your data is displayed.

Working with Fields

Now that you are familiar with how to create a custom field, you're ready to learn how to effectively develop fields. This section will not only deal with custom fields, but also relate to the fields already existing in Outlook 2000.

Working with shared fields

Shared fields are fields that are utilized on both the Compose page and the Read page of a form. The Compose page of a form is used when creating a message, as shown in Figure 22-5.

The Read page of a form is used when reading a message, as shown in Figure 22-6. In order to avoid confusion, we'll use the terms *compose page* and *read page* when the form is in Design mode (since it's the same form). However, when not in Design mode, it seems as though two different forms are being used instead of one, so we'll use the terms *compose form* and *read form* when referring to a form outside Design mode.

Notice the difference between the two forms. Although both forms have the To:, Cc:, and Subject: fields, these fields are enabled only in the Compose form. These are shared fields, because they are linked to the same data on both forms.

In order to create shared fields, you first need to know how to move between the Compose and Read views of a form. To do so, toggle between the Edit Compose Page and Edit Read Page buttons on the toolbar at the top of the page. Follow these steps to create a shared field:

1. Create the control and link it to a field in the Compose view.

Cross-
Reference

Chapter 21 details the steps involved in creating controls.

2. Switch to the Read view, add the control, and link it to the same field you linked to in the Compose view, as shown in Figure 22-7.

Note

If your form includes a reply form, your shared field will not automatically appear on the reply form. You must manually add the control and link it to the shared field in the same manner as explained in the preceding steps.

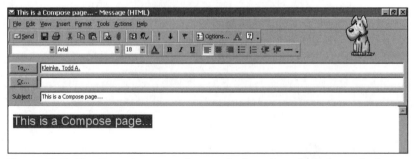

Figure 22-5: The Compose page of a standard message form is used when creating a message.

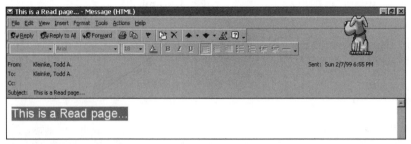

Figure 22-6: The Read page of a standard message form is used when reading a message.

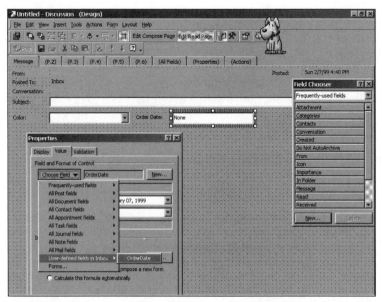

Figure 22-7: In the Read view, link the control to the same field you linked to in the Compose view.

Using combination fields

A *combination field* is a type of custom field used to combine two or more fields into one. For example, you may want to display a contact's name in the format *Last name, First name*. The following example will walk you through creating a combination field.

1. While in Design view in the Outlook 2000 Forms Designer, create a new label from the Toolbox menu on your sample form.

2. Right-click the label and select Properties from the pop-up menu.

3. On the Value tab of the Properties window, click New to create a new custom field.

4. Give the custom field a name and select Combination under the Type menu.

5. Now to define the contents of the field: Click the Edit button to the right of the Formula field to bring up the Combination Formula Field.

6. Once the Combination Formula Field window opens, click the Field button in the bottom-right corner to begin the process of choosing the fields you wish to display.

7. Select Last Name and First Name from the Name Fields menu, accessible from the Field button menu, and type in a comma and a space to the right of "[Last Name]", as shown in Figure 22-8.

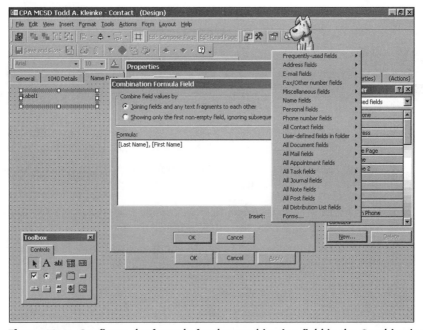

Figure 22-8: Configure the formula for the combination field in the Combination Formula Field window.

8. Click OK to close the Combination Formula Field window, click OK to create the field, and click OK again to close the Properties window.

The end result will be a field with the combined information of two fields, as shown in Figure 22-9.

Figure 22-9: The resulting combination field displays the information of two fields.

Using formula fields

Formula fields are similar to combination fields, but rather than fuse fields together, formula fields perform calculations. An example of why you may want to utilize a formula field may be to calculate income tax. The following describes this process:

1. While in design view in the Outlook 2000 Forms Designer, create a new label from the Toolbox menu.

2. Right-click the label and select Properties from the pop-up menu.

3. On the Value tab of the Properties window, click New to create a new custom field.

4. Give the custom field a name and select Formula under the Type menu.

5. Next, you need to define the contents of the field. Start by clicking the Edit button to the right of the Formula field.

6. Once the Formula Field window opens, click the Field button in the bottom-right corner to choose the fields you want to display.

7. Select TaxableIncome and TaxRate from the Field button menu and type a * to the right of "[TaxableIncome]", as shown in Figure 22-10.

8. In addition, you can select a function to use from the menu accessible through the Function button in the bottom-right corner.

9. Click OK to close the Formula Field window, click OK to create the field, and click OK again to close to the Properties window.

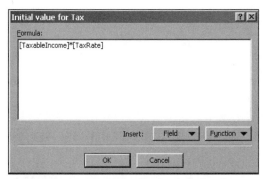

Figure 22-10: Configure the formula for the formula field in the Formula Field window.

The end result will be a field with the calculated information, as shown in Figure 22-11.

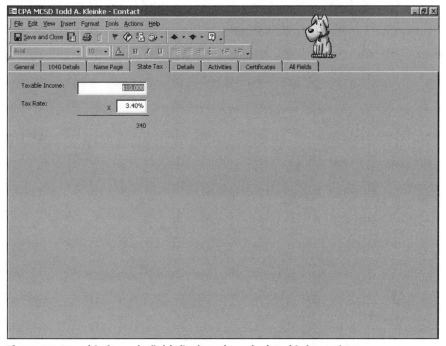

Figure 22-11: This formula field displays the calculated information.

Validating user input

To maintain the integrity of your data, you may need to validate the information the user enters. In order to accomplish this task, you can configure the Validation tab of the Properties window. For example, the following steps demonstrate how to verify that taxable income is not entered as a negative number.

1. Select the Taxable Income text box, right-click the control, and select Properties from the pop-up menu.

2. Select the Validation tab, and click the Edit button to the right of the Validation Formula field.

3. Enter **>=0** in the Validation Formula window, as shown in Figure 22-12. (Note that you can also select fields and functions in this window by accessing the Field and Function button menus in the lower-right corner.)

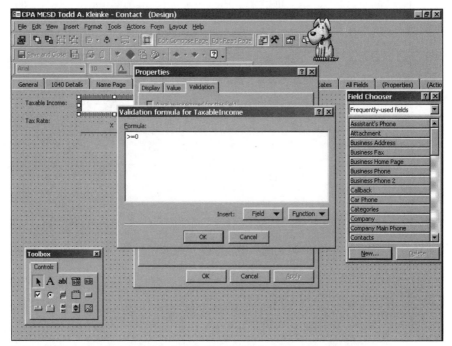

Figure 22-12: Configure validation in the Validation Formula window.

4. Click OK, and then select the Edit button to the right of the validation message field (that is, the *Display this message if the validation fails* field).

5. As you can see, the Validation text window has the same field and formula selection options. Enter your validation message, as shown in Figure 22-13, and click OK. Click OK again to close the Properties window.

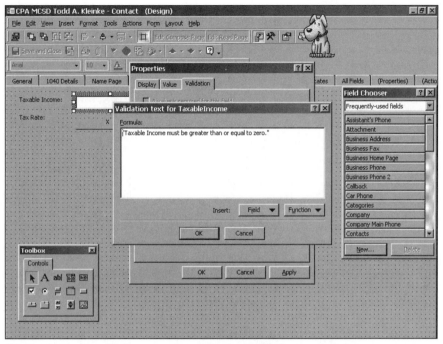

Figure 22-13: Specify the message text in the Validation text window.

Because you may select multiple fields from the Field menu, you can also compare the values of fields against others. For example, if your form has a due date field, you could verify that the due date is greater than the date created. With the extensive list functions, the possibilities are endless.

Specifying default values for fields

The Value tab of the Properties window allows you to specify default values for your controls. Therefore, the value that you specify will automatically be in place when the user opens the form. However, the user may still have the ability to change the value. Default values are appropriate in fields that frequently hold a particular value. For example, in the United States, a country field may typically store the value "USA". To specify a default value, do the following:

1. Select the control, right-click the control, and select Properties from the pop-up menu.

2. Select the Value tab and type a default value in the Initial Value section of the tab. In addition, select the *Set the initial value of this field to* and *Calculate this formula automatically* checkboxes. The example shown in Figure 22-14 uses the current date as the default value, as indicated by "Date()".

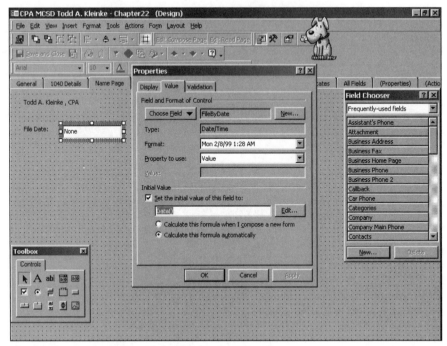

Figure 22-14: Specifying a default value for a text box

Alternatively, you may use the Edit button to specify a default value. As you might guess, this window is similar to the other formula configuration windows.

Summary

In this chapter, you learned how to work with custom fields within Outlook 2000. Here we covered the following points:

✦ The time you spend planning for your custom fields in the initial stages of development will save you time later.

✦ When planning your custom fields, consider how your business needs may change in the future. Try to develop your application in a manner that will easily accommodate such changes.

✦ Custom fields are created on the Value tab of the Properties window. A custom field may be created from any control that interfaces with data.

✦ Shared fields are the fields used on both the Compose and Read pages of a form. To share a field, configure one control on the Compose page and one control on the Read page to point to the same field.

✦ Combination fields fuse the data from two different fields into one. For example, a First Name field and a Last Name field may be fused together into a

LastFirst combination field, which would display the last name followed by the first name.

✦ Formula fields are used to perform calculations. In addition to standard mathematical operations, an extensive list of functions is built into the formula edit tool.

✦ User input may be validated in order to protect data integrity. The capability of including more than one field in the validation enables you to compare fields against one another.

✦ Default values may be specified for a field on the Value tab of the Properties window. Default values are appropriate when the same information is frequently entered into a field.

✦　　✦　　✦

Adding Functionality to Outlook Forms

So far, we've covered everything you need to know about creating a basic application in Outlook 2000. This chapter gets a bit more specific and covers some of the elements of more complex applications.

Compose Versus Read: Changing Form Appearance

As mentioned previously in this book, the interface to provide users with messaging information within a Windows environment is typically known as a form. In terms of Outlook 2000, users typically design forms within the Outlook 2000 Forms Designer (OFD). From your experience in sending e-mail to your friends, family, and coworkers, you probably understand the basic elements of an e-mail message. Typically, an e-mail message consists of a recipient, a sender, a subject, and a body. However, the manner in which a user interfaces with these elements is dependent on whether the user is a sender or a recipient. What we're getting at is this: The user interface seen by the composer of the e-mail message is different from the interface seen by the recipient of the e-mail message. Does this mean you need two forms for one e-mail message? Yes, to a certain extent, but not really. A standard e-mail message actually uses the same form for both the composer and recipient. However, there are two modes to a standard e-mail message—a Compose mode and a Read mode.

The Compose mode in a standard message form is exactly what it sounds like—it's the mode used for composing an e-mail message. In a standard message, notice how all text boxes in the form are enabled.

In contrast, the Read page does not enable all text boxes. In addition, text boxes displaying who the message is from and when the message was received are characteristics of a standard message form in Read mode.

Switching between Compose and Read Mode

So how do you customize your form's appearance in Compose and Read mode? You do so from within the Outlook 2000 Forms Designer (OFD), of course. When you view the standard message form in Design view, notice the two toggle buttons on the design menu, as shown in Figure 23-1. Because the Edit Compose Page toggle button is selected, the form is displayed in the Compose mode.

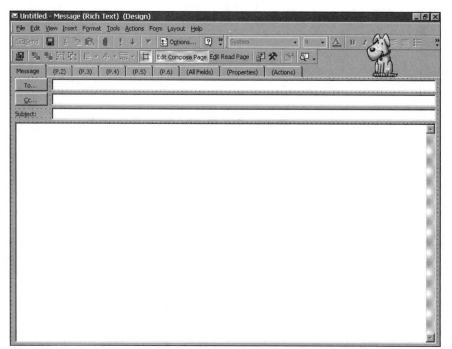

Figure 23-1: The standard message form as it appears in Compose mode in the Outlook Form Designer

Once the Edit Read Page toggle button is selected, the form is shifted to Read mode, as shown in Figure 23-2.

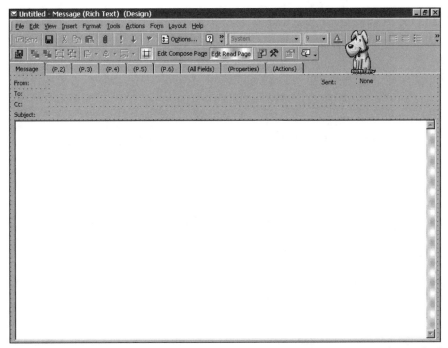

Figure 23-2: The standard message form as it appears in Read mode in the Outlook Form Designer

Although the Compose and Read modes of a form can be handy when differentiating between how the author and viewer interact with information, these modes can also be a curse. When developing a form of this nature, it's a good idea to double-check that the appropriate fields are present in both Compose and Read modes.

Tip   Although the Compose/Read mode forms are appropriate when the viewer needs to interact differently with data than the author, Compose/Read mode forms are not appropriate when the viewer and author interact with the data in the same manner. In fact, if you designed a Compose/Read mode form that displayed information in the same manner for both the author and viewer, you would basically have to do the same work twice. For this reason, the Compose/Read modes may be disabled by deselecting the Separate Read Layout option from the Form menu.

Caution   Once again, be careful. If you disable the Compose/Read mode on a form, any changes you've made to the Read mode portion of the form will be lost.

Adding Form Pages

Form pages are the tabs seen on multiple tab forms, such as the Contacts form. Often in the context of software applications, *tab* commonly refers to the tab on the top of a form, as well as the page associated with it. Note, however, that in Outlook the tab-and-page combo are commonly referred to as a *page*. Forms without multiple tabs simply have one page.

Pages are most appropriate when a form utilizes a large number fields or controls that require a large amount of space. Pages enable fields and controls to be categorized and/or temporarily kept behind the scenes, thereby allowing the user interface to accommodate a wide range of information without overcrowding the form.

For example, one page may contain all information relating to the shipping address. Another page may relate to specific billing information. The multiple pages allow for both shipping and billing information to be incorporated into a single form in an organized and noncrowded manner.

Adding a page is simple. While your form is in Design view within the Outlook 2000 Forms Designer (OFD), select the page you wish to display and simply choose Display This Page from the Form menu.

Note   Once the page has been displayed, the parentheses surrounding the title disappear.

To change the title of the page, you must select Rename Page, enter the new title, and click OK, as shown in Figure 23-3.

Figure 23-3: Use the Rename Page dialog box to rename the newly created page.

Using Form Properties

The form's Properties page is the second-to-last page displayed on a form in Design view within the OFD. The Properties page is used to configure certain characteristics (or properties) of the form as a whole. The Properties page can be thought of as a catchall for form properties that are not specified in any other location. In addtion, the Properties page may store information to assist the developer in the management of Outlook forms, such as a description of the form, version control, and so on. An example of a Properties page is shown in Figure 23-4.

Assign a MS Word template to message text   Change application icon

Categorize your forms here   Assign version, in order to track changes

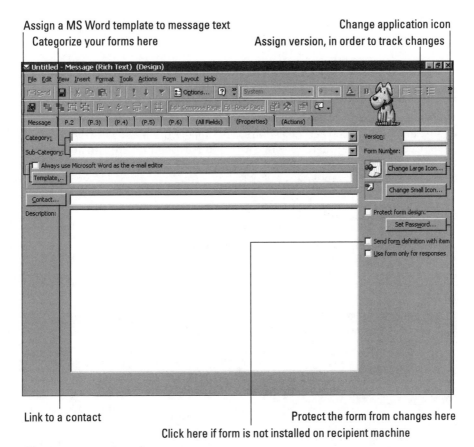

Link to a contact   Protect the form from changes here

Click here if form is not installed on recipient machine

Figure 23-4: A Properties page

Certain elements of the Properties page are self-explanatory. The Category and Sub-Category fields simply assign category classifications. An example of a category could be Sales, and one subcategory could be Midwest. The Description text box provides a free-form area for adding any necessary comments and/or documentation for the form.

Version control

The Version and Form Number fields assist the developer in tracking what changes, fixes, or enhancements have been made to the form. An example of when a version number comes in handy is when a user comments that she does not have a new feature in her form. The developer can investigate the form the user is currently using and determine whether or not it is the most current by checking the version number.

Tip   Because the difference in forms may be buried in a bunch of VBScript code, utilizing version numbers can save the developer time and energy.

Icons and Word templates

The Change Large Icon and Change Small Icon buttons specify which icons are displayed in Outlook 2000 and elsewhere. The *Always use Microsoft Word as the e-mail editor* checkbox integrates MS Word with the composition area. In addition, if the checkbox is selected, the Template button enables you to associate a MS Word template with the composition area of your form.

Linking a form to a contact

The Contact button enables the developer to associate the Outlook form with a Contact record within Outlook. Click the Contact button to open the Address Book and select the Contact record you wish to link to, as shown in Figure 23-5.

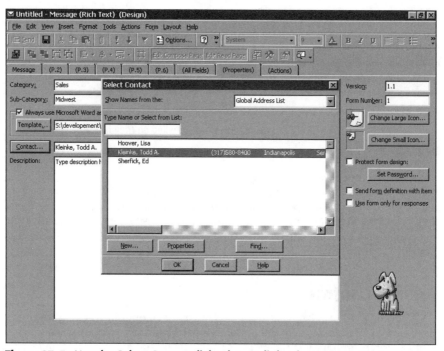

Figure 23-5: Use the Select Contact dialog box to link a form to a contact.

Protecting your form

If you are using your form in a multiuser environment, you may want to protect your form with a password. This will prevent users from viewing your underlying code as well as protect the form from tampering or accidental changes. To protect your form with a password, you simply check the *Protect form design* checkbox and set the password in the Password dialog box that opens. You may change the password using the Set Password button, as shown in Figure 23-6.

Figure 23-6: Protect your form with a password.

Including form definition

If you need to send your form outside of your organization, or if your form is not published to the Organizational Forms Library, you may include a definition in your form. To do so, simply select the *Send form definition with item* checkbox. The definition enables the recipient to view your form in the way you intended the form to appear. In order for users to protect themselves, they are prompted to either enable or disable the code within the custom form, as shown in Figure 23-7. However, if your form is published to the Organizational Forms Library by an Exchange Administrator, users will not be prompted. In such a case, it is the responsibility of the Exchange Administrator to verify the integrity of the form.

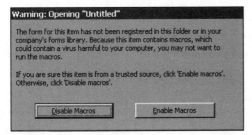

Figure 23-7: Users are prompted to enable or disable code when a definition is included with a form.

Limiting to a response

Perhaps you want to send a survey to a number of your coworkers. In addition, you would like to limit the responses of the survey in order to focus the survey on a specific topic. In this case, you would want to configure your form to be utilized only when your coworkers are returning the results of your survey (that is, when your coworkers are responding to the survey). To do so, just select the *Use form only for responses* checkbox.

Modifying Behavior with the Actions Page

The Actions page is located to the far right of a form displayed in Design view within the Outlook 2000 Forms Designer (OFD). The Actions page defines the type of routing for a form. For instance, the Actions page can define whether or not a form has the following capabilities:

✦ Post to a folder

✦ Reply to sender

✦ Reply to all recipients and sender

✦ Forward to another user

An example of how an Actions page may appear is shown in Figure 23-8. As you can see, the first line represents a standard reply. A standard message form will be created, the message will be addressed using whatever the user has defined as the default, and the subject line will be preceded by "RE:". The second line accomplishes the same task, only the message will be addressed to all recipients of the original message. The third line forwards the message and precedes the subject line with "FW:". The fourth line posts the message to a folder and does not add anything to the subject line.

To manipulate any of these attributes, double-click the attribute you want to change to open the Form Action Properties dialog box. This dialog box is shown in Figure 23-9.

New actions may be created with the New button in the bottom-left corner of the form, and actions may be deleted using the Delete button. The Form Action Properties dialog box may also be accessed by clicking the Properties button.

As you can see in Figure 23-9, an action can be enabled by selecting the Enabled checkbox, and form type and characteristics can be assigned as well. Additional behavior characteristics are assigned with the radio buttons under *This action will*. In addition, a prefix may be added to the subject field.

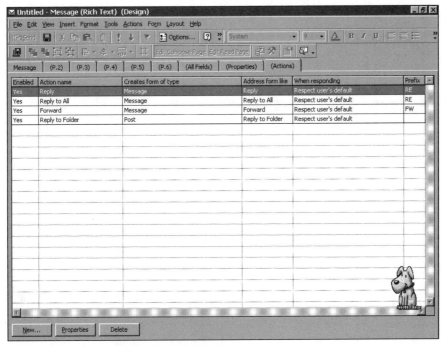

Figure 23-8: Example of a typical Actions page

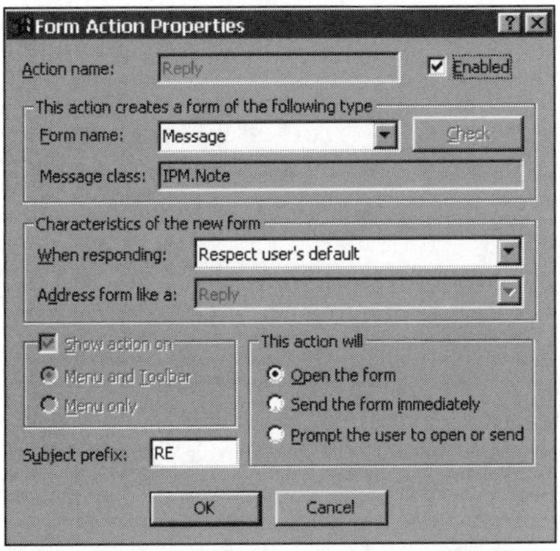

Figure 23-9: Make changes to the attributes of the Actions page using the Form Action Properties dialog box.

Once the actions have been configured to your specifications, they will become a part of the toolbar of the form to which the actions are associated. In the case of the Reply action in a message form, a Reply button will appear in the toolbar of a form in Read mode.

Changing the Tab Order

When designing a form, it's a good idea to keep a certain amount of usability in mind. Part of maintaining proper usability involves setting the tab order on your forms. What is tab order? It is the order in which the control focus changes as the user hits the Tab key, not to be confused with changing the order of pages in a form. Tab order is especially important to those users who prefer to use their keyboard over their mouse.

To better understand tab order, think of when you're composing a message, and you just entered the recipient's e-mail address. After entering the recipient's e-mail address, you hit the Tab key. Which field becomes activated? The answer is the Cc field, located right below the To field. If the user hits Tab again, the focus moves to the Subject field, and so on. It's the tab order that specifies the order in which these fields receive the focus.

To change the tab order of a form in Design view, do the following:

1. Right-click the first control to receive focus, and then select Advanced Properties from the pop-up menu.

2. Move to the TabIndex property in the Advanced Properties list and enter **0**. This signifies the first control to receive focus.

3. Verify that the TabStop property is set to "-1 - True". If it is not, change it to "-1 - True". This property identifies the control as being included in the group of controls that receive focus when the Tab key is pressed.

Note   Certain controls, such as labels, do not typically participate in the tab order. However, the controls that enable the user to manipulate data typically do.

An example of how your tab properties should appear is shown in Figure 23-10.

4. Once you have the first control configured, move to the next control that you would like to receive focus.

5. This time, enter **1** for the TabIndex property. The "1" places the control next in line.

6. Verify that the TabStop property is set to "-1 - True". If it is not, change it to "-1 - True".

7. Proceed to the other controls and increase the numeric value of the TabIndex property by one for each subsequent control.

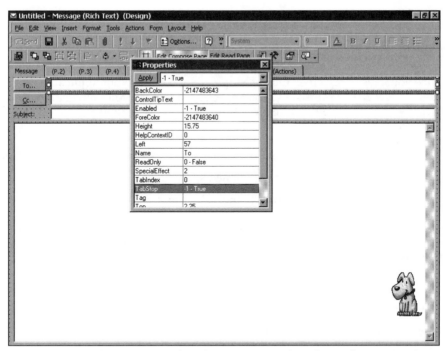

Figure 23-10: Make changes to the tab properties in the Advanced Properties form

Tip

Keep in mind that your tab order will be affected every time you add a new control to your form. By default, the new control will be last in line to receive focus.

Testing Design-Time Form Applications

While designing your applications, you'll probably want to test your forms as you develop them. This will allow you to catch a problem in its infancy, rather than catching the problem after other functions have been based on the particular part of the form that has the problem. If other functions are based on the problem part, then the other functions may have to be changed as well. Testing throughout makes more sense than developing the entire application and then testing all functionality after you publish the application.

To quickly test your form while in the middle of development in the OFD, you can select Run This Form from the Form menu.

A copy of the form is opened in run-time.

Installation and Deployment of OFD Applications

Once you have completed your development and tested your application using the methods described previously, you are ready to publish your application. However, before you publish your application, there are a few questions your need to ask yourself:

✦ Does this application need to be accessed by everyone in the organization?

✦ Should this application have offline capabilities?

✦ Will this application be sent to individuals outside of the organization?

Although these questions address how your application should be distributed, they also relate to where the forms should be stored. The forms can be stored in these places:

✦ Personal Forms Library

✦ Organizational Forms Library

✦ Personal Folders file (.pst)

✦ Subfolder of an existing Outlook folder, such as Inbox

In the following sections, you learn how to publish a form, and then you get a chance to explore some other options relating to publishing forms.

Publishing a form

To publish a form from the Outlook 2000 Forms Designer (OFD), complete the following steps:

1. Select Forms ➪ Publish Form from the Tools menu. Or, if you choose to use the Form Design Toolbar, click the Publish Form icon (the one with a floppy disk and triangle).

The Publish Form As dialog box will open, as shown in Figure 23-11.

2. Select from the Look In combo box the location of where you would like to publish your application. For this example, the form will be published to the Personal Forms Library.

 Note   The Personal Forms Library is exactly as it sounds—a place (or library) to store your personal forms. In this case, *personal* means only you can see the forms.

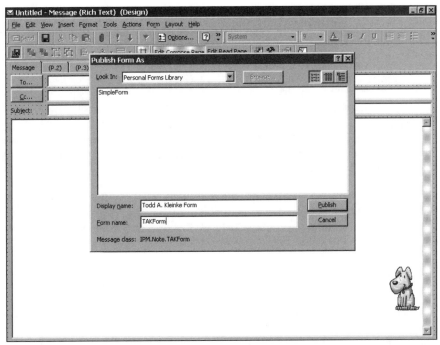

Figure 23-11: Use the Publish Form As dialog box to specify options for publishing your form.

3. Enter the display name of the form and a name for the form in the appropriate text boxes.

4. Click Publish to publish your form.

Publishing to Public Folders

Publishing to a Public Folder involves the same steps as described in the preceding section, but you would select a Public Folder from the Look In combo box rather than the Personal Forms Library. However, there are a few things you need to be aware of when publishing to a Public Folder:

✦ As indicated by the word *public*, everybody with access to the folder will have access to the form.

✦ Even though you may have access to a Public Folder, only owners of Public Folders have the sufficient rights to publish a form.

✦ You should typically remove the checkmark from the *Send form definition with item* checkbox when publishing to a Public Folder, because it's not needed and would require additional resources. An exception would be if the form is to be sent outside the organization.

Note   The Organizational Forms Library is similar to the Personal Forms Library, but is shared by the entire organization. Only an Exchange Administrator has sufficient rights to publish a form to the Organizational Forms Library.

Publishing to a Personal Folder file

A Personal Folder file (one with the extension .pst) is a file located on your local machine in which you can store Outlook items, such as custom forms. Because the file is stored locally, you have the ability to access the contents of the form when you're offline. It's not always convenient to dial into a server, so offline capabilities can be very handy.

On the CD-ROM   The CD-ROM distributed with this book contains the sample file used in the demonstration discussed in this chapter. This file, PSTFolder.pst, is provided in the Chapter 23 folder on the CD-ROM. It shows an example of how Personal Folder files may be distributed. See Appendix A for details

Once again, the steps involved with publishing to a Personal Folder file are the same as previously mentioned in the section "Publishing a form," but you select your Personal Folder file from the Look In menu. However, you may need to create a Personal Folder file to store your application. If so, follow these steps:

1. From the File menu, select New ⇨ Personal Folder File (.pst). This should open the Create Personal Folders dialog box, as shown in Figure 23-12.

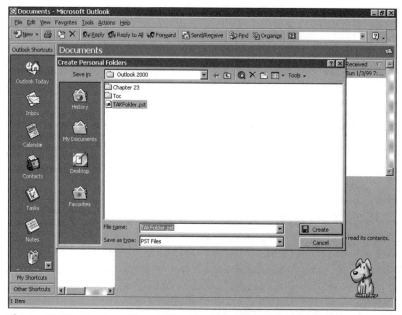

Figure 23-12: Create a Personal Folder file using this dialog box.

2. Select a location for the file, enter a name for your file in the File name field, and click Create.

Note   The .pst files created for Personal Folders may be distributed to other users.

Summary

In this chapter, you learned how to add functionality to Outlook 2000 custom forms. The chapter covered the following points:

✦ Some forms have two modes — Compose and Read. The Compose mode sets forth layout and functionality for the author, whereas the Read mode is designed for the recipient.

✦ Form pages are similar to tabs in a tab control. Additional form pages can be added to a form in order to organize information and provide the flexibility to include a greater number of fields and controls.

✦ A form's Properties page can be used to configure various properties relating to the form as a whole.

✦ The Actions page plays a significant role in the routing capabilities of a form.

✦ Close attention should be devoted to tab order, as it is often overlooked.

✦ Design-time form applications should be tested periodically while being developed.

✦ When considering how to deploy an application, issues surrounding who will be using the application, whether or not the users are within the organization, and whether or not offline capabilities are necessary should first be addressed.

✦   ✦   ✦

Advanced Messaging Development

Part VI covers advanced application development tasks within Outlook 2000 and its related technologies. These chapters describe how to incorporate Exchange folders into your applications effectively, provide an introduction to collaborative messaging, and introduce the Outlook 2000 Object Model. You also learn how to incorporate COM add-ins into Outlook 2000, what Collaborative Data Objects and Exchange Routing Objects are, and when they are appropriate to use.

Working with Application Folders

From this point on, we focus on issues you may face when developing advanced messaging applications. An entire book could be written on the subject of messaging, so we focus only on issues often faced by developers — particularly those that relate to Outlook 2000.

This chapter looks at application folders. Application folders are the folders that house Outlook 2000 applications. Here you have the opportunity to explore how to create different types of folders and learn when each type is appropriate.

Application Folder Types

To accommodate the functionality difference between applications, Outlook makes available different types of folders. These folder types can be classified in three categories:

✦ Discussion folders

✦ Tracking folders

✦ Built-in module folders

In order to get a better idea of each folder type, let's examine each one individually.

Discussion folders

In basic terms, discussion folders provide a way for people to discuss whatever topics they choose. Discussion folders provide an excellent means for collaboration. *Collaboration* refers to the sharing of ideas and information with the intent of accomplishing a specific task.

Chapter 25 discusses collaboration in greater detail.

For all discussion participants to be able to see the discussion folder, the folder must be set up as a Public Folder. To set up a discussion folder, follow these steps:

1. If your folder list is not displayed, select Folder List under the View menu.

2. Go to the Public Folders section.

3. Right-click All Public Folders and select New Folder.

4. Type a name for the new discussion folder. For this example, enter **Discussion Group**.

5. Because discussion postings act in the same manner as e-mail messages, select Mail Items in the Folder Contains field and click OK.

The folder should appear as a new Public Folder under All Public Folders.

In order to see for yourself how a discussion folder works, post a new item in the folder. To do so, click the New button in the upper-left corner, as if you were creating a new e-mail message. A post message form should appear, as shown in Figure 24-1.

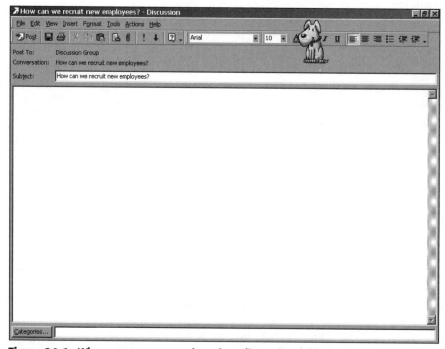

Figure 24-1: When you post a new item in a discussion folder, a post message form with a new subject/conversation defined appears.

Notice how the discussion topic "How can we recruit new employees?" is displayed on both the Subject and Conversation lines. This is because the Conversation line is based on what is entered as the subject. The Conversation line defines the discussion topic. However, when responding to a posted message, the Conversation line of the conversation you're responding to will remain the same, but you will have the opportunity to enter new text into the Subject line. We discuss the specifics behind this later in the chapter.

If you take a look in the Discussion Group folder, you can see that your message has been posted (see Figure 24-2).

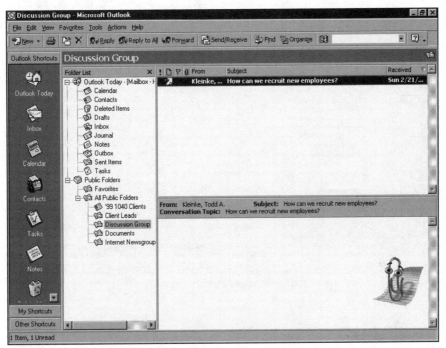

Figure 24-2: A message has been posted to the Discussion Group Public Folder.

By double-clicking the message, any user with access to the Public Folder may view the message. In addition, by clicking the Post Reply button on the message, the user can respond to the initial posting.

The user's response will appear in the Discussion Group Public Folder. However, it may be difficult to differentiate between conversations unless you organize your view of your discussion folders. To group the messages with the conversation to which they apply, select Current View ➪ By Conversation Topic from the View menu.

Cross-Reference   We discuss the details behind folder views and their capabilities later in this chapter.

Now that the current view is grouped by conversation, you can add as many conversation topics as you choose. Because the topics may be either expanded or collapsed, you can easily manage a large number of conversation topics and message postings, as you can see in the example in Figure 24-3.

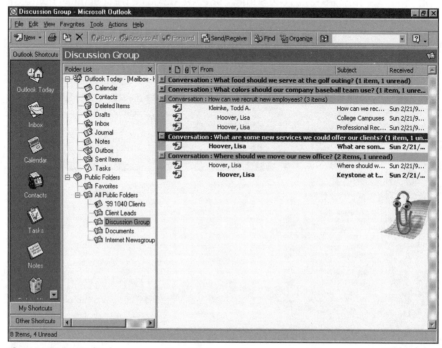

Figure 24-3: Multiple conversation topics and message postings can easily be managed once you've grouped messages by conversation.

Tracking folders

As you may have guessed, tracking folders track specific information, usually relating to some kind of business process. Because the information may be constantly updated, the Compose and Read pages of the form are often the same. In other words, there is typically not a separate Read form.

Tracking information

For example, Figure 24-4 shows a lead-tracking form that keeps track of potential client leads.

Cross-Reference   Chapters 20 and 21 discuss the details involved in creating the form in Figure 24-4.

Unlike a discussion post form, this form does not include reply functionality. A reply actually creates a new message, whereas simply editing the content does not. The original message is preserved, but the content stored within the message changes. Therefore, any changes to the data are merely saved.

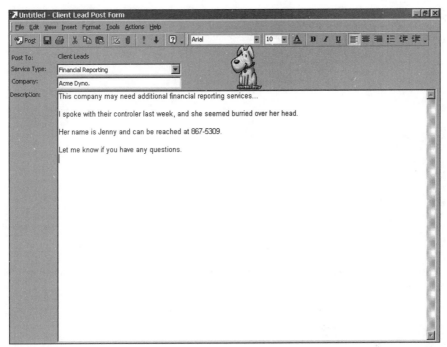

Figure 24-4: This custom lead-tracking form is used in conjunction with a tracking folder.

The CD-ROM distributed with this book contains a copy of this form. It is called ClientLead.oft and can be found in the Chapter 24 folder. See Appendix A for more details.

As with discussion folders, tracking folders are based on mail item folders. The lead-tracking form used in our example features a custom view that groups the service disciplines and potential/existing clients together.

Custom views are created by right-clicking the headings and adjusting the Group by This Field and Group by Box items. Additional information on custom views can be found later in this chapter.

Figure 24-5 demonstrates how the information is grouped.

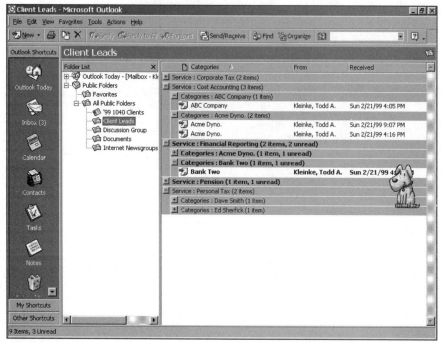

Figure 24-5: The messages in this tracking folder are grouped by service and the names of potential and existing clients.

Tracking documents

In addition, tracking folders can assist in the management of Office 2000 documents. For instance, suppose you want to keep track of company-wide contacts, all information pertaining to those contacts, and all correspondence and documents relating to those contacts. To do so, create a Public Folder named Documents. As you recall, you can create a Public Folder by right-clicking the All Public Folders folder and selecting New Folder. Within this folder, you can store Office 2000 documents, as shown in Figure 24-6.

To post a document to a Public Folder, you can use one of the following three methods:

✦ From your office application, such as MS Word 2000, select Send To ⇨ Exchange Folder from the File menu. Next, select the folder you wish to post to.

✦ From Outlook 2000, select Office Document from the drop-down menu of the New button in the upper-left corner. Select the option Post the Document in this Folder.

✦ Drag a document from Windows Explorer into the folder.

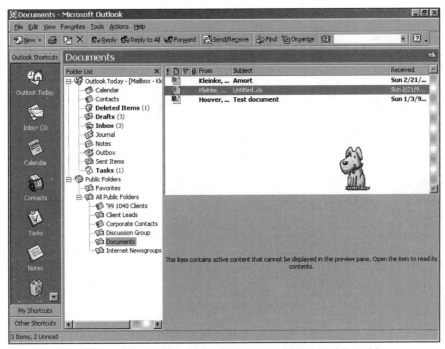

Figure 24-6: Office 2000 documents can be stored within a Public Folder.

To open the document, simply double-click the item.

To tie a document to a contact stored within a Public Folder (let's say you have a custom folder for business contacts called the Corporate Contacts Public Folder), do the following:

1. Right-click the document you wish to assign and select Options from the pop-up menu. The Message Options dialog box will open, as shown in Figure 24-7.

2. Click the Contacts button and assign the document to the contact of your choice.

Once the document has been assigned, the document is associated with that particular contact. The document may then be accessed through the Activities tab of the Contact form, as shown in Figure 24-8, as well as from the Documents folder.

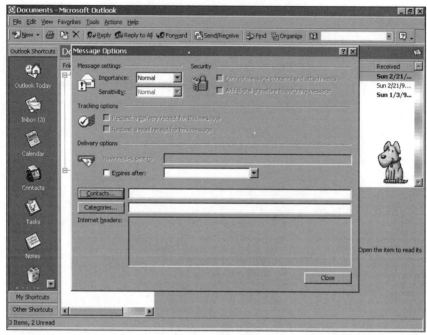

Figure 24-7: Use the Message Options dialog box to tie a document to a contact.

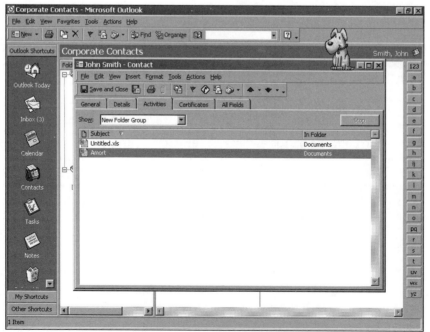

Figure 24-8: Accessing the document through the Activities tab of a Contact form

Note In order for the Activities tab to display the document, it must be pointed to the Public Folder containing the appropriate documents (in this case, the Document Public Folder). This may be done on the Activities tab in the Properties dialog box for the Public Folder containing the contacts (the Corporate Contacts folder in our example) and is explained in greater detail later in this chapter.

In fact, there are third-party manufacturers, such as Eastman Kodak, who design document-tracking applications through the use of messaging technologies. Not only do the applications help manage your documents, but they also assist in version control by enforcing a check-out policy. In other words, an employee must check out a document before he or she can make any changes. While the document is checked out, others may view the document, but not make any changes. If the document is checked out for too long, an e-mail message is generated and sent to the employee with notification of the overdue check-in date.

Built-in module folders

Built-in module folders are folders based on an Outlook 2000 built-in module. For instance, if you wanted to create a Corporate Contacts Public Folder like the one in the preceding example, an easy way to do so would be to base the folder on the standard Contacts folder.

To create the Corporate Contacts Public Folder, follow the same steps as for the Discussion Groups Public Folder example earlier, but select Contacts Items instead of Mail Items from the Folder Contains field. To enable the folder to view a contact's associated documents, you must add the Public Folder containing the documents (in this example, the Documents Public Folder) to the Activities tab of the Properties dialog box. To add the Documents Public Folder to the Activities tab, select New, and then select the Documents Public Folder (see Figure 24-9).

In addition to Contacts, built-in module folders can be configured to act as a Calendar, Tasks List, or other Outlook 2000 built-in module. Calendar Public Folders are good for corporate calendars, whereas public task lists may assist in identifying and tracking corporate goals.

Keep in mind that these types of folders are only based on built-in folders. They may be customized in order to suit your individual needs.

Managing Folder Properties

Although we've touched on folder properties earlier in this chapter, we haven't really gone into the specifics behind folder properties. As you'll recall, folder properties may be accessed by right-clicking the folder you wish to configure and selecting Properties from the pop-up menu.

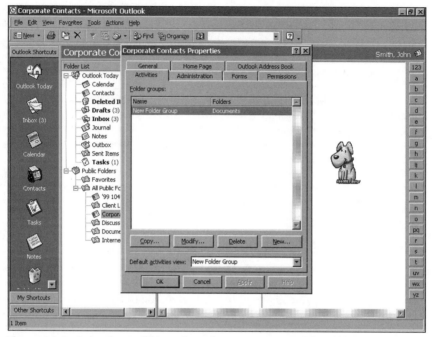

Figure 24-9: Point the Activities tab to the Documents Public Folder.

Depending on the type of folder you are working with, the Properties dialog box will be different. The differences are organized as tabs in the Properties dialog box. Because many of these property settings are covered in earlier chapters, this chapter only focuses on those properties that greatly affect the applications you program in Outlook 2000.

Specifying a default form

Because most Outlook 2000 applications use custom forms, you will most likely want to assign a particular form as the default form to the folder that houses your application. To do so, perform the following steps:

1. Select the Forms tab of the Property dialog box, as shown in Figure 24-10.

2. Click the Manage button to open the Forms Manager dialog box.

3. Click the Set button, select your form, and click OK.

4. Next, select the form name and click the Copy button, as shown in Figure 24-11. This copies the form to a location where it can be used by the folder.

5. Click the Close button to close the Forms Manager dialog box.

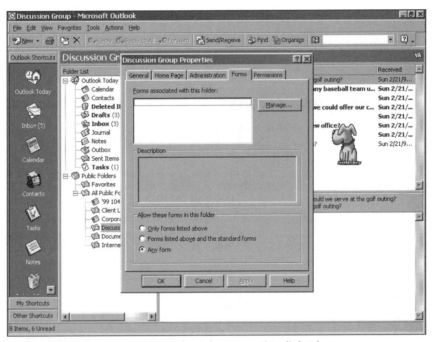

Figure 24-10: Select the Forms tab of the Properties dialog box.

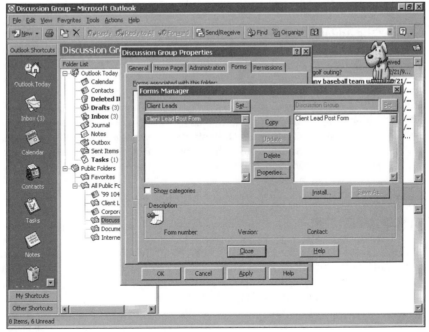

Figure 24-11: Copy the form via the Forms Manager dialog box.

At this point, the form is available to be used within the folder. However, if you want to force the users to only use the form you designed, make sure you select *Only forms listed above* in the Properties dialog box. The other two options, of course, do not limit which forms are used within the folder.

Defining permissions

Security almost always plays an important role when building applications within Outlook 2000. For this reason, be sure to review and test the permissions assigned to your application folder.

Chapter 17 discusses the details of defining folder permissions.

Be especially careful about assigning the role of Owner to users. Your application is more likely to "break" if the users have too many rights.

Using rules

Traditionally, rules are used to forward e-mail messages to another account. However, rules can be useful for applications that require certain actions when particular information enters a folder. These actions can be defined within the Edit Rule window, shown in Figure 24-12.

Under the Administration tab of the Properties dialog box, the rules pertaining to the folder can be defined by clicking the Folder Assistant button. This will, of course, open the Folder Assistant window. By clicking the Add Rule button, rules may be created.

Before creating rules using the method just explained, it's recommended that you initially attempt to define your rule using the Rules Wizard. The Rules Wizard is one of the best new features of Outlook 2000 and is easy to use. To access the Rules Wizard, select the folder for which you wish to define the rule, and then select Rules Wizard from the Tools menu.

Using Views

Views are very important when it comes to application development. Folder views not only organize information by providing structure, but can also provide a friendly interface for interaction. The remainder of the chapter will demonstrate why views play such an important role in developing Outlook 2000 applications.

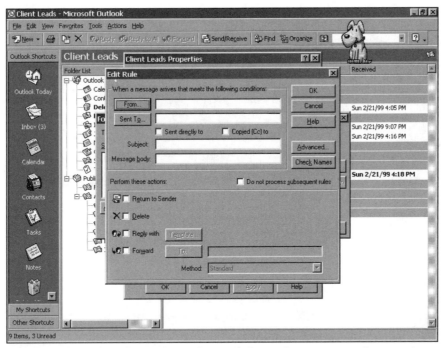

Figure 24-12: Use the Edit Rule window to define actions to occur when certain information enters the folder.

Customizing versus defining a view

In order to manipulate the view of a folder, you first select the folder, and then select Current View from the View menu. From that point, another menu will open displaying a number of predefined views. Because the focus here is on application development, you don't need to be particularly concerned with the predefined views. However, you should be concerned with two of the choices at the bottom of this menu: Customize Current View and Define Views.

The Customize Current View choice enables the user to modify the folder view on his or her computer. However, the Define Views choice enables the user to define how the folder will be viewed by default. Therefore, when designing the view for an application, you want to use the Define Views choice.

Figure 24-13 illustrates the Customize Current View choice. Note the descriptions to the right of each button. To the right of the Fields button, the Icon, Categories, From, and Received fields are displayed. On the next line, the information is grouped in ascending order by the Service and Category fields. The information is sorted by the PotentialClient field, and so on.

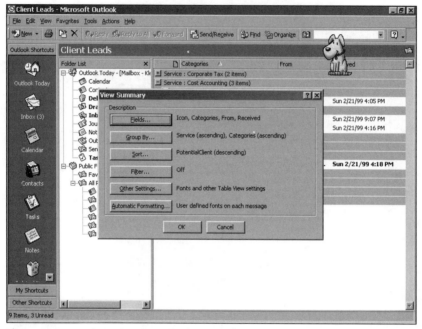

Figure 24-13: Customize Current View window.

Figure 24-14 illustrates the Define Views choice. On the bottom half of the form, you can see that the Icon, Categories, From, and Received fields are defined in the current view. The information is grouped in ascending order by the Service and Categories fields. The information is sorted by the PotentialClient field and is not filtered.

Although the windows look different in comparison, the Modify button of the Define Views window opens a window that looks exactly like the Customize Current View window. Therefore, the only important thing to know is when one or the other is appropriate. Just remember, a customized view in this case pertains only to the view the user that performs the customization sees; a defined view is inherent to the folder itself. Therefore, all users of a particular folder see the view that has been defined for that folder.

Manipulating field headings

By selecting the Fields button of the View Summary window, you may define which fields will appear in the view. To define which fields appear in the view, select the field you wish to include on the left and click the Add button, as shown in Figure 24-15. You also have the flexibility to add, remove, move up, or move down any field in the view.

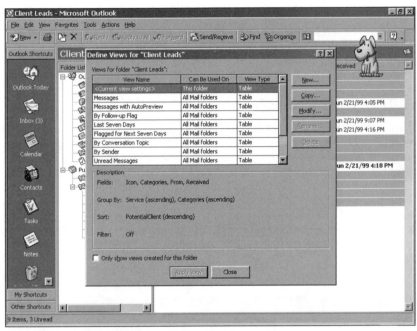

Figure 24-14: Define Views window.

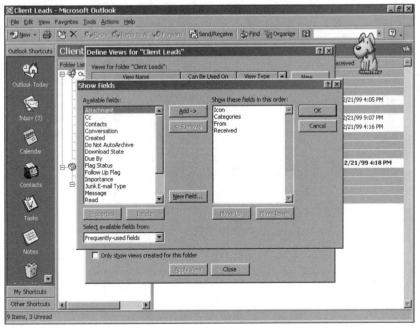

Figure 24-15: Use the Show Fields dialog box to manipulate the field headings of a view.

Tip

Outside of the customize/define view windows, the column headings may also be modified (for the current view) by right-clicking the column header, selecting Field Chooser from the pop-up menu, and then simply dragging and dropping the fields onto the header.

Grouping information

Grouping information is one of the best ways to organize your items within a folder. By grouping items together, the items suddenly have meaning and are easy to browse. Up to three levels of grouping may be used, giving the view a hierarchical structure.

Grouping may be defined by selecting Group By from the View Summary window. As you recall, the View Summary window may be accessed either through Custom Current View or Define Views from the View/Current View menu, or by right-clicking within a view. The Group By dialog box is displayed in Figure 24-16. As you can see, defining the groups is as simple as selecting a field.

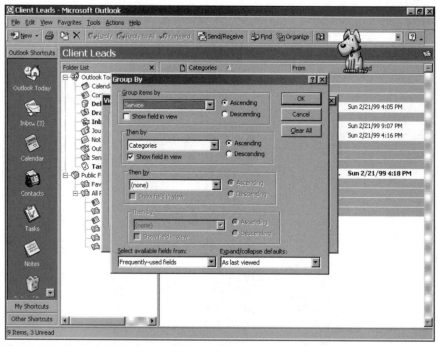

Figure 24-16: Defining groups within a view

> **Tip** Grouping (for the current view) may also be controlled by right-clicking the column header and selecting Group By Box from the pop-up menu.

Sorting and filtering

Sorting and filtering configuration is also accessed through the View Summary window. Sorting is used to present information in an ascending or descending manner, whereas filtering presents only the information specified by your criteria. The sorting window defines which field the information will be sorted by within each group. Figure 24-17 shows what the Sort dialog box looks like.

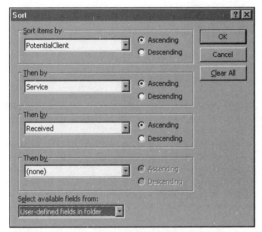

Figure 24-17: Use the Sort dialog box to sort information when defining a view.

The Filter dialog box, shown in Figure 24-18, filters according to the information you specify.

Other view settings

The remaining view settings, referred to as Other Settings, represent various font formatting options. Figures 24-19 and 24-20 show what font formatting options are available. Automatic Formatting enables the format choices to be implemented throughout each selected item.

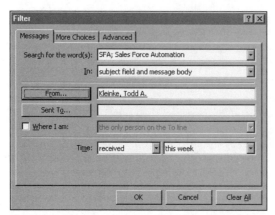

Figure 24-18: Use the Filter dialog box to filter information when defining a view.

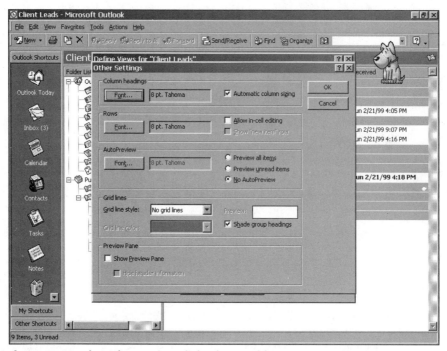

Figure 24-19: The Other Settings dialog box enables you to specify font options when defining a view.

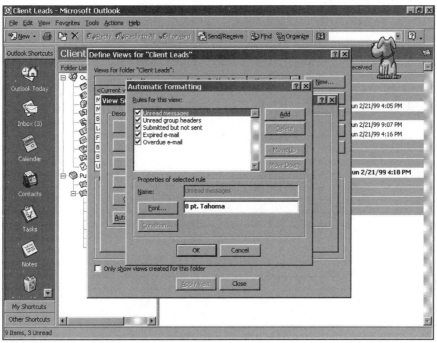

Figure 24-20: The Automatic Formatting dialog box enables format choices to be implemented on selected items when you define a view.

Summary

In this chapter, you learned how to work with folders when designing applications in Outlook 2000. The chapter covered the following points:

✦ Application folder types can be classified in three categories: Discussion folders, tracking folders, and built-in module folders.

✦ Discussion folders are designed to assist in collaboration by providing a convenient means for discussing a topic.

✦ Tracking folders can be used to house information in a central location in an organized manner. The information can be in the form of text or documents.

✦ Built-in module folders borrow from the characteristics inherent in Outlook 2000 built-in folders.

✦ Folder properties vary depending on the type of folder you are maintaining.

✦ When designing a custom application in Outlook 2000, you need to keep in mind certain key considerations in terms of folder management. These considerations partially consist of specifying a default form, defining permissions, and defining rules.

✦ Views are an important aspect of Outlook 2000 development. Careful choice of fields, grouping, sorting, and filtering are what define a friendly and effective folder interface.

✦   ✦   ✦

Collaborative Messaging Basics

In Part IV and Chapter 24, we've shown you how to configure, utilize, customize, and integrate the key elements of Outlook 2000. Now we're going to shift gears and get a bit more technical and a bit more theoretical. But don't worry — we'll keep the theory to a minimum. In this chapter, you learn basic methodologies that surround collaborative messaging applications. These methodologies are the backbone to the solutions that save companies fat cash! In addition, you get a chance to look at some sample applications and learn what makes them so powerful so you can apply the same concepts to your custom solutions.

Understanding the Lingo

Word of warning: Even as Microsoft Solution Providers, we sometimes feel like we have to be MCASs (Microsoft Certified Acronym Specialists) to understand what Microsoft is talking about. (Just kidding, there's no such certification.) However, when developing in Outlook 2000, it's important to understand collaboration and messaging, as well as how they relate to collaborative solutions. It's important for you to know that collaborative messaging has a meaning similar to the dictionary definition, but varies somewhat when addressing the topic at hand. Also, we promise to keep the acronyms to a minimum.

Collaboration

In general terms, *collaboration* describes the sharing of information among a group of individuals who intend to accomplish a common goal. Examples include brainstorming, group discussions, and simple teamwork. When implemented within an organization, large or small, collaboration can accomplish the following:

✦ Establishes a shared location for related information

✦ Organizes the information in an understandable and easily accessible manner

✦ Enables people to work as a team without being hassled by continuous meetings

✦ Allows people to be more productive, which saves money

A collaborative solution that utilizes Outlook 2000 (especially when used with Exchange Server) has the ability to accomplish each of these goals. The central location could be a Public Folder, and the organization could be accomplished through a hierarchy of folders within the Public Folder. Because the information is available through a common, shared application (that is, Outlook 2000), the information is easily accessible via a familiar interface. Sharing information in this manner would enable people who are located in different cities to participate on the same project team without the need for traveling between cities. That saves time, makes people more productive, and, of course, saves money.

Collaborative solution

Common elements of a *collaborative solution* include the integration of multiple sources of information. For instance, Figure 25-1 demonstrates a collaborative solution that integrates SAP (an enterprise-level accounting system used by large corporations that integrates all aspects of business), multiple SQL Server 7.0 databases, Exchange Server 5.5, an Outlook 2000 custom form, Internet Information Server 4.0, and a custom e-form developed in Visual Basic 6.0. Although the individual functions of each piece of the solution are explained later in the chapter, it's important to understand that the integration of applications and communication among people with various business roles are what classify the example as a collaborative solution.

Note The custom e-form (developed in Visual Basic 6.0) and the Outlook 2000 custom form are interfaces that display information specific to a custom application. Both e-forms and Outlook 2000 custom forms have the capability of being transmitted as an e-mail message. Both e-forms and Outlook 2000 custom forms are discussed in detail later in the chapter.

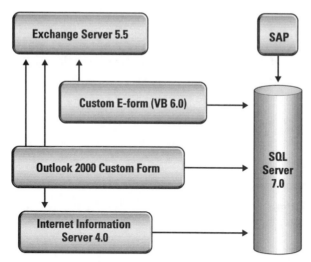

Figure 25-1: An example of a collaborative solution

The flow of this scenario would be as follows:

1. Data from SAP is stored within SQL Server 7.0 along with other databases.

2. The custom e-form, the Outlook 2000 custom form, and the Internet Information Server 4.0 (IIS) Web server all pull data from the SQL Server databases.

3. The custom e-form and Outlook form are routed to various individuals within the organization through Exchange Server. As the forms are routed to each individual, the data contained within the forms is manipulated.

4. Once the changes to the data within the forms are complete, the data is synchronized with a SQL Server database.

Collaborative messaging

When we speak of *collaborative messaging,* we're referring to the elements of a collaborative solution that involve the transmission of data through an e-mail message. For example, when a user clicks the Send button on an e-mail message asking a friend in Cincinnati what he's doing New Year's Eve, it's messaging that transmits the question from that user's Windows 98 machine over the Internet to the friend's iMac. Even though the machines utilize two different operating systems, they are still able to communicate with one another. If the e-mail message was transmitted as part of a team effort to accomplish a common goal, such as to coordinate a trip to New York Times Square on New Year's Eve, the entire process could be considered a collaborative messaging solution. Figure 25-2 identifies the elements of the collaborative solution example that relate to collaborative messaging — in other words, the elements of the solution that involve the transmission of data through an e-mail message. The grayed-out elements in Figure 25-2 represent the elements that do not involve the transmission of data through an e-mail message.

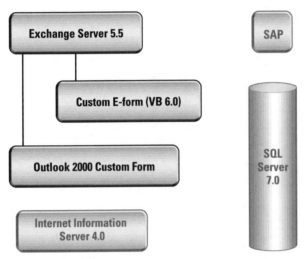

Figure 25-2: Elements relating to collaborative messaging

Workflow applications

Oftentimes, collaborative messaging processes replace business processes that formerly involved a great deal of paper and manual manipulation. For example, a coworker of ours designed an Outlook application that scheduled boys and girls sports teams to appropriate athletic facilities. Before the application, the scheduling was performed manually. A *workflow application* replaces these paper and manual processes by accomplishing the flow of the business process through the use of collaborative messaging. For instance, the Outlook 2000 custom form that is part of Figure 25-2 could represent an office supply request form.

The office supply request form would be considered a workflow application. An example of an office supply request process is represented in Figure 25-3. Keep in mind that the request is routed to the various individuals through the use of collaborative messaging.

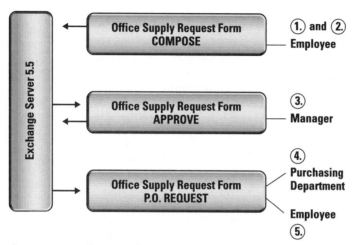

Figure 25-3: Office supply request processes through collaborative messaging

The office supply request form process is as follows:

1. An employee who needs a new calculator initiates a request by opening the office supply request form from within Outlook 2000.

2. The employee enters the proper information into the form and clicks the Send button.

3. The form is sent to a manager who is in charge of office supply approval. When the manager opens the form, she has the option of either approving or rejecting the request. In this case, the manager clicks the Approve button.

4. The form is sent to the purchasing department for processing. When a member of the purchasing department views the form, all the relevant information relating to the request is displayed.

5. A copy of the approved request is also sent to the employee, so he or she knows that the request has been approved.

6. If the manager had rejected the request, the purchasing department would not have received the form. However, the employee would receive the form stating the request has been rejected.

Before collaborative messaging, this process would probably have involved a carbon copy form completed by the employee, and then manually routed to the manager and purchasing department. If any one individual required a record of the request, a paper copy would be made and filed. There's no question that the automated collaborative messaging process is much more efficient.

Messaging application programming interface

Outlook 2000 uses messaging to provide its underlying functionality. Specifically, messaging refers to the *messaging application program interface* (MAPI). MAPI is the interface that enables different e-mail systems to speak to one another. Because system-based messaging APIs (application programming interfaces) are integrated with many different operating systems (including Windows 95, 98, and NT, and the Apple Macintosh OS), cross-platform messaging is possible, assuming the API provides simple messaging functions. Whew! What does this all mean? It means that your Windows 98 machine can talk to any Macintosh, which can also talk to a mainframe computer that can talk to your Windows 98 machine. Everybody can talk to everybody.

If there were no messaging standard available to different e-mail applications, each software vendor would be forced to write code to accommodate the specific e-mail application interfaces of other vendors. Nobody wants to do that, so MAPI has a lot of supporters. Through MAPI, vendors only need to support one specific standard. Figure 25-4 demonstrates how an application utilizing MAPI is able to communicate among multiple environments. In other words, MAPI acts as the pipeline between the various platforms.

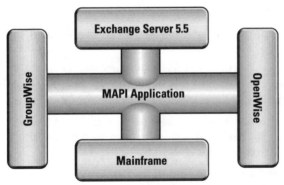

Figure 25-4: Cross-messaging system support with MAPI application

Today, many applications use MAPI to communicate with other applications in a manner more sophisticated than traditional e-mail. Specifically, MAPI can be used to initiate actions in other applications, based on the commands transmitted. However, due to the complexity of MAPI, this type of application development can require a great deal of technical expertise.

Outlook 2000 Custom Forms

Outlook 2000 provides an environment for developers to utilize MAPI technologies without the headache of traditional MAPI programming. Outlook 2000 includes an extensive object model that provides a simplified method of using a complex interface.

The majority of the Outlook 2000 user interface consists of Outlook forms. The forms provide a friendly means of accessing the underlying code. These forms can be customized to accommodate specific business needs. The forms are created within the Outlook Forms Designer, as shown in Figure 25-5.

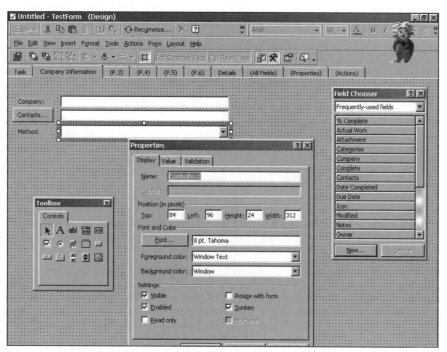

Figure 25-5: Outlook Forms Designer

As you may recall, we explained the details of the Outlook Forms Designer and how to design Outlook 2000 custom forms in Chapters 20 through 23. It's important to understand that these forms can be customized to suit specific needs and that they provide an interface to the underlying messaging system.

E-form Basics

The name *e-form* is a short name for *electronic forms*. The term *electronic form* came from the idea of creating an electronic version of an existing paper form. However, e-forms are more than just a replacement for a paper form. Typically, e-forms are key components of workflow applications. In addition to replacing the paper form, the e-form accomplishes the underlying business process that surrounded the paper form. By embedding the business logic into the e-form, the process can be automated. All the user needs to do is enter the information, submit the form, and let it do its thing.

For example, suppose your company surveys employees in each department about the performance of their supervisor. Each employee receives the same survey. Each department head is only interested in the surveys of employees in his or her department when evaluating the performance of the supervisor. In a traditional paper-process model, each employee would complete a form by giving his or her name, the supervisor's name, and responses to the questions. Under this scenario, the surveys would have to be printed, distributed, completed, returned, sorted, and tabulated.

However, by embedding the survey into an e-form, the survey does not have to be printed. In addition, the e-form can be distributed, completed, and returned to the proper department head via business rules embedded into the form. The department head may then view an automated report based on the results of the survey. By implementing the e-form solution, you can replace the slow, inefficient, paper-intensive process with a fast, efficient, automated process.

Although Outlook 2000 custom forms can often accomplish these same goals, e-forms enable you to do more things for a greater degree of functionality. For instance, e-forms can be written to fully exploit the full capabilities of Visual Basic and ActiveX controls to provide a more robust, high-performance application with a complex user interface. Outlook 2000 custom forms use VBScript to perform tasks, whereas e-forms can be created in Visual Basic, Visual Basic for Applications, Visual C++, or Visual J++. Because these development platforms offer a greater degree of functionality, it sometimes makes sense to develop forms in the more flexible environment these platforms provide.

Dow AgroSciences e-form application

To give you a real-world example of an e-form in action, let's examine an application that Brad Hehe developed for Dow AgroSciences. The e-form was developed in Visual Basic 5.0 and utilizes the Sax mPower ActiveX control to simplify the underlying MAPI procedure calls. In other words, you can program against the Sax mPower ActiveX control as you would any other COM object without having to understand the complexity of direct MAPI procedure calls.

The application is used to process claims against herbicides and pesticides manufactured by Dow AgroSciences. The e-form interface is shown in Figure 25-6.

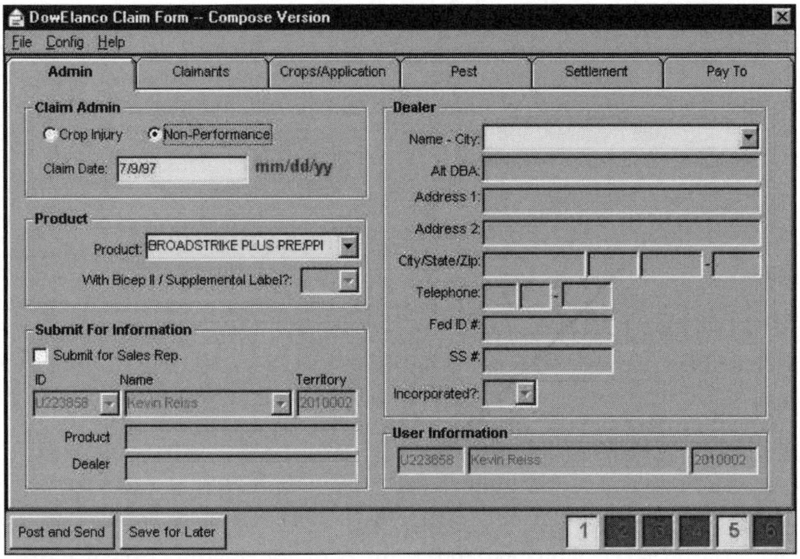

Figure 25-6: Dow AgroSciences e-form interface

Without going into too many details, the e-form proceeds through the following steps.

1. After careful examination of a customer's crops and determining that a claim is in order, a sales representative at the customer site initiates a claim.

2. Once the information regarding the claim is entered into the form, the sales rep clicks the Post and Send button to submit the claim. If any required information is missing, the application will not allow the claim to be processed.

3. Based on the information pertaining to the claim, the information is routed to various levels within the organization to obtain proper approval. The claim may be rejected at any point during the approval process.

4. Assuming the claim has obtained approval from all levels, the claim data is inserted into an Oracle 8.0 database and electronically transmitted to a check-writing agency for payment distribution.

5. Once the check has been processed, the claim's corresponding check number and check date is electronically delivered back to Dow AgroSciences and inserted into the database.

The manual process that took months to complete is now accomplished in a fraction of the time. The time and effort spent on developing the application has been surpassed by the time and effort saved in regards to processing claims.

The CD-ROM contains the PowerPoint presentation presented at the 1998 Microsoft Exchange Conference in Boston. The presentation highlights in greater detail how Dow AgroSciences used this technology to streamline a claims approval process common to many companies. Additional details regarding the Dow AgroSciences claims application can also be obtained from the Microsoft Web site (www.microsoft.com) under the Exchange Server Case Studies.

Summary

In this chapter, you learned about the basic methodologies that surround collaborative solution development. In addition, you learned how Outlook 2000 and collaborative messaging can play an important role in providing an overall solution. The chapter covered the following points:

✦ Collaboration describes the sharing of information among a group of individuals with the intention of accomplishing a common goal.

✦ Collaboration can establish shared sources of information, organize the information in a logical and easily accessible manner, assist in working with teams, and make people more productive.

✦ Collaborative solutions typically integrate many different applications containing a wide-range of information.

✦ Collaborative messaging is an element of a collaborative solution that transmits information through the Exchange Server, Outlook 2000 custom forms, custom e-forms, or any application that utilizes MAPI.

✦ Workflow applications resemble business processes by routing information through the use of collaborative messaging. Workflow applications often replace paper-based manual business processes.

✦ The messaging application programming interface (MAPI) is the interface that allows different e-mail systems to speak to one another.

✦ Outlook 2000 custom forms are created within the Outlook Forms Designer and can accommodate specific individual needs.

✦ Applications that require greater flexibility and a high degree of functionality are developed as e-forms, as opposed to Outlook 2000 custom forms.

✦   ✦   ✦

Using the Outlook 2000 Object Model

To fully exploit the capabilities of Outlook 2000 and integrate with other applications, you need to understand the Outlook 2000 Application Object Model. By understanding the model, you will be able to manipulate your applications into performing the same complex tasks inherent in Outlook 2000, but without having to understand the minute details of the messaging application programming interface (MAPI).

 Cross-Reference For more information on MAPI, see Chapter 25.

What's an Object Model?

An object model can be thought of as the blueprint of a component-based application. When we refer to component-based applications, we are stating that the application is broken-down into individual objects and fits into Microsoft's component software model know as the Component Object Model (COM). An object model is a diagram of all the individual components working together to form an application. To give you an idea of what an object model looks like, Figure 26-1 displays the object model for the Office Assistant, which is referred to as the Assistant Object from a programming standpoint.

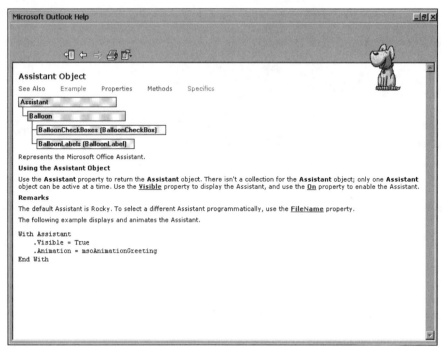

Figure 26-1: Object model for the Assistant Object

Component Object Model

Applications designed using COM can be broken down into individual components known as *objects*. Depending on the specifics, these objects go by a number of names, but all refer to the same basic concept. Some common terms referring to these objects include COM-object, ActiveX .dll, ActiveX control, ActiveX component, component, or simply just object.

So why are applications designed under the COM software model? There are a number of reasons why it's a good idea to build component-based applications, and here are a few of them:

✦ *Reusability*—Because the functionality of component-based applications is divided into objects, the functionality can be borrowed for use in another application.

✦ *Integration*—Because the components can be shared between two different applications, the applications can easily be integrated.

✦ *Language independence*—Components built as ActiveX components can be shared among programming languages that support ActiveX, such as Visual Basic, Visual C++, and Visual J++. Therefore, an ActiveX component built in Java can just as easily be used in a Visual Basic or Visual C++ application as it can in a Visual J++ application.

✦ *Scalability*—By utilizing certain application architectures and the Distributed Component Object Model (DCOM), applications can be very scalable. Scalability touches on how easily the application can be distributed to users and how well the application responds to a large number of users.

Outlook 2000 Application Object Model

As explained previously in the chapter, an object model can be thought of as the blueprint of an application. Therefore, the Outlook 2000 Application Object Model can be thought of as the blueprint for Outlook 2000. To view the Outlook 2000 Application Object Model, select Microsoft Outlook Object Library Help from the Help menu with the Script Editor open. A diagram of the object model should open, as displayed in Figure 26-2. The diagram is interactive—you can click on an object to view additional information.

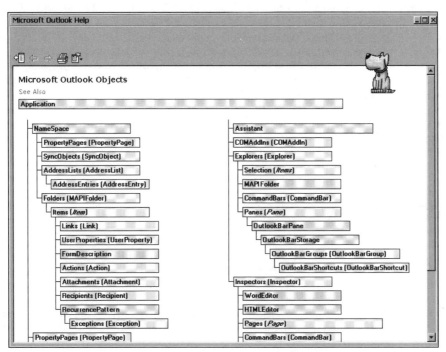

Figure 26-2: Outlook 2000 Application Object Model interactive diagram

The items in yellow represent the object and collection, whereas the items in blue represent an object only. *Collections* refer to objects that have a set of related objects associated with them. For example, the Folders collection has all the individual folders associated with the object.

Methods versus properties

To understand how to work with an object model, it's important to understand the methods and properties of an object. In simple terms, a method is described as an action associated with an object, whereas a property can be described as a characteristic of the object. In order to get a better understanding, let's look at the following code:

```
Function Item_Open()

    Dim strFolder
    Set myNameSpace = Application.GetNameSpace("MAPI")
    Set myFolder = myNameSpace.GetDefaultFolder(13)
    strFolder = myFolder.Name
    msgbox strFolder

End Function
```

In this example, we use the GetNameSpace method of the Application object to assign the name space to MyNameSpace. Next, we use the GetDefaultFolder method of the NameSpace object to assign folder number 13 to myFolder. Finally, we assign our string to the name property of our folder object. Therefore, the methods completed the actions of obtaining the objects we needed, and the property stored the name characteristic we needed. The end result is a message that states "Tasks" when the form opens.

In order to relate this example back to our explanation of the Object Browser, Figure 26-3 shows how we could have used the Object Browser to find the GetDefaultFolder method of the NameSpace object.

Using the OFD Script Editor

As discussed in Chapter 20, the Outlook 2000 Forms Designer (OFD) Script Editor is the tool to use to program your VBScript functions and subroutines within Outlook 2000. In order to access the Script Editor from within the OFD, select View Code from the Form menu.

The function is designed to display a message box when the form is closed. In order to accomplish this task, we used the Item_Close event. You learn more about events in the next section.

 Cross-Reference   For details on creating a simple function or subroutine, see the introduction to the Script Editor in Chapter 20.

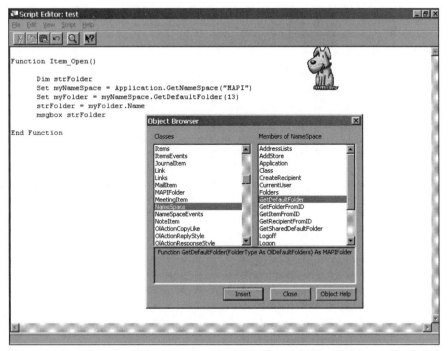

Figure 26-3: Using the Object Browser to obtain the GetDefaultFolder method of the NameSpace object

Event handlers

Events are user actions that trigger the execution of any code associated with that particular event. Without events, your code would never be executed. In other words, when an event occurs, such as an On_Click event, the code specified underneath the event will be executed. In order to assist with programming against events, the Script Editor has a built-in event handler. To access the Event Handler dialog box, select Event Handler from the Script menu. The Insert Event Handler dialog box should appear, as shown in Figure 26-4.

The list box contains a list of all the possible events. A description of when each event occurs is indicated at the bottom of the Insert Event Handler dialog box. To view a description, simply select the event. To insert an event into the Script Editor, select the event, and then click the Add button. Alternatively, you can just double-click the event. A function with the specified event will automatically be created in the Script Editor.

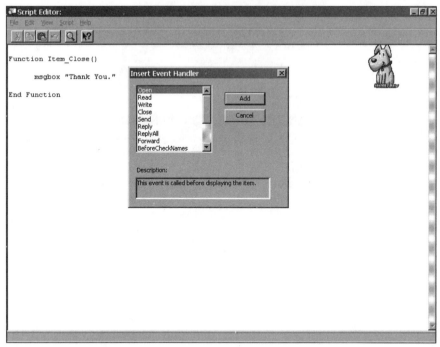

Figure 26-4: An option on the Script menu brings up the Insert Event Handler dialog box.

Object Browser

The Object Browser is another component of the Script Editor that aids the programmer in his or her development. The Object Browser is a quick reference for determining the members of the selected object. To access the Object Browser from the Script Editor, select Object Browser from the Script menu (or press F2). Figure 26-5 gives you an idea of what the Object Browser looks like.

The list on the left provides a list of classes, including the objects, and the list on the right provides a list of the corresponding members. By selecting a member and then clicking the Insert button, the Object Browser will insert the member text into the Script Editor, as shown in Figure 26-6.

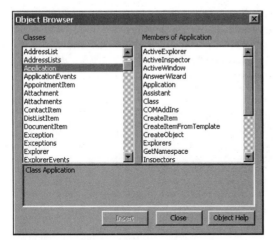

Figure 26-5: Object Browser window

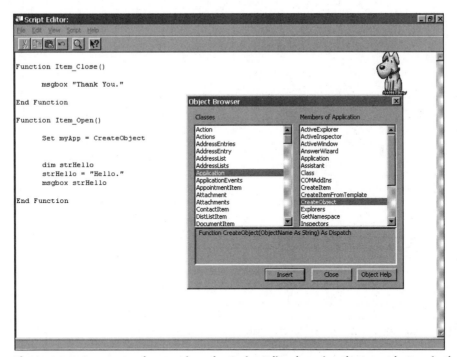

Figure 26-6: Insert member text into the Script Editor by using the Insert button in the Object Browser.

Tip   By clicking the Object Help button from within the Object Browser, you will open the Help file for that particular object, as shown in Figure 26-7. The Outlook 2000 Object Model Help files are extremely helpful in giving you an understanding of how to work with an object. In addition, the actual models are set up as links to help on the piece of the model you click.

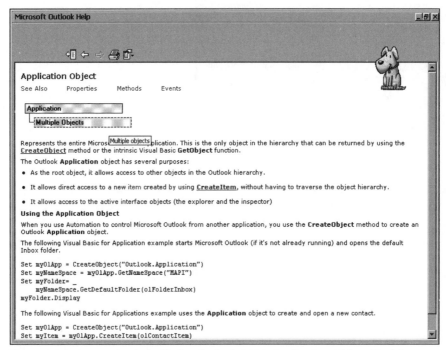

Figure 26-7: Interactive help file for Outlook 2000 Application Object Model

Debugging Your Code

Once you get started writing your own code, chances are your code will not always work on your first try. However, don't feel bad — you'll be no different than any other programmer in the world. Thankfully, there are tools to assist in finding where the problems lie within your code. For Outlook 2000, that tool is known as the Script Debugger. The Script Debugger released with Office 2000 has vast improvements over older versions. The new version seems to provide more feedback when debugging, and the break mode support is especially helpful.

To access the Script Debugger, you must first be running your form:

1. To run your form from the OFD, select Run This Form from the Form menu.

2. Next, to open the Script Debugger, select Forms ➪ Script Debugger from the Tools menu.

The Script Debugger is empty at this point.

Break mode

When code is executed in break mode, there is a pause before each line of code. By analyzing the behavior of your application as it relates to each line of code, you can determine in which lines problems exist. To see how the Script Debugger can step though code, set the Script Debugger to run the application in break mode by doing the following:

1. To set the Script Debugger to run the application in break mode, select Break from the Debug menu (or you can press Ctrl+Break).

2. Because the Script Debugger will not step through code until an event is fired, close your form to fire off the Close event.

Figure 26-8 shows the Script Debugger stepping through the code.

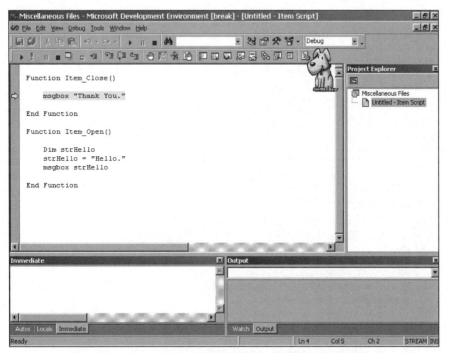

Figure 26-8: Script Debugger steps through the code in break mode.

Note   The form used for this example displays a "Thank You" message when the form is closed. If there was no code written for this event, the Script Debugger would not have any code to step through.

By selecting Step Into from the Debug menu, or pressing the F11 key, you can step though each line of code.

In Figure 26-9, the code for the Close event has changed to utilize a string value to represent the text of the message box. As we step through our example code with the F11 key, the string "strThanks" is assigned the value "Thank You.". As you can see, when the mouse is hovered over "strThanks", the value of the string can be viewed in the form of a tip (strThanks = "Thank You.").

```
Function Item_Close()

    Dim strThanks
    strThanks = "Thank You."
    msgb strThanks = "Thank You."

End Function

Function Item_Open()

    Dim strHello
    strHello = "Hello."
    msgbox strHello

End Function
```

Figure 26-9: View the value of a string by hovering the mouse over the string (strThanks = "Thank You.").

Setting Break Points

Break points enable you to pause your code at a specified point, but without stepping though several lines of code. This is particularly useful when you have several lines of code. To set a break point, do the following:

1. Run your form.

2. Open the Script Debugger by selecting Forms ➪ Script Debugger from the Tools menu.

3. Set the Script Debugger to run the code in break mode by selecting Break from the Debug menu. Another approach is to put your cursor where you want to add your breakpoint in the code window, and then choose Insert Breakpoint from the Debug menu.

4. Set your break point on the desired line by clicking in the left-hand margin.

5. Select Continue from the Debug menu, or press F5.

The code should stop at the break point you specified, as shown in Figure 26-10.

Break point

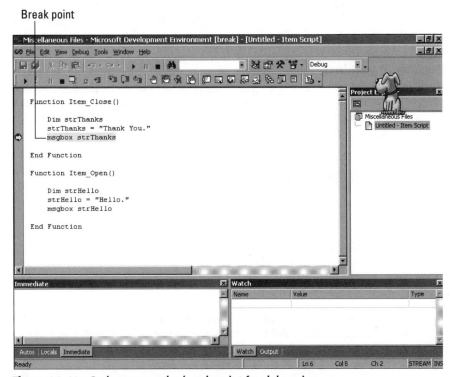

Figure 26-10: Code stops at the break point for debugging.

Debug windows

In addition to the methods of debugging discussed previously, you may also wish to use the additional debug windows offered through the Script Debugger. These debug windows are accessed by selecting the Debug Windows option from the View menu within the Script Debugger. The additional debug windows include the following:

✦ Immediate (Ctrl+Alt+I)

✦ Autos (Ctrl+Alt+A)

✦ Locals (Ctrl+Alt+L)

✦ Watch (Ctrl+Alt+W)

✦ Threads (Ctrl+Alt+H)

✦ Call Stack (Ctrl+Alt+C)

✦ Running Documents (Ctrl+Alt+R)

These windows provide various information relating to the code being executed. You probably will not use much of the information provided in these additional windows, as it is a bit too detailed. However, a few of these windows are definitely beneficial when it comes to debugging.

Immediate window

The Immediate window is used to execute single lines of code. In addition, you can execute code from within the Immediate window even when you are stepping through the actual code in break mode. This can be useful when you need to change or assign a value to a variable, as shown in Figure 26-11.

Immediate

```
strThanks = "No Thank You."
```

Figure 26-11: A value of a string being can be changed from within the Immediate window.

Notice that even though the form code specifies to set "strThanks" to "Thank You.", "strThanks" is actually assigned the value "No Thank You.", which you can see by hovering the mouse over the string.

Locals Window

The Locals window is another debug window that can be useful in troubleshooting your code. The Locals window summarizes current information about the form and the values associated with the current state. For example, Figure 26-12 summarizes the current state of the form as we step through the code.

Locals

Item_Close <VBScript>

Name	Value	Type
Item_Close	Empty	User-defi
strThanks	"Thank You."	String

Figure 26-12: Locals window summarizing current state of the form and the associated values.

Summary

In this chapter, you learned some of the basics behind object models, COM, and, specifically, the Outlook 2000 Application Object Model. The chapter covered the following points:

✦ Object models are the blueprints of applications.

✦ The Component Object Model (COM) is Microsoft's component software model and is what the Outlook 2000 Application Object Model is based on.

✦ There are many reasons to develop component-based applications, but some of the main reasons touch on sharing components, integrating with other applications, language independence, and scalability.

✦ The Insert Event Handler window can assist in identifying events within the OFD Script Editor.

✦ The Object Browser can aid in navigating through the Outlook 2000 Application Object Model.

✦ The Script Debugger has a number of features to assist you in troubleshooting your code.

✦ Running the Script Debugger in break mode will enable you to step through each line of your code individually.

✦ Setting break points enables you to pause your code at designated points.

✦ There are a number of additional debug windows designed to provide information regarding the current state of the form.

✦ Documentation for the Outlook 2000 Application Object Model can be accessed through the Help menu of the Script Editor.

✦ When working with object models, it's important to understand that methods represent the actions of an object, whereas properties represent the characteristics of an object.

✦   ✦   ✦

Outlook 2000 COM Add-ins Primer

Although the capabilities of Outlook 2000 are vast, there may come a point in time when you need to go beyond what Outlook 2000 has to offer. You may also find on some occasion that you want to integrate an existing application into Outlook 2000. In such cases, COM add-ins may be able to help.

What's a COM Add-in?

Support for COM add-ins is a new feature with Outlook 2000. COM add-ins are applications built either in Visual Basic, Visual C++, or Visual J++ and accessed from another application, such as Outlook 2000. Outlook 2000 COM add-ins often integrate with Outlook, but could also be designed to not utilize any features included in Outlook 2000.

The idea behind a COM add-in is to provide a piece of functionality that you did not have before. In addition to automating functionality within an application, a COM add-in can implement functionality within an application that initially did not exist. COM add-ins can be thought of as separate programs integrated within Outlook 2000. Visual Basic, Visual C++, and Visual J++ are extremely powerful programming tools, so the possibilities are endless. In addition, COM add-ins are designed with the Component Object Model (COM) methodologies in mind, so their functionality can be designed to work within other applications as well.

Cross-Reference See Chapter 26 for additional information regarding COM .

Creating a Simple COM Add-in

This section describes how to create a simple COM add-in for Outlook 2000. We illustrate the discussion with an example COM add-in that was built using Visual Basic, because the language is similar to VBScript and Visual Basic is widely used among programmers.

Three basic steps

There are three basic steps to the process of creating a COM add-in:

1. Create the necessary code to provide the functionality you seek for your COM add-in.

2. Provide the necessary entries within the Registry.

3. Configure your office application to use the COM add-in.

AddInDesigner

The easiest way to build a COM add-in is by using an Office AddInDesigner. An AddInDesigner is a Visual Basic project that has a Designer file to assist with making changes to the Registry settings when creating a COM add-in. An Office AddInDesigner should be included as an ODE tool within the Office 2000 Developer Edition. An example of an Office AddInDesigner is shown in Figure 27-1.

Our example COM add-in includes a single form with two buttons. One button displays a message box, and the other button closes the form. Figure 27-2 shows the form as it was designed within Visual Basic.

As you can see, many similarities exist between the Outlook 2000 Forms Designer (OFD) and Visual Basic. However, there are also quite a few differences. Some tasks are more easily accomplished in Visual Basic, and other tasks are more easily accomplished in the OFD. For instance, it's much easier to program the code behind a button in Visual Basic. To do so, simply double-click the button, and an on_click subroutine will automatically be created.

In addition, as you program the code for an item, command hints appear to let you know what parameters to include, such as the ones shown in Figure 27-3 that popped up when we coded our message box. This is another advantage over the OFD, which does not provide programming hints.

Once you have the code in place to provide the functionality you need, it's time to configure the Designer. To do so, double-click the Connect file under the Designers folder from within the Project window. Connect(AddInDesigner) should appear in your workspace.

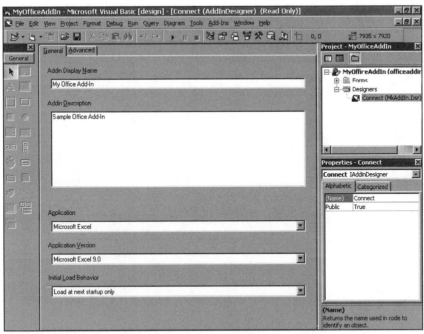

Figure 27-1: Use an Office AddInDesigner to build COM add-ins the easy way.

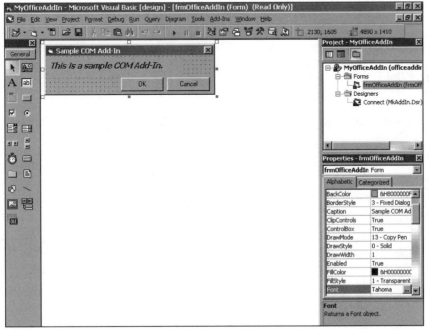

Figure 27-2: Our example COM add-in form was designed within Visual Basic.

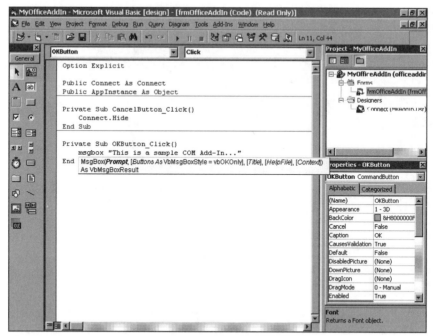

Figure 27-3: Programming hints appear in Visual Basic when we program the code for a message box.

You can provide a display name and description of your COM add-in in the Addin Display Name and Addin Description fields, respectively. The Application field is where you designate the application with which your COM add-in will interact. The Application Version designates the version of the Office application you wish to run your COM add-in. Because we want our example to run in Outlook 2000, we selected Microsoft Outlook from the Application drop-down menu.

> **Note**   Because COM add-ins are supported in only the most recent version of Outlook (Outlook 2000), there is only one choice available under Application Version when Microsoft Outlook is selected as the application. In addition, "Microsoft Outlook 9.0" refers to Microsoft Outlook 2000.

The Initial Load Behavior setting designates how the COM add-in will be initialized with the Office application. There are four options to choose from:

✦ *Load at next startup only* — This option will load your COM add-in at the same time Outlook 2000 is started. However, the COM add-in will only be available the next time Outlook 2000 is opened. After that, the COM add-in will not be available.

✦ *Load on demand*— This option will not load your COM add-in when Outlook 2000 is opened, but will wait until the user chooses to open the COM add-in before loading it.

✦ *Startup*— This option loads the COM add-in at the same time Outlook 2000 is loaded.

✦ *None*— This option indicates that the load behavior is not designated.

Caution

Be careful on which load behavior you choose to initiate your COM add-in. The option you choose can have a significant effect on how quickly Outlook 2000 loads or, conversely, how quickly your COM add-in loads when selected.

For our example, we chose to load the COM add-in on startup.

Creating the .dll file

Once you have configured the Connect(AddInDesigner) to your liking, you are ready to create a .dll file. The .dll file will store all the necessary information to run your COM add-in. Outlook 2000 will access this .dll file in order to open your COM add-in. To create the necessary .dll file, select Make MyOfficeAddIn.dll (where MyOfficeAddIn is whatever you've named your add-in) from the File menu from within Visual Basic.

You may store your .dll file anywhere on your local hard drive, but be sure to remember where you save it.

Tip

It's a good idea to also save the Visual Basic Project file. The Project file is also referred to as the source code. This will enable you to add functionality to your COM add-in in the future without having to re-create the entire COM add-in from scratch.

Once you click OK, Visual Basic compiles the project and then writes the .dll file, as indicated by the activity within the progress bar in the upper-right corner. You're now ready to access the file from within Outlook 2000.

Accessing a COM Add-in

Because we configured our COM add-in to load when Outlook 2000 is opened, our COM add-in should be available when we open Outlook 2000. To access a COM add-in, select it from the Tools menu.

Once the item is selected, the COM add-in should open, as shown in Figure 27-4 below.

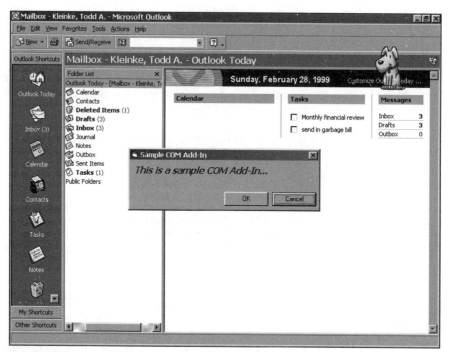

Figure 27-4: Our example COM add-in displays after the item is selected from the Tools menu.

When the OK button is clicked, a message box should appear, as shown in Figure 27-11, just as was specified within Visual Basic.

Figure 27-5: A message box displays when the OK button is selected.

When the OK button is clicked again, the main form will reappear. When the Cancel button is selected, the form will close.

Using the COM Add-ins Manager

Now that you know how to create a COM add-in, you may be wondering how to get rid of one. To do so, you need to access the COM Add-ins Manager from within Outlook 2000.

Accessing the COM Add-ins Manager

The COM Add-ins Manager may be accessed as follows:

1. Select Options from the Tools menu.
2. Select the Other tab.
3. Click the Advanced Options button.
4. Click the COM Add-ins button.

Once you've done so, you should see a list of any COM add-ins you've created in the Add-Ins available list box. Checkmarks appear beside the add-in or add-ins that are enabled, as shown in our example in Figure 27-6.

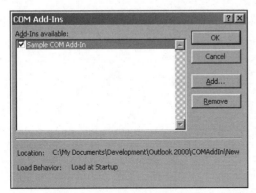

Figure 27-6: Our example COM add-in is listed in the COM Add-ins Manager.

Disabling a COM add-in

In order to disable a COM add-in, simply deselect the checkbox next to the COM add-in you wish to disable, and click OK. This will remove the ability to access any functionality of the COM add-in.

Restoring a COM add-in

If you reselect the checkbox next to a COM add-in from within the COM Add-ins Manager, the functionality of that COM add-in will be restored.

Note A COM add-in cannot be restored after it has been removed, as opposed to disabled. To reinstate functionality of a COM add-in that has been removed, you must add the COM add-in by using the Add button from within the COM Add-ins Manager.

Removing a COM add-in

To remove a COM add-in, do the following from within the COM Add-ins Manager:

1. Select the COM add-in you wish to remove.

2. Click the Remove button.

Note Removing a COM add-in from within the COM Add-ins Manager does not physically remove the .dll from your local hard drive. To remove the .dll from your local hard drive, you must actually delete the file.

Adding a COM add-in

To add a COM add-in, do the following from within the COM Add-ins Manager:

1. Click the Add button.

2. Select the .dll or .exe file that represents the COM add-in.

3. Click OK.

Note When distributing COM add-ins to other machines, make sure you include not only the .dll file for your COM add-in, but also the .exp and .lib files of the same name. In addition, if your COM add-in has any other dependency files, include those as well. Once copied to the new machine, the COM add-in may be added, as explained in the preceding steps.

Using Your COM Add-in in Other Office 2000 Applications

As we discussed earlier, you can use your COM add-in within other Office 2000 applications as well. In fact, you can use your COM add-in in any one of the following applications:

✦ Microsoft Access

✦ Microsoft Excel

✦ Microsoft Outlook

✦ Microsoft PowerPoint

✦ Visual Basic for Applications IDE

✦ Microsoft Word

✦ Visual Basic

✦ Microsoft Development Environment

To use your COM add-in within another Office 2000 application, you need to create another .dll for any other Office 2000 application you wish to run your COM add-in. To accomplish this, do the following:

1. Open the Visual Basic Project file you used to create the COM add-in for Outlook 2000.

2. Double-click the Connect(AddInDesigner) file under the Designers folder within the Project window.

3. Change the Application item to the new Office 2000 application within which you wish to use your COM add-in. For the example shown in Figure 27-7, we chose Excel.

4. Select the version from the Application Version drop-down menu. For the example shown in 27-7, we specified Excel 2000.

5. Adjust the initial load behavior as necessary.

Cross-Reference For more information on the initial load behavior, refer to the section "AddInDesigner" earlier in this chapter.

6. Select Make MyOfficeAddIn.dll (where MyOfficeAddIn represents the name of your add-in) from the File menu, point to where you want to save your .dll, and click OK.

7. Open the other Office 2000 application.

8. Open the COM add-in from the Tools menu of the Office 2000 application. In the example shown in Figure 27-7, the specifications we made earlier enables us to run our COM add-in in Excel 2000.

When the COM add-in menu item is selected, your COM add-in should open in the same manner as it did in Outlook 2000. Figure 27-8 shows our example COM add-in being used in Excel 2000.

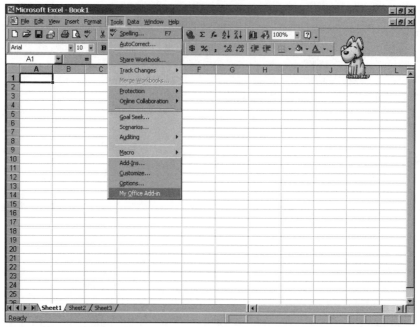

Figure 27-7: The My Office Add-In menu item appears at the bottom of the Tools menu in Excel 2000.

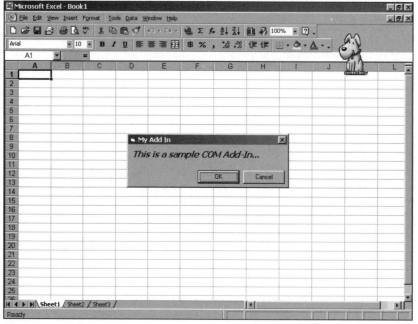

Figure 27-8: The example COM add-in can now be used within Excel 2000.

The Power of COM Add-ins

Given the capabilities of Visual Basic, the power of COM add-ins is never-ending. You're limited only by the capabilities of Visual Basic, Visual C++, and Visual J++. In addition, each one of these tools is extremely powerful.

In the near future, you'll probably see a number of applications designed around Outlook 2000 using COM add-ins. Because Outlook has inherent functionality that is needed by a wide range of custom solutions, such as contact management, scheduling, and so on, it makes sense to build on top of this technology, rather than re-create the wheel.

Summary

In this chapter, you learned how to create COM add-ins to be used not only within Outlook 2000, but also in other Office 2000 applications as well. The chapter covered the following points:

✦ COM add-ins are component-based applications that can be built using Visual Basic, Visual C++, and Visual J++. These applications are accessed from within certain Office 2000 applications.

✦ COM add-ins may or may not utilize the functionality of the parent Office 2000 application.

✦ There are three basic steps in creating a COM add-in to be used within an Office 2000 application: 1) create the code for the specific functionality you need, 2) make the necessary Registry entries, and 3) configure the parent application to accept the COM add-in.

✦ COM AddInDesigners can assist with the creation of COM add-ins, as they insert the necessary Registry entries for you.

✦ The default method of accessing COM add-ins is through the COM Add-ins Manager.

✦ You can disable, restore, remove, and add COM add-ins from within the COM Add-ins Manager.

✦ By opening your project file, reconfiguring the COM AddInDesigner, and creating a new .dll file, your COM add-in can be utilized within other Office 2000 applications.

✦ Because the capabilities of COM add-ins are only limited by the capabilities of tools such as Visual Basic, Visual C++, and Visual J++, COM add-ins can be very powerful tools.

✦   ✦   ✦

Collaborative Data Objects

CHAPTER

28

◆ ◆ ◆ ◆

In This Chapter

What are CDO
and CDONTS?

Where can CDO
be used?

Requirements for
using CDO

Requirements for
using CDONTS

Utilizing CDO
for the Web

Mass e-mailing
with CDO

◆ ◆ ◆ ◆

Collaborative Data Objects (CDO) and Collaborative
Data Objects for NT Server (CDONTS) can both assist
in providing messaging solutions in a number of different
environments. This chapter provides you with an introduction to the types of solutions you can create with CDO and
CDONTS.

What Are CDO and CDONTS?

CDO and CDONTS are object-based technologies used to
deploy messages. However, the underlying technology is messaging. CDO and CDONTS are merely programmable objects
that sit on top of messages. As a result, CDO and CDONTS
provide a perfect means to interface messaging with object-
oriented programming languages, such as Visual Basic.

What's the difference between the two? The difference lies
within the layer at which the CDO object model and the
CDONTS object model fall in relation to the underlying
message. Although CDO uses the messaging application
programming interface (MAPI) to accomplish messaging
tasks, CDONTS works directly with the messages themselves.
In addition, the CDONTS object model does not support the
same degree of functionality as the CDO object model. The
CDONTS object model supports only simple e-mail functions,
such as the sending of messages to specified recipients, the
creation and manipulation of message text, and the inclusion
of attachments, whereas the CDO object model extends the
capabilities to include such features as the Address Book
listing, message filters, and support for custom fields.

**Cross-
Reference**
For more information on MAPI, refer to Chapter 25.

Where Can CDO and CDONTS Be Used?

CDO and CDONTS are used within applications that require messaging capabilities. These applications are typically not used for day-to-day e-mail sending, as there are many applications already designed to meet this need. Instead, these types of applications serve specific needs that are perhaps not well met by an off-the-shelf e-mail application.

For example, suppose you are in the business of selling vintage guitars over the Internet. There are certain clients looking for specific guitars, and you store that information in a database. An application that makes use of CDO or CDONTS could fire off an e-mail message to notify all clients in search of a particular guitar that the item is in inventory. An example of such an e-mail message is shown in Figure 28-1. Because the e-mail message is generated on the fly, it is customized for each individual.

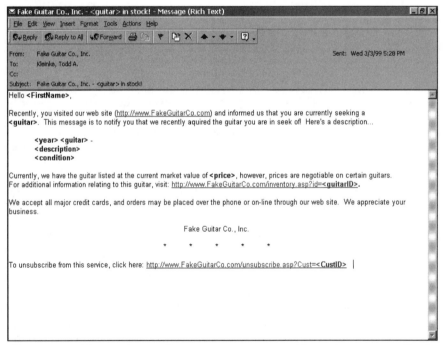

Figure 28-1: This sample e-mail message was generated by an inventory application.

The items shown in bold and surrounded by angular brackets (< >) represent the database fields used to personalize the message. When the user actually receives the e-mail message, his/her personal information appears in place of the database fields. For example, if the message was sent to Ed Sherfick, the first line of the message would read "Hello Ed," rather than "Hello <FirstName>,".

To expand on this concept even further, you could send the message using the Multipurpose Internet Mail Extensions HTML (MHTML) format, which enables you to embed images in your e-mail messages (see Figure 28-2).

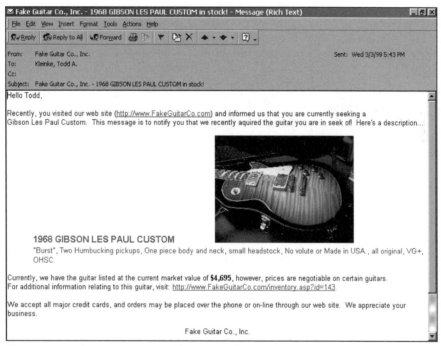

Figure 28-2: The same message in MHTML format, featuring an embedded image

As you can see, applications similar to the one shown in the figure utilize CDO and/or CDONTS to create complex, highly customizable, personalized messages. Typically, these types of applications are integrated with a database of some sort. Chances are, you will not find an off-the-shelf application that can accomplish the same degree of functionality. Therefore, CDO and/or CDONTS are your best bet when confronted with similar needs.

Requirements for Using CDO and CDONTS

CDO is designed to run with Microsoft Exchange Server 5.5. The CDO.DLL and CDOHTML.DLL files are the dynamic link libraries used by CDO, so these files are installed with Microsoft Exchange Server. The CDO.DLL file is not installed with Outlook 2000, but may be installed with Exchange Client. The CDOHTML.DLL file, on the other hand, is used for server-side programming. Therefore, if your CDO application is running on your Exchange Server, you won't need to install any additional software. However, if your CDO application is running on the client, you may need to install Exchange Client in addition to Outlook 2000.

CDONTS is designed to run on server-side applications and has the ability to run with or without Microsoft Exchange Server. If CDONTS is running without Exchange, either Internet Information Server (IIS) or MCIS server must be run in its place.

CDO Example

In order to get a better understanding of CDO, let's go through the creation of a simple application step by step.

On the CD-ROM The CD-ROM distributed with this book contains this example in the Chapter 28 folder. The CDO project example can be found in the CDO Sample subfolder; the CDONTS examples are located in the CDONTS Sample subfolder. See Appendix A for details.

In this example, you create an application in Visual Basic that uses CDO to send a simple e-mail message.

1. Open Visual Basic, select Standard EXE as the type of application under the New tab, and click Open.

   At this point, you should see a blank form, the Toolbox on the left, and the Project Explorer on the right with the Project Properties dialog box directly underneath, as shown in Figure 28-3. As you can see, the Visual Basic interface has many characteristics similar to those of the Outlook 2000 Forms Designer (OFD).

2. From the Toolbox window on the left, select the CommandButton control and draw a button on the form, as shown in Figure 28-4.

Toolbox   Project Properties   Project Explorer

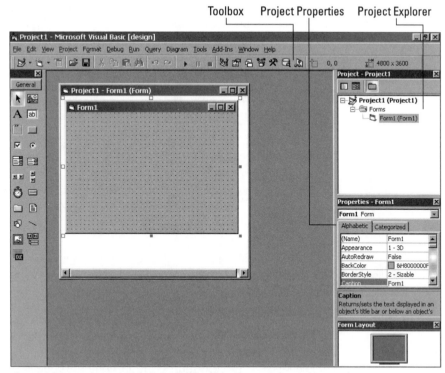

Figure 28-3: Bring up the default Visual Basic project workspace layout.

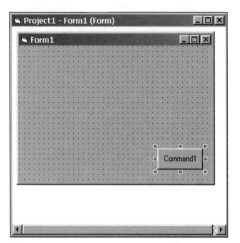

Figure 28-4: Draw a command button on the form.

3. Double-click the button in order to enter code for the Command1_Click event. A subroutine should automatically be created, as shown in Figure 28-5.

Figure 28-5: A subroutine is automatically created when the command button is double-clicked.

4. Enter the following code into the subroutine, or copy the code from the sample file on the CD-ROM and paste it into the Project1 window, but use the Exchange profile specific to your machine. This example uses the profile "Todd A. Kleinke".

```
Dim objSession As MAPI.Session
Dim objMessage As Message
Dim objMailRecip As Recipient

Set objSession = CreateObject("MAPI.Session")
objSession.Logon profileName:="Todd A. Kleinke", _
     profilePassword:="1313"
Set objMessage = objSession.Outbox.Messages.Add
objMessage.Subject = "Here is my subject"
objMessage.Text = "I enter my message text here."
Set objMailRecip = objMessage.Recipients.Add
objMailRecip.Name = "lhoover"
objMailRecip.Type = CdoTo
objMailRecip.Resolve
objMessage.Send showDialog:=False
```

As you can see, the code defines a MAPI session, a message, and recipient information. Once everything is defined, the message is sent to the recipient — in this case, "lhoover".

Note Your profile name can be viewed from within the Mail configuration window within the Windows Control Panel. To view your mail profile name, select Show Profiles on the Mail configuration window, as shown in Figure 28-6.

Figure 28-6: View your Profile name(s) in the Mail configuration window.

As the program runs, it needs to log in to the Exchange Server in order to send a message. If the profile information is not entered within the code, the user will be prompted to select a profile. Therefore, if more than one profile is configured on the machine, the user will have an opportunity to select the appropriate profile.

5. Close the Form1(code) window and apply any cosmetic changes to the form that you want, such as those shown in Figure 28-7.

Figure 28-7: Make any cosmetic changes to your form after closing the Form1 window.

You are now ready to test the project:

1. Select Run ➪ Start With Full Compile. The project should compile, and Form1 should appear in run mode, as shown in Figure 28-8.

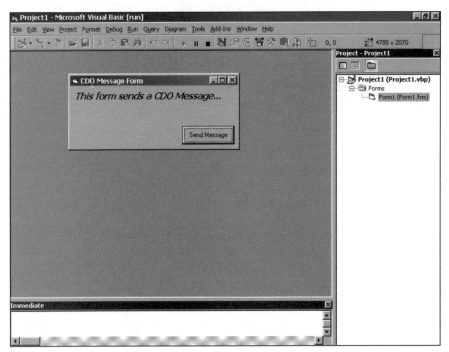

Figure 28-8: Test the CDO example.

2. Click the button within the form to send the message.

The recipient ("lhoover" in this case) should receive a message similar to the one in Figure 28-9.

CDONTS Example

In order to demonstrate CDONTS, let's examine another application that generates an e-mail message. However, because CDONTS can utilize the SMTP (Simple Mail Transfer Protocol) service when installed with Internet Information Server, we show you how to develop this sample application as an active server page.

Note

Active server pages are files with .asp extensions and are viewed with an Internet browser. Active server pages have the capability to utilize VBScript and JavaScript. In addition, Active server pages have the capability to execute code on both the client side and server side of the application. In the case of CDONTS, the code is executed on the server.

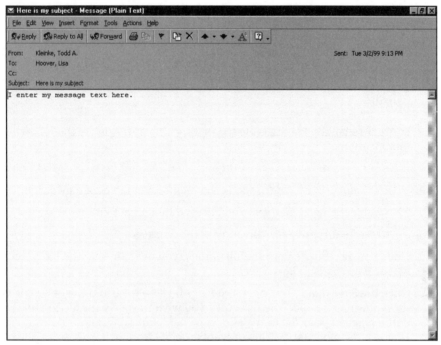

Figure 28-9: The message as seen by the recipient

For this example, use Notepad to create your active server page. Notepad is a simple text editor installed with Windows 95/98/NT. It can be found generally by selecting Start ➪ Programs ➪ Accessories.

On the CD-ROM For your convenience, this example has been included on the CD-ROM. See Appendix A for details.

1. To create the Active Server Page, type the following code into Notepad, or copy the code from the sample file on the CD-ROM and paste it into Notepad.

```
<%@ LANGUAGE="VBSCRIPT" %>
<%
Dim sampMail
Set sampMail = CreateObject("CDONTS.NewMail")
sampMail.Send "Info@Sender.com", "lhoover@Recipient.com",
"Subject Line", "Msg Text"
Set sampMail = Nothing
%>
<HTML>
<HEAD>
```

```
<TITLE>Simple CDONTS Example</TITLE>
</HEAD>
<BODY>
<FONT SIZE=6 FACE="Arial" COLOR=Blue>
A message has been sent via CDONTS...
</FONT>
</BODY>
</HTML>
```

2. In order to customize the code to your specifications, make the following modifications:

   - Info@Sender.com is an outgoing mail account on your SMTP server.

   - lhoover@Recipient.com is the recipient of the e-mail message.

   - Subject Line is the (yes, you guessed it!) subject line.

   - Msg Text represents the body of the message.

3. Once you have made your modifications, you need to save the file as an active server page. Select File ➪ Save As.

4. Once the Save dialog box opens, select All Files (*.*) from the Show file types drop-down menu. Find the directory you wish to save your file to and type the entire name of your file in the File name field, but add ".asp" at the end (for example, "sample.asp"). This prevents the file from being saved as a text file. Figure 28-10 demonstrates this step.

Caution If your file is saved as a text file (that is, with the default .txt file extension), your active server page will not function.

5. Once the file has been saved, you need to copy the file to your Web server. Keep in mind that this file will only function on a Web server that supports active server pages and has an e-mail engine, such as SMTP Server.

Tip If you do not have access to a Web server, you may download (for free) the Windows 95/98 version of Option Pack 4 from www.microsoft.com/ntserver. Option Pack 4 contains Internet Information Server 4.0 for NT Server. However, the Windows 95/98 version contains Personal Web Server, which enables your personal computer to act as a Web server. Therefore, you can develop active server page applications without having to constantly upload to a Web server.

When the active server page is accessed through a browser from the Web server, the page will send a message to the recipient, and it will resemble the page in Figure 28-11.

The body of the message is stored within a text file as an attachment.

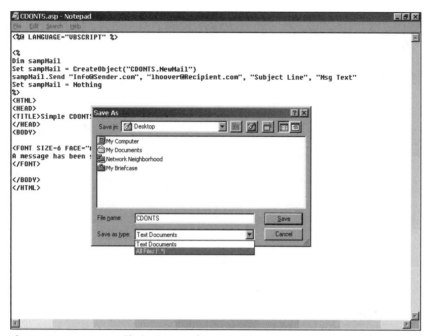

Figure 28-10: Save a file in Notepad as an active server page.

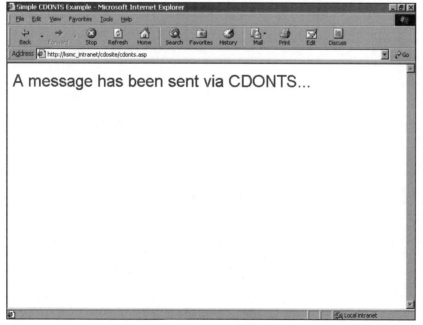

Figure 28-11: A CDONTS active server page as it appears in a browser

Alternatively, you can generate an e-mail message in HTML format by slightly modifying the code shown earlier. For example, the following code will send a message in HTML format:

```
<%@ LANGUAGE="VBSCRIPT" %>
<%
Dim sampMail
Set sampMail = CreateObject("CDONTS.NewMail")
HTML = "<!DOCTYPE HTML PUBLIC ""-//IETF//DTD HTML//EN"">" & NL
HTML = HTML & "<html>"
HTML = HTML & "<BODY>"
HTML = HTML & "<FONT SIZE=6 FACE=Arial COLOR=006600>"
HTML = HTML & "Here's an HTML message"
HTML = HTML & "</FONT>"
HTML = HTML & "</BODY>"
HTML = HTML & "</html>"
sampMail.MailFormat = 0
sampMail.BodyFormat = 0
sampMail.From = "tkleinke@ksmconsulting.com"
sampMail.To = "lhoover@ksmconsulting.com"
sampMail.Subject = "Test CDONTS msg"
sampMail.Body = HTML
sampMail.Send
Set sampMail = Nothing
%>
<HTML>
<HEAD>
<TITLE>Simple CDONTS Example</TITLE>
</HEAD>
<BODY>
<FONT SIZE=6 FACE="Arial" COLOR=Blue>
A message has been sent via CDONTS...
</FONT>
</BODY>
</HTML>
```

The end result will be a message that appears similar to the message displayed in Figure 28-11.

Mass E-mailing with CDONTS

By using CDONTS in combination with a database, you have the ability to create a powerful mass e-mailing application. Although sending mass e-mail messages to people without their request (or *spamming*) is considered impolite, it is not considered impolite to send subscription e-mail this way. For instance, many companies send electronic newsletters via e-mail, others send the status of a work in process, and still others send electronic invoices. These companies are most likely storing their subscriber information in a database.

The following code can be used to create such an application. This application begins by linking to a database through the use of a Data Source Name (DSN) created within the Windows Control Panel, under ODBC Data Sources (32-bit). Next, the application grabs a list of subscriber e-mail addresses from the database. If there is data present, the application creates a message to be sent. By assigning the e-mail address to a variable ("strAddress"), the code loops through the set of e-mail addresses from the database and sends the message.

```vbscript
<%@ LANGUAGE="VBSCRIPT" %>
<%
Dim sampMail
Dim strAddress
'**********Connect to database
    Set DataConn = Server.CreateObject("ADODB.Connection")
    DataConn.ConnectionTimeout =
Session("DataConn_ConnectionTimeout")
    DataConn.CommandTimeout =
Session("DataConn_CommandTimeout")
    DataConn.Open "DSN=Subscribe;UID=TAK;PW=passtak;"
    Set cmdTemp = Server.CreateObject("ADODB.Command")
    Set rsSQLQuery = Server.CreateObject("ADODB.Recordset")
'**********Get list of subscribers
    cmdTemp.CommandText = "SELECT Email FROM Subscribers" _
& " WHERE Type='Y';"
    cmdTemp.CommandType = 1
    Set cmdTemp.ActiveConnection = DataConn
    rsSQLQuery.Open cmdTemp, , 1, 3
    If rsSQLQuery.EOF=True and rsSQLQuery.BOF=True Then
'*****i.e., if there's no data
        Resume
    Else
        Set sampMail = CreateObject("CDONTS.NewMail")
        HTML = "<!DOCTYPE HTML PUBLIC ""-//IETF//DTD" _
            & "HTML//EN"">" & NL
        HTML = HTML & "<html>"
        HTML = HTML & "<BODY>"
        HTML = HTML & "<FONT SIZE=6 FACE=Arial COLOR=006600>"
        HTML = HTML & "Here's an HTML message"
        HTML = HTML & "</FONT>"
        HTML = HTML & "</BODY>"
        HTML = HTML & "</html>"
        sampMail.MailFormat = 0
        sampMail.BodyFormat = 0
        sampMail.From = "tkleinke@ksmconsulting.com"
        sampMail.Subject = "CDONTS msg content."
        sampMail.Body = HTML
    rsSQLQuery.MoveFirst
        strAddress = rsSQLQuery("Email")
        '**********Loop through recordset of subscribers and
send message
```

```
        While Not rsSQLQuery.EOF

              sampMail.To = strAddress
              sampMail.Send

          rsSQLQuery.MoveNext
              strAddress = rsSQLQuery("Email")

      Wend
          '**********End Loop
        End If
        Set sampMail = Nothing
        rsSQLQuery.Close
%>
<HTML>
<HEAD>
<TITLE>Simple Mass E-mail Example</TITLE>
</HEAD>
<BODY>
<FONT SIZE=4 FACE="Arial" COLOR=Blue>
Messages have been sent via CDONTS...
</FONT>
</BODY>
</HTML>
```

That's it! Good luck with it.

Summary

In this chapter, we covered the basic concepts surrounding Collaborative Data Objects (CDO) and Collaborative Data Objects for NT Server (CDONTS):

✦ CDO and CDONTS are object-based technologies used to deploy messages.

✦ CDONTS does not support the same degree of functionality as CDO; however, CDONTS can function over a wider range of platforms.

✦ CDO and CDONTS are typically utilized within applications that require messaging functionality that is not well supported within off-the-shelf e-mail applications.

✦ CDO and CDONTS applications can be programmed using Visual Basic, active server pages, or any other language that supports the CDO and CDONTS dynamic link libraries.

✦ CDO is designed to run with Microsoft Exchange Server. The CDO.DLL and CDOHTML.DLL files are the dynamic link libraries used by CDO.

✦ CDONTS is designed to run on server-side applications and has the capability to run with or without Microsoft Exchange Server. If CDONTS is running without Exchange, either Internet Information Server (IIS) or MCIS server must be run in its place.

✦ CDONTS is a good tool to use in designing custom mass e-mailing applications.

✦　　✦　　✦

Exchange Server Scripting and Routing Objects

I n Chapter 28, we discussed server-side scripting within active server pages on a server running Internet Information Server. This same concept is also inherent in Microsoft Exchange in the form of Exchange Server scripting and routing. In this chapter, we discuss Exchange Server scripting and routing and what each of these technologies can do for you.

What Is Exchange Server Scripting?

Exchange Server scripting is exactly what it sounds like — server-side scripts executing on the Exchange Server. As with active server pages, these scripts can either be written in VBScript or JavaScript. The scripts are designated to run within folders. Depending how you set things up, these scripts will execute when one of the following events occur:

- ✦ A scheduled event occurs
- ✦ A new item is posted in the folder
- ✦ An item is changed in the folder
- ✦ An item is deleted from the folder

However, before you are able to run Exchange server-side scripts, you must configure both the client and server machines to allow for Exchange scripting. We cover these details later in this chapter.

What Are Exchange Server Routing Objects?

Exchanger Server routing objects are similar to Exchange scripts in that they are executed on the Exchange Server. However, Exchange Server routing objects are set up as Microsoft routing engine agents, rather than as scripts. Typically, Exchange Server routing objects route certain information to specified individuals. Those individuals may either accept or reject the information as it flows through the chain. When a message is routed through an application using Exchange Server routing objects, the following events occur:

1. A message is created.

2. The routing engine agent receives the message.

3. Criteria stored within the message are evaluated.

4. The message is forwarded to another recipient, based on the results of the criteria.

5. The second individual reviews and manipulates the information stored in the message.

6. The message is forwarded back to the agent.

What Is an Agent?

Generally speaking, an agent is a mechanism that monitors the activity of a folder. When an action occurs within the folder, the agent evaluates what happened, and then reacts in the appropriate manner. Based on the definitions of Exchange Server scripting and Exchange Server routing objects given earlier, both of these technologies act as agents.

Figure 29-1 demonstrates an agent that monitors messages between a sales force and an Oracle database. As you can see, the appropriate information is routed among the individuals and the database based on the activity within the folders and the content of the messages.

Requirements for Using Exchange Server Scripting and Routing Objects

On the server, you should be running Microsoft Exchange Server version 5.5 or higher with Service Pack 1 installed. On the client, you will want to install the Microsoft Exchange Routing Wizard (for Exchange Server routing objects only). The application may be installed from the Microsoft Exchange 5.5 Service Pack 1, or downloaded from Microsoft's Web site (for free) at the following URL (after registering with Technet):

www.microsoft.com/technet/download/exchange/default.htm

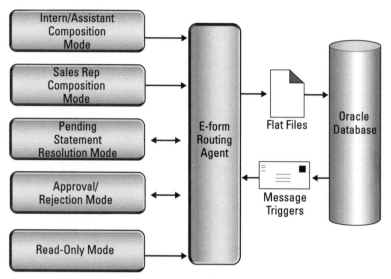

Figure 29-1: The agent routes information to the sales force and database based on folder activity and information within the messages.

Exchange Routing Wizard is available here:

```
http://technet.microsoft.com/reg/download/exchange/misc/rwsource.exe
```

Exchange 5.5 Service Pack 1 is available here:

```
http://technet.microsoft.com/reg/download/service/ExchangeSvr55sp1.htm
```

If you download the application from the Microsoft Web site, you will have access to the Visual Basic 5.0 source code. The source code is beneficial if you plan on developing a custom workflow routing application, since the code can be modified to suit your own specific needs. However, you will still need to obtain the following .dll files from the Microsoft Exchange Server 5.5 Service Pack 1 CD to be able to run the application:

✦ CDO.DLL (Microsoft CDO 1.21 Library)

✦ EXRTOBJ.DLL (Microsoft routing objects)

✦ ESCONF.DLL (Microsoft Exchange Event Service Config 1.0 Type Library)

In addition, you will need to specify these references before you attempt to run the project file from within Visual Basic. To do so, select Project ➪ References and choose the appropriate references, as shown in Figure 29-2.

If you install the Microsoft Exchange Routing Wizard from the Service Pack 1 CD, the referencing will be taken care of for you. However, you will not have access to the source code.

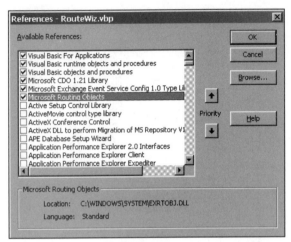

Figure 29-2: Specify appropriate references in Visual Basic.

Microsoft Exchange Server Configuration

Because these technologies involve executing code on the server, they involve an element of security risk. Code will be executing directly on the Exchange Server, so it may be a good idea to limit the number of programmers with administrative rights. As an administrator, a programmer will have the ability to cause serious damage if not experienced in Microsoft Exchange Server administration. You may also want to consider running your application in a test environment before actually implementing in the production environment. Keep in mind, the configuration requires both server-side and client-side configuration.

Server-side configuration

In order to use these technologies, you need to perform the following server-side configuration:

1. Appropriate authoring rights must be assigned to the user(s) who will be creating the scripts and/or routing objects. To assign these rights within the Microsoft Exchange Administrator, go to Events Root under System Folders as shown in Figure 29-3.

2. Double-click "EventConfig_<SERVER NAME>" in the right window of Microsoft Exchange Administrator to display the Properties dialog box, as shown in Figure 29-4.

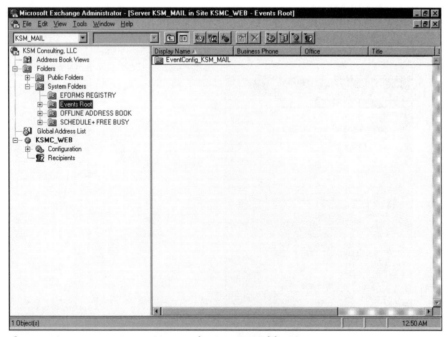

Figure 29-3: Access Events Root under System Folders.

Figure 29-4: Double-click EventConfig_<SERVER NAME>
to display its properties.

3. Click the Client Permissions button to open the Client Permissions dialog box. Click the Add button to select the developer's user account and assign the appropriate rights, as shown in Figure 29-5.

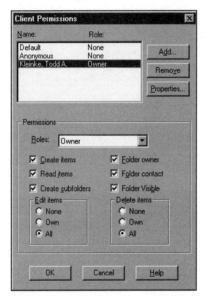

Figure 29-5: Configure appropriate rights for the developer in the Client Permissions dialog box.

Client-side configuration

In addition to the server-side configuration, there is also a setting you need to configure on the client-side in Outlook 2000.

1. After selecting Tools ➪ Options, click the Other tab.

2. Click the Advanced Options button to display the Advanced Options dialog box, shown in Figure 29-6.

3. Click the Add-In Manager button to open the Add-In Manager dialog box. Select Server Scripting, as shown in Figure 29-7, and then click OK.

Click OK two more times to close the dialog boxes, and you should be ready to go!

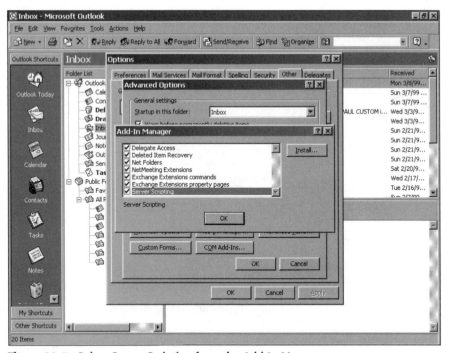

Figure 29-6: Advanced Options dialog box

Figure 29-7: Select Server Scripting from the Add-In Manager.

Creating an Exchange Server Script

To create an Exchange Server script, begin by selecting or creating a folder from within Outlook 2000 in which you would like to create your script. Once you have determined which folder to use, complete the following steps:

1. Right-click the folder and select Properties from the pop-up menu.

2. Select the Agents tab in the folder's Properties dialog box.

Note   If you do not see an Agents window, either the proper rights are not assigned on the Exchange Server, or you do not have Server Scripting selected in the Add-In Manager.

3. Click the New button to open the New Agent dialog box.

4. Enter a name for your agent in the Agent Name field and select the appropriate event(s) for your agent to monitor, as shown in Figure 29-8.

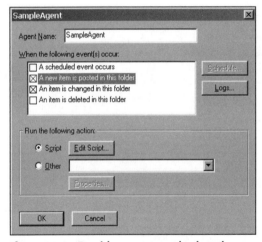

Figure 29-8: Provide a name and select the appropriate event(s) for the agent.

5. Click the Edit Script button to type code for each event, as shown in Figure 29-9.

6. Click OK to close the agent window and click OK again to close the property window.

Note   Debugging your code may either be accomplished through the Script Debugger or by clicking the Log button from within the Agent window.

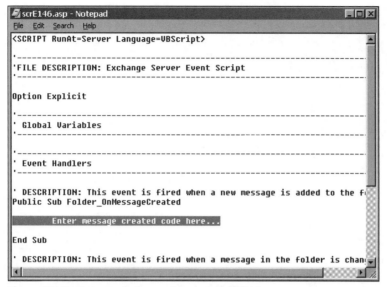

Figure 29-9: Enter code for each event specified.

Creating an Exchange Server Routing Object

Exchange Server routing objects are typically components of workflow applications. This technology provides a perfect medium for routing information through various levels of approval. Let's take a look at what's involved with creating an Exchange Server routing object.

1. Open the Microsoft Exchange Routing Wizard.

2. Click Next to begin and select your Exchange profile if prompted.

3. Click the Choose Folder button and select the appropriate folder to house the agent, as shown in Figure 29-10. Click OK.

4. Select the appropriate routing type and number of recipients.

Note   Sequential routing will forward information to each recipient one by one, whereas Parallel routing will forward the information to everybody at the same time.

5. Select the appropriate recipients (in the order you wish to route the information), as shown in Figure 29-11. Click Next.

6. Specify whether to send the item as a link or as an attachment. Click Next.

7. Enter the text you wish to appear in the body of your message/attachment. Click Next.

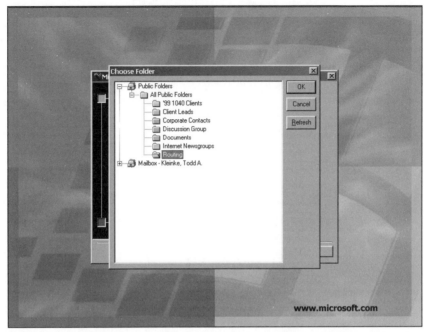

Figure 29-10: Select the appropriate folder to house the agent.

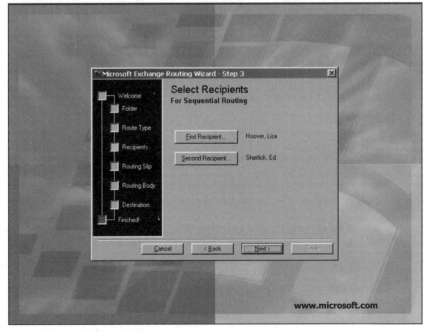

Figure 29-11: Select recipients.

8. Select final destination options, as shown in Figure 29-12. Click Next.

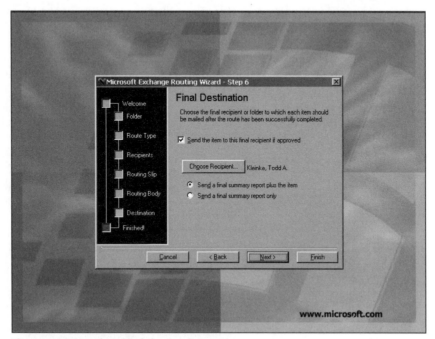

Figure 29-12: Select final destination options.

9. Click Finish. You should get a message to inform you of a successful installation.

10. In order to test the routing object, go to the folder where you created the routing object, click the New button in the upper-left corner, and post an item to the folder.

The item should be routed to the first recipient. Figure 29-13 demonstrates what the message looks like to the first recipient.

Figure 29-14 shows what the message looks like once it has been routed to all the appropriate individuals and reached its final destination.

Note   If the message had been rejected by the first recipient, the second recipient never would have received the message. However, the message would still have been forwarded to the final destination.

As you can imagine, Exchange Server routing objects have the potential to replace many of the paper approval processes your office may currently use. When these technologies are combined with forms, the potential is even greater. Therefore, the possibilities are unlimited.

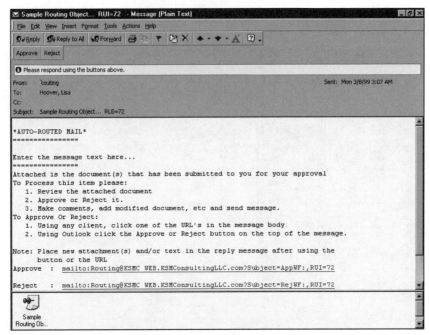

Figure 29-13: Routed message to initial recipient

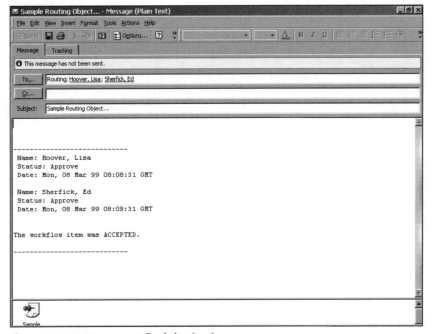

Figure 29-14: Message at final destination

Summary

In this chapter, we covered the basic concepts surrounding Exchange Server scripting and Exchange Server routing objects:

✦ Exchange Server scripting involves executing VBScript or JavaScript within a specified Exchange folder.

✦ Exchange Server scripting is similar to running a server-side active server page in that the processing is accomplished on the server.

✦ Exchange Server routing objects are similar to Exchange Server scripts, but are executed as a Microsoft routing engine agent.

✦ Agents are applications that monitor the activity of a folder and react when certain events occur within the folder.

✦ In order to use Exchange Server scripting and Exchange Server routing objects, you need to be running Microsoft Exchange version 5.5 with Service Pack 1 on the server. Running the Microsoft Exchange Routing Wizard requires three additional .dll files (found on the Service Pack 1 CD). Source code for the wizard may be downloaded from Microsoft's Web site.

✦ Server-side configuration as well as client-side configuration is required to create Exchange Server scripts and Exchange Server routing objects from the client.

✦   ✦   ✦

What's on the CD-ROM?

The CD-ROM at the back of this book contains sample files referred to in the text. Feel free to modify these files as you wish in order to create your own custom applications.

Because Outlook 2000 in general is designed to integrate with the Internet, we've provided a full installation copy of Microsoft Internet Explorer 5.0.

For your convenience, we have also provided a searchable, electronic copy of the chapters in this book in Adobe Acrobat PDF format. You should install the copy of Adobe Acrobat Reader on this CD-ROM to read those files.

Installing the Sample Files

The files on the CD-ROM may be accessed in two ways. The first is via a Personal Folders File (.pst); the second is directly from the CD-ROM.

In order to access the files via a Personal Folders File (.pst), follow these steps:

1. Copy the "Outlook 2000 Bible.pst" file from the CD-ROM to a location on either a network or local drive.

2. Right-click the file within Windows Explorer and select Properties from the pop-up menu.

3. Remove any selections on the Attributes section of the form (that is, Read-only, Archive, Hidden, System), and click OK.

4. Launch Microsoft Outlook 2000.

5. Select File ➪ Open ➪ Personal Folders File (.pst).

6. Highlight the "Outlook 2000 Bible.pst" file you just copied and click OK.

7. A folder titled "Outlook 2000 Bible" will appear in your folder list in Outlook. If you do not see a folder list, select View ⇨ Folder List to show that pane.

If you choose to browse the files in this manner, be sure to read the respective Readme.txt file in each folder, because some of the examples will not function directly within Outlook 2000; they require that you open the files directly from a drive.

In order to access the files directly from the CD-ROM instead, choose the appropriate file(s) from the chapter folders on the CD-ROM. For example, the files for Chapter 19 are located in the Chapter 19 folder.

Using the Sample Files

Following is a description of the sample files included on the CD-ROM.

Outlook Today sample

This example from Chapter 19 demonstrates how to create your own customized Outlook Today interface. By customizing Outlook Today, you can effectively communicate information throughout your entire organization.

Outlook form sample

This example from Chapter 20 introduces the basic concepts behind creating a simple form in Outlook 2000.

Utilizing controls sample

This example from Chapter 21 demonstrates how the various controls within Outlook 2000 can be utilized to develop custom solutions within your organization. (When opening this file, click the Enable Macros button in the warning dialog box that appears.)

Custom fields sample

In order to capture relevant information within your custom application, you may need to define a set of custom fields. This example from Chapter 22 shows you how.

Application distribution sample

Once you've created your application, you need to distribute the application among the users. This example from Chapter 23 demonstrates how to distribute applications via .pst files. Be sure to view the Readme.txt for details on removing read-only, archive, and other rights from the .pst file.

Application folder sample

In order to exploit the full capabilities of your application within Microsoft Exchange, you will need to understand the concepts behind application folders. This example from Chapter 24 walks you through what you need to know.

CDO Visual Basic sample

In addition to the solutions you can create within Outlook 2000, you have the capability to create message-based custom solutions within other platforms as well. This example from Chapter 28 demonstrates how Collaborative Data Objects (CDO) can provide effective solutions within Visual Basic.

CDONTS active server page sample

In addition to the solutions you can provide using CDO, Collaborative Data Objects for NT Server (CDONTS) can also provide effective solutions. CDONTS works well within active server page applications. The three examples from Chapter 28 demonstrate these capabilities.

Installing Microsoft Internet Explorer 5.0

Chapter 19 discusses the tight integration between Outlook and Microsoft Internet Explorer. For instance, Outlook Today actually uses Internet Explorer 5.0 in its display of information, so any functionality that can be built into an HTML document, active server page, XML page, or Dynamic HTML document can be utilized in your own Outlook Today page. For this reason, we include a full installation copy of MSIE 5.0.

To install MSIE 5.0, you must meet the following minimum system requirements:

✦ i486 or Pentium processor-based personal computer

✦ Microsoft Windows 95, Windows 98, Windows NT 4.0

✦ 16MB application RAM on Windows 95 and Windows 98

✦ 32MB application RAM on Windows NT

✦ 27MB hard disk space for browser only; 58MB for typical installation (up to 89MB required during actual installation procedure)

To install Microsoft Internet Explorer 5.0, run the IE.EXE program found in the MSIE 5.0 folder on the CD-ROM.

For more information online about this product, check out the official Microsoft Internet Explorer home page at `http://www.microsoft.com/windows/ie`.

Reading the Chapter PDFs

For your convenience, we have provided a searchable, electronic copy of the chapters in this book in Adobe Acrobat PDF format. To view these files, launch the Adobe Acrobat Reader, select File ➪ Open, and open the appropriate chapter PDF file in the Chapter PDFs folder on the CD-ROM.

Installing Adobe Acrobat Reader

If you do not already have a copy of Adobe Acrobat Reader installed on your computer, you will need to install it to view the chapter PDFs on the CD-ROM.

To install the Acrobat Reader, you must meet the following minimum system requirements:

✦ i486 or Pentium processor-based personal computer

✦ Microsoft Windows 95, Windows 98, or Windows NT 4.0

✦ 8MB application RAM on Windows 95 and 98 (16MB RAM recommended)

✦ 16MB application RAM on Windows NT (24MB RAM recommended)

✦ 8MB hard disk space

To install the Acrobat Reader, run the RS32E301.EXE program found in the Acrobat Reader folder on the CD-ROM. This version of Acrobat Reader allows you to open the chapter PDFs and search through them.

For more information online about this product, check out the official Adobe Acrobat Free Reader Web site at `http://www.adobe.com/prodindex/acrobat/readstep.html`.

✦   ✦   ✦

Object Model References

igure B-1 shows the Outlook 2000 Object Model. To view it, select Help ⇨ Microsoft Outlook Object Library Help while in the Script Editor. If you need assistance accessing the Outlook 2000 Script Editor, refer to Chapter 20.

```
Microsoft Outlook Help                                              _|8|×|
⬚| ← → 🖨 📑

Microsoft Outlook Objects
   See Also
   Application

      NameSpace                              Assistant
         PropertyPages (PropertyPage)        COMAddIns (COMAddIn)
         SyncObjects (SyncObject)            Explorers (Explorer)
         AddressLists (AddressList)             Selection (Items)
            AddressEntries (AddressEntry)       MAPIFolder
         Folders (MAPIFolder)                   CommandBars (CommandBar)
            Items (Item)                        Panes (Pane)
               Links (Link)                        OutlookBarPane
               UserProperties (UserProperty)          OutlookBarStorage
               FormDescription                           OutlookBarGroups (OutlookBarGroup)
               Actions (Action)                             OutlookBarShortcuts (OutlookBarShortcut)
               Attachments (Attachment)        Inspectors (Inspector)
               Recipients (Recipient)             WordEditor
               RecurrencePattern                  HTMLEditor
                  Exceptions (Exception)          Pages (Page)
         PropertyPages (PropertyPage)            CommandBars (CommandBar)
         LanguageSettings                        Item
         AnswerWizard

   Legend
      ⬚ Object and collection
      ⬛ Object only
```

Figure B-1: Outlook 2000 Application Object Model
interactive diagram

The diagram is interactive, so you can click an object to view additional information. For example, suppose you click the Application object. A screen describing the details of the Application object, as well as an example of the Application object being utilized, appears, as shown in Figure B-2.

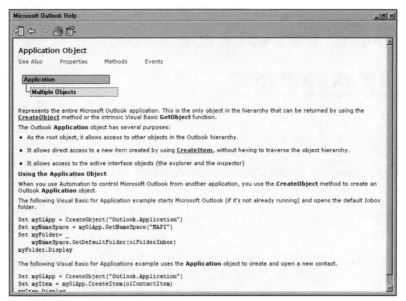

Figure B-2: Application object details and example

CDO Object Model Reference

Figure B-3 shows the Collaborative Data Objects (CDO) Object Model. The following tables list all properties and methods associated with each CDO object. Details summarizing the properties and methods for each object follow the object model. The details describing the parameters of the object methods are italicized, and the parameter instantiation types are displayed in bold text

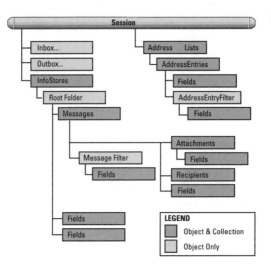

Figure B-3: CDO Object Model

Session object

As you can see from Figure B-3, Session is the top-level object. The word *session* is very descriptive of what the Session object accomplishes, as the object is the occurrence of a CDO instance, or session. In other words, anything that happens using CDO happens under the Session object. Table B-1 lists all properties of the Session object. Table B-2 lists all methods of the Session object.

Table B-1	
Session Object Properties	
Name	**Type**
AddressLists	AddressList object or AddressLists Collection object
Application	String
Class	Long
Current User	AddressEntry object
Inbox	Folder object
InfoStores	InfoStore object or InfoStores Collection object
MAPIOBJECT	IUnknown object
Name	String
OperatingSystem	String
Outbox	Folder object
OutOfOffice	Boolean
OutOfOfficeText	String
Parent	Object; set to Nothing
Session	Session object (itself)
Version	String

Table B-2
Session Object Methods

Name	Parameters
Name	(optional) *recipients* as **Object**, (optional) *title* as **String**, (optional) *oneAddress* as **Boolean**, (optional) *forceResolution* as **Boolean**, (optional) *recipLists* as **Long**, (optional) *toLabel* as **String**, (optional) *ccLabel* as **String**, (optional) *bccLabel* as **String**, (optional) *parentWindow* as **Long**
CompareIDs	*ID1* as **String**, *ID2* as **String**
CreateConversationIndex	(optional) *ParentIndex* as **String**
DeliverNow	(none)
GetAddressEntry	*EntryID* as **String**
GetAddressList	*ObjectType* as **Long**
GetArticle	*ArticleID* as **Long**, *FolderID* as **Long**, (optional) *storeID* as **String**
GetDefaultFolder	*ObjectType* as **Long**
GetFolder	*FolderID* as **String**, (optional) *storeID* as **String**
GetInfoStore	*StoreID* as **String**
GetMessage	*MessageID* as **String**, (optional) *storeID* as **String**
GetOption	*OptType* as **String**
Logoff	(none)
Logon	(optional) *profileName* as **String**, (optional) *profilePassword* as **String**, (optional) *showDialog* as **Boolean**, (optional) *newSession* as **Boolean**, (optional) *parentWindow* as **Long**, (optional) *NoMail* as **Boolean**, (optional) *ProfileInfo* as **String**
SetLocaleIDs	*LocaleID* as **Long**, *CodePageID* as **Long**
SetOption	*OptType* as **Long**, *OptValue* as **Variant**

Folder object (Inbox or Outbox)

The Folder object represents a folder within the mail system. Table B-3 lists all properties of the Folder object. Table B-4 lists all methods of the Folder object.

Table B-3 Folder Object Properties	
Name	*Type*
Application	String
Class	Long
Fields	Field object or Fields Collection object
FolderID	String
Folders	Folders Collection object
HiddenMessages	Messages Collection object
ID	String
MAPIOBJECT	IUnknown object
Messages	Messages Collection object
Name	String
Parent	Folders Collection object or InfoStore object
Session	Session object
StoreID	String

Table B-4 Folder Object Methods	
Name	*Parameters*
CopyTo	*FolderID* as **String**, (optional) *storeID* as **String**, (optional) *name* as **String**, (optional) *copySubfolders* as **Boolean**
Delete	(none)
IsSameAs	*ObjFolder2* as **Object**
MoveTo	*FolderID* as **String**, (optional) *storeID* as **String**
Update	(optional) *makePermanent* as **Boolean**, (optional) *refreshObject* as **Boolean**

InfoStores Collection object

The InfoStores Collection object stores one or more InfoStore objects. Table B-5 lists all properties of the InfoStores Collection object. There are no methods to list for this object.

	Table B-5 InfoStores Collection Object Properties	
Name	**Type**
Application	String
Class	Long
Count	Long
Item	InfoStore object
Parent	Session object
Session	Session object

Root Folder object (same as Folder object)

The Root Folder object represents a folder within the mail system. Refer to Tables B-3 and B-4 for the properties and methods of this object.

Messages Collection object

The Messages Collection object stores Message objects. Note that the object model diagram in Figure B-3 represents, for purposes of simplicity, both the Collection and Message object(s) as one item. Table B-6 lists all properties of the Messages Collection object. Table B-7 lists all methods of the Messages Collection object.

	Table B-6 Messages Collection Object Properties	
Name	**Type**
Application	String
Class	Long
Count	Long
Filter	MessageFilter object
Item	GroupHeader object or Message object

Name	Type
Parent	Folder object
RawTable	IUnknown object
Session	Session object

Table B-7
Messages Collection Object Methods

Name	Parameters
Add	(optional) *subject* as **String**, (optional) *text* as **String**, (optional) *type* as **String**, (optional) *importance* as **String**
Delete	(none)
GetFirst	(optional) *filter* as **String**
GetLast	(optional) *filter* as **String**
GetNext	(none)
GetPrevious	(none)
Sort	(optional) *SortOrder* as **Long**, (optional) *PropTag* as **Long**, (optional) *PropId* as **String**

Attachments Collection object

The Attachments Collection object stores Attachment objects. Note that the object model diagram in Figure B-3 represents, for purposes of simplicity, both the Collection and Attachment object(s) as one item. Table B-8 lists all properties of the Attachments Collection object. Table B-9 lists all methods of the Attachments Collection object.

Table B-8
Attachments Collection Object Properties

Name	Type
Application	String
Class	Long

(continued)

Table B-8 *(continued)*	
Name	**Type**
Count	Long
Item	Attachment object
Parent	Message object
Session	Session object

Table B-9 **Attachments Collection Object Methods**	
Name	**Parameters**
Add	(optional) *name* as **String**, (optional) *position* as **String**, (optional) *type* as **String**, (optional) *source* as **String**
Delete	(none)

Recipients Collection object

The Recipients Collection object stores Recipient objects. Note that the object model diagram in Figure B-3 represents, for purposes of simplicity, both the Collection and Recipient object(s) as one item. Table B-10 lists all properties of the Recipients Collection object. Table B-11 lists all methods of the Recipients Collection object.

Table B-10 **Recipients Collection Object Properties**	
Name	**Type**
Application	String
Class	Long
Count	Long
Item	Recipient object
RawTable	IUnknown object
Parent	Message object
Resolved	Boolean
Session	Session object

Table B-11
Recipients Collection Object Methods

Name	Parameters
Add	(optional) *name* as **String**, (optional) *address* as **String**, (optional) *type* as **Long**, (optional) *entryID* as **String**
AddMultiple	*names* as **String**, (optional) *type* as **Long**
Delete	(none)
GetFirstUnresolved	(none)
GetFreeBusy	*StartTime* as **Variant**, *EndTime* as **Variant**, *Interval* as **Long**
GetNextUnresolved	(none)
Resolve	(optional) *showDialog* as **Boolean**

AddressEntries Collection object

The AddressEntries Collection is the object that stores the account information regarding e-mail users within the Address Book. Table B-12 lists all properties of the AddressEntries Collection object. Table B-13 lists all methods of the AddressEntries Collection object.

Table B-12
AddressEntries Collection Object Properties

Name	Type
Application	String
Class	Long
Count	Long
Filter	AddressEntryFilter object
Item	AddressList object
Parent	Session object
RawTable	Iunknown object
Session	Session object

Table B-13
AddressEntries Collection Object Methods

Name	Parameters
Add	*emailtype* as **String**, (optional) *name* as **String**, (optional) *Address* as **String**
Delete	(none)
GetFirst	(none)
GetLast	(none)
GetNext	(none)
GetPrevious	(none)
Sort	(optional) *SortOrder* as **Long**, (optional) *PropTag* as **Long**, (optional) *PropID* as **String**

Fields Collection object

The Fields Collection object stores the fields beneath the various parent objects shown in the object model. Table B-14 lists all properties of the Fields Collection object. Table B-15 lists all methods of the Fields Collection object.

Table B-14
Fields Collection Object Properties

Name	Type
Application	String
Class	Long
Count	Long
Item	Field object
Parent	AddressEntry object, AddressEntryFilter object, AddressList object, AppointmentItem object, Attachment object, Folder object, InfoStore object, MeetingItem object, Message object, or MessageFilter object

Name	Type
Session	Session object

Table B-15
Fields Collection Object Methods

Name	Parameters
Add	*Name* as **String**, *Class* as **Long**, *Value* as **Variant**, (optional) *PropsetID* as **String**, *PropTag* as **Long**
Delete	(none)
SetNamespace	(optional) *PropsetID* as **String**

AddressEntryFilter object

The AddressEntryFilter object stores the criteria for searching within the AddressEntries Collection. Table B-16 lists all properties of the AddressEntryFilter object. Table B-17 lists the one method of the AddressEntryFilter object.

Table B-16
AddressEntryFilter Object Properties

Name	Type
Address	String
Application	String
Class	Long
Fields	Field object or Fields Collection object
Name	String
Not	Boolean
Or	Boolean
Parent	AddressEntries Collection object
Session	Session object

Table B-17	
AddressEntryFilter Object Method	
Name	Parameters
IsSameAs	*ObjAddrEntryFilter2* as **Object**

CDONTS Object Model Reference

Figure B-4 shows the Collaborative Data Objects for NT Server (CDONTS) object model. The following tables list all properties and methods associated with each CDONTS object.

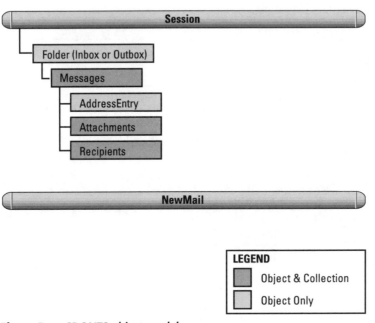

Figure B-4: CDONTS object model

Session object

As you can see from Figure B-4, the Session object is the top-level object. The word *session* is very descriptive of what the Session object accomplishes, as the Session object is the occurrence of a CDONTS instance, or session. In other words, anything that happens using CDONTS happens under the Session object. Table B-18 lists all properties of the Session object. Table B-19 lists all methods of the Session object.

Table B-18 Session Object Properties	
Name	**Type**
Application	String
Class	Long
Inbox	Folder object
MessageFormat	Long
Name	String
Outbox	Folder object
Parent	Object; set to Nothing
Session	Session object (itself)
Version	String

Table B-19 Session Object Methods	
Name	**Parameters**
GetDefaultFolder	*FolderType* as **Long**
Logoff	(none)
LogonSMTP	*DisplayName* as **String**, *Address* as **String**
SetLocaleIDs	*CodePageID* as **Long**

Folder object (Inbox or Outbox)

The Folder object represents a folder within the mail system. Table B-20 lists all properties of the Folder object. There are no methods to list for this object.

Table B-20 Folder Object Properties	
Name	**Type**
Application	String
Class	Long

(continued)

Table B-20 *(continued)*	
Name	*Type*
Messages	Messages Collection object
Name	String
Parent	Session object
Session	Session object

Messages Collection object

The Messages Collection object stores Message objects. Note that the object model diagram in Figure B-4 represents, for purposes of simplicity, both the Collection and Message object(s) as one item. Table B-21 lists all properties of the Messages Collection object. Table B-22 lists all methods of the Messages Collection object.

Table B-21 **Messages Collection Object Properties**	
Name	*Type*
Application	String
Class	Long
Count	Long
Item	Message object
Parent	Folder object
Session	Session object

Table B-22 **Messages Collection Object Methods**	
Name	*Parameters*
Add	(optional) *subject* as **String**, (optional) *text* as **Object** or **String**, (optional) *importance* as **Long**
Delete	(none)

Name	Parameters
GetFirst	(none)
GetLast	(none)
GetNext	(none)
GetPrevious	(none)

AddressEntry object (Inbox or Outbox)

The AddressEntry object defines addressing information within the mail system. Table B-23 lists all properties of the AddressEntryFilter object. There are no methods to list for this object.

Table B-23
AddressEntry Object Properties

Name	Type
Address	String
Application	String
Class	Long
Name	String
Parent	Message object
Session	Session object
Type	String

Attachments Collection object

The Attachments Collection object stores Attachment objects. Note that the object model diagram in Figure B-4 represents, for purposes of simplicity, both the Collection and Attachment object(s) as one item. Table B-24 lists all properties of the Attachments Collection object. Table B-25 lists all methods of the Attachments Collection object.

Table B-24
Attachments Collection Object Properties

Name	Type
Application	String
Class	Long
Count	Long
Item	Attachment object
Parent	Message object
Session	Session object

Table B-25
Attachments Collection Object Methods

Name	Parameters
Add	(optional) *name* as **String**, (optional) *type* as **Long**, (optional) *source* as **String** or **Object**, (optional) *ContentLocation* as **String**, (optional) *ContentBase* as **String**
Delete	(none)

Recipients Collection object

The Recipients Collection object stores Recipient objects. Note that the object model diagram in Figure B-4 represents, for purposes of simplicity, both the Collection and Recipient object(s) as one item. Table B-26 lists all properties of the Recipients Collection object. Table B-27 lists all methods of the Recipients Collection object.

Table B-26
Recipients Collection Object Properties

Name	Type
Application	String
Class	Long

Name	Type
Count	Long
Item	Recipient object
RawTable	IUnknown object
Parent	Message object
Session	Session object

Table B-27
Recipients Collection Object Methods

Name	Parameters
Add	(optional) *name* as **String**, (optional) *address* as **String**, (optional) *type* as **Long**
Delete	(none)

✦   ✦   ✦

Index

continued

continued

continued

continued

continued

NOTES

NOTES

NOTES

NOTES

NOTES

NOTES

NOTES

NOTES

NOTES

NOTES

NOTES

NOTES

NOTES

NOTES

IDG BOOKS WORLDWIDE, INC.
END-USER LICENSE AGREEMENT

READ THIS. You should carefully read these terms and conditions before opening the software packet(s) included with this book ("Book"). This is a license agreement ("Agreement") between you and IDG Books Worldwide, Inc. ("IDGB"). By opening the accompanying software packet(s), you acknowledge that you have read and accept the following terms and conditions. If you do not agree and do not want to be bound by such terms and conditions, promptly return the Book and the unopened software packet(s) to the place you obtained them for a full refund.

1. **License Grant**. IDGB grants to you (either an individual or entity) a nonexclusive license to use one copy of the enclosed software program(s) (collectively, the "Software") solely for your own personal or business purposes on a single computer (whether a standard computer or a workstation component of a multiuser network). The Software is in use on a computer when it is loaded into temporary memory (RAM) or installed into permanent memory (hard disk, CD-ROM, or other storage device). IDGB reserves all rights not expressly granted herein.

2. **Ownership**. IDGB is the owner of all right, title, and interest, including copyright, in and to the compilation of the Software recorded on the disk(s) or CD-ROM ("Software Media"). Copyright to the individual programs recorded on the Software Media is owned by the author or other authorized copyright owner of each program. Ownership of the Software and all proprietary rights relating thereto remain with IDGB and its licensers.

3. **Restrictions On Use and Transfer**.

    (a) You may only (i) make one copy of the Software for backup or archival purposes, or (ii) transfer the Software to a single hard disk, provided that you keep the original for backup or archival purposes. You may not (i) rent or lease the Software, (ii) copy or reproduce the Software through a LAN or other network system or through any computer subscriber system or bulletin-board system, or (iii) modify, adapt, or create derivative works based on the Software.

    (b) You may not reverse engineer, decompile, or disassemble the Software. You may transfer the Software and user documentation on a permanent basis, provided that the transferee agrees to accept the terms and conditions of this Agreement and you retain no copies. If the Software is an update or has been updated, any transfer must include the most recent update and all prior versions.

4. **Restrictions On Use of Individual Programs**. You must follow the individual requirements and restrictions detailed for each individual program in Appendix A of this Book. These limitations are also contained in the individual license agreements recorded on the Software Media. These limitations may include

a requirement that after using the program for a specified period of time, the user must pay a registration fee or discontinue use. By opening the Software packet(s), you will be agreeing to abide by the licenses and restrictions for these individual programs that are detailed in Appendix A and on the Software Media. None of the material on this Software Media or listed in this Book may ever be redistributed, in original or modified form, for commercial purposes.

5. **Limited Warranty.**

    (a) IDGB warrants that the Software and Software Media are free from defects in materials and workmanship under normal use for a period of sixty (60) days from the date of purchase of this Book. If IDGB receives notification within the warranty period of defects in materials or workmanship, IDGB will replace the defective Software Media.

    (b) **IDGB AND THE AUTHORS OF THE BOOK DISCLAIM ALL OTHER WARRANTIES, EXPRESS OR IMPLIED, INCLUDING WITHOUT LIMITATION IMPLIED WARRANTIES OF MERCHANTABILITY AND FITNESS FOR A PARTICULAR PURPOSE, WITH RESPECT TO THE SOFTWARE, THE PROGRAMS, THE SOURCE CODE CONTAINED THEREIN, AND/OR THE TECHNIQUES DESCRIBED IN THIS BOOK. IDGB DOES NOT WARRANT THAT THE FUNCTIONS CONTAINED IN THE SOFTWARE WILL MEET YOUR REQUIREMENTS OR THAT THE OPERATION OF THE SOFTWARE WILL BE ERROR FREE.**

    (c) This limited warranty gives you specific legal rights, and you may have other rights that vary from jurisdiction to jurisdiction.

6. **Remedies.**

    (a) IDGB's entire liability and your exclusive remedy for defects in materials and workmanship shall be limited to replacement of the Software Media, which may be returned to IDGB with a copy of your receipt at the following address: Software Media Fulfillment Department, Attn.: *Microsoft Outlook 2000 Bible,* IDG Books Worldwide, Inc., 7260 Shadeland Station, Ste. 100, Indianapolis, IN 46256, or call 1-800-762-2974. Please allow three to four weeks for delivery. This Limited Warranty is void if failure of the Software Media has resulted from accident, abuse, or misapplication. Any replacement Software Media will be warranted for the remainder of the original warranty period or thirty (30) days, whichever is longer.

    (b) In no event shall IDGB or the authors be liable for any damages whatsoever (including without limitation damages for loss of business profits, business interruption, loss of business information, or any other pecuniary loss) arising from the use of or inability to use the Book or the Software, even if IDGB has been advised of the possibility of such damages.

    (c) Because some jurisdictions do not allow the exclusion or limitation of liability for consequential or incidental damages, the above limitation or exclusion may not apply to you.

7. **U.S. Government Restricted Rights.** Use, duplication, or disclosure of the Software by the U.S. Government is subject to restrictions stated in paragraph (c)(1)(ii) of the Rights in Technical Data and Computer Software clause of DFARS 252.227-7013, and in subparagraphs (a) through (d) of the Commercial Computer — Restricted Rights clause at FAR 52.227-19, and in similar clauses in the NASA FAR supplement, when applicable.

8. **General.** This Agreement constitutes the entire understanding of the parties and revokes and supersedes all prior agreements, oral or written, between them and may not be modified or amended except in a writing signed by both parties hereto that specifically refers to this Agreement. This Agreement shall take precedence over any other documents that may be in conflict herewith. If any one or more provisions contained in this Agreement are held by any court or tribunal to be invalid, illegal, or otherwise unenforceable, each and every other provision shall remain in full force and effect.

my2cents.idgbooks.com

CD-ROM Installation Instructions

The CD-ROM at the back of this book contains sample files referred to in the text, as well as a searchable, electronic copy of the chapters in this book in Adobe Acrobat PDF format. Also included are full installation copies of Microsoft Internet Explorer 5.0 and Adobe Acrobat Reader.

You access the sample files via a Personal Folders File (.pst):

1. Copy the "Outlook 2000 Bible.pst" file from the CD-ROM to a location on either a network or local drive.

2. Right-click the file within Windows Explorer and select Properties from the pop-up menu.

3. Remove any selections on the Attributes section of the form (that is, Read-only, Archive, Hidden, System), and click OK.

4. Launch Microsoft Outlook 2000.

5. Select File ⇨ Open ⇨ Personal Folders File (.pst).

6. Highlight the "Outlook 2000 Bible.pst" file you just copied and click OK.

7. A folder titled "Outlook 2000 Bible" will appear in your folder list in Outlook. If you do not see a folder list, select View ⇨ Folder List to show that pane.

Be sure to read the respective Readme.txt file in each folder, because some of the examples will not function directly within Outlook 2000; they require that you open the files directly from a drive.

To install Microsoft Internet Explorer 5.0, run the IE.EXE program found in the MSIE 5.0 folder on the CD-ROM.

To install the Acrobat Reader, run the RS32E301.EXE program found in the Acrobat Reader folder on the CD-ROM.

To view these files, launch the Adobe Acrobat Reader, select File ⇨ Open, and open the appropriate chapter PDF file in the Chapter PDFs folder on the CD-ROM.

For more information about the contents of the CD-ROM, please read Appendix A.